The Slave Trade and Culture in the Bight of Biafra

The Slave Trade and Culture in the Bight of Biafra dissects and explains the structure, dramatic expansion, and manifold effects of the slave trade in the Bight of Biafra. By showing that the rise of the Aro merchant group was the key factor in trade expansion, G. Ugo Nwokeji reinterprets why and how such large-scale commerce developed in the absence of large-scale centralized states. The result is the first study to link the structure and trajectory of the slave trade in a major exporting region to the expansion of a specific African merchant group – among other fresh insights into Atlantic Africa's involvement in the trade – and the most comprehensive treatment of Atlantic slave trade in the Bight of Biafra. The fundamental role of culture in the organization of trade is highlighted, transcending the usual economic explanations in a way that complicates traditional generalizations about work, domestic slavery, and gender in precolonial Africa.

G. Ugo Nwokeji is assistant professor of African American studies at the University of California, Berkeley. His research focuses on the cultural history and political economy of Africa since 1500, with particular focus on international commerce in the Nigerian Niger Delta and its hinterland. Professor Nwokeji is the author of the James A. Baker III Institute for Public Policy's *The Nigerian National Petroleum Corporation and the Development of the Nigerian Oil and Gas Industry: History, Strategies, and Current Directions* (2007) and multiple journal articles and book chapters, as well as co-editor of *Religion, History and Politics in Nigeria* (2005).

The Slave Trade and Culture in the Bight of Biafra

An African Society in the Atlantic World

G. UGO NWOKEJI

University of California, Berkeley

CAMBRIDGE
UNIVERSITY PRESS

CAMBRIDGE
UNIVERSITY PRESS

32 Avenue of the Americas, New York NY 10013-2473, USA

Cambridge University Press is part of the University of Cambridge.

It furthers the University's mission by disseminating knowledge in the pursuit of education, learning and research at the highest international levels of excellence.

www.cambridge.org
Information on this title: www.cambridge.org/9781107662209

© G. Ugo Nwokeji 2010

This publication is in copyright. Subject to statutory exception and to the provisions of relevant collective licensing agreements, no reproduction of any part may take place without the written permission of Cambridge University Press.

First published 2010
First paperback edition 2013

A catalogue record for this publication is available from the British Library

Library of Congress Cataloguing in Publication data
Nwokeji, G. Ugo.
The slave trade and culture in the Bight of Biafra: an African society in the Atlantic world / G. Ugo Nwokeji.
   p.   cm.
ISBN 978-0-521-88347-4 (hardback)
1. Slave trade – Biafra, Bight of, Region – History.   2. Slavery – Biafra, Bight of, Region – History.   3. Biafra, Bight of, Region – Social conditions.   I. Title.
HT1334.B5N87 2010
306.3′620916373–dc22   2010021039

ISBN 978-0-521-88347-4 Hardback
ISBN 978-1-107-66220-9 Paperback

Cambridge University Press has no responsibility for the persistence or accuracy of URLs for external or third-party internet websites referred to in this publication, and does not guarantee that any content on such websites is, or will remain, accurate or appropriate.

This book is dedicated to the memory of Don Ohadike, historian and gentleman

Contents

List of Tables and Figures	page	ix
Map of the Bight of Biafra and Its Hinterland		xi
Preface		xiii
Foreword by Paul E. Lovejoy		xxiii
1 Introduction		1
2 The Aro in the Atlantic Context: Expansion and Shifts, 1600s–1807		22
3 The Trade Diaspora in Regional Context: Aro Commercial Organization in the Era of Expansion, 1740–1850		53
4 Culture Formation in the Trading Frontier, c. 1740 to c. 1850		82
5 Household and Market Persons: Deportees and Society, c. 1740–c. 1850		117
6 The Slave Trade, Gender, and Culture		144
7 Cultural and Economic Aftershocks		178
8 Summary and Conclusions		204
Notes on Sources		209
Sources Cited		223
Index		265

Tables and Figures

TABLES

0.1. Estimated Volume of Biafra Captive Exports, 1551–1850, by Twenty-Five-Year Period   *page* xiv

2.1. Estimated Volume of the Transatlantic Captive Departures from the Bight of Biafra and All African Regions Combined, Primarily Five-Year Intervals, 1531–1740   33

2.2. A Sample of Captive Prices (in Copper Bars) in New Calabar and Old Calabar, 1678–1704   36

2.3. The Volume of the Transatlantic Captive Departures from the Bight of Biafra and All African Regions Combined, Five-Year Intervals, 1701–1805   38

2.4. Time Spent by Ships at African Ports, 1751–1800   39

2.5. Daily Average Number of Captives Loaded Per Vessel, 1701–50   41

2.6. Daily Average Number of Captives Loaded Per Vessel, 1751–1800   41

2.7. Estimated Departures of Captives from Bight of Biafra Ports by Quarter Century, 1651–1850 (in thousands)   46

3.1. Division of Spheres among Aro Lineage-Groups   61

3.2. Principal Aro Settlements at the Edge of the Igbo Heartland   62

4.1.	Arondizuogu Lineage-Groups before 1890 and the Probable Original Occupiers of the Land	89
4.2.	Sequence of Nucleation of Arondizuogu Lineage-Groups	92
4.3.	Lexicostatistics of Arochukwu, Arondizuogu, Nri-Awka, and Non-Aro Communities Around Arondizuogu	109
6.1.	Proportion of Females Leaving the Gold Coast, the Bight of Benin, and the Bight of Biafra, 1601–1864	151
6.2.	Women, Girls, Men, and Boys Leaving Major Embarkation Points in the Bight of Biafra, Selected Quarters, 1651–1850 (in percents)	155

FIGURE

2.1.	Arochukwu Structure	28

THE BIGHT OF BIAFRA AND ITS HINTERLAND

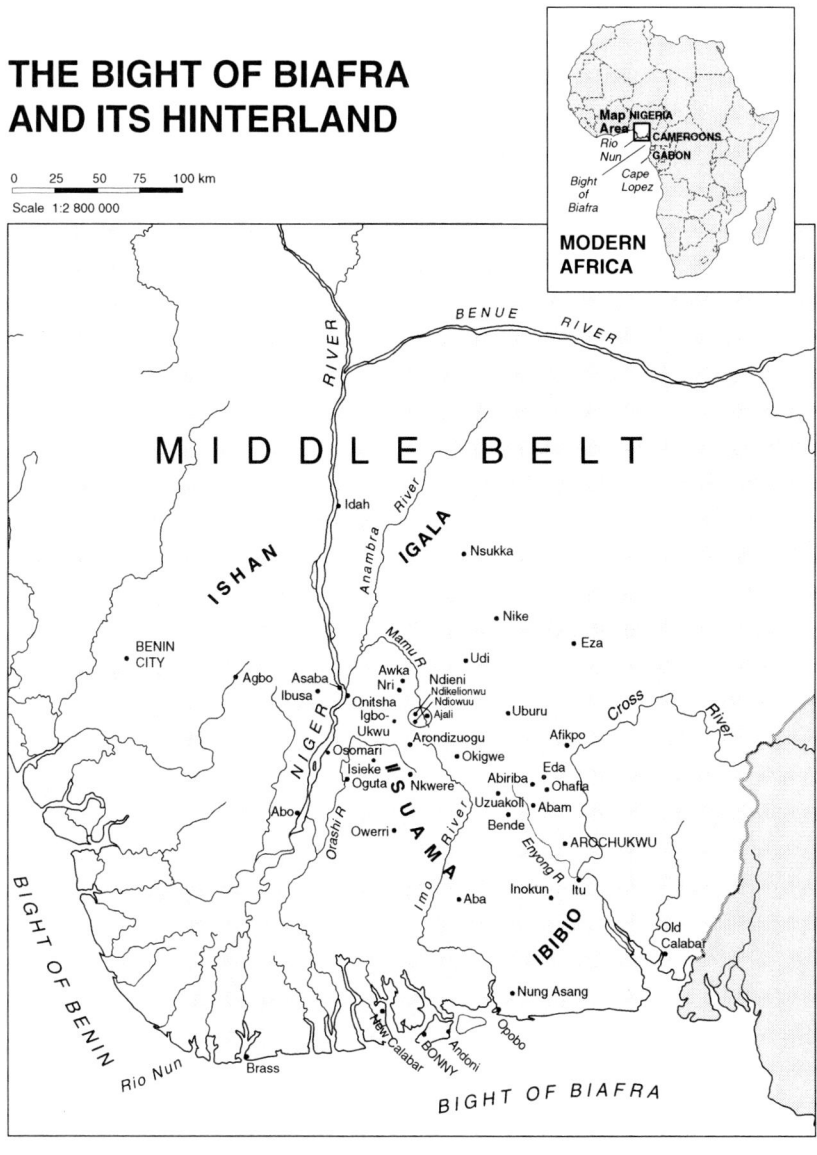

Preface

The human traffic through which African societies supplied the labor needs of the Americas invokes many fundamental questions. Some of the most persistent questions are why Africa supplied so many captives; how the trade was organized; what its political, social, and cultural implications were; what the gender and ethnic composition was; and how the trade affected the societies involved. The answers to these questions are the primary focus of this book. They are addressed from the vantage point of the Bight of Biafra, a major exporting region, extending from the Niger Delta (exclusive of the River Nun) in modern Nigeria to Cape Lopez in modern Gabon. The region supplied an estimated 13 percent of all captives exported between 1551 and 1850, which made it the third most important supply region after West-Central Africa and the Bight of Benin. What marked out the Bight of Biafra slave trade was its unusual trajectory. Departures of captives from the region increased fivefold between the last quarter of the seventeenth century and the last quarter of the eighteenth century (Table 0.1). Concomitantly, the majority Igbo of the hinterland were probably the largest single African group arriving in North America and several Caribbean destinations for much of the eighteenth century. The traffic closed down quickly in the 1840s, but for most of the preceding century, the Bight of Biafra had been the second most important region for captives taken to the Americas (though lagging well behind West-Central Africa). How did a region that once supplied a small number of captives so quickly become the second most important supply region in the eighteenth century, in spite of the absence of large centralized states? In comparison to the well-known ever-increasing demand for African slave labor that the sugar revolution stirred in the

TABLE 0.1. *Estimated Volume of Biafra Captive Exports, 1551–1850, by Twenty-Five-Year Period*

Period	Bight of Biafra	All Africa	Biafra Percentage of African Total
1551–1575	3,383	61,007	5.5
1576–1600	2,996	152,373	2.0
1601–1625	2,921	352,843	0.8
1626–1650	33,540	315,050	10.6
1651–1675	80,780	488,064	16.5
1676–1700	69,080	719,674	9.6
1701–1725	66,833	1,088,909	6.1
1726–1750	182,066	1,471,725	12.4
1751–1775	319,709	1,088,909	16.6
1776–1800	336,008	1,471,725	16.7
1801–1825	264,834	1,925,314	14.1
1826–1850	230,328	2,008,670	13.0
Grand Totals	1,592,478	12,231,600	13.0

Slavevoyages.org. Numbers with decimal points are not precise because of rounding.

Americas, there is still much to explore about how African regions met this demand.

The Aro, who call themselves "Aru," inhabit a conspicuous place in the history of the inglorious slave trade. They dominated the slave trade in inland Bight of Biafra from their Arochukwu homeland, north of the Cross River–Enyong Creek estuary in the southeastern portion of the Nigerian section of the region. The Aro were a peculiar group. Though the region was marked by "stateless" societies, Aro organization did in fact have characteristics of a state. Yet, it was rather a peculiar organization as a diaspora – rather than a state – which explains the rise and expansion of the region's transatlantic slave trade. The following chapters elaborate this proposition.

This study treats the Aro trading network as a trade diaspora, in spite of the relatively small geographic space of the Bight of Biafra. The enormous ethnolinguistic diversity and the evolution of ethnic identity of the region warrant such a perspective and explain the treatment in this study of the slave-trade-era Aro as a separate cultural phenomenon, even though they are today little more than a subgroup of the Igbo. By the seventeenth century, Arochukwu culture and dialect had emerged as a hybrid of Igbo, Ibibio, and Akpa elements; Arochukwu itself is located in the Igbo-Ibibio-Ejagham borderland. Hybridity – a process undergone in

Preface

different forms and degrees by much of Atlantic Africa during the slave trade era – continued in the Aro diaspora. The process was perhaps more marked among the Aro than was the norm in the Bight of Biafra.

Although the vast majority of present-day Aro people either identify themselves or are identified by others as Igbo, to impose such an identity on the period covered in this study is an anachronism. Arochukwu's multiethnic origin shaped Aro social structures and identity during the period covered in this study. Contrary to the sections of pre-twentieth-century Aro population that originated among groups that came to see themselves as Igbo, the case with the Aro tracing their own origins elsewhere is different. Neither can we simply conflate as Igbo the Aro communities that still remain outside Igboland, principally among the Ibibio in the Cross River region and the Igala in the Middle Belt. It should be noted that the Igbo group covered a much smaller area before the late nineteenth century than they came to occupy in the twentieth century. That an Igbo group in the sense that we have come to know them in the twentieth and twenty-first centuries did not exist in the era of the transatlantic slave trade is not in question; what is subject to debate is whether there were any people who identified themselves as Igbo and, if so, when they began to do so.[1]

For the most part, the application of "Igbo" to much of the period covered in this book is not meant to project a pan-Igbo identity as currently exists but to refer to a group of societies that later constituted Igboland. A reading of historical and anthropological studies of the region, as well as ethnographic observations during the late twentieth century, suggests that Igboness came to involve (perhaps not exclusively) four basic elements in addition to a common language – two deities, the *Ala/Ani/Ana* earth deity and *Chi* personal god, and reverence for two crops/foods, yam (*ji*) and kolanut (*oji*). Except for peripheral societies that migrated into the Igbo area after the overseas slave trade had gathered momentum in the region, the societies that became Igbo seem to have in the main shared a strong social and spiritual attachment to yam and kolanut, but only those within the perimeter referred to as the Igbo heartland and which had additionally subscribed to *Ala* and *Chi* deities are assumed to have

---

[1] The earliest written reference to the group was when Spanish missionary in the Americas Alonso Sandoval entered "Ibo" in his collection of ethnolinguistic groups, which was how some people located in a place we now know as Igboland were referred to and probably how some people referred to themselves as well ([1627] 1956:94). For various perspectives, see Leith-Ross 1939:56; Oriji 1994:5; Gomez 1998, chapter 6; Nwokeji 2000:629–33; Northrup 2000; Chambers 2002; Byrd 2008:17–33, 56, 261n

become Igbo at the onset of the overseas slave trade.[2] At any rate, the process of Igboization would seem to have begun with – at least in part – the embrace of yam and kolanut reverence.[3] These two foods/crops – as will be shown in this study – played important roles in shaping the structure of the slave trade in the Bight of Biafra.

[2] Explicitly and implicitly, anthropologists have identified *Ala* as the most important deity among the Igbo (Meek 1937:20, 24–33; Ottenberg 1959:136). There was a larger number of units in the Igbo pantheon, but some of these were not pan-Igbo even at the turn of the twentieth century, in the sense that nearly all the groups that referred to themselves as Igbo had come to be associated beyond *Ala* and *Chi*. The heartland is the home of an inner core, the "autochthonous" communities of Igboland – a group of societies whose peoples have continuously occupied the area for so long that their traditions locate their origins in the vicinity of their present abodes. For the autochthones, see J.O. Ijoma 1986c:11; Ifemesia 1979:21; Isichei 1976:67; G.I. Jones 1963; Ohadike 1994:12; Oriji 1994. The autochthones may be deemed the first-order Igbo, followed by the rest of the heartland. Beyond the heartland, we find an outer ring of groups that had significant non-Igbo elements, such as Arochukwu, several other Cross River Igbo groups, southern Igboland – principally the Ngwa, Ndoki, and communities to their south – as well as the societies around and beyond the city of Enugu. Finally, there are groups that migrated into the region in the course of the transatlantic slave trade, mostly in riverine regions, such as Onitsha, Oguta, Abo, Igga, and many of the West-Niger Igbo societies. Historian John Oriji (1994:5) has drawn attention to the presence in the Igbo heartland of *Amaigbo* (Ama-Igbo, meaning "Igbo Square"), the ancient town to which many Isuama Igbo communities trace their origins, and the historic *Igbo-Ukwu* ("Grand Igbo"), in which the archeologist Thurstan Shaw (1970a, 1970b) uncovered artifacts of ninth-century vintage, which suggests that the nucleus of Igboland was perhaps the Amaigbo/Igbo-Ukwu axis of the so-called Igbo heartland. The human figures found among the artifacts had the distinctive *ichi* marks on their faces, a practice that continued in the Nri-Awka area up to recent decades (Ifemesia 1979:18–19, 89). There is a dialectical variation in the ways people of the Amaigbo and Igbo-Ukwu subregions of the Igbo heartland pronounce the earth cult – *Ala* in the case of Amaigbo and *Ani/Ana* in the case of Nri. There are no dialectical variations in the pronunciation of the other key terms – *oji* (kolanut), *ji* (yam), and *Chi*, except for the nasalization that mark some dialects. The cultural landscape of the region was, however, more fluid than this schema might imply. A given group may have combined cultural forms that related more to groups outside than the ones inside the category it is placed in, a reflection of relentless movement of people and ideas. Aro diaspora communities were in very recent centuries established in areas long settled by autochthones and heartland groups.

[3] Originally, *Ikeji* itself celebrated the beginning of yam harvest among the Aro, although the festival changed significantly after trading became the principal occupation of the Aro. Kolanut also played a central role in Aro covenants with their trading and political allies as well as in inducting newly acquired slaves into the household (Kanu-Igbo 1996b; J.G. Okoro 1996). The present writer has not seen any evidence in support of the existence of *Chi* and the *Ala* cult among the Aro before the nineteenth century. An instance of *Ana* emerges among the Aro diaspora of the Ndieni cluster, located in the Nri-Awka region, in the late nineteenth century. *Ikeji*, *Ihu*, and to an extent the *Ana* cult (*Ajana*) are discussed in detail in Chapter 4. The role of yam and kolanut in shaping the structure of the slave trade is analyzed in Chapter 6. Aro traditions refer to gifts of kolanuts and yams accompanying the *Ihu* "homage" rite, and to wives giving their husbands kolanuts during the *Ikeji* festival (Arodiogbu 1996; Nwankwo and Okereke 1996).

Preface

With their Arochukwu homeland located in the southeastern periphery of what we now call Igboland and having significant sections of their population speak languages and subscribe to customs significantly different from what was later recognized as Igbo, the Aro had not subscribed to *Ala* and *Chi* at the onset of the overseas slave trade, even though most of them seem to have adopted kolanut and yam reverence. The process of Aro Igboization intensified with Aro expansion into the Igbo heartland in the mid-eighteenth century, and the process accelerated during the twentieth century. As emerges in the following pages, there is a difference between the Aro who left the Igbo-Ibibio-Efik borderland to establish settlements in the Igbo heartland and present-day inhabitants of those settlements, themselves mostly descendants of non-Aro Igbo immigrants who joined incoming Aro charter groups. The ethnolinguistic diversity of the Bight of Biafra, the close relationship of trade and culture, and the need to cast light on the background of the African diaspora in the Americas justify a cultural perspective to the study of the region's slave trade.

The pivotal role the Aro diaspora played in the rise of the Biafra Atlantic trade shaped and was shaped by both external forces and the region's political economy, defined as the totality of the region's economic, political, cultural, social, and ideological processes. The Aro built their influence mainly by extending preexisting commercial infrastructure and adapting spiritual norms to new circumstances (Ijoma and Njoku 1991:307; Northrup 1978b:142). And expanding trade in the eighteenth century was, in the first instance, the function of increasing Euro-American demand. Although shaped by internal developments, the trade and its aftermath affected the region in many ways. By asserting the collaborative relevance of both internal *and* external factors, this study departs from the strong tendency in African studies to see historical agency as deriving from either one *or*, and the other. The interactive approach seeks agency in both internal and external processes and examines how their interaction produced change. This approach throws light on the Atlantic world into which the Aro sold people, not only for pecuniary ends but also for other reasons touching on particular visions of the political and social order. By focusing on one region of Atlantic Africa, the present study provides some basis for understanding developments in the Atlantic region. The following chapters explore African patterns of supply, American patterns of demand, and the sociocultural processes underpinning them. This study should thus be read more than simply as an analysis of the slave trade in the Bight of Biafra. It makes pertinent connections and comparisons with other regions at many junctures; two of these connections – the use of the average daily loading rates of slave ships to measure the intensity of slaving interregionally and the implication for the gender structure of the slave trade of the culture and commerce that developed around kolanut – are introduced here for the first time.

The arrangement of the chapters is both chronological and thematic. There are chronological overlaps, but even within the affected sections, I have strived to present the material chronologically. Chapter 1 details the historical and historiographical contexts of the Biafra Atlantic slave trade, and stakes out the claim that the rise and expansion of the Aro merchant group and their organization as a trade diaspora were pivotal to the massive expansion of the Biafra trade in the mid-eighteenth century. In Chapter 2, I relate the chronology of Aro expansion during its first and second phases to the oscillations in the Biafra Atlantic trade up until 1807, when the British, carriers of the bulk of the region's trade, abolished the traffic. Focusing on the second and third phases, Chapter 3 situates Aro slaving in the regional context with an emphasis on Aro organization between the 1740s and 1850s, a period that captured both the expansion and decline of the Biafra Atlantic slave trade. I link cultural and economic processes within the Bight of Biafra to the Atlantic slave trade in Chapters 4–6, presenting slaving within the region, not just in terms of economic relationships, but also in terms of collateral, social, cultural, and ideological systems. Chapter 4 illustrates how the formation and expansion of the Aro diaspora as a result of the expanding overseas slave trade reconfigured the geocultural landscape of the Bight of Biafra hinterland. On the other hand, endogenous sociocultural practices, such as slavery, means of enslavement, and conceptions of the Atlantic world helped to shape the composition of export captives. The means, process, and structure of slaving are thus the subject of Chapter 5, with a focus on who got enslaved or retained in the region, and who got shipped to the Americas, how and why. Chapter 6 engages with the unusual gender structure of the Biafra slave trade and explains it by patterns of domestic consumption, ritual, warfare, gender division of labor in agriculture, and long-distance trade. Chapter 7 continues the story of cultural changes imposed by the Atlantic slave trade into the final phase of Aro expansion between 1850 and 1902, highlighting the increased incidence of warfare both as the long-term effect of slaving and as the immediate impact of the end of the overseas slave trade. Detailed analysis of the demographic impact has been left out because it has received attention elsewhere (Nwokeji 2000). It suffices here to affirm that the demographic impact was less severe in the Bight of Biafra and its hinterland than in most other regions, not because fewer captives were removed from here, but because the region gained population from immigration from outlying inland areas, and did not suffer the adverse effect of the additional slave trade from across the Sahara. Unlike other West African regions, that trade was marginal in the region. Chapter 8 summarizes and concludes the study. A detailed note on the sources appears at the end.

In the course of writing this book, I have accumulated debts of gratitude to numerous individuals and organizations. At the University of Toronto Ph.D. program where it all began, the history department, School of Graduate Studies, and the Center for International Development gave generous funding. Over the years, funding has also come from the history department and the Institute for African American Studies, both of the University of Connecticut (UConn), as well as from the African American studies department and the Chancellor of the University of California, Berkeley. This book has benefited from the congenial atmospheres and resources afforded me in the following institutions where I have held visiting positions over the years – the history department of Emory University, the DuBois Institute for Afro-American Research at Harvard University, the Gilder Lehrman Center at Yale University, and Zentrum Moderner Orient, Berlin, Germany. I enjoyed the assistance of many librarians and archivists in several countries, but I would like to single out U.O.A. Esse of the Nigerian National Archives, Enugu, and Father Leo Laden of the Holy Ghost Provincialate, Dublin, Republic of Ireland. Among the elders who taught me aspects of Aro and Igbo history are the late Eze John O. Dike and Eze Jonas Ekemezie Uche, as well as K.G. Ufere, the late Aaron Muotoh, Michael Sunday Igwe, the late Jacob Okoro, Ukobasi Kanu-Igbo, J.G. Okoro, Thomas Okereke, the late Eneanya Akpu, and Azubuike Nkemakonam Nwaokoye-Emesuo (Periccomo). The late Princewill Imo gave me an insight into the Izuogu lineage in a way few are able and willing to offer. Obi and Ngozi Uche helped me clarify some items in the Aro vocabulary. Ohiaeri Okoro, Aloy Igbo and Fritz-Canute Ngwa, and my cousins Ifeanyi Ike and Emeka Okoronkwo, helped during crucial junctures of the fieldwork; Udi Ojiako provided me invaluable material about and insight into Nri-Awka history. I would like to single out J. Okoro Ijoma and the late Rev. Canon Amos Egwuekwe D. Mgbemene ("AED") for their assistance during my fieldwork, including giving access to sources and contacts and their own invaluable intellectual reflections on Aro history. All my colleagues in the history department of UConn during 1999–2003 and in the African American studies department at Berkeley since 2003 have given me every support possible.

Numerous scholars have contributed in many ways to the extent that it is possible to inadvertently omit several, and I apologize to those who I may leave out. I count myself extremely lucky to have been a student of Martin Klein, who introduced me to slavery studies and supervised the dissertation that gave rise to this book. He always asked the hard questions, gave generously from his time and personal financial resources, and has tirelessly motivated me over the years to publish this work. Almost like a guardian angel, Paul Lovejoy has always been there from the time of my introduction to slavery studies to now, giving me as much attention as he would his own formal students, and he shared generously from his extensive knowledge of the slave trade. David Eltis has been a wonderful mentor, inspirer, and friend, and has always done more than I could ask for. Michael Levin and Nakanyike Musisi were of great assistance at the University of Toronto. Southeastern Nigerian scholars of my generation owe enormous intellectual debt to those who have paved the way for us, most prominently the late Adiele Afigbo, Ebiegberi Joe Alagoa (my teacher), the late K. Onwuka Dike, the late Felicia Ekejiuba, Robin Horton, the late G.I. Jones, Elizabeth Isichei, David Northrup, and Simon Ottenberg.

Many others deserve credit for comments on drafts of this book – five anonymous reviewers for Cambridge University Press; Toyin Falola who commented extensively on an advanced draft and has always provided useful advice; Gloria Chuku, Jonathan Sadowsky, and Bob Shenton who offered insightful comments on a very early draft, just as Steve Behrendt, Robin Law, and Sean Hawkins did on several draft chapters. John Thornton has been extremely supportive of this work and my career over the years, among other things, drawing my attention to useful sources and sharing his translations of pertinent passages from the writings of Christian Georg Andreas Oldendorp (2000). Three other friends have also helped me with translations – Heike Raphael-Hernandez Onyinye Obidoa with portions of Oldendorp 1995a and 1995b, and Victor Madeira with passages of Alonso Sandoval's book. David Dickson, the late Felicia Ekejiuba, Jane Guyer, Susan Hargreaves, the late Martin Lynn, Obi Nwakanma, Ikem Stan Okoye, John Peel, Richard Rathbone, Obiora Udechukwu, and Innocent Uzoechi graciously helped with various resources when I intruded in their lives.

Over the years, I have benefited enormously from advice by Jerome Handler, the late Ogbu Kalu, Richard Roberts, David Richardson, and Chris Youé. The following people – many of whom are also great friends – have supported me in various ways: Ibrahim Abdullah, Bendi Agocha, Andrea Arrington, Johnson Asiegbu, Edna Bay, Eli Bentor, Carolyn

Brown, Alex Byrd, Michael Echeruo, Felix Ekechi, Peter Ekeh, Michael Gomez, Gwendolyn Hall, Axel Herneit-Sievers, Jocelyn Jacquot, Joseph Inikori, Ray Kea, Tony Kirk-Greene, Joseph Miller, Kristin Mann, Phil Morgan, Ben Naanen, Onwuka Njoku, Chidi Nwaubani, Onaiwu Ogbomo, Andrew Okolie, Rachel Sullivan, Vincent Bakpetu Thompson, Maureen Warner-Lewis, and Hans Zell. My thanks also go to the late Don Ohadike, to whom this book is dedicated.

Finally and by no means the least, I salute my family for doing everything for me. My parents, Godwin Ukobasi and Christiana Ejenene Nwokeji, challenged me to be the best I can be but they are no longer around to see this book. I am grateful to my wife Nnenna and our children Anaezi, Nwaka, and Ukaobasi, who have come to enrich my life and have sacrificed much in the long course of writing this book. I also salute my siblings and their spouses for their support: Georgy Umenaa and Philip Umunnakwe, May Enda and Tony Okafor, Uche Cele and Fab Amobi, Oby and Uche Ikoro, and Maureen and Obi Anadi. For many stimulating intellectual exchanges, I am grateful to my father-in-law, His Royal Highness Eze (Professor) Green Nwankwo. Of course, I alone am responsible for any remaining errors.

Foreword

Paul E. Lovejoy

The interior of the Bight of Biafra has been somewhat of an enigma in the attempt to reconstruct the history of Africa during the era of transatlantic slavery. Its importance in the peopling of the Americas is clear. Perhaps one in six enslaved Africans came from the region. And while there is disagreement in estimating the relative proportions of people who can be identified as Igbo, Ibibio, and other ethnic categories and, indeed, in the meaning of these categories, it does seem certain that most people came from the relatively densely populated areas immediately inland from the coast behind the Niger Delta. Although Portuguese and other European traders did acquire some enslaved Africans from the Bight of Biafra in the sixteenth and seventeenth centuries, the overwhelming majority of people from the region left in the eighteenth and nineteenth centuries, and especially in the century after circa 1730. The enigma is that it has been difficult to document this migration, the causes of enslavement, and any relevant political and economic factors that might explain the phenomenon and its timing.

The reason for this difficulty relates to two factors. First, there is a paucity of documentary and oral sources that might be used in historical reconstruction for the eighteenth and early nineteenth centuries. Second, there seems to be what might be called a "wall of silence" in the region about the past. Perhaps the lack of centralized institutions that can preserve details of the past explains this problem. There seem to be few historical benchmarks, such as the accession to office of political figures, their deaths, major battles, and such chronologically specific details that can be useful in historical reconstruction. There is historical memory, of course, but it is often connected with titled societies and associations that require initiation and secrecy rather than the accumulation of knowledge about the chronological past. The political and social titles were related to positions of rank, but these are difficult to identify with specific individuals within a precise chronology. History tends to be telescoped, therefore, which has meant that historians have had to be innovative in attempting to provide a structure to analyze change over time.

For these reasons, G. Ugo Nwokeji's study of the Aro is important. One of the exceptions, the Aro have retained memories and traditions that help to establish a chronology for the interior of the Bight of Biafra. As the principal merchants in slaves and other commodities of long-distance trade, Aro merchants have left traditions of origin, settlement, and internal migration that coincide with the expansion of the slave trade in the Bight of Biafra. Nwokeji follows in the footsteps of K.O. Dike, F. Ekijuiba and David Northrup, whose pioneering work established the Aro role in the history of the Bight of Biafra. But the difficulty of historical reconstruction tied to a chronological framework plagued their research. By drawing on the latest estimates of the scale and timing of slave departures from the Bight of Biafra, Nwokeji is able to establish a chronology that can be correlated with Aro settlement patterns and oral traditions in the interior. The results of his analysis will be subject to debate and refinement, but the methodological breakthrough deserves notice.

How are historians to deal with gaps in documentation and historical memory that is telescoped? Why is it that in some places there is a wealth of historical documentation, while in other places it is difficult to reconstruct the basic chronology of the past? It seems as if some societies and some eras want to remember and document events, whereas in other contexts, such detail is not considered necessary and perhaps is even not desirable. Does the effort to restrict knowledge as "secrets" of titled societies interfere with historical memory? Can we talk about the interior of the Bight of Biafra as an area that was "without history" in that historical details were secondary to the focus on attainment, as measured in titles and membership, in which inheritance and tradition were tailored to the future rather than to chronicling the past? How did such constructions of knowledge and society affect those who were taken to the Americas as slaves? Nwokeji attempts to confront these questions in a provocative new interpretation of the history of the interior of the Bight of Biafra.

1

Introduction

In about 1733, Izuogu Mgbokpo, an Aro merchant from Arochukwu, in the Cross River region of what is now southeastern Nigeria, settled his people, or *ndi̯* (a generic term for offspring, henchmen, followers, clients, and slaves), on a major trade route located some 30 kilometers west of the upper Imo River in the densely populated central Igboland. Called *Aro-ndi-Izuogu* (Izuogu's people's Aro, conventionally written as *Arondizuogu*), this settlement eventually became the largest and most populous Aro settlement. Other Aro merchants soon established settlements farther northwest and in the densely populated part of Ibibioland south of Arochukwu. These merchants were part of an intricate network that accounted for the huge increase in the numbers of captives leaving the Bight of Biafra after 1740. Neighboring people supplied the Aro with produce, captives, and some porterage services, while the Aro, in turn, provided foreign goods, indicating the extent of the region's entanglement with the emerging world economic system. Among these goods, guns and gunpowder came from various European centers, "george" cloth from the Netherlands and most other cloth from India, while tobacco was being produced in the Chesapeake Bay region in today's United States, principally by Biafrans who had been exported as captives of the overseas traffic.[1]

[1] I reconstruct the foregoing detail from the following sources: NAE 81/27-OKIDIST 4/9/70; NAE OR/C/823-ORLDIST 3/1/359; NAE 12481A-MINLOC 16/1/1326; NAE OKIDIST 19/1/1 1908–25; NAE ORLDIST 14/1/3; NAE 35/1920-OKIDIST 4/2/32; NAE 38/22 OKIDIST 4/4/29; NAE CSE 1/85/6197A; Arodiogbu 1996; J.O. Dike 1996; K.O. Dike and Ekejiuba 1990:205–08; Goodlife 1933, 1952; Heslop 1936; M.S. Igwe 1996; Michael Ike 1995; Mayne 1935; J.C. Nwankwo 1973; C. Okoli 1996; J.G. Okoro

The Atlantic slave market provided attractive profits, but the Aro always ensured that they retained within their group many of the people they traded. As a small group, the Aro concentrated on group expansion and depended economically on slaves as both merchandise and laborers. Aro political contests, such as the civil wars and succession disputes, as well as such social facts as marriage, tribute, and the incest prohibition were deeply entangled with slaving. The people's belief system and their media of worship were grounded in, and reinforced by, slaving related processes. Their value system celebrated the ownership and proliferation of people and encouraged the sale of captives into Atlantic slavery. The decision regarding whom to send into Atlantic slavery and whom to retain was central to Aro political economy and, ipso facto, to this study.

Aro slave trade involved both business and social engineering. The overwhelming majority of captives that Aro traders bought from the non-Aro people were random victims of war, kidnapping, and sundry methods but many were innocent. The Aro welcomed craftsmen, artists, medicine men, fortune seekers, refugees, and others who desired the prestige and protection that Aro citizenship conferred during that time. But even these noncaptive immigrants found that they could enter Aro society only as protected persons under Aro patrons – normally males – who were already well established there. The Aro concept of *mmuba*, meaning, at the most basic level, "proliferation," captured the phenomenon of expansion. Aro oral history and folklore often refer to *mmuba* as an end in itself, but this ideology also encapsulated the people's desire to increase the labor pool and to strengthen the Aro population for geopolitical purposes.

By the mid-nineteenth century, the Aro world comprised more than 150 diaspora settlements across the Biafra hinterland. These communities celebrated common observances and maintained linkage institutions, such as the annual *Ikeji* festival, the *Ekpe* society, and the *Ibu* routine homage system. These institutions fostered and sustained a strong pan-Aro identity that facilitated Aro political interests and commercial hegemony. Yet, in spite of these linkage institutions, the Aro diaspora was susceptible to the cultural influence of host societies and

---

1985:23–28; J.E. Uche 1996; Umo n.d. One enslaved African of Ibibio origin told German Moravian missionary Christian Georg Andreas Oldendorp in Pennsylvania in the late 1760s that the Aro, whose land "was not too far from [Ibibioland]," supplied the Ibibio with "riffles, sabres, powder, lead, linen, and the like" (Oldendorp 1987: 167).

Introduction

of the societies from which the Aro drew immigrants. For example, an estimated more than 1 million inhabitants of the Aro settlements in central Igboland, the vast majority of whom descended from people who were not Aro 250 years ago, speak a dialect that deviates substantially from the one spoken in metropolitan Arochukwu.[2] The frontierspeople also brought with them new media of worship and developed new taboos and even notions of class consciousness. These developments did not result simply from the routine domestication that is associated with frontier societies, colonists, or immigrant groups adapting to a new environment; they were also shaped by the Aro struggle to dominate trade in various parts of the Biafra hinterland. Ironically, while the Aro diaspora altered Aro ways, sometimes radically, the Aro nevertheless often remained aloof and distinct from the preexisting communities in their immediate neighborhood, ostensibly in order to maintain strict fidelity to Aro culture.

After the trade in palm oil replaced the Atlantic slave trade in the mid-nineteenth century, most of the region's food-producing groups devoted more of their efforts to the production of palm oil and palm kernel oil. Other groups became actively involved in the new trade, giving the Aro keener competition than they had had in the days of the overseas slave trade. These developments restructured the Aro economy and affected Aro relationships with the non-Aro. By the 1890s, the Aro had begun to produce foodstuffs for domestic consumption and, increasingly, for the market, while continuing to dominate what was left of the slave traffic, until the British Aro Expedition of 1901–02 overthrew the Aro and imposed a new order. The present study elaborates the foregoing story and situates it in Atlantic and regional contexts.

---

[2] This estimate is from a 1.5 percent compounded annual growth rate of 45,000 inhabitants in 1927 for Arondizuogu, by far the largest Aro diaspora settlement, plus a roughly equal number of inhabitants for the rest of Aro settlements in central Igboland. A 1927 estimate put Arondizuogu's population at 30,000 (see NAE 81/27-OKIDIST 4/9/70. "Anthropological Report on Aros of Ndizuogu and Others"). The report itself shows that colonial officials made their estimate based on one part of the town alone, the part that fell into the Orlu District (making up most of the Arondizuogu territory west of the Imo), leaving out the part that fell into the Okigwe District (east of the Imo and some territory on the west bank). One 1935 report again covered only the Orlu part, as did the map accompanying it (see Mayne 1935). I have increased this figure to 45,000 because the 1927 estimate underrepresented the population after leaving out east-Imo Arondizuogu. This situation obviates any attempt to derive reliable census figures. Theresa Nwankwo (1991:10) has claimed that a 1931 census put the population at 180,000, which would drastically escalate present estimates. I have not seen this census.

MAIN FEATURES, ORGANIZATION, AND EXPANSION OF THE OVERSEAS SLAVE TRADE

Although the Biafra trade grew dramatically in the eighteenth century, it represented a small part of the overall African Atlantic trade before the 1740s. The region's share of captives exported from all African regions combined was only 5.5 percentage points in the first half of the seventeenth century. Although there was an appreciable increase in trade in the third quarter of the seventeenth century, the Biafra trade quickly entered a long period of decline.[3] By the 1670s, Bende, the principal slave mart in the Biafra hinterland, was already well established (Nwokeji 1997a). Captives leaving Bight of Biafra ports were carried mainly on English ships; some 80 percent of Biafra captives ended up in English America colonies during the eighteenth century.[4] The region's share of total African trade rose by 13.6 percentage points between the 1700s and the end of the century. Eighteenth-century British slave trader John Hippisley must have echoed his contemporaries' sentiments when he wondered "how Africa [was] able to supply ... such prodigious numbers" (Hippisley 1764:1).

In the Bight of Biafra, the big surge in slave trade took place in the 1740s. The region exported an annual mean of about 13,800 captives between 1741 and 1800; that number increased to about 20,000 a year in the 1780s. Taking up only about 270 kilometers of coastline, the southeastern Nigerian portion of the Bight of Biafra was during this period the site of the most intensive slaving in Atlantic Africa, accounting for 90

---

[3] Except when otherwise stated, overall Biafra export figures are calculated from the *Expanded Online Trans-Atlantic Slave Trade Database* (Slavevoyages.org). There are many contending estimates. See Anstey 1975; Behrendt 1997; Curtin 1969, 1976; Eltis 1978, 1987, 1989b, 1995; Eltis and Richardson 1995a; Inikori 1976a, 1976b, 1978, 1992b; Lovejoy 1982b; Richardson 1989a, 1989b; Richardson and Behrendt 1995. See Henige 1986; Inikori 1994a, 1994b, 1998; Lovejoy 1989; and Manning 1998b for analyses of the historiography.

[4] For the Biafra Atlantic slave trade to 1700, see Thornton 1999. John Thornton states: "Undoubtedly ... the greatest source of slaves for New Calabar [then the dominant port] was the Igbo-speaking region" (11). As early as 1627, Spanish missionary priest Alonso de Sandoval reported that *Caravalies*, as Biafra captives were then called, were "innumerable" in Spanish America and spoke a variety of tongues (de Sandoval [1627] 1956:94, 96). A 1790s British House of Lords survey shows that the Bight of Biafra and West-Central Africa accounted for 78 percent of all captives arriving in Jamaica from known African ports. This pattern reflects that of other English colonies. Between these two regions, the Bight of Biafra exported more (H. Klein 1978, 147–48, 150, 173). It accounted for 40 percent of all British purchases just before abolition in 1807 (Law and Lovejoy 1996).

percent of the region's overseas trade. The mid-century surge had implications for Biafra's major ports. Bonny, serving mainly the trade from the Igbo heartland, superseded Old Calabar as the region's preeminent port between 1726 and 1750; by 1750 it was the single busiest slaving port in Africa north of the Equator. Turnaround rates at Biafra's ports also became significantly shorter than they were elsewhere. Indeed, the 1740s marked a turning point in the Biafra Atlantic trade. By the third quarter of the century, the "trust" system, by which Europeans advanced goods to African merchants on credit, had been well established (Lovejoy and Richardson 1997, 1999). In addition to this extraordinary expansion of trade, the Bight of Biafra exported higher proportions of females than any other major coastal region. This characteristic deviated from the focus of New World demand, which tilted heavily toward males. To properly understand these unique features of the Biafra Atlantic slave trade, a close examination of the institutions and processes that underpinned the trade in Africa is imperative.[5]

The Nigerian section of the Bight of Biafra was home to numerous ethnolinguistic groups. The Igbo and Ibibio people predominated in the region south of the Benue River, known today as southeastern Nigeria. These two groups had long provided most of the export captives.[6] German-born Moravian missionary Christian Georg Andreas Oldendorp reported a substantial Igbo and Ibibio presence in the Caribbean and North America during the late 1760s. By the mid-eighteenth century, Biafrans had become the largest African group in the Chesapeake.[7] They were also a substantial presence in the British Caribbean. Most of the captives exported from Biafra – some 70 percent, according to most estimates – passed through the Aro network (K.O. Dike and Ekejiuba 1990, 250; Ijoma and Njoku 1991:300). The Aro were also the largest slaveholders in the hinterland. More than any other group, they were linked directly to region-wide institutions. Along with the coastal city state of Old Calabar and Cross River Igbo warrior groups, the Aro participated in

---

[5] Eltis 1986; Eltis and Engerman 1992, 1993; Galenson 1986:97–114; Geggus 1989:37–38, 40–41; Inikori 1992a; H. Klein 1978:174, 241–42; 1983:35–37; Lovejoy and Hogendorn 1979; Robertson and Klein 1983; Thornton 1991, 1998.

[6] A 1953 census shows that the Igbo and the Ibibio made up respectively 68.56 percent and 10.36 percent of the region south of the Benue River known today as southeastern Nigeria. *International Population Census* 1953. (See "Population Census of Eastern Region of Nigeria 1953.")

[7] Oldendorp [1777] 1995, 2000: ms. 427–28, 431–32, 459, 462, 464, 466. For the Virginia evidence see Chambers 2005:10–11; Gomez 1998:115–16; Kulikoff 1986:321–23; Morgan 1998:62, 63; Sobel 1987:5; Walsh 1997:67.

the *Ekpe* confraternity.[8] This society settled credit matters and provided local law enforcement, as well as monopolized the *Nsibiri* writing system. The Aro controlled the *Ibiniukpabi* oracle, which served as the highest court of appeal, including for the coastal city-states and communities on the west side of the Niger River. Further, they maintained alliances with Cross River Igbo warrior communities that facilitated Aro wars in different parts of the region, operated the region's rotational slave fairs, and zoned virtually all parts of the region to individual Aro lineage-groups as spheres of influence (*mbia*). Overseeing these *mbia* on a day-to-day basis were a variety of permanent diaspora settlements corresponding to the respective Aro lineage-groups. These settlements ranged from small, peacefully established Aro presences within preexisting non-Aro lineage-groups to large conquest settlements. The existence of Aro settlements in areas separated by distance, language, and cultural practices within the Biafra hinterland was an Aro hallmark.

In spite of this highly visible role, Aro organization and its basic chronology are still in need of integration into Atlantic scholarship. Perhaps the most promising line of inquiry is to relate Aro expansion to the expansion of the Biafra Atlantic trade and to explain the correlation of the two processes. Aro expansion occurred in four main phases. The first phase – lasting from the beginning of the seventeenth century to the end of the 1730s – witnessed the consolidation of the Arochukwu metropole, the establishment of Aro influence in the Cross River Region, the foundation of the principal market at Bende, Aro forays into Ibibioland and central Igboland, and the rise of Old Calabar (the city closest to Arochukwu) as Biafra's principal port. The second phase – beginning in about 1740 – witnessed great expansion in the Biafra export slave trade, the establishment of Aro settlements in the Biafran hinterland, and Bonny's supersession of Old Calabar as Biafra's principal port. This period ended in 1808 when the British, carriers of some 80 percent of Biafra captives, abolished slave traffic. The third phase of Aro expansion began in 1808, following British abolition, to the end of the Atlantic slave trade by 1850, the region's deeper involvement in the overseas palm oil trade, and the expansion of the domestic slave market. The fourth and final phase began in the 1850s and ended in 1902, when the British

---

[8] This society took the name *Okonko* in other areas, such as the Niger delta states and southern Igboland where the Aro exported this institution. The role of this variant of the society comes out most clearly in the work of John Oriji (Oriji 1982, 1983). The examination of the role of the *Ekpe* society as an agency of slave procurement awaits future research.

conquered Arochukwu. By the 1890s, the Aro had vigorously embraced agriculture in an effort to minimize the pangs of the world depression in the oils trade and to cope with their food needs. Along with a host of domestic social implications, Aro adoption of agriculture generated conflicts when the group expanded into agricultural regions at the expense of the preexisting communities. The Aro case highlights the interconnectedness of major changes in the Bight of Biafra with changes in the overseas trade and its aftermath over three centuries.

THE ARO IN THE HISTORIOGRAPHY OF THE BIAFRA SLAVE TRADE

The literature of the Bight of Biafra slave trade has often dealt separately with the hinterland and coastal sections of the region rather than considering the two in their relationship within the Atlantic system. This tendency has impeded the effective study of the region's involvement in the Atlantic slave trade. Consequently, Joseph Inikori has lamented the neglect of the region in the production of studies dealing with the Atlantic slave trade, despite a massive surge in captive export there in the second half of the eighteenth century (Inikori 1994a:9). The literature of the Atlantic slave trade has dealt with the coastal states rather than the hinterland, even though much of the trade was subject to influences from the hinterland, while the work dealing with the hinterland did not actively link the Aro to the Atlantic context.[9]

Aro historiography effectively began in the mid-nineteenth century, when Europeans and Sierra Leone–based African returnees from Atlantic slavery traveled the Niger River and began to pay special attention to the Aro. Based mostly on hearsay, their reports focused on Aro omnipresence in the region via trade and/or oracular activities.[10] British attention to the Aro and efforts to suppress them left a trove of paperwork, ensuring that Anglo-Aro relations and the Aro role in the domestic slave trade during the postoverseas slave trade era – rather than the overseas trade itself – loom large in the historiography. Interest in the Aro continued into the early colonial period, although much of the colonial-era literature was nonhistorical. Even the historical work that

---

[9] For studies dealing with the Atlantic slave trade with a focus on coastal states, see Alagoa 1964, 1970, 1971a, 1971b, 1972, 1986; Cookey 1974; Hargreaves 1987; Latham 1973; Nair 1972; Noah 1980; Wariboko 1991.

[10] Allen and Thomson 1848a; Baikie 1856; Burdo 1880; Crowther and Taylor 1859; J.A.B. Horton 1863:183–85; Hutchinson 1861.

germinated during that era did not produce much notable information on the Aro trading system. Instead, it concentrated on Aro origins (G.I. Jones 1939:101). In tune with the Hamitic hypothesis – the tendency to attribute "civilizations" found in Africa to descendants of the Biblical Ham – the British seemed bent on locating external provenance for the Aro, one that would ultimately be linkable to Caucasian influence. The resulting theories of Aro origins were so speculative that historian Adiele Afigbo has insisted on putting them on the same footing as Aro sagas. Afigbo's analysis has itself come under severe criticism, illustrating the continued interest in the subject.[11]

Major Arthur Leonard's firsthand account of the Aro market at Bende during 1896 was the first published work on the Aro. While Leonard provided useful glimpses into a changing Aro society, as a harbinger of British invasion, he was interested mainly in immediate strategic matters (Leonard 1898). Several British military officers generated useful ethnographic information in a round of publications that appeared in the wake of the Aro Expedition of 1901–02.[12] The multivolume work by colonial officer and anthropologist Amaury Talbot, published in 1926, provided equal measures of useful and chimerical information on Aro organization.[13] In the 1920s and 1930s, the colonial government commissioned "intelligence" and anthropological reports that produced significant knowledge of the Aro.[14] From the 1930s through the 1960s, local historians and other scholars in many communities in the region did much spadework.[15] The aforementioned sources did not, however,

---

[11] Afigbo (1971b, 31; 1972a). Afigbo's critique has, with some justification, been termed a stretch (Nwauwa 1995, 110). As made clear in Chapter 2, however, Afigbo's comments on the genealogies collected by colonial administrators should be taken seriously.

[12] A.G. Leonard 1906:34, 175, 183, 308–09, 287, 486; MacAlister 1902; Mockler-Ferryman 1902:127, 222; Steel 1908; Venour 1902; Vickery 1906. For an illuminating scholarly account of Aro-British relations up until the invasion, see Anene 1959.

[13] Instances of the latter category are his claims that the Aro were of Carthaginian provenance and that they ran a theocracy (Talbot 1926a:183; 1926b:50, 52, 338; 1926c: 592, 821).

[14] See Anthropologists' Papers 1927; Mathews 1922; Mayne 1935; Shankland 1933.

[15] See Nwana [1933] 1950; Ojike 1947; Umo n.d. [1947?]; Igwegbe 1962, and Uku 1993. A portion of Uku's account that appeared in the *West African Review* (Dec. 1953) is quoted widely. For more recent works see A.O. Anyoha 1977; Irono 1988; Mbadiwe 1991; E.O. Mmeregini n.d; E.O. Okoli 1977; J.G. Okoro 1985. For a representative sample of theses, see Agu 1985; Anaba 1988; Chuku 1989; Emeruwa 1992; C. Eze 1987; C.E. Igwe 1992; Imo 1980; G.C. Mmeregini 1978; Monye 1991; I.O. Nwankwo 1986; J.C. Nwankwo 1973; T. Nwankwo 1991; D.C. Nwosu 1978; Onyensoh 1985; B.N.N. Orji 1978.

provide reliable chronologies and did not explicitly place the Aro in regional trade, let alone the Atlantic system.

Serious historical inquiry into the Aro role in regional trade, however, began with the seminal work of historian K. Onwuka Dike. Although he focused on the coastal trading states, Dike referred to the Aro as the "economic dictators of the hinterland," and emphasized the role of their oracle, *Ibiniukpabi* (K.O. Dike 1956:38). The role of oracles in Igbo social organization has since been studied, as have the workings of Aro influence and the importance of *Ibiniukpabi*, leading to the finding that this oracle was not a major source of captives (S. Ottenberg 1958; 1971:24–26).[16] It was, however, the former British colonial officer and anthropologist G.I. Jones who began to place the Aro in a regional chronological framework. Based on the traditions of the coastal port states, Jones suggested that the Aro had been formed by the mid-seventeenth century (Jones 1963, 134). This means that the Aro had been well established by the eighteenth century when the Biafra Atlantic trade became prominent. Together, the aforementioned works established the significance of the Aro in the region's political economy and commercial history. Unfortunately, however, these important contributions did not stimulate scholarship in the hinterland.

Systematic analysis of hinterland trade began during the late 1960s. The genealogy of this historiography starts with regional geographer Ukwu I. Ukwu's pioneering study of the regional marketing system, trade routes, and delivery systems. Ukwu identified the conscious coordination of diaspora settlements with fairs and trade routes as the distinctive feature of the Aro system (Ukwu 1967:1969). His work foreshadowed the scholarly interest in regional trade, as well as in Aro operations and the institutions that underpinned them, that developed during the 1970s. Similar studies proliferated in the early 1970s (Ekejiuba 1972a, 1972b; Northrup 1972; Ofonagoro 1972). Further, Afigbo mapped the extent of regional trade and highlighted the hitherto neglected trade links between southeastern Nigeria and the Middle Belt to the north, complementing extant studies on Igbo–Middle Belt relations.[17] It is noteworthy that the relevant scholarship of the late 1960s and early 1970s concentrated on trading mechanisms, trade routes, goods, and supply systems. It had little to say on the implications of these processes for politics, culture, and social organization.

---

[16] K.O. Dike and Ekejiuba 1990, 250; Ekejiuba 1972b, 12; J.O. Ijoma 1986c; Ijoma and Njoku 1991:206, 300; Northrup 1978, 138; Ofonagoro 1972:83.

[17] Afigbo 1973b, 1977; Boston 1968; Shelton 1971; Sargent 1999:173–89, 252–59.

A holistic approach to regional history developed from the mid-1970s. Elizabeth Isichei's (1973, 1976:49–67) work dealing with Igbo history was the most notable example of this trend. The underlying theme of Isichei's work is transformations in the Igbo social economy. She traces the process by which trade-induced migrations between the seventeenth and nineteenth centuries helped to shape modern Igboland. The efforts of many other scholars – university thesis authors, nonprofessional local historians of increasing sophistication, and professional historians – have since further clarified our understanding of this process through a plethora of cases studies. These contributions did not, however, relate Aro expansion to the Atlantic slave trade.[18]

In their study of West Africa as whole, historians Paul Lovejoy and Jan Hogendorn see the rise of the Biafra Atlantic trade in the mid-eighteenth century as the culmination of four developments: expansion in the structure and organization of the coastal states; the role of the *Ekpe* society in guaranteeing credit; the division of the lower Niger trade among the Ijo and the Niger riverine states; and the consolidation of the Aro network in the hinterland (Lovejoy and Hogendorn 1979:225–31). Lovejoy and Hogendorn's critical insight that the African slave trade was organized around self-conscious regional cartels has received implicit support from empirical findings about the institutional basis of the Aro network in southern Igboland (Oriji 1982, 1983, 1987). Because Lovejoy and Hogendorn's study did not primarily focus on the Bight of Biafra, it did not resolve the important question of the timing of the developments they identified, an essential step in establishing the extent to which the trading groups caused or resulted from them. The developments may have been repercussions of major environmental and geopolitical changes in late-sixteenth- and early-seventeenth-century West Africa, as Robert Sargent has argued (Sargent 1999:15–20).

One common limitation of the Biafra literature is that, while gender relations in the societies of the region have sometimes received attention, the gender structure of the Atlantic slave trade has suffered neglect, even though it has long been discernible to scholars not primarily focused in

---

[18] For examples of pertinent studies done by professional historians, see Afigbo 1977, 1981a, 1981b, 1987; Ifemesia 1978, 1979; Ijoma and O.N. Njoku 1991; Oguagha 1991; Ohadike 1994; Oriji 1987; O.N. Njoku 2000; Uya 1984. Of no less significance is the work of anthropologist M. Angulu Onwuejeogwu 1975, 1981, 1987. For published work dealing specifically with aspects of Aro history by a variety of authors, see K.O. Dike and Ekejiuba 1990; Eni 1973; Ezekiah Muotoh 2000; Igwegbe 1962; Ijoma 1986b, 1994; Pita Nwana 1933; Ohia 2007; J.G. Okoro 1985; Uku 1993; Umo n.d. [1947?].

the region.[19] The gender structure of the slave trade has only recently been the focus of analysis in the region (Nwokeji 1997b, 2000a, 2001). Yet, the Bight of Biafra is of particular interest in understanding African conceptions of gender. If, in other regions, the Euro-American drive to secure men was only partially successful, it all but broke down in the Bight of Biafra. In this region, the character of African warfare and the role of women in the indigenous economy and in social institutions shaped the age and gender structure of the slave trade differently from elsewhere. Key elements in this process were African conceptions of slavery and the division of labor, reproduction in the context of the lineage, polygyny, and methods of enslavement. Because of the failure to tie the Biafra trade to its Atlantic context, the implications for the aforementioned processes of the Aro being the preeminent trading group remain unexplored.

Despite its limitations, the scholarship since the mid-1970s has represented two significant shifts. First, it reintegrated trade with its politics in the manner Onwuka Dike enunciated in 1956. Some scholars now argue that the Aro dominated regional trade precisely because they developed strong state structures (see also K.O. Dike and Ekejiuba 1978, 1990; Ijoma 1986b; Stevenson 1968). Second, this scholarship located the Aro within the region-wide socioeconomic process. The Aro phenomenon became central to the analysis of the regional political economy.

STATE AND DIASPORA

If there is a consensus about the Aro role in regional political economy, the exact character of their social organization has been the subject of fierce debate among specialists, best exemplified in David Northrup's *Trade without Rulers* (1978) and Onwuka Dike and Felicia Ekejiuba's *The Aro of Southeastern Nigeria* (1990). Each of these studies has been up until now the basic reference on its subject – Northrup's on regional trade and Dike and Ekejiuba's on Aro political economy, two themes that are central to this study. Because these studies share a key concern with Aro organization, the questions they raise are essential to the present study.

---

[19] For gender relations in the region, see Hargreaves 1987; Martin 1988, 1995; Oriji 1982. For studies that have commented on the gender structure, see Eltis 1986, 1998; Eltis and Engerman 1992, 1993; Eltis and Richardson 1997; Geggus 1989; Inikori 1992a; H. Klein 1983, 35–37; Manning 1998a.

Like the present study, Northrup's admirable and meticulously researched work attempts to explain the existence of a complex commercial structure in a region where decentralized political arrangements were the norm. In a chapter titled "The God Men of the Slave Trade," Northrup correctly observes that the Aro were neither the only nor the oldest trading group in the region, but that they transcended and combined "into a single marketing grid the already existing regional networks of trade through alliances with other leading trading people to bring them into this economic structure" (Northrup 1978, 142). Northrup argues that the people of the region evolved this complex commercial organization without corresponding complex political institutions.

The uncommon nature of Aro organization does in fact invite scrutiny. Perhaps the most conspicuous question mark on Aro statehood is the fact that many Aro wars were indeed orchestrated and prosecuted by Aro lineages and, increasingly, by individual merchant-warriors, rather than the Aro as a whole. This was certainly not the case with such prominent West African states as Benin, Dahomey, Asante, and even Oyo in its heyday.[20] Northrup's argument refreshingly departs from state-centric approaches to the study of precolonial African history by making a genuine attempt to study and understand noncentralized societies on their own terms. Indeed, the existence of states was not essential to the development of the slave trade.

Northrup insists, however, that Aro organization closely resembled that of the rest of the Igbo. For him, the Aro "differed more by degree than by kind" because they depended on, rather than transcended, the segmentary organization that pervaded the region. He points to brutal intra-Aro disputes as evidence of the weakness of Aro political organization, and to their supposed lack of "substantial state structures and military force" as being responsible for their "inability to break through to the coast to trade directly with European ships" (Northrup 1978:137, 139, 140–42, 145). Such far-reaching assertions deserve scrutiny given that more evidence on Aro institutions has percolated in the more than thirty years since Northrup's remarkable work first appeared; that interest in questions about the state persists; and that Aro organization and regional trade are pivotal to the present study.[21]

---

[20] This observation has been confirmed by Martin Klein's recent survey of slaving in decentralized societies, of which the Igbo region provides a prime example (M. Klein 2001, 63). Peter Ekeh has gone as far as arguing that slaving was actually heaviest in decentralized societies (Ekeh 1990:680–82).

[21] Although the Aro were central to Northrup's work, his respondents were overwhelmingly Ibibio (Nwauwa 1995:114). Northrup's interviews with Aro people, although not

Introduction 13

To argue that politics played an insignificant role in Aro organization is to separate economics from politics. It is not otherwise possible to claim both that local alliances were indispensable to Aro organization and that Aro expansion was economic, not political, as Northrup has done (Northrup 1978:121, 142).[22] Aro alliances have been widely linked to Aro warfare precisely because they were a political phenomenon.[23] The reality of social existence can be more complicated than the heuristic distinctions scholars may seek to make between the concepts of trade and politics. The people of the Bight of Biafra and, indeed, the rest of Atlantic Africa, did not distinguish the political, spiritual, and material aspects of their life as sharply as these categories imply at first sight.

Aro "inability to break through to the coast" and intra-Aro conflicts have no necessary connection with state structures. A polity's ability and/or disposition to conquer all states in a given region is not a precondition for a state. The Aro, in fact, experienced many more disputes than Northrup highlighted, but such disputes do not necessarily mean the absence of state structures; conflicts occur in all societies.[24] Political philosophers tell us that cooperation, competition, and conflict normally characterize relations within the "political class" (see, e.g., Bottomore 1964:9). Much more than in the Aro case, brutal civil wars visited eighteenth-century Kongo Kingdom, often resulting in the overthrow of constituted authority, decimation of the population of the capital, and its recolonization with out-of-province people (Thornton 1992). Yet, the appeal of Kongo political institutions and the legitimacy of the capital remained intact. As Northrup himself recognizes, the "ability to achieve voluntary agreement in time of crisis was the key to Aro organization," and their tendency to set up permanent diaspora settlements and commitment to a common identity distinguished them from other groups (Northrup 1978b:104, 140, 142, 143). Contrary to Northrup's claim, the diasporic characteristic

---

always indicated or necessarily borne out by respondents' names, are self-evident in the content of the interviews. In my estimation, seven of Northrup's forty interviews were among the Aro. They are Asiegbu 1973; Inokun 1972; Merem and Nwankwo 1973; K. Oji 1972; F.E.S. Okoro 1973; Okori 1972; J. Udo 1972. For the transcripts, see Northrup 1972–73.

[22] Northrup argues that the Aro were a political force only in Afikpo in Cross River Igboland but were only economic imperialists elsewhere (Northrup 1978b, 121). Such a distinction is unstainable given that such settlements as Inokun, Arondizuogu, and the Ndieni cluster dominated both economic and political affairs.

[23] Bentor 1994:104–08; K.O. Dike and Ekejiuba 1990:165–71, 174–86; Isichei 1976:82–87.

[24] See, for example, K.O. Dike and Ekejiuba 1990:180–81; Igwegbe 1962:15–16, 43, 46–47, 91–93, 114–19; J.G. Okoro 1985:40–42.

of the Aro was a difference in kind, not simply of degree. The Aro were the only group in the region that deliberately and consistently established settlements abroad for the purposes of trade that were tied to the homeland through systemwide institutions.

Fitting the Aro tightly into a stateless mold merely draws from and reinforces the idealized notions of Igbo segmentarism rampantly assumed in the literature.[25] A detailed study of the Niger riverine states of Abo, Oguta, Onitsha, and Osomari revealed that generalizations about an Igbo political framework are only meaningful after each Igbo "cultural area" has been studied in detail (Nzimiro 1972). Such research as has been carried out in the past forty years or so no longer sustains the idea that the region lacked rulers, or what Northrup (1981) called a "ruling class."[26] For example, after examining the empirical evidence the members of a multidisciplinary panel of Igbo social scientists generated, a colloquy declared in 1986: "It will probably come as a surprise to many of us, nurtured as we are on the principle [that is] now clearly under severe pressure that *Igbo enwegh eze* (the Igbo have no king), to learn that in traditional Igboland the ultimate authority figure was very often a monarch of some kind" (*Ahiajoku Lecture Colloquium* 1986:ii). The fact that the region had many rulers is not evidence that it had none (Afigbo 1981b). We cannot understand indigenous slavery and the Atlantic slave trade by laying undue emphasis on leveling structures. The power held by some individuals in the region over others determined people's fate – whether they would be enslaved and, if so, whether they would be enslaved within the region or sent to the Americas.

Some of the most effective arguments against overemphasis on leveling mechanisms come from Dike and Ekejiuba, who focus on stratification and state institutions, as these characteristics concerned the historical development of trade in the region. They insist that analyzing what the Aro did, instead of pinpointing what they did not do, is more useful in determining the true nature of their political organization. The ultimate measure of Aro hegemony should emerge from a comparison with regional polities unanimously acknowledged to have evolved state structures: the Middle Belt Igala kingdom suffered decentralization, disintegration, and defections; Bonny (Biafra's premier port state) split after a

---

[25] Meek 1937; Green 1964; Carlston 1968:190–210; Echeruo 1979; Horton 1976; Henderson 1972; Nwaubani 1994.
[26] Afigbo 1973a; Anikpo 1985; Anyanwu 1993a:31–32; P.C. Dike 1986; Ubah 1987:168–72.

civil war in 1869; and the Niger riverine Onitsha kingdom simply lacked military muscle. Decentralization and disaggregation usually happened to states – including Arochukwu – as a result of trade (K.O. Dike and Ekejiuba 1990:81, 83–85). Dike and Ekejiuba periodize the history of the Aro state into three phases – the pre-1650 period, the post-1650 period, and the nineteenth century. The pre-1650 period corresponded with the segmentary lineage system usually ascribed to the entire Aro history. The period after 1650 was when King Akuma initiated state building, when primogeniture prevailed, and *Omu Aro* (Aro coat of arms) was introduced as a symbol of central authority.[27] Finally, the nineteenth century witnessed the accommodation of ethnic heterogeneity and a "dynamic response" to external regions, such as "the absence of a centralized power to challenge and compete with the Aro in the control of the [trade] of the vast hinterland" (K.O. Dike and Ekejiuba 1990:81–82, 96–103, 123). The existence of spheres of influence among the respective Aro lineage-groups is characteristic of state organization.

Yet, it is unlikely that the Aro had a high degree of centralization at any point in their history. For instance, if the wars that produced Aro settlements resulted from the initiatives and efforts of "a handful of Aro households," as Dike and Ekejiuba posit, these settlements can hardly have simultaneously been private enterprises and state-sponsored projects (K.O. Dike and Ekejiuba 1990:165). The crucial point perhaps is that Aro expansion up to the early eighteenth century was state sponsored – as illustrated in the appointment in a newly settled area of a resident *Mazi* (Consul), usually a trusted confidant of the Aro king (K.O. Dike and Ekejiuba 1990:69) – but had become the responsibility of private individuals just before mid-eighteenth century. This change perhaps resulted from the rapid proliferation of diaspora settlements and the concomitant expansion of the Bight of Biafra slave trade. This scenario contrasts sharply with Dike and Ekejiuba's own characterization of a trend toward

---

[27] Okoro Kanu stresses Eze Agwu before Akuma was the first Aro to be addressed as "Eze" as a title rather than a first name (Okoro Kanu 2000:15). Possibly, "Eze" was his first name but because he turned out to be – in the words of Kanu – a "powerful" and "accomplished ruler," the largely acephalous Igbo adopted the name as a title to refer to a person who exhibited authoritarian power, barring contrary evidence from elsewhere in Igboland, notably Nri. Scholars are unsure of when such an institution emerged in Nri, but they generally suggest a date much later than indicated by ninth-century artifacts suggesting concentration of power in the hands of an individual or individuals. While M. Angulu Onwuejeogwu asserts that the institution of Eze Nri did not emerge until "the late seventeenth and early eighteenth centuries," Thurstan Shaw suggests the end of the fifteenth century (Onwuejeogwu 1975:49; Shaw 1978:124).

increased centralization. Further, placing too much emphasis on a high degree of centralization overstates the "assimilation" of immigrants and slaves into Aro culture. While immigrant assimilation was crucial to the Aro system, overemphasizing it obscures the profound impact that the incorporated groups made on Aro culture, especially in the diaspora.[28] Finally, the penchant for the centralized-state model promotes reference to Aro settlements as "colonies," a term that fails to capture Aro communities in their variety and complexities.

However, as is typical of the debate about precolonial African political organization, which seems to assume that despotism is an essential state characteristic, the aforementioned studies share a fixation with the presence or absence of a *centralized* state. A state is effectively assumed to be present wherever despotism exists and absent where it is lacking. While Northrup showed successfully that nothing of the kind existed in the region, he equates this absence with the absence of state structures. On the other hand, political theorist Robert Stevenson who, like Northrup, could not locate a despotic regime, lamented that, although the Aro developed a state, it was not "full blown" (Stevenson 1968). Finally, Dike and Ekejiuba constructed an early autocratic state that never was. Rather than accept the proliferation of settlements as an essential feature of a trade diaspora in the context of expanding trade, they bemoan the fact that this development "eroded the monopoly of power by the central government" (K.O. Dike and Ekejiuba 1990:72). A high degree of centralization is not a necessary attribute of a state and was not necessary for Aro expansion. Social scientists have only recently begun to realize that the functions and effects of states – including the most powerful ones – are enacted outside "institutionalized politics and established bureaucracies" (see Trouillot 2001:133). Like Michel Rolf-Trouillot, who made this observation, some scholars may perhaps view this as a characteristic specific to the state in the age of globalization; but states have exhibited this characteristic for ages.

One can speak of an Aro state. The anthropologist Ronald Cohen offers a simple but nuanced insight into state theory, which is relevant to this argument. For Cohen, the distinguishing characteristic of a state is "the formation and development of institutions counteracting the normal fissioning of the polity," and he holds that "if a society fissions as a

---

[28] Judith Okely (1996) has reiterated the pitfalls of the nondialectical characterization of culture contact.

normal or expectable part of political process," it is not a state, regardless of the central government's continuing ability to enforce decisions. This is because states are "highly adaptive," irrespective of the location or specific characteristics of its constituent parts (R. Cohen 1981:81, 87, 92, 95). The Aro fit neatly into this formulation. Critically important is the fact that no Aro groups ever seceded from the Aro fold at any point in Aro history, in spite of their dispersion. The operations of specific Aro institutions that promoted Aro interests and enabled the state to counteract fissioning are analyzed in the following chapters.

Even though one can speak of an Aro state, however, the key to understanding Aro organization and regional trade is not the presence of a state system or, for that matter, its absence, but in seeing the Aro as a trade diaspora. Although so far ignored in regional literature, the systematic study of trade diasporas has been growing since the late 1960s.[29] What Northrup described merely as Aro "predilection for commerce" or "skill and single-mindedness" was, as anthropologist Abner Cohen (1969:9, 98) illustrates with the Hausa experience, "not associated with a basic personality trait, but with a highly developed economico-political organization."

Placing Aro settlements in the context of a trade diaspora throws light on crucial aspects of trade organization, commercial politics, institutional change, and cultural development. Thus, neither the variation in the sizes of Aro diaspora communities nor their mode of organization was fundamentally peculiar. These elements made them a diaspora and gave the Aro a distinct advantage in regional trade. "In short," writes Abner Cohen, who originated the concept of trade diasporas, a diaspora "is a nation of socially interdependent, but spatially dispersed, communities" (A. Cohen 1971:267). If there is a dominant theme to Aro history, it ought to emerge from a systematic understanding of trade diasporas, not in the existence or absence of a centralized-state system. The concept of the trade diaspora has theoretical significance because trade diasporas are a universal phenomenon (Curtin 1975:62–63; 1984). They exist today in the form that modern economic anthropologists refer to as ethnically homogenous middleman groups (EHMGs) (see, e.g., Landa 1994). The Aro trading network was, therefore, a cultural phenomenon. Anthropologist Karl Polanyi was correct in observing that the market is only one of, and susceptible to, "a great variety of institutions" that

---

[29] Baier 1980:57–67; A. Cohen 1969, 1971; Curtin 1971b, 1975, 1984; Eades 1993; Lovejoy 1980:28–45; 1982a; Lovejoy and Hogendorn 1979; Meillassoux 1971a; Roberts 1987.

underpin human existence.³⁰ Thus, this study takes into account, not only the market mechanisms, but also the geocultural context and implications of the slave trade.

The Aro diaspora presents a challenge for contemporary Igbo and Nigerian cultural studies. The settlements are incompatible with the existing taxonomies of Igbo subcultural areas. Daryll Forde and G.I. Jones identify five subcultural groups for the Igbo: northern, or Onitsha; southern, or Owerri; western; eastern, or Cross River; and northeastern (Forde and Jones 1950). This spatial framework has advanced regional cultural studies, but it is singularly inadequate for understanding the Aro cultural experience. It restricts Aro settlements to Igboland, whereas many Aro settlements existed and still exist in non-Igbo areas, such as Idomaland, Igalaland, and Ibibioland. Inokun in Ibibioland was one of the largest Aro settlements. Second, the Forde-Jones taxonomy locates the "Aro" in the eastern or Cross River subgroup where the Aro metropole of Arochukwu is located, and places Aro diaspora settlements in the cultural categories of their respective vicinities. This framework implies that Aro settlements lacked cultural personalities and had completely assimilated into neighboring subcultures. Also, by not applying the Aro cultural category to these Aro settlements, the taxonomy unwittingly collapses Aro (a group) with Arochukwu (a place). Perhaps, a more appropriate taxonomy is the one, advanced by Afigbo, based on interregional variations in the manifestations of pan-Igbo achievement norms. For Afigbo, two distinctive ways by which rewards and recognition were allocated to individuals sprouted two subcultures – Igbo-Ọzọ, which emphasized title – taking, prominently the Ọzọ, and Igbo-Abamaba, which emphasized membership of secret societies (Afigbo 1991d). The Aro diaspora, like the homeland, clearly falls into the latter category. Although this taxonomy is based on more measurable criteria and does not claim to embrace all Igbo communities, it shares the focus in Forde-Jones's model in "areas" and so places different Aro settlements in different "culture areas". In short, the aforementioned taxonomies ignore the distinctiveness of the Aro. Certainly, the Aro factor renders futile any attempt to subdivide Igboland into subculture "areas" and to straitjacket the Aro into being one more Igbo group.

There is a distinction between the terms "Arochukwu" and "Aro," and recognizing this distinction is crucial to understanding the Aro. Arochukwu is a place, and Aro refers to a people and/or their culture

---

³⁰ Polanyi 1957:245–46; Polanyi et al. 1957b:241; Bohannan and Bohannan 1968:220; Curtin 1984:14; Ekkehart 1998.

found in many Igbo and non-Igbo locations, including Arochukwu. This distinction is distinguishable from art historian Eli Bentor's claim that the Aro diaspora has little cultural similarity with the Aro metropole. For Bentor, Aro is primarily an identity – a way in which groups of people represent(ed) themselves, rather than a cultural reference per se – and the cultural and linguistic forms of Aro settlements are similar to the communities in their immediate neighborhoods (Bentor 1994). By implication, the Aro diaspora settlements cannot be located within an Aro cultural frame and are not even a diaspora. Like Forde and Jones's approach, Bentor's glosses over the cultural dimension of Aro-ness, a conclusion he derived primarily from his observations of masquerading in Arondizuogu – the most spectacular aspect of the Aro annual *Ikeji* festival in the late twentieth century. Bentor is correct in observing that deviations from Arochukwu practices are particularly striking in masquerading, which is a "a complex mixture of Aro, local, and innovative cultural practices" (Bentor 1994:211).[31] However, this observation does not warrant conflating Aro diaspora cultures and those of their neighbors or a conception of Aro-ness defined solely in identity terms. Rather, it underscores the persistence of aspects of Aro cultural practices, despite the incorporation of non-Aro ways. This was the case for both homeland and diaspora; the *Ikeji* festival is in itself a pan-Aro institution, which by virtue of its inherent yam reverence was rooted in Igbo culture. The performance aspects of *Ikeji* may have changed in the diaspora, but the rituals remained essentially the same as in the homeland during the twentieth century. The most radical observation possible is that "Aro" is primarily an identity and secondarily a cultural reference, but as *Ikeji* rituals show, the cultural dimension has remained significant. Culture was thus a principal element of Aro-ness. The development of the Aro culture was tied to the history of the Atlantic slave trade.

PERSPECTIVE

The rise and expansion of the Aro was the key influence that shaped the character of the Biafra Atlantic slave trade. Aro incursions into the densely populated Igbo heartland and the establishment there of their most important settlements in about the mid-eighteenth century coincided with the steady increase observed in the Biafra trade during this

---

[31] For the *Ikeji* festival, also see K. Ike 1972; C. Okafor 1986:127–28; N. Okoli 1972 and for masquerading in Igboland, see Nwabueze 1984.

time. The establishment of Aro frontiers in close proximity to the densely populated Nri-Awka region coincided with another major shift in the Biafra Atlantic slave trade; centrally located Bonny superseded easterly Old Calabar as Biafra's premier port during 1726–50. No previous studies have made the foregoing claims. The 1726–50 estimate locates the time of this change more firmly than the recent estimate of 1730–79 offered by Lovejoy and Richardson (2004, 368–72). The shift of major activity from Old Calabar to Bonny has been attributed to developments in the port states and, especially, to the preferences of Euro-American buyers (Hargreaves 1987; Latham 1973). So also are "important political advantages at Bonny in credit security, commercial efficiency and the promotion of impersonal exchanges" (Lovejoy and Richardson 2004, 372). While these developments at Bonny are important, they provide at best a partial explanation for the shift. In actual fact, the shift in the relative importance of the ports, the dramatic growth in the Biafra trade, and higher volumes of captives largely reflected changes in existing trade routes that accompanied the establishment of the Aro diaspora settlements in densely populated central Igboland. Several of these communities were unusually large. Arondizuogu and the Ndieni cluster (including Ujari, now Ajali, and Ndikelionwu) on the banks of the Mamu River were established virtually contemporaneously and through violence in the mid-eighteenth century.[32] Inokun in Ibibioland was the only other Aro settlement that shared all these characteristics. This expansion followed such seventeenth-century internal developments as consolidation of Arochukwu in the Cross River region, the formation of the Niger riverine states, and the expansion of the coastal states and changes in their organization, including the introduction of the credit-regulating *Ekpe* society in Old Calabar.[33]

This study is self-consciously interactive, highlighting relationships between the Aro and the rest of the region, between the Bight of Biafra and the rest of Atlantic Africa, and between Atlantic Africa and external

---

[32] Ndieni is a cluster of several Aro settlements on the northeastern fringes of the Nri-Awka region in present Anambra State. The rest of Ndieni more or less proliferated from Ujari and Ndikerionwu (Ndikelionwu) over time. For example, Ndiokwaraeze proliferated from Ujari when the descendants of Ujari's founder's first son Okwareze and their dependents and clients left Ujari to establish it. Another Ndieni settlement Ndiowuu proliferated when the descendants of Owuu Mgboro and his people, who had existed as an appendage of Ndikerionwu, left Ndikerionwu to establish it (see Eni 1973:19–21).

[33] Old Calabar adopted *Ekpe* "as early as the seventeenth century" from the Ekoi (Aye 1967:70).

regions – trans-Atlantic and trans-Saharan. Without suggesting that Aro history is synonymous with the history of the Bight of Biafra, West Africa at large, or the external world, it can be said that Aro history makes sense only in the context of regional and Atlantic history. Aro expansion took form within the framework of the political economy of the Bight of Biafra and West Africa, and it correlates with the expansion of the Atlantic trade. The Aro were associated with region-wide institutions, were central to regional commerce, and incorporated persons from virtually every part of the Bight of Biafra. The Aro were affected by economic, environmental, and political change that originated elsewhere in West Africa and beyond.[34] These identifiable sociocultural processes in the hinterland accompanied and mutually complemented the rise and expansion of the Biafra slave trade, and shaped its composition.

---

[34] Fred Cooper (1996) has explicated the interactive approach, distinguishing it from the comparative method. Sargent (1999) has shown how environmental, economic, and political change in one place in West Africa could affect other regions.

2

The Aro in the Atlantic Context

Expansion and Shifts, 1600s–1807

The dramatic rise of the slave trade in the Bight of Biafra during the seventeenth and eighteenth centuries was remarkable, notwithstanding the dense population of the region's hinterland. Of all the captive-exporting regions of Atlantic Africa, Euro-American buyers had the least incentive to trade in the Bight of Biafra. Its harbors were apparently the most unpleasant, discouraging Euro-American slavers from building permanent bases. The mortality rates of captives from the region were significantly higher than other African regions – 18.3 percent, compared to 10.8 percent among captives from all other regions combined. In the Americas, Euro-American slavers got lower prices for captives from Biafra than from any other African region. The region supplied the largest proportion of females in a trade that placed a premium on males. During the seventeenth century, when the proportion of females embarked on African ports was at its highest, only the Bight of Biafra actually sent more females than males to the Americas – 50.6 percent as opposed to the African average of 41.5 percent (Table 6.1). That the region's slave trade experienced rapid expansion after 1650 despite the aforementioned impediments is attributable, at least in part, to its ability to deliver captives quickly and efficiently during the sugar revolution in the Americas.

The outlines of the process by which the Aro attained dominance of the inland Bight of Biafra trading system that fed the region's ports are clear enough, but linking the process to oscillations in the Biafra Atlantic trade and working out its basic chronology are another matter.[1] The

---

[1] For these outlines, see K. O. Dike and Ekejiuba 1990; Ijoma and Njoku 1991; Northrup 1978b; Ukwu 1969:132–36.

challenge, then, is to periodize Aro expansion and correlate its dynamics with those of the Biafra Atlantic trade, mapping how the development of the Aro trading complex and demand conditions impacted each other. What emerges is that the foundation of Arochukwu and the development of the Aro diaspora corresponded neatly with basic trends in the region's Atlantic trade. The Aro case is unusual because, unlike the West African states whose commercial expansion during the slave trade era relied on the imposition of direct suzerainty over large areas, such as Oyo in the Bight of Benin and Asante in the Gold Coast, the Aro built a trading pax in the Bight of Biafra through a network of diaspora settlements. By placing the Aro trading system in the Atlantic context, therefore, we gain a fuller understanding of how African societies helped shape the overseas slave trade.

Efforts to describe and explain the expansion of the region's Atlantic trade have focused on the coastal city-states and concentrated on structural changes related to trade in the nineteenth century.[2] Detailed studies of the individual trading states Bonny, Brass, Opobo, New Calabar (Elem-Kalabari), and Old Calabar (Calabar) have thrown light on the patterns and dimensions of regional trade but, except for studies emphasizing the role of internal long-distance trade in the institutional development of the coastal states, little work has been done on the hinterland, encouraging the implication that the hinterland did no more than reflect coastal impulses. This paradigm was perhaps inevitable for two reasons. With few exceptions, these studies dealt with the nineteenth century, especially the later part, that is, after the Atlantic slave trade era, when coastal traders had taken some initiative in hinterland trade.[3] Second, such studies drew heavily on European sources and explained Biafra trade from the European perspective.[4] A critical reading of this literature is necessary to understand the system that produced the captives sent to the Americas from the Bight of Biafra.

Attempts to understand this system must involve analysis of the relevant structures and processes with a focus on the Aro. The captive, which had become the principal "commodity" of the Aro by the eighteenth century at the latest, opens a vista into the Aro political economy and Aro expansion.

---

[2] Dike 1956; Jones 1963; Alagoa 1970, 1971a, 1971b, 1972; 1986.
[3] Notable among these exceptions are Alagoa 1970, 1971a, 1971b, 1986; Cookey 1974; Latham 1973; Lovejoy and Richardson 1997, 1999.
[4] On Bonny, Hargreaves 1987; Brass, Alagoa 1964; Opobo, Cookey 1974; New Calabar, (Elem – Kalabari), Wariboko 1991; and Old Calabar (Calabar), Latham 1973:26–28; Nair 1972; Noah 1980).

To the Aro, the captive was both a commodity and a resource within an institution of slavery. This connection between indigenous African slavery and the Atlantic slave trade is an important theme of African history. The question of whether slavery was important in African societies before the Atlantic slave trade era or whether it resulted from the slave trade itself has been of particular interest.[5] Did the Atlantic slave trade feed on an entrenched slave system or did slavery emerge because of the trade? Both sides of the debate agree that the Atlantic slave trade interacted intimately with indigenous slavery, but any role of preexisting slavery in the development of the overseas slave trade – would likely differ from region to region, according to the extent and spread of slavery.[6]

The extent of slavery in the Bight of Biafra vis á vis the export slave trade unfolds from a few pertinent facts of regional history. First, up to the beginning of the seventeenth century, the coastal city-states were still fledgling formations. Second, the later large-scale slaveholders of the hinterland – Arochukwu, Abo, Asaba, Oguta, and Osomari – were only just emerging at this time, out of a series of migrations.[7] Third, if the theory that abundant land (relative to population) promoted slavery has any validity, the case for large-scale slavery in the Bight of Biafra is weak. The region does not seem to have experienced abundant land at any point in the last millennium. Localized cases of depopulation resulted from the Atlantic slave trade, but they were a consequence of the overseas slave trade rather than a cause of indigenous slavery (Nwokeji 2000a:632–33; 1997c:707–10).[8] But none of the foregoing observations in itself proves the nonexistence of slavery in the Bight of Biafra prior to the Atlantic slave

---

[5] For the first view, see Fage 1969, 1975, 1980; Thornton 1998: chap. 3. The second view is most closely associated with Davidson 1961, 1971; Rodney 1966, 1967; Inikori 1982b, 1992a, 1994a; Noah 1980:76–77; Thompson 1987. Other scholars have explained the expansion, not the origin, of slavery in terms of the influence of the Atlantic slave trade (see M. Klein 1978, 2001:56, 58; Klein and Lovejoy 1979; Lovejoy 1979, 1983, 1989; Manning 1981, 1982:10; 1990; Meillassoux 1982). Except for Meillassoux, the scholars in the third category describe nineteenth-century political economies as slave modes of production.

[6] For details, see Nwokeji forthcoming

[7] K.O. Dike 1956:25–26; Henderson 1972:41–65; Noah 1980:1–19; Northrup 1978b:45–47; Ogedengbe 1971; Ohadike 1994:xvi, xviii–xix, 46–48, 49–50; Onwuejeogwu 1987:34; Oriji 1994:11, Nwokeji 2000a:629–30. As Latham explicitly states, "it is unlikely that the Efik [of Old Calabar] were owners of many slaves when they were simple fishermen" (Latham 1973:31). The coastal city-states had also come to depend on slavery by the end of the eighteenth century, about which period relevant work exists (Hargreaves 1987:87, 91–92, 93, 101; Nair 1972:37).

[8] For surplus land as a determinant of slavery, see Nieboer 1900; Hopkins 1973:24–25.

trade era. Our concern here is not the existence of slavery per se – because it most likely existed in some form – but the extent to which it was practiced and its relationship to the export slave trade. The "crucial issue," Inikori persuasively argues, "is what the export slave trade [Saharan and Atlantic] did to the extent and character of slavery in the region" (Inikori 1982b:45; 1992a:127, 130, 157).[9] The Atlantic slave trade was however but one of the factors that shaped domestic slavery in the region.

Slavery does seem to have become widespread by the second half of the eighteenth century, however. Even if we assume that Olaudah Equiano's description of Igboland was based on accounts he garnered from Igbo-speaking people in the Americas, his references to gifts of slaves and fines paid in slaves, and to a man's "family and slaves" sometimes being "numerous" are instructive (Equiano 1995:37). We also know that a few of the Aro settlements were founded in the mid-eighteenth century by men whom Arochukwu slaveholders had enslaved as boys.[10] Whereas the available evidence points to widespread domestic slavery only in the heyday of the Atlantic slave trade in the region, the question of whether slavery in Africa aided the development of the Atlantic slave trade is not as critical as once supposed. First, Africa was only one of many world regions in which this ancient institution existed, so that its mere existence cannot satisfactorily explain why the continent supplied slave labor to the Americas. Second, there is no necessary connection between the extent of preexisting slavery and the volumes of captives exported. The Bight of Biafra became one of the most important supply regions, but regions with well-established preexisting slave regimes – of which the kingdom of Benin is a prime example – were not necessarily the most important supply regions (Ekeh 1990:677n). Other reasons consigned Africa to the role of captive supplier at that point in history.[11] In fact, some recent major studies have avoided altogether the relationship between slavery in Africa and the Atlantic slave trade, without detracting from their impact

---

[9] See also Ekeh 1990:677n. Cookey believes that slavery existed, but like Thornton (1998: 86–88) and Kopytoff and Miers (1977) later claimed for all of Africa, he argues that the slave status "lacked the odium which it subsequently acquired" (Cookey 1974:18).

[10] Nevertheless, the initiative of ex-slaves in founding Aro settlements has sometimes been overstated. Although K.O. Dike and Ekejiuba do this in an attempt to theorize the slave element as the motive force of Aro dispersal, their own data show that this element was relevant only in a handful of cases (K.O. Dike and Ekejiuba, 1990:71, 75, 78, 97–98, 99, 120, 176, 206, 217).

[11] Curtin 1990, 1993:171–76; Eltis 1993, 2000:57–84; H. Klein 1978:3–8; Menard and Schwartz 1993; Walvin 1997:24; E. Williams 1944:6–10; Wolf 1982:201–04.

on the historiography (e.g., Law 1991b). Slavery was integral to Aro political economy, but the origins of slavery within the group are not as important in galvanizing the Biafra Atlantic trade as are the origins, structure, development, and expansion of the Aro trading network. An understanding of these issues must begin with a reconstruction of the origins of the group.

FIRST PHASE: ARO RISE AND THE BIAFRA SLAVE TRADE, 1600S–1720S

All of what we know about Aro origins comes from oral traditions. These traditions, like those of the other Cross River Igbo-speaking groups, recall "Igbo" and non-Igbo Cross River origins, and Igbo influence predominated, as is reflected up to the present in their customs and dialects of the Igbo language. Prior to the formation of the Aro, the area of Arochukwu, was inhabited originally by what K.O. Dike and Ekejiuba characterized as "ethnically unrelated groups – the Losi, Nkalagha and Nchai" – whom the Igbo and the "Ibibio" referred collectively to as Iwerri and Unene, respectively (K.O. Dike and Ekejiuba 1990:45). This area was also the site of immigration for various groups, principally the Igbo and Ibibio. The incoming Igbo lineages derived principally from two regions – the Igbo heartland and Cross River Igbo groups, particularly Ohafia, Abam, and Ada. A civil war, known in present-day Aro lore as Aha Ibibi (Ibibio War), between the Igbo and the Ibibio led to the arrival of a third major immigrant group known as the Akpa, an itinerant collectivity said to have settled various locations in the southeastern Nigerian Middle Belt and the northern Cross River area. Aro traditions are unanimous that it was the Igbo faction that invited Akpa warriors to intervene in the conflict on their behalf. Akpa intervention was decisive, according to most accounts, because the Akpa introduced firearms into the equation.[12]

At the conclusion of the war, the victorious "'Igbo'-Akpa" alliance formed the Arochukwu confederacy. The structure of this confederacy and the changes it has witnessed over time reflect not only the heterogeneity of Aro origins but also, perhaps, a history of power struggles and shifts among the confederates over time, which the modern day Aro

---

[12] For details of the events described here, see K.O. Dike and Ekejiuba 1990: Ch. 2; Ijoma 1986c:10–11; Okoro Kanu 2000:10–40. See also Ifemesia 1979:39; G.I. Jones 1963:30–31; Northrup 1978b:34–35.

never seem keen to dwell on. At the apex of the confederacy were three confederates – Ezeagwu, Okennachi, and Ibom Isii – which the Aro refer to as "kindreds" (Figure 2.1). The three confederates comprised uneven numbers of a grand total of nine inalienable lineage components called the Ọtụsị, all of which were conceptually equal politically, culturally, and spiritually. Each of the nine Ọtụsị, in turn, served as an umbrella for a number of the nineteen Arochukwu lineage-groups (or sections of them), which the British referred to as "towns," and Aro themselves as "villages."[13] The various Aro diaspora settlements were connected to these units, from which the founders of the respective diaspora settlements were drawn. The heads of the nine Ọtụsị (singular form: Eze Ọtụsị) constituted Ọkpankpọ, the highest ruling council headed by a troika – Nna Atọ (Three Fathers) – chaired by Eze Aro (Aro king), who must be the senior Ọtụsị of his lineage-group cluster or confederate. In effect, Eze Aro was not an absolute ruler but a committee man.

The resulting confederacy reflected the defeat and marginalization of the Ibibio. Many, if not most, of the Ibibio would have fled the site, and those that remained behind would have been subsumed into Igbo and perhaps Akpa collectivities or lineage-groups because none of the three confederates or lineage-group clusters was Ibibio dominated. Ezeagwu was constituted by the descendants, relatives, and associates of Ezeagwu, said to have been a distant descendant of the legendary pioneer immigrant from the Igbo heartland called Ụrụ. Okennachi was constituted by the relatives, followers, and associates of Nnachi, said to have immigrated from Ada, a Cross River Igbo group claiming origins in Akunakuna, a Cross River non-Igbo group to the northeast. Ibom Isii was constituted by the Akpa group led by Akuma Nnubi. Instead, we see lineage-groups and lineages claiming Ibibio origins staggered across Arochukwu towns or villages.

The uneven distribution of the Ọtụsị among the confederates suggests long-standing power struggles among the component parts. In an ideal world, the three confederates would have had an equal number of Ọtụsị, to march the putative equality of the Ọtụsịs and, by extension, the confederates. Yet, while Ezeagwu and Okennachi were composed of two and three Ọtụsị, respectively, Ibom Isii was composed of four. The number of

---

[13] Some of the villages or towns are split between the two Ọtụsị, but parts of the same village belonged to Ọtụsịs in different "Igbo" confederates – Ezeagwu and Okennachi. In the case of the "non-Igbo" Ibom Isii, this kind of overlap occurred only within the confederate.

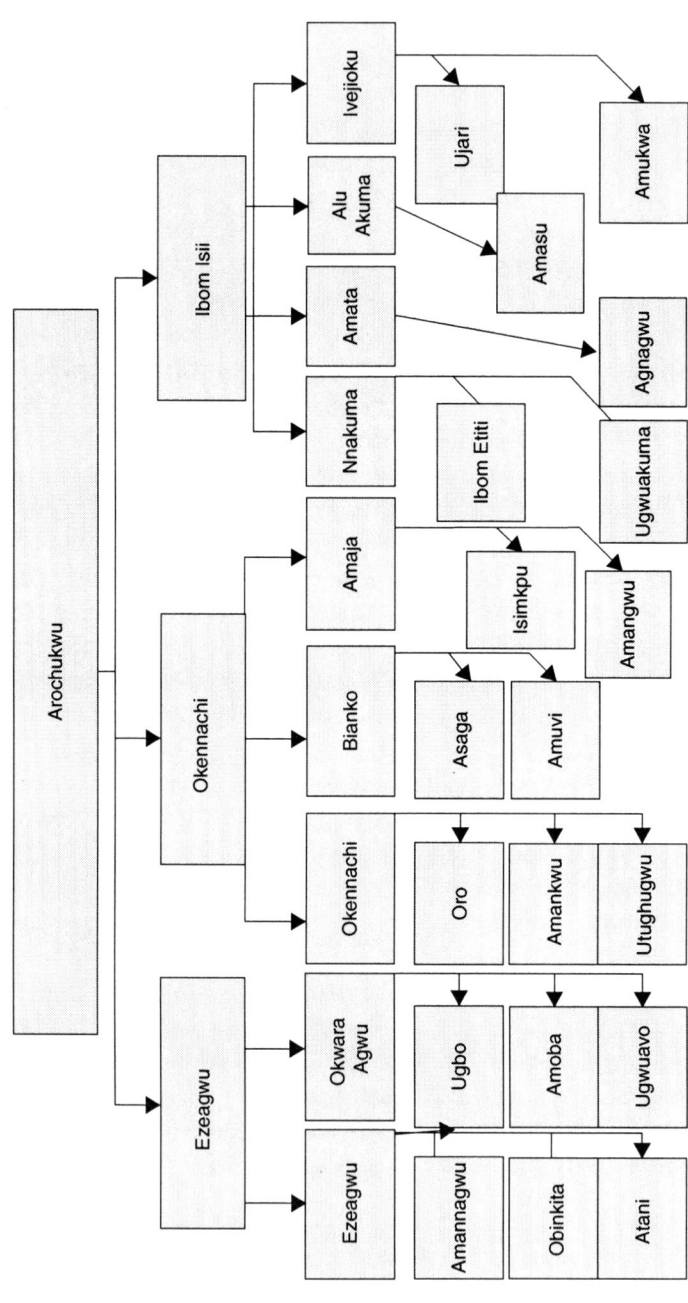

FIGURE 2.1. Arochukwu Structure

Otusi in each of the confederates is roughly proportional to the role it played during the war. By all accounts, the non-Igbo Ibom Isii (Akpa confederate) initially wielded effective suzerainty over the two Igbo confederates. They had been invited by the Nnachi (Okennachi) group, whose role in the war up to the time of Akpa intervention seems to have exceeded that of the Amagwu group, even though the latter were and are still recognized as the originally leading group. The name Ibom Isii (six Iboms) suggests that the Amagwu group may have started out with even more Otusi than it came to have in subsequent centuries, which would have given the non-Igbo enormous leverage in decision making. The apparent reduction of the number of Ibom Isii Otusi reflected perhaps the shift of power over time from the non-Igbo Akpa group, which had wielded effective power after its intervention in Aro affairs, to the Igbo. All this also indicates that historically the Otusi have perhaps not been as inalienable Aro traditions suggest.

There have been spirited efforts to date Aro origins since the colonial period. The vast outpouring of the discourse came in the wake of the Aro Expedition of 1901–02, through which the British subordinated the Aro to colonial rule. The first systematic attempt to date Aro formation was made by colonial anthropologist, H.F. Mathews, who in 1927 wrote that it took place not "earlier than 1700 or 1730 but most probably around 1750." Mathews's heavy dependence on the genealogies of relatively recent Aro families led him to conclude, erroneously, that Aro formation had taken place only 150 or 160 years before 1927. This places Aro foundation at either 1777 or 1767. Also, Mathews learned that blunderbusses had played a decisive role in the war that produced the Aro state. His investigations led him to believe that the first blunderbusses arrived in Biafra early in the eighteenth century.[14] Mathews's conclusions have promoted the view that the Aro were formed in the second half of the eighteenth century, which effectively implies that the Aro, who actually dominated the hinterland trade, arrived on the scene only after the slave trade in the region had fully come into its own.[15]

---

[14] Many of the details on Aro origins as presented by colonial officials are contained in NAE ARODIV 20/1/15:Anthropologists Papers on Aro Origin: Discussion and the Basis of the Widespread of Aro Influence, 1927.

[15] For this view, see Latham (1973:26–28); Bentor (1994:79). The genealogies that Mathews used are so flawed that even Apollos Nwauwa's rigorous reinterpretation yielded conspicuously improbable results. Nwauwa's chronological charts place the genealogies of almost all the major characters of Aro formation in the generation 1690–1720 and the establishment of "many of [Arochukwu's] constituent villages … in the next generation (ca. 1720–1750)" (Nwauwa 1990:227, 233–36; 1991:296, 308). This chronology, which places the foundation of Arochukwu in 1690–1720, is about one century late and does not correlate Aro expansion with the expansion of the Biafran export slave

Using the traditions of the Niger Delta corporate kin groups, G.I. Jones (1963:134) concluded that the Aro oracle, Ibiniukpabi, played a crucial part in their formation. He attributed the blunderbusses' element in Aro traditions of origin to telescoping and places Aro formation at the period before the mid-seventeenth century. This view is widely accepted. Still, there have been suggestions that the Aro had been formed by the early seventeenth century and probably before.[16] These suggestions are realistic, given the uncertainty about the length of the time lag between the occupation of the Unene region (the Arochukwu area) and the foundation of Arochukwu. If Arochukwu was formed in the early seventeenth century, the region seems to have been occupied before then, probably long before.

The chronology of the wider regional history brings early Aro history into sharper relief. Developments relating to the Middle Belt state of Kwararafa in particular throw light on Aro origins and political structure, and on the Biafra trade. The demise of the long troubled state of Kwararafa dovetailed with the formation of the Aro state. The firearm-bearing Akpa who intervened in the crisis that produced Arochukwu appear to have represented advance elements of Kwararafa migrants, in an exodus that had commenced in the sixteenth century.[17] The Kwararafa diaspora groups that crystallized in the seventeenth century as a result of the centralizing project of the successor state of Jukun shared a political culture in which power

---

trade. It places the foundation date of Arondizuogu within 1795–1825 and identifies two settlements, Amawom and Nkalunta in the western Cross River Igbo area, as the earliest diaspora settlements, formed in the mid-eighteenth century. If they were the first diaspora settlements, they would have been established considerably earlier. At any rate, if the location of these two obscure settlements outside the Igbo heartland would hardly have generated the high volumes of captive exports observed in the mid-eighteenth century. The genealogies from which these chronologies were derived came from families of relatively recent origins, from whom the British drew the early warrant chiefs. To legitimate their claim to authority, these individuals impressed on the British that their lineages began with the establishment of Arochukwu (Ekejiuba 1972a:13n). Fieldwork and information from local histories provide a better insight into dating Aro expansion than is available in the colonial texts informed by such traditions.

[16] For the first group, see K.O. Dike and Ekejiuba 1990:44; Isichei; 1976:6, 58, 76; Oriji 1994. The second group comprises Northrup 1978b:36; Ijoma 1986c:16; Ijoma and Njoku 1991:204.

[17] According to Sargent, the Jukun migrated into the region just north of Cross River region in c. 1610. "Apa later became known as their homeland" (Sargent 1999:226, 236, 249). Apa probably refers to the land of the "Akpa," the group that decisively intervened in Aro formation. If claims to Akpa origins of a section of the Aro are accurate, the Aro would have been produced in the same process associated with Kwararafa's conflict with Kano and Bornu, as well as resulting migrations and internal conflicts.

devolved among major blocs in a multiethnic setting. Each bloc was represented in central administration, as an alternative to the centralized model of Benin-derived kingdoms of the Middle Belt (Sargent 1999:218–19, 243–51). The multiethnic confederacy the Aro established in the Cross River basin, described earlier in this chapter, resembled the pre-Jukun Kwararafa political structure. The Akpa's reputation as seasoned warriors and strategists fitted into a culture shaped in the context of the volatile Benue valley geopolitics associated with Kwararafa's disintegration.

The notion that Arochukwu was founded in the early seventeenth century at the latest is also compatible with new evidence regarding the antiquity of the major slave market at Bende. The Bende market was organized around the Aro trading network; its major and minor fairs, respectively, were named after the Aro families Agbagwu and Bianko, so that evidence of its existence implies Aro trading activity. Indeed, Bende was thriving by the 1670s. French mariner John Barbot, who made at least two voyages to the Biafra coast between 1678 and 1682, wrote in 1682 that "There is ... a large market for slaves in Belli, a large town *west of Old Calabar inland*" (John Barbot 1732:381, emphasis added). In July 1699, James Barbot and John Grazilhier (1699:109), referred to a "Bendi" market where 247 bars exchanged for twenty-three captives. The inland market was, according to them, three or four days away from the New Calabar port. The descriptions of both "Belli" and "Bendi" fit into the location of Bende, situated in Cross River Igboland. These observations were made a century before Mathews's projected date of Aro formation – the second half of the eighteenth century.

Although the Bende market was in existence by the 1670s, exactly when it came into being or when the Aro took control of it is unclear. It is likely, however, that it would have taken considerable time – perhaps several decades – between the foundation of Arochukwu and the 1670s, when the market had attained such a strategic status in the slave trade that information about developments there reached European traders on the coast, who never ventured inland. It would likely have taken more time still between Aro formation and Aro establishment of the market or Aro control of it and its conversion to a slave mart. Given the forgoing logic, it seems plausible that the Aro came into prominence in the mid-seventeenth century (Afigbo 1980:87; Ekejiuba 1972a:13). Nothing suggests that any other group controlled the Bende slave mart before the Aro. In light of this new information about Bende and other evidence, blunderbusses are not central to dating Aro formation. Firearms certainly came into the region well before John Latham's 1713 date. Guns and gunpowder are known to have been imported in the second half of the seventeenth century: over £1,000 worth of these goods were imported between 1662 and 1703, and importation may well have begun even earlier.[18] Not surprisingly, the blunderbuss that Mathews saw in Arochukwu was, by his own testimony, of "a primitive type." It is now clear, based on the foregoing, that Arochukwu was formed during the early Atlantic slave trade era in the Bight of Biafra. This event fits into a general pattern of immigration into the region, aimed at taking advantage of the coastal trade in captives. The contemporaneous formation in the seventeenth century of the Niger riverine states – Abo, Oguta, Onitsha, and Osomari – has been linked to non-Igbo people interested in the slave trade (K.O. Dike and Ekejiuba 1990:56, 57). Indeed, these societies all came to be deeply involved in the slave trade.

The Aro formation appear to have resulted from three related developments.

1. Conflict between expanding "Igbo" and "Ibibio" over a frontier region.
2. Migration of Kwararafa elements away from their troubled homeland under the weight of conflicts with Sudanic and, later, with emergent Middle Belt states.
3. The fledgling Atlantic trade in which the Kwararafa diaspora and, perhaps, local Igbo and Ibibio sought to partake.

The Atlantic trade provided the incentive for Aro expansion, just as Aro modes of organization made the expansion possible and enduring.

Aro expansion correlates closely with the rise of the Biafra Atlantic slave trade. The Biafra trade was in its infancy up to the mid-seventeenth century, a period for which we lack evidence of Aro expansion (Table 2.1). Between 1501 and 1650, captives leaving the region's ports accounted for only 4.7 percent of captives from all African regions combined. If the sample of enslaved Biafrans in the Americas that Alonso de Sandoval recorded in 1627 is anything to go by, the proportion of the Igbo in the Biafra trade was still small; there was only one captive who was of "Igbo" origin among fifteen slaves from the Bight of Biafra.[19] This indicates that the slave trade still drew heavily on coastal populations.

---

[18] For gun importation during 1662–1703, see Eltis 2000:300. Latham's 1713 date seems to refer to commercial importation, while firearms could have trickled into the region during more than 150 years of trade with Europeans (Nwauwa 1990:235).

[19] De Sandoval ([1627] 1956:94). See also Hair (1967:263n).

TABLE 2.1. *Estimated Volume of the Transatlantic Captive Departures from the Bight of Biafra and All African Regions Combined, Primarily Five-Year Intervals, 1531–1740*

Period	B. of Biafra	All Africa	Biafra %*
1531–1600	8458	255,173	3.3
1601–1605	0	35,799	0.0
1606–1610	0	56,127	0.0
1611–1615	0	46,184	0.0
1616–1620	1,142	102,749	1.1
1621–1625	1,779	111,985	1.6
1626–1630	468	71,509	0.6
1631–1635	0	59,380	0
1636–1640	1,630	60,820	2.7
1641–1645	11,323	67,119	16.9
1646–1650	20,119	56,222	35.8
1651–1655	7,679	60,171	12.6
1656–1660	17,112	95,516	17.9
1661–1665	17,236	102,954	16.7
1666–1670	20,432	126,585	16.1
1671–1675	18,321	102,839	17.8
1676–1680	16,072	119,552	13.4
1681–1685	13,481	145,546	9.3
1686–1690	8,228	115,018	7.2
1691–1695	10,603	128,356	8.3
1696–1700	20,696	211,201	9.8
1701–1705	12,981	211,590	6.1
1706–1710	8,999	182,651	5.0
1711–1715	17,323	210,977	8.2
1716–1720	17,292	242,431	7.1
1721–1725	10,238	241,259	4.2
1726–1730	31,591	307,133	10.3
1731–1735	28,647	282,593	10.1
1736–1740	27,936	315,410	8.9
Totals	349786	4,124,849	8.5

Note: *Numbers with decimal points are not precise because of rounding.
Source: http://www.Slavevoyages.org.

The opening up of new plantation regions in the Americas generated significant increases in the volume of captives exported from Africa in the second half seventeenth century. Between 1651 and 1680, the Bight of Biafra supplied as much as 16 percent of all captives exported from Africa. Although absolute numbers remained strong for the remainder of the century, captives from the Bight of Biafra, as a percentage of all

African captives exported to the Americas, entered a period of decline after 1680 (Table 2.1). The result is that, while the volume of captives exported from all African regions combined increased by 68 percentage points during the twenty-five-year period between 1676 and 1700, the number of exports leaving the Bight of Biafra actually declined by 14.5 percentage points (Table 2.1). And the Biafra share generally remained small between 1700 and 1740, when overall captive exports continued to increase appreciably. The upsurge of captive departures that began in the 1651–75 period suggests that there was a concentration of Aro activities in neighboring Ibibioland at a time when the Aro had not yet expanded westward and northwestward, and when Old Calabar was still Biafra's principal port. It seems that the Aro could no longer meet the expanding Atlantic market demand with captives procured from their relatively limited area of operation at the time. The mid-seventeenth-century rise in exports soon ceased, and captives began to trickle to the coast once again. John Barbot writes in 1682 that "trade is not so brisk" in Bende "east of river Calabar," and in the delta port of New Calabar. "[S]everal ships are obliged to stay eight or ten months, *according to the circumstances of the natives*"[20] (emphasis added). John Barbot made his observation out of frustration at the low turnaround rate of the New Calabar trade, which did not abate until the end of the century; James Barbot and Grazilhier commented in similar vein in 1699 (James Barbot and Grazilhier 1699:109–16). Up to this time, New Calabar was the only port in the Bight of Biafra to which European slave vessels paid regular visits (Thornton 1996:1, 5–6, 7). But trade was shifting eastward to Old Calabar, closer to Arochukwu than New Calabar. Captain William Snelgrave estimated that only a total of 20,000 captives had been exported from Old Calabar by 1730 (Snelgrave 1730:505). Aro organization seems to have already had more impact on the coastal trade in the mid-seventeenth century, but it was not yet able to meet Euro-American

---

[20] John Barbot (1732:381, 383). John Barbot "made at least two voyages to the West coast" between 1678 and 1682. His *A Description* was originally written in French in 1682 and translated into English in 1732 (Donnan 1930:282). While Elizabeth Donnan's version implies that Barbot may have made more voyages, Paul Hair, Adam Jones, and Robin Law pinpoint only 1678–79 and 1681–82. They doubt that Barbot made any further voyages after 1682 (Hair, Jones, and Law 1992b:ix, xiii). But they conceded that the John Barbot reference may have been made in connection with the journey of the *Griffin* or with that of the *Dragon*, which apparently made its journey later, in 1699, and which involved his brother, James Barbot. John Barbot may have borrowed from the journal of his brother and his mates or may himself have been part of the *Dragon*'s 1699 trip (Hair, Jones and Law 1992b:cxlix, lxxiii, xciii).

demand for captives, even though that demand still was much smaller than it was to become.

Two demand conditions also influenced the trend observed in export volumes in the Bight of Biafra before the eighteenth century. The first was that captives from the Calabars "were not in high favor with the English." Discrimination against captives from the Old Calabar, in particular, was reported in Barbados as early as 1675–76 (see Donnan 1930:108, 205). They were referred to as "supernumerary Negroes" in 1679 (Stede and Gascoigne 1679). Reinforcing this negative attitude was what European sailors in the late seventeenth century described as the turbulence of Old Calabar waters and its "intemperate air" (John Barbot 1682:300; Van Nyendael 1702:467–68). "Intemperate air" conspired with malaria and high mortality to discourage Europeans from establishing a permanent presence in the region, as they did elsewhere in Atlantic Africa (Thornton 1996:1).

Though significant increase in the Biafra slave trade did not happen until after 1650, there was some increase during the first half of the seventeenth century. Out of recorded to have been enslaved 5,278 Africans who were enslaved in Peru between 1560 and 1650, entries for "Biafra" and "Caravali" total 682, or nearly 13 percent (see Bowser 1974:40–41). Indeed, Biafrans "became quite numerous" in Peru between 1610 and 1640 (Thornton 1996:5). The Spaniards at Jamaica and Barbados were buying captives from the Bight of Biafra as early as the 1660s (see Donnan 1930:108). In about 1668 and about 1693, a total of about 215 captives from "Callebar" were imported into the island of Bermuda (Bennett 1704:48).[21] In 1672, a Royal African Company (RAC) document concerning New and Old Calabar read in part, "whither many ships are sent to trade [and where] slaves and teeth … are to be had in plenty."[22] Up to 1705, the British were trailing the Dutch, who had "the greatest share" in the Old Calabar trade (John Barbot 1682:299–300; James Barbot, Jr. 1705:14). In June 1699, James Barbot learned of an English ship commanded by one Captain Edwards, who "got his compliments" of 500 captives in three weeks' time in New Calabar (James Barbot 1699:432). James Barbot, Jr., claimed to have seen ten or more slave ships in New Calabar in October 1700 (James Barbot, Jr., 1705:14). In October 1702, it was expected that there might be too many ships in New Calabar, but

---

[21] Slightly more than a half of the captives were reshipped to North Carolina and Virginia.
[22] See "The Royal African Company, 1672." See Donnan (1930:193).

TABLE 2.2. *A Sample of Captive Prices (in Copper Bars) in New Calabar and Old Calabar, 1678–1704*

Date	Men	Women	Girls	Boys	Place
Feb. 1678[a]	36	30	NA	NA	N. Calabar
1682[b]	38	36 or 37	NA	NA	O. Calabar
1688[c]	56 or 60	NA	NA	NA	N. Calabar
1698[d]	40–48	28–36	17–30	20–40	O. Calabar
1699[e]	52	36	NA	NA	N. Calabar
1703/1704[f]	48	36	NA	NA	N. Calabar

Note: 5s or 6s equaled 1 iron bar (i.e., 4 copper bars) (see Donnan 1931:14n).
Sources: [a] "Journal of the Arthur, Dec. 5, 1677 – May 25, 1678." See Donnan (1930:226). [b] John Barbot (1682:300n). [c] Dapper, cited by Meek (1937:5).1 [d] John Barbot (1698:419). [e] James Barbot (1699:420).2 [f] James Barbot, Jr. (1705:14); Donnan (1931:2n).

the situation was much worse again in Old Calabar (see Starke 1702:81). Prices correspondingly increased, though James Barbot, Jr.'s comment in December 1705 that New Calabar suppliers "rais'd price of negroes from 40s.–50s. to £12 or £14" probably reflected short-term phenomena (James Barbot, Jr. 1705:14n) (Table 2.2). Supply had fallen behind demand, and although the market was still not as tight here as it was elsewhere in Atlantic Africa, this trend could indicate a hinterland situation in which protracted resistance on the part of central Igbo checked captive supplies before the Aro eventually gained influence in the region.

In spite of increasing prices, probably due in part to fluctuations in the value of the iron bar, which was in use then as currency, the British Board of Trade reported in 1709 that, along with the situation at the ports below the Equator, prices of captives were lowest in the Bight of Biafra, "from whence the greatest number of Negroes are exported" (Board of Trade 1709:56–57, 59). The Board of Trade was either behind the times in its appraisal of the volume of the Bight of Biafra trade or it based its report on a short-term fluctuation. Relatively smaller numbers of captives left the region during the first four decades of the eighteenth century. Shortfalls in supply and competition from independent traders compelled the RAC to send factors[23] "to try if an allyance cannot be made with the princes of the Country of the Bight, and to learn what sort of Trade may be carried on there," according to an internal report of February 1721

[23] A "factor" was a resident trade representative of European companies. The factor operated out of the company's "factory" (basically a buying and warehousing structure/building) or fort as the case may be. The factor was the one in regular contact with African traders, making deals and purchases on behalf of his company.

The Aro in the Atlantic Context

(Royal Africa Company 1721:251).[24] Clearly, demand was increasing at a faster rate than supply because of the expansion of the American plantation complex. This condition provided an incentive for hinterland slave traders to expand the sources of captives.

SECOND PHASE, 1740S TO 1807: SURGE IN TRADE

Aro efforts had yielded results by the 1740s, when captive exports from the Bight of Biafra increased dramatically. During the 1740–45 period, the volume of captives leaving the ports of the Bight of Biafra increased 61 percent over the previous five-year period, representing a 7 percent increase in the Biafra share of African total (Table 2.3). Whereas the region supplied 66,833, or 6.1 percent, of a total of 1,088,909 captives exported from all African ports in the first quarter of the eighteenth century, it supplied 182,066, or 12.4 percent, of an Africa total of 1,471,725 during the second quarter. This upward trend continued more or less until the end of the second phase of Aro expansion in 1807. The slave trade was expanding across the board, but the Bight of Biafra branch was expanding at a higher rate.

The rise in the Biafra Atlantic trade during this period was accompanied by a drastic increase in the turnaround rates for ships buying captives at Bight of Biafra ports. This phenomenon was obvious to Alexander Falconbridge, who sailed frequently to the region as a slaver's surgeon in the third quarter of the eighteenth century.

> The time during which the slave ships are absent from England, varies according to the destination of the voyage, and the number of ships they happen to meet on the coast. To Bonny, or Old and New Calabar, a voyage is fully performed in about ten months. Those to the Windward and Gold Coasts, are rather more uncertain, but in general from fifteen to eighteen months. (Falconbridge 1788:11)

Falconbridge's observation is consistent with the quantitative evidence. Two kinds of quantitative data are used here: the average number of days a ship spent in African regions and the average daily number of captives a ship loaded per day in African ports. Both measures show the Bight of Biafra as having the fastest rates of loading captives during the second half of the eighteenth century. During this period, a ship spent an average of 109 days in the Bight of Biafra, compared to 203.6 days

---

[24] RAC wrote the Bonny king on September 15, 1702, asking to be supplied "three men ... to two women" (cited in Eltis 2000:106).

TABLE 2.3. *The Volume of the Transatlantic Captive Departures from the Bight of Biafra and All African Regions Combined, Five-Year Intervals, 1701–1805*

Period	Bight of Biafra	All Africa	Biafra %*
1701–1705	12,981	211,590	6.1
1706–1710	8,999	182,651	4.9
1711–1715	17,323	210,977	8.2
1716–1720	17,292	242,431	7.1
1721–1725	10,238	241,259	4.2
1726–1730	31,591	307,133	10.3
1731–1735	28,647	282,593	10.1
1736–1740	27,936	315,410	8.9
1741–1745	45,382	287,564	15.8
1746–1750	48,509	279,025	17.4
1751–1755	57,975	361,496	16.0
1756–1760	35,319	281,462	12.6
1761–1765	59,566	367,023	16.2
1766–1770	86,975	451,937	19.2
1771–1775	79,873	463,396	17.2
1776–1780	30,124	292,271	10.3
1781–1785	61,245	362,658	16.9
1786–1790	89,997	505,335	17.8
1791–1795	83,022	459,366	18.0
1796–1800	71,620	389,040	18.4
1801–1805	80,287	453,906	17.7
Totals	984,901		14.2

Note: *Numbers with decimal points are not precise because of rounding.
Source: http://www.Slavevoyages.org.

for Sierra Leone, 215.9 in Windward Coast, 137.4 in Gold Coast, 145 in the Bight of Benin, 162.3 in West-Central Africa, and 126.8 in Southeast Africa (Table 2.4). Only Senegambia records fewer days – 103.7 – but this figure is misleading and requires an explanation. The Bight of Biafra consistently posted significantly higher loaded-captives-per-ship numbers than Senegambia, and the volume of captives embarked there far outnumbered those that embarked at Senegambia (Table 2.4).

The relatively short times vessels spent in Senegambia ports reflects the intention of ships' crews to spend less time in the region more than the ports' capacity to supply captives quickly. Ships departed Senegambia ports quickly because captives from there had a high tendency to rebel. According to David Richardson, captives on ships leaving Senegambia had the highest tendency to revolt of all other African regions, and ships leaving Senegambia ports were fourteen

TABLE 2.4. *Time Spent by Ships at African Ports, 1751–1800*

Region	Mean (No. of Days in Port)	No. of Vessels in Sample	Standard Deviation
Senegambia	103.7468	154	79.0894
Sierra Leone	203.6883	77	132.0673
Windward Coast	215.94	50	130.6919
Gold Coast	137.4759	374	95.1905
Bight of Benin	145.0172	232	75.9383
Bight of Biafra	109.702	245	82.4087
West-Central Africa	162.3577	601	73.381
Southeast Africa	126.8	20	63.9651
Unknown	159.2143	84	106.3542
Total	145.8258	1837	90.5224

Note: Numbers with decimal points are not precise because of rounding.
Source: Data generated by David Eltis.

times more likely to experience revolts than those leaving the Bight of Biafra (Richardson 2001:77). Before the mid-eighteenth century, ships visiting Senegambia were generally larger than the ones sent to the Bight of Biafra before mid-century, but they consistently loaded fewer captives than those that traded in the Bight of Biafra. This means that ships often left Senegambian ports with either unloaded space or loaded with other African commodities. Perhaps as a result of this phenomenon, slavers at mid-century began to send smaller ships to low-yield Senegambia. The decline in the average tonnage of ships that traded in Senegambia after mid-century certainly reflected the decline in the general tonnage of French vessels during the second half of the century as did the decline in the tonnage of Portuguese vessels, which became very active in the region after 1790. The average size of French ships was 258 tons during 1701–50, compared to 238.3 during 1751–1800. This decline was progressive. The average size of French ships declined from 250.1 during the 1751–1775 quarter to 189.3 during 1776–1800. The decline in the size of Portuguese/Brazilian ships took similar trajectory and was of an even greater magnitude during the last quarter of the century when they became more active in Senegambia, 222.1 tons compared to 342.2 tons in the preceding quarter. This decline was steepest in the 1790s, when the size of Portuguese ships declined to 146.7 tons from 266.7 tons in the 1781–1790 decade (Slavevoyages.org).

Incidentally, mid-century witnessed a significant increase in the tonnage of ships sent to the Bight of Biafra, in response to the region's high yield of captives. During the 1751–1775 period, the mean tonnage of ships sent to the Bight of Biafra rose to 205, while that of Senegambia declined to 162 over the same period. This trend escalated during the 1776–1800 period, when the tonnage for the Bight of Biafra rose further, to 233.6, while that of Senegambia declined further to 125.6. The contrast in the availability of captives between the two regions highlights the disparities in the volumes of captives and numbers of voyages recorded, the turn-around rates at principal ports, and the mean tonnages of the ships sent to those ports. According to the *Expanded Online Trans-Atlantic Slave Trade Database* (Slavevoyages.org), the total number of captives that left Bight of Biafra ports between 1751 and 1800 was 655,717, from 2030 voyages and with a mean tonnage of 214.6, compared to Senegambia's total of 220,214 from 1046 voyages with a mean tonnage of only 174.74 over the same period. The high turnaround rate observed in Senegambia does not reflect a greater availability of captives. After controlling for unloaded space per ship, turnaround rates as an indicator of availability of captives on the coast were far higher in the Bight of Biafra than in Senegambia.

This fact is brought in sharp relief by the average daily number of captives loaded per vessel. This represents the first time the average rate of daily number of captives loaded per vessel has been used to analyze the slave trade. The method is introduced here to control for uneven-ness in the data, such as ship size, the number of days a vessel spent in a port, and any nonhuman commodities that ships often loaded. The daily average number of captives embarked per ship is derived by dividing the total number of captives embarked on a particular port during a particular period with the average number of days a vessel spent on the port over the same period. In other words, this method measures how fast a ship loaded, irrespective of size and total duration of call on a particular port. Tables 2.5 and 2.6 show the average numbers of captives that ships calling on major African ports loaded per day for the 1701–50 and 1751–1800 periods, respectively. While the principal ports of the Bight of Biafra were not important enough for much of the first half of the eighteenth century and are thus excluded from Table 2.5, which shows Whydah as the fastest loading port, we see the two principal ports of the region – Old Calabar and, particularly, Bonny – leapfrog Whydah during the second half of the century. Whydah's loading rate had declined to 3.2 captives per ship per day from 4.7 captives per ship per day in the first half-century, compared to Old Calabar, which had risen to 3.7, and Bonny to 5.5 (Table 2.6).

TABLE 2.5. *Daily Average Number of Captives Loaded Per Vessel, 1701–50*

Imputed Principal Port of Slave Purchase	Average No. of Captives Embarked Per Vessel Per Day	No. of Vessels in Sample	Number Embarked	Standard Deviation
Gambia	2.5	16	35,425	2.1
Anomabu, Adja, Agga	3.0	38	43,218	3.4
Whydah	4.7	200	198,537	2.9

Note: Numbers with decimal points are not precise because of rounding.
Source: Data generated by David Eltis.

TABLE 2.6. *Daily Average Number of Captives Loaded Per Vessel, 1751–1800*

Imputed Principal Port of Slave Purchase	Average No. of Captives Embarked Per Vessel Per Day	No. of Vessels in Sample	Number Embarked	Standard Deviation
Gambia	1.7	56	66,459	1.4
Anomabu, Adja, Agga	2.7	81	122,820	2.5
Whydah	3.2	87	109,010	1.7
Bonny	5.5	65	279,898	3.6
Old Calabar	3.7	53	131,144	2.8

Note: Numbers with decimal points are not precise because of rounding.
Source: Data generated by David Eltis.

This method is not foolproof for a number of reasons. The daily average number of captives that were loaded on a vessel at a particular port depended in part on the total number of vessels that called there. For example, a port hosting five ships would likely have loaded at faster rate than when the same port had ten ships competing for the same trade – all things being equal. While the daily average number of captives loaded per vessel may not necessarily reflect a port's actual supply capacity, we can assume that in the long run the number of ships that called on a particular port depended largely on its perceived ability to deliver captives. The daily average number of captives loaded per vessel is a useful, if imperfect, reflection of the actual rates at which ships loaded captives at African ports because information about trading conditions in the different ports, including supply capabilities, had become in the eighteenth century more widely available to Euro-American slavers.[25] Nevertheless, the daily average number of captives loaded per vessel has a number of advantages over the turnaround rates of ships. It focuses analysis on the vessels about which we have the necessary information – dates of arrival and departure and the actual average number of captives embarked in specific African ports during sustained periods. The method gives an estimate, as close as possible, of loading rates of ships than does the simple matrix of how frequently ships arrive and depart.

The dramatic rise of the Biafra Atlantic slave trade from the 1740s onward reflected not only the supply conditions that facilitated the fast loading rate described above but also trajectories in Euro-American demand. While captives from the region were generally not considered premium grade by the planters, there seemed always to be pockets of plantation Americas that desired them, reflecting ambivalent perceptions about the enslaved Igbo, sometimes in the same regions, and perhaps a rising profile of Biafra captives in the New World over time. Planters of the Carolinas and to an extent those of Saint-Domingue rejected Igbo captives, but not those of Jamaica; Virginian planters accepted them enthusiastically (Gomez 2003:84–85). While Michael Gomez is able to quote a report that described that the Igbo in sixteenth-century Mexico as "difficult to manage and disposed to committing suicide when subjected to the slightest punishment or ridicule," Colin Palmer reports that they "were considered tractable and hence were highly sought after by some of the slaveholders" in early seventeenth-century Spanish America (Gomez 2003:85; Palmer 1981:29). Writing in 1793, Jamaica-based British planter Bryan Edwards dwelled on suicide as cause for "the great objection to the Eboes as slaves," and after heaping scorn on the Igbo and their ways, he still took care to add that he could not "draw any conclusion of natural inferiority in these people to the rest of the human race" (Edwards 1793:73, 74–75). Despite Edwards's somber characterization of the Igbo, the course of the eighteenth century reveals what seems to be an incremental willingness to accept Igbo captives. One Theodore Morris ([1730/1?]:431) in Barbados bemoaned to Bristol merchant Isaac Hobhouse in January 1730 or 1731 that "there has not been a cargo of Ebbo Slaves Sould here a long time, and many People are Enquiring for them."

---

[25] The reader should note that the major ports of West-Central Africa, such as St. Paul and Malembo, have been excluded from this comparison. These ports offer a different landscape because much of the inland organization of the slave trade that fed them was under Portuguese control; thus they are not a true reflection of African organization.

Some slaveowners even had reasons to prefer the Igbo. Gwendolyn Hall has suggested that Chesapeake planters – and to a lesser extent planters in Lousiana as well – sought Igbo females, probably because of the high reproductive powers that were ascribed to Igbo women (Hall 2005:141–42). In his memoirs, published in 1789, Olaudah Equiano stated that "[t]he West India planters prefer the slaves of Benin or Eboe to those of any other part of Guinea, for their hardiness, intelligence, integrity, and zeal" (Equiano 1995:39). Equiano's observation corroborates that of Captain Hugh Crow, who made regular trips to the Bight of Biafra in the last twenty years of the eighteenth century. Crow gives the impression that favorable comments on captives from the Bight of Biafra had become the norm in his day.

The Eboes [are] a superior race, and the inhabitants, generally, are a fair dealing people, and much inclined to a friendly traffic with the Europeans, who humor their peculiarities. Their general honesty, when the loose nature of their laws as respects Europeans. ... The Eboes, tho' not generally robust, are a well-formed people, of the middle stature: many of their women are of remarkably symmetrical shape, and if white, would in Europe be deemed beautiful. This race is ... of a more mild and engaging disposition than the other tribes ... and though less suited for the severe manual labor of the field, they are preferred in the West India colonies for their fidelity and utility, as domestic servants, particularly if taken young, as they then become the most industrious of any of the tribes taken to the colonies. (Crow 1830:197–99)

Impressions were mixed, but captives from the Bight of Biafra had gained wide acceptance by the second half of the eighteenth century, and possibly, half a century earlier. Although he noted in 1788 that Biafra captives were "weakly, and more liable to disorders," Liverpool merchant James Jones (1788:590) considered "the Trade [in Biafra] most Advantageous ... both as to Our Manufactures and the Number had from thence." All this suggests a shift in Euro-American attitudes toward Biafra captives or, at the very least, that an ever-increasing need for labor left planters with no choice but to take captives from wherever they could be found. Some who expressed very negative views of the Igbo even offered advice on how to make them better slaves. In 1864, physician and poet James Grainger opined that they needed to be "bought young" and Edwards recommended "the gentlest and mildest treatment" (Edwards 1793:74).

The entry of Liverpool merchants and their subsequent takeover of the trade from their Bristol counterparts in the Bight of Biafra is relevant to understanding the expansion of trade despite the negative reviews of the region's captives. Liverpool merchants preferred to buy lower priced captives and were willing to accept lower prices in New World ports (Drake 1976:141). The conditions in the Bight of Biafra suited this strategy well. Whereas the Bristol ships alone carried 300,000 captives between 1680 and 1700, Liverpool became dominant toward the mid-eighteenth century (Blindloss 1898:171). At least two-thirds of the voyages in which the Liverpool tycoon of the second half of the eighteenth century, William Davenport, invested, were dedicated to the trade in Old Calabar and the Cameroons, both in the Bight of Biafra. Of 144 of these voyages that have been traced, out of a total of some 160, as many as 98 went to the Bight of Biafra – 55 to Old Calabar and 43 to the Cameroons (Richardson 1976:65).[26] In January 1736, two mariners wrote to their owner in Britain that "we buy Callabar and Angola Negroes ... on which account we take as many ... as possibly we can, in order to render the Negroe Account proffitable to the Company" (Merewether and Manning 1736). Thus, Liverpool operations emphasized turnover, illuminating why the increase in the size of slave ship between 1664 and 1807 was greatest in the Bight of Biafra, where it rose by 50 percentage points in comparison to the previous 200 years.[27] Liverpool domination of the Biafra trade correlates with this development.

Certain demand factors, including a continuing New World demand for labor and the rising profile of Biafra captives, especially the "Eboes" from the port of Bonny, justified this strategy and contributed to the expansion of the Biafra trade. These demand factors drove prices, notwithstanding increased supply. While supply variables were important, there is in the long run a direct relationship between price and the quantity of captives (Eltis 1983:260). This appears to have been the case in the Bight of Biafra. The average prices of Biafra captives in the New World, especially the "Eboe," hovered at quite competitive rates during the peak years of trade (see G. Williams 1897:539–40). This phenomenon was particularly striking in late eighteenth-century Spanish Louisiana, according to Hall. "If Igbo men were despised ... this is not reflected in the prices during the Spanish period in Louisiana, when the mean price of Igbo men was highest among the most numerous ethnicities" (Hall 2005:141). The trend reversed with the advent of the U.S. period from 1804 onward, but the fact that enslaved Igbo men commanded

---

[26] See E. Williams (1944:61, 63), Hopkins (1973:96), and Minchinton (1976) for informative details concerning the Liverpool slave trade.

[27] For changes in ship size, see Behrendt 1998:7, 8–9.

high prices in different regions and over long spells complicates planters' apparent lukewarm attitude to them.

If increases in volumes of captive exports from the Bight of Biafra reflected increasing demand for captives, they also manifested greater organization, on both sides of the Atlantic, to meet the labor needs of a rapidly expanding plantation complex in the Americas. On the Biafra coast, the "trust" system of credit had become operative by the 1760s.[28] Through this system, European buyers advanced goods to coastal traders on deferred payment basis, to be repaid in captives. In turn, coastal traders advanced these goods to the Aro. The rise of the Biafra trade has been attributed to this peculiar practice, which was made possible by the operation of the indigenous Ekpe society (Drake 1976:149; Forde 1956:16; Latham 1973:27-28, 35-39; Lovejoy and Richardson 1999). This institution was important, but like other important factors, it only partially explains the rise of the region's trade. Developments in the hinterland anchored by Aro organization facilitated the supply of captives to the coast and justified European credit investment in the region.

COASTAL PORTS AND THE HINTERLAND

The pivotal relationship of Aro organization to developments on the coast manifested by the mid-eighteenth century in Bonny's supersession of Old Calabar as Biafra's principal port just as the Aro expanded westward. The shift occurred during the 1726-50 period, when the volume at Old Calabar rose to 66,800, nearly doubling the 34,400 in the previous quarter century, while Bonny's rose to 93,200 – 22 times the paltry 4,200 in the previous period. Thereafter, the numbers embarked at both Old Calabar and Bonny continued to rise, but while exports from Old Calabar rose appreciably to 103,800 or 55.3 percentage points in the 1751-75 period, the rise at Bonny was again exponential – 193,000 or 107 percentage points. In the last quarter of the century, the volume from Old Calabar declined to 82,500 while the number embarked at Bonny rose even further to 207,900 (Table 2.7). Bonny not only became the busiest port in the Bight of Biafra; it also became the busiest in Atlantic Africa north of the Equator (Table 2.6).

Concomitant with the expansion of trade was the exceptionally fast loading rate that occurred at the Bonny port. Captain Simmons of the

[28] Cowan (1936:53-54); Latham (1973:27); Hargreaves (1987); Lovejoy and Richardson (1997, 1999).

TABLE 2.7. *Estimated Departures of Captives from Bight of Biafra Ports by Quarter Century, 1651–1850 (in thousands)*

	Bonny	New Calabar	Old Calabar	Cameroon	Gabon/ Corisco	All Others	Total
1651–1675	1.0	31.7	25.8	0	0	0	58.5
1676–1700	2.8	15.5	33.2	0	0	0	51.5
1701–1725	4.2	4.7	34.4	0	1.3	1.4	45.9
1726–1750	93.2	3.3	66.8	0	2.1	1.3	166.8
1751–1775	193.0	29.0	103.8	17.7	9.5	0.9	354.0
1776–1800	207.9	37.8	82.5	16.6	11.3	2.6	358.7
1801–1825	161.8	17.7	41.8	17.6	9.3	9.2	257.4
1826–1850	82.6	5.4	49.2	12.3	21.4	27.4	198.2
1676–1850	746.5	145.1	437.5	64.2	54.9	42.8	1491

Source: Eltis et al. 2000.

Vine, from Liverpool, "apparently [broke] the record" in 1766 when he sailed with 400 captives from Bonny to Dominica. He "accomplished the round voyage in seven months and ten days" (G. Williams 1897:529). The development at Bonny was phenomenal.

Why did trade at Bonny expand so dramatically and why was the turnaround rate exceptionally high? Historians have pondered how this change came about, and many cite the declining demand at Old Calabar as a factor. They have paid considerable attention to the role of Euro-American buyers in bringing about the relative decline of Old Calabar. Relatively poor health conditions at Old Calabar, the disinterest of West Indian planters in Old Calabar captives, high *comey* rates (duty paid to coastal rulers to secure trading rights), and the rivalry between the Liverpool and Bristol ships over captives regularly feature as factors that promoted the shift. According to this view, European traders could make £60–62 per head from Bonny and New Calabar captives, "against only £28–30 for slaves from Old Calabar" (Hargreaves 1987:181; Latham 1973:19–20). Indeed, the Liverpool-Bristol rivalry seems to have been more intense at Old Calabar and may have put off some buyers by 1767, when one Liverpool sailor wrote in 1767 that he "never saw a worse prospect for making a voyage than at present" (see G. Williams 1897:535). Also, exactions of *comey* at Old Calabar had reached notable proportions and could well have deterred Euro-American buyers (see Crosbies and Trafford et al. 1762:486; G. Williams 1897:529–48). Further, Bonny's more convenient anchorage relative to Old Calabar and its consolidation of "the perpetual alliance" with boat-producing Brass against the other city-states, notably rival New Calabar, have been cited as giving Bonny an advantage over Old Calabar (Cookey 1974:19–20). While transatlantic demand explains the take-off of the overseas slave trade, to attribute Bonny's supersession of Old Calabar to Euro-American factors or solely to coastal conditions glosses over the crucial reasons for the change. The rest of this chapter will show that the reasons Old Calabar gave way to Bonny as the leading port in Biafra are more complicated.

The one demand condition that seems to have had significant impact has barely received attention. The poor reputation of Biafra captives in the Americas affected Old Calabar much more than Bonny. The exceptionally poor reputation of captives from Old Calabar continued to inhibit the demand for captives that sailed from that port. That captives from the Bight of Biafra had a tendency to revolt aboard slave ships was a "common stereotype" among eighteenth-century British slavers (Richardson 2001:73, 79). That they were prone to suicide was another stereotype of the Igbo held by planters in several regions of the Americas (Gomez 2003:84–86). James Jones, who sent ships regularly to Bonny in the 1780s, claimed that he "always declined sending" ships to Old Calabar (and the Cameroons) because the ports "are Sickly, and Slaves inferior to any other, very Weakly and liable to great mortality" (J. Jones 1788:590). Indeed, mortality rates among captives leaving the Bight of Biafra were 7.5 percentage points higher than among those leaving from the rest of Atlantic Africa, and within Biafra, the mean mortality rate involving vessels from Old Calabar was a significant 5.7 percentage points higher than those departing Bonny (Eltis et al. 2000; H. Klein 2001:101). One Euro-American and coastal element that may have been instrumental to the shift and high turnaround rates in the region is the possibility that the Aro moved captives to the ports where they could obtain higher prices, in this case Bonny, and where they could sell their captives as "Eboe" rather than the opprobrious "Calabar." This phenomenon buttresses the importance of Euro-American preferences.

A combination of factors – external and domestic – accounts for the ascendancy of Bonny. Eltis, Lovejoy, and Richardson have identified a number of conditions that favored the major ports – their proximity to "large stocks of potential slaves," accessibility to slave vessels, greater information there about commercial conditions, personal and commercial ties between indigenous merchants of the ports and their European counterparts, and domestic political factors. This perspective offers a greater range of possibilities than explanations that focus exclusively on external or internal factors, but as the authors themselves make clear the particular factors they identified do not necessarily explain the trajectories of any one port (Eltis, Lovejoy, and Richardson 1999:20, 23–24). Indeed, the explanation offers a clarification of why the major ports generally remained important between 1626 and 1832, but not why the relative fortunes of particular ports changed at particular periods. It was the changes taking place in supply within inland trading networks that gave Bonny the edge over its closest competitor, Old Calabar.

Captive supplies were actually shrinking at Old Calabar. One unidentified European eyewitness' report from Old Calabar, dated August 12, 1767, is quite informative.

> There are now seven large vessels in the river, each of which expects to purchase 500 slaves, and I imagine there was seldom ever known a greater *scarcity of slaves than at present*, and these few *chiefly from the low country* (emphasis added). The natives [are engaged in a bloody internal conflict]. The river of late has been very fatal both to whites and blacks. There have three captains belonging to Bristol died within these few months, besides a number of officers and sailors .... The major part of the vessels here have very dangerous disorders amongst the slaves, which makes me rejoice that I have very few on board. I do not expect that our stay here will exceed eight months. *The adjoining coasts of trade seem all to be very much thronged with shipping* .... (reproduced by G. Williams 1897:535)

The gist of this report is that European buyers went to Old Calabar with large vessels, and each vessel was to collect as many as 500 captives. Earlier in 1762, the Liverpool owners of the *Marquis of Granby* had sent Captain Ambrose Lace hoping for a "larger than ... expected" cargo of 550 captives (Crosbies and Trafford et al. 1762:486). But the reality was that captives were becoming comparatively scarce in Old Calabar, and coastal middlemen calculated their prices based on supply and demand. European demand at Old Calabar had placed pressure upon supply, a situation that local rulers sought to exploit sometimes by hiking the *comey*. Violent rivalry between two leading factions of Old Calabar symptomized a structural problem. Old Calabar and European factions hankered over dwindling supplies of captives (relative to demand) in a series of messy, complicated, and violent incidents (see G. Williams 1897:535–36). Declining supplies at Old Calabar and increasing supplies at Bonny as a function of the shifting focus of Aro operations, rather than Euro-American demand patterns, best explain Bonny's supersession of Old Calabar as Biafra's principal port.

If demand-side explanations fail to illuminate Bonny's supersession of Old Calabar, explanations based exclusively on coastal conditions offer, at best, a limited perspective of the shift. High European mortality rates at this time resulted, not from the intrinsic unhealthiness of Old Calabar relative to other ports in the region, but from the long waits caused by the shortage of captives at that port. In the post–slave trade era, the British vice consul in the Bight of Biafra during the 1880s, Harry Johnston, found Old Calabar to be "relatively healthy" – in comparison to other ports, including Bonny (Johnston 1888b:753). Unless the climatic conditions had changed significantly during the preceding century, conditions at Bonny could not have been healthier than at Old Calabar.

Other coastal conditions do not satisfactorily explain the shift either. Comey rates do not seem to have played a crucial role in decision making in the Biafra slave trade and certainly not in the case of Bonny, where comey was just as great. Neither did they hamper the palm oil trade at Old Calabar that became important in the second half of the eighteenth century (see Adams 1832; Northrup 1976; Ryder 1980:242). Nor did they prevent the ascendancy of Bonny, where, as in New Calabar, the comey rates were, after all, also considerable. By 1788, James Jones could declare that "the Dutys paid [at Bonny and New Calabar are] very high *much more than at any other part of the Coast* (emphasis added), and on every ship alike without distinction as to size" (J. Jones 1788). In Bonny, the custom duty for each ship was as high as £400 in 1792 (see Crow 1830:43). Rather than trade shifting away from Bonny because of high comey rates, Bonny posted phenomenal sales despite its high comey rates. Thus, comey rates had less impact on the shift than often suggested.

Nor does Bonny's favorable anchorage explain its rise as a major outlet for captives. After all, Euro-American buyers were aware of this advantage by the turn of the eighteenth century, and probably before (see Starke 1702:74). Yet, it was not until the 1726–50 period that Bonny superseded Old Calabar. If good and safe anchorage was a key factor in Bonny's rise, why then did Opobo later supersede Bonny, after 1869, in spite of Opobo having an exceeding shallow channel? No do Bonny's apparent alliances with neighboring trading states pass muster as a reason for the shift. While a strategic alliance could have been relevant in Bonny's rise to prominence, and while Bonny's alliance with westerly Brass could have given Bonny an advantage over New Calabar (which was sandwiched by Bonny and Brass), this alliance has no necessary connection with Bonny overtaking Old Calabar, located some distance away to the east of Bonny. Further, it is impossible to gauge the relevance of this supposedly crucial political alliance to the shift in trade that had become noticeable by the 1750s, since it is unclear when the alliance took effect. The explanation for Bonny's rise lies elsewhere.

The relative attractiveness of the ports to overseas buyers was largely dependent on the ports, supply links with the hinterland, from where the vast majority of export captives were drawn. The location of Bende (eastern Igboland), which had been well established since the 1670s, suggests the existence of a trade-route network that crisscrossed Igbo and the Ibibio countries down to Calabar (Nwokeji 1997a). These routes led southward to the ports of Bonny and New Calabar and northward into the Igala and Idoma lands in the Nigerian Middle Belt, probably from the early eighteenth century and toward the end of the second phase or beginning of the second phase of Aro expansion. This would partly have resulted from the policies of the Atta dynasty of the Igala kingdom of Idah, which came into existence in c. 1687–1717. The Atta dynasty "turned energetically to the development of slave trading, and became a major supplier to the Niger River markets and the Aro overland system" (Sargent 1999:8, 61). Of particular interest are the changes that took place in trade-routes network. Four north to south routes had emerged by 1750, according to Afigbo (1987).

1. The Niger waterway in the westernmost extreme of the region.
2. An overland route from the Middle Belt towns of Ejure and Idah on the Benue River, through Nsukka, central Igboland, and Akwete in southern Igboland to Bonny.
3. An overland route from the Middle Belt town of Ibi on the Benue through Ejure to central Igboland and "to the coast."
4. The easternmost route from Ibi through Wukari and Ogoja in the Ejagam region, Ezza in northeastern Igboland, to Cross River Igbo towns of Uburu and Bende, Arochukwu, and the Ibibio town of Itu. This route most likely terminated at Calabar.

The second and third of these routes passed through central Igboland and headed toward the central Niger delta, and the second route terminated at Bonny. The Niger route was probably the oldest (Afigbo 1987:41). This picture squares with the trends in Biafra Atlantic exports. The pattern of exports from Old Calabar suggests that the easternmost route was also older than the central routes; New Calabar was the oldest port of significance and received most of its trade from the Niger route closest to it, as did Brass, the westernmost port in the region. As

Biafra's easternmost port, Old Calabar, "dealt with the Ibibio along the lower Cross River" and bought captives from the Aro (Cookey 1974:19). Whereas the captives sold at Brass included significant numbers of non-Igbo from farther north, Bonny received its trade principally from the Aro network (Alagoa 1986:127). It was more practicable to reach the Niger through the Brass River than through the Bonny River; the Bonny River was not even a branch of the Niger (Burdo 1880:95; Whitford 1967:159). Thus, Bonny received its captive supplies almost exclusively from central Igboland. Its rise as the principal port had to await the development of the central route. Old Calabar, which superseded New Calabar, received its trade from the easternmost route via Arochukwu, so that a higher proportion of non-Igbo captives were exported from there than from Bonny (Nwokeji 2000a:621). The two central routes leading to Bonny through the Igbo heartland were the new elements in the trade-route system during the eighteenth century. The Bonny port, which became preeminent by the mid-eighteenth century, linked these two routes via the major Aro settlements in the greater upper Imo River area. Thus it is clear that both internal and external dynamics were linked. The Aro mobilized captives from the hinterland, and Euro-American traders bought and transported those captives overseas, underscoring the fact that both internal processes and external Euro-American circumstances shaped the region's trade.

CONCLUSIONS

This chapter correlates with uncommon specificity changes in coastal trading activities – in particular the rise of slave exports and shifts in the relative importance of embarkation ports – not just with external factors or internal developments confined to coastal trading societies, but also with changes in inland organization of the slave trade. Aro expansion into the Igbo heartland and the rise of the Biafra Atlantic slave trade were linked. Aro incursions, manifested in the establishment of the principal Aro diaspora settlements, were both a cause and effect of the Biafra Atlantic system. The Aro had been trading in the Igbo heartland prior to the shift in export activity from Old Calabar to Bonny in the mid-eighteenth century, and their setting up of settlements in the heartland resulted from the quest to satisfy increasing demand for captives. Trade with Europeans encouraged Aro forays in the hinterland, which in turn both increased Biafra's supply of captives and shifted the thrust of trade from Old Calabar to Bonny. As the Aro network matured in the Cross River region, Old Calabar, situated near Arochukwu, became dominant in the first half of the eighteenth century, as a result of the supply situation at Old Calabar, where the Aro channeled most of their captives before the 1740s. This initial shift of trade eastward skipped Bonny, which was located between New Calabar and Old Calabar, because the central trade routes had not yet developed. Further expansion of trade escalated Aro expansion. But Aro forays northwestward into the densely populated central Igboland, and especially their creation of new settlements there, shifted trade away from Old Calabar to Bonny – a port that was more convenient port to these settlements. It is significant that, although the overall reputation of Biafra captives may have risen over the period among Euro-American buyers, the poor reputation of captives sold at Old Calabar remained unaltered throughout the shifts and trends observed, a fact that strongly suggests the centrality of the supply side to these changes. The remarkably fast loading rate at Bonny relative to other ports in the Bight of Biafra must have been the function of the delivery system from hinterland sources of captives to the coast. More detailed analyses are needed across African regions, which delineate the role of inland trading organizations in shaping the structure of the Atlantic slave trade, in particular, the trajectories of specific embarkation ports during different periods. Chapter 3 fleshes out the empirical details of the role of Aro institutions and trading mechanisms in the expansion of their operations and in changes in the Bight of Biafra slave trade.

3

The Trade Diaspora in Regional Context

Aro Commercial Organization in the Era of Expansion, 1740–1850

The Aro trading complex had not only an Atlantic context but also a regional political and economic one.[1] The Aro created what K. Onwuka Dike termed a regional "pax" under which large-scale trade flourished in a multiethnic region, and their operations eased exchange and "brought rapid impetus to economic expansion" in a region with a multitiered currency system. Some further argue that the Aro brought stability to the region.[2] It bears noting, however, that the Aro were only one of several groups in the seventeenth century that resulted from migrations into the Bight of Biafra to partake in the slave trade. Both Arochukwu and the Niger riverine states underwent a period of growth and consolidation throughout the seventeenth century and after. Yet, it was the Aro, rather than these states or any other groups, who came to dominate the hinterland trade. Did the Aro weave their trading network using an organization similar to the organizations of other communities in the region or did they fashion a truly unique model?

That the Aro used an organization based on a fundamentally different model seems to have been the case. While Abo and Igala established a few trading outposts, they did not open up new markets for captives per se.

---

[1] For the regional context, see Dike and Ekejiuba 1990; Ekejiuba 1972a, 1972b; Ifemesia 1978:32–37; Ijoma and Njoku 1991; G.I. Jones 1989:34–36; Northrup 1978b; Ofonagoro 1972; Oriji 1981, 1982; S. Ottenberg 1958, 1971:24–27; Stevenson 1968:Ch. 9; Ukwu 1967, 1969.

[2] For the first view, see Crowder 1978:65; K.O. Dike 1956:38–39; Ekejiuba 1991:313–14; Isichei 1976:64 and, for the second, see Grier 1922.

These settlements only dotted the banks of the lower Niger.³ The most spectacular development of the eighteenth century was the establishment of Aro settlements virtually everywhere in the region. In fact, the Aro soon carried their trade into the turfs of some of these immigrant trading communities and even their parent communities outside Igboland, where the Aro established settlements, including the main Igala market at Idah at the northern reaches of the Lower Niger.⁴ These diaspora settlements also enabled the Aro to participate actively in the Niger riverine trade. Thus, they played a vital role in Aro trade, probably accounting for more than 85 percent of all the captives that resulted from Aro operations (K.O. Dike and Ekejiuba 1990:250). The diasporic character of Aro organization was the decisive factor in Aro ability to meet the demands of the expanding Biafra Atlantic trade. Aro settlements coordinated activities and strongly identified with the metropole.

Aro settlements were more than permanent settlements in the common sense because their routine contact with, as well as determined cultural and political fidelity to, the Arochukwu metropole were an essential feature. As a pivotal element in Aro expansion and the expansion of the Biafra Atlantic trade, the diaspora phenomenon calls for detailed examination. Placing Aro settlements in the diaspora context highlights, on the one hand, the internal relations among Aro groups and, on the other, their relations with the host communities. In this way, too, we can establish the process and direction of cultural evolution, the incorporation of outsiders into Aro groups, and how the Aro system both resembled, and deviated from, other trade diasporas.

THE DIASPORA CONTEXT

The Aro had five key elements of trade diasporas. First, a "central place" that performed roles "which all require but it alone can perform" (Curtin 1975: 64) was often an important component of a trade diaspora. In the Aro case, the central place was Arochukwu in the Cross River region. Arochukwu was the seat of major Aro institutions, such as the central council (Ọkpankpọ), the Ibiniukpabi oracle, and Eze Aro (Aro king), and each diaspora settlement was institutionally tied to the Aro world only

---

³ These outposts included Akri-Atani, Akri-Uteri, Akri-Ugidi, Nsugbe and Oko See Afigbo (1977:131), Isichei (1976); K.O. Dike and Ekejiuba (1990:83).
⁴ For Oguta, see Ofonagoro (1972:89); Isichei (1976:62); Northrup (1978b:130); G.I. Jones (1989:36). For Igala, see Dike and Ekejiuba (1990:200).

through its parent Arochukwu lineage-group. A second element is in the relationship of trade diasporas to their host communities, which range from dominated diasporas to dominant ones, with most falling into the former category. The third similarity between the Aro and other trade diasporas is cultural aloofness from the host population. Whatever their size, structure or specific history, Aro settlements stood out from the local population. Fourth, in spite of the tendency to emphasize cultural exclusiveness, trade diasporas were "cross-cultural carriers of culture" or "cultural brokers." For example, although the trade diasporas of the Senegambian trade, such as the Maraka, the Juula and the Jahaanke, "adopted the language[s] and some aspects of the culture of the [host societies]," they continued to claim Soninke origin.[5] The Aro diaspora settlements, too shared, much and mixed with the groups among whom they lived, notably the Igbo, but they steadfastly held on to a separate Aro identity. Fifth, trade diasporas historically made ideological and/or religious references to universalist monotheism, and often claimed a special place within it. The best example is the Jews, who were the most widespread of all trade diasporas. The known African trade diasporas, such as the Hausa and the Sonninke-speaking groups of West Africa, and the Swahili of East Africa, operated within the framework of Islam. These Muslim merchants presented themselves to, and were accepted among, most African groups, operating as standard bearers of Islam. Although the Aro were non-Muslim, their religion also espoused a universalist monetheist deity, Chukwu, and the Aro alone were its children. Like other trade diasporas, the Aro successfully inserted themselves into a special place in the world of Chukwu. These characteristics distinguished the Aro from other groups in the Bight of Biafra.

While being non-Muslim made the Aro unique among most other African trade diasporas, they also differed from most other trade diasporas anywhere. Unlike other diasporas, the Aro diaspora almost always had access to military resources, which was often a decisive factor in their dealings with hinterland groups. Trade diasporas also tended to be slow, if not always averse, to incorporate outsiders, but the Aro embarked on a programmatic incorporation of non-Aro into the Aro group (Chapter 6). In addition, the Aro invariably wielded political influence over their host communities, a marked departure from other trade diasporas, which tended

---

[5] The theoretical and comparative insights in this paragraph are drawn from Curtin (1975:63–64; 1984:2, 3, 5, 25). See Kea (1982:ch. 2) for an elaboration of a central place in a different context.

to be politically marginal within their host societies. These differences compel a detailed examination of Aro methods.

The number and diversity of Aro settlements in a region as small as the Nigerian section of the Bight of Biafra are bewildering. The complex historical circumstances that accompanied the formation and development of about 150 Aro trade diaspora communities during the Aro expansion have given rise to competing taxonomies, from which two to five types have emerged depending on the criteria used. These taxonomies derive from mode of establishment, size, or function of the diaspora settlements.[6] The most useful typology eschews function as a comparative criterion and uses mode of formation, size, and structure to derive the following types: (1) large settlements founded by conquest that grew to dominate the land, superimposing their names on it (as in Arondizuogu, the communities of the Ndieni cluster, and Inokun); (2) those founded peacefully that constituted separate villages or wards within preexisting non-Aro communities (as found in Oguta, Bende, Umuahia, and the Port Harcourt area); and (3) the numerous compounds or lineages within preexisting non-Aro villages that peacefully sprouted as trading posts (C. Okafor 1986:116–19). All typology is of course merely heuristic, and exceptions obtain even in this classification.

Although no single model can account for all trade diasporas, the principal Aro settlements – Arondizuogu and the Ndieni cluster – exhibited remarkable uniformities in the timing, spacing, and patterns of establishment. They were all established around the mid-eighteenth century at the edge of the densely populated Igbo heartland, and force was typically used. The perimeter of the Igbo heartland had the largest concentration of large Aro settlements. Among the many features of the Aro expansionist strategy, five stand out: (1) the timing and location of the major settlements in the densely populated central Igboland; (2) the virtual partitioning of the Biafra hinterland among Arochukwu lineage-groups; (3) alliances with non-Aro groups through the agency of Aro private enterprise; (4) the use of force in establishing the large settlements; and (5) conscious efforts at group expansion and inherent motivation for successful merchants to create new settlements. The rest of this chapter examines these processes and the institutions that articulated them, in order to explain the hinterland dimensions of the expansion of the Biafra Atlantic trade.

---

[6] See Umo (n.d.:10); S. Ottenberg (1958:301); Stevenson (1968:204); Dike and Ekejiuba (1990:196–97); Ijoma and Njoku (1991:305).

TIMING AND LOCATION OF THE MAJOR SETTLEMENTS

As was common among trade diasporas, the Aro settlements were established in areas with existing channels of exchange.[7] The Aro established settlements whenever any trader or kin-related traders deemed it necessary to do so in furtherance of trade. Settlements therefore tended to follow existing trade routes that linked the principal markets that had been adopted by the Aro. In areas with rudimentary market infrastructures, such as Ikwereland in southern Igboland and other peripheral areas, the Aro established new markets (Ifemesia 1978:33; Ukwu 1969:134, 135). The Aro found reliable exchange structures in the upper Imo River/Nri-Awka region, which they had in fact used for some time before the 1740s. This region maintained a complex trade network that encompassed Igbo-Ukwu, a community that had acquired items produced outside Africa as far back as the ninth century AD and established trading groups of Awka and Nkwere. It was not a surprise, therefore, that the most important Aro settlements were concentrated in central Igboland between Nkwere and the Nri-Awka region.

Aro traders seem to have commonly established settlements in familiar territories. The founding of these settlements was the culmination of long-established trading contacts with the people of the greater central Igbo region. The founders of the Aro settlements of the Igbo heartland either had already acquired dependents from the Nri-Awka area (and beyond) or had themselves been acquired originally as children from the region. For example, Izuogu Mgbopko, the founder of Arondizuogu, had as dependents Amazu from Oro (Awlaw) in the Oji-Mmam River area, west of Awgu in the savanna, and Iheme from Nise near Awka in the Igbo heartland. Izuogu is said to already have had a key contact in the upper Imo region – Nzeadachie of Umulolo (see J.G. Okoro 1985:23; 1996). In time, Umulolo traditions even claimed that the clan's legendary projenitor, Lolo, was an Aro man (see Goodlife 1933:7, NAE CSE 1/1/5 28935). The founders of the Ndieni cluster had also had long-standing contact with the greater central Igboland, including Nri-Awka. The founder of Ujari (Ajalli), Oti Emesinwa, is said to have acted at the prompting of his father who had traded in the Nri-Awka area. The Nri-Awka origins of some of these mid-eighteenth-century traders show that the Aro had traded with the region sometime before, in part because these men had been acquired as small boys a few decades earlier. The Aro traders who made regular

---

[7] Dike and Ekejiuba 1990:197; Ukwu 1967, 1969.

trips to the Nri-Awka axis included men the Aro merchant–warlords had acquired from the greater central Igboland. Ikerionwu Ufere, who soon established a settlement north-northwest of Arondizuogu, had been acquired from Ifite in Awka, also in the Nri-Awka area. Owuu Mgbori, whose descendants founded Ndiowuu, had himself also been acquired from the Nri-Awka region.[8] All this seems to support the suggestion that most of the Igbo who were sent to the export slave trade were drawn from the Nri-Awka area, and Douglas Chambers specifically mentions the U.S. Chesapeake region up to the 1740s (Chambers 2005:30, 37; S. Martin 1995:174; Oriji 1987:159–60). Indeed, the two Igbo place names Oldendorp gathered from enslaved Igbo in North America during 1767 and 1768 – Alo (Alor) and Okwa (Ukwa) – are in the Nri-Awka region (Oldendorp 2000: ms. 432, 434). The region seems to have begun to supply significant numbers of captives through Aro operations prior to the establishment of the Aro settlements in central Igboland.

The most important Aro settlements to be established during the eighteenth century were in the area that had the highest population densities in the Biafra hinterland and Atlantic Africa. Arondizuogu in particular was "situated in the heart of the Ibo country with easy access from this broken country to the uplands in the west and north, through gaps in the encampment to the Cross River basin in the east, as well as to the southern coastal plains" (Ukwu 1967:651; 1969:134). With the Ndieni cluster, this settlement commanded the trade routes from the Igbo heartland in all directions, leading ultimately to destinations outside Igboland (Cookey 1974:6). Another basic rationale for the strategic siting of settlements was the Aro need for a constant supply of provisions for their ever-growing populations and for transit captives.

If Arondizuogu was the first full-fledged diaspora settlement of the Aro, as is generally accepted, the date of its foundation should clarify the timing of the Aro diaspora. In the absence of written records, genealogies provide a guide to the chronology. Early Arondizuogu writers give great antiquity to the settlement – 1620 or 1635 (Umo n.d. [1947?:17]; Igwegbe 1962). Others have put forth later dates – 1728 or 1720–30 (K.O. Dike and Ekejiuba 1990:205; B. Orji 1978:8). Based on six generations of genealogy and his awareness of the role of the Atlantic slave trade in Aro expansion, Jonathan Okoro suggests that the settlement was founded in

---

[8] See Umo (n.d.); Igwegbe (1962) and J.G.Okoro (1985) for Arondizuogu; J.C. Nwankwo (1973) for Ndikerionwu; and Eni (1973:9) for Ujari. Eni claims that Ujari was established in the 1730s.

1750. Notably, he observes that this period was "still within the peak period of the slave trade in West Africa, and the colony was set up as a convenient base for the collection of slaves" (J.G. Okoro 1985:43). One calculation from the genealogies collected by colonial officers during the early twentieth century suggests 1790–1820 (Isichei 1976; Nwauwa 1990). According to this scheme, the Atlantic slave trade was almost over when the community was founded. This faulty date resulted from genealogies collected among descendants of recent immigrants, who sought to advance their position within the colonial-era indirect-rule system whereby the British apparently ruled the people through their traditional rulers. Clearly, the foundation of the settlement happened considerably before the late eighteenth century.

Researchers in the Bight of Biafra commonly use thirty years as the standard for the male generational marker (Nwauwa 1990; Sargent 1999). There should never be a standard to apply to all societies, except where too little is known to allow for special circumstances and specific cultural practices that influence the demographic process. Each society is different, and special circumstances might exacerbate differences in generational averages among different societies. The thirty-year paradigm assumes that a male was always the first child and that first male children (who were not necessarily first born or by the first wife) all survived. High infant mortality and late marriages on the part of men ensured that these constants hardly applied to any real situation. According to an Aro elder, Michael Igwe, "Before a man could say in those days that he was getting married, he would be up to fifty years, or at least forty" (M.S. Igwe 1996). His testimony most likely exaggerates the phenomenon, but it does indicate that early marriages cannot be assumed. When men eventually did marry, it sometimes took several years and additional wives before they had male children. The problem is further complicated by the fact that one can hardly trace the lines of first sons with consistency. Because Arondizuogu leadership is based on gerontocracy, rather than promogeniture, there are few traces left in oral tradition on which one can base the genealogies of the ruling house on first sons. Reliance on later sons, whose genealogies are nonetheless known, stretches the generational gap even wider. For example, the following calculation based on the genealogy of the late Eze, John Dike II, exhibits such a problem. Dike II was one of his father's last children, born when Dike Oti would have been well into his seventies (P. Imo 2003). Given the foregoing demographics, forty-five years seems a more accurate marker in this case. John Dike was born in about 1918 as the son of Dike, and using the forty-five-year rule, this date puts the hypothetical birth date of Dike Oti at 1873.[9] John's grandfather, Oti Okoronkwo, would have been born about 1828. Oti's father, Okoronkwo, would have been born in 1783. From this, we derive at 1738 birth date for Awa, Izuogu's second son, born of Izuogu's junior wife.[10] This would have put Izuogu's own birth date in about 1693. As Izuogu seems to have traded in the area for some time when he founded the settlement, he would have been sufficiently advanced in age, perhaps forty years. This puts the date of the formation of Arondizuogu at about 1733, with a five-year margin of error. This range is largely correspondent with genealogies collected from the pioneer lineage-groups. Izuogu was the great grandson of Nnachi, the Igbo pioneer of the Aro state.

The intensification of Aro activities in central Igboland that is evident from the concentration of the major Aro settlements there, starting about the 1740s, suggests strongly that the trade of these Aro communities was oriented toward Bonny and New Calabar. Given that this trend was the most significant element in Bonny's supersession of Old Calabar (and New Calabar) during the 1726–50 period, the correlation of these byproducts of Aro expansion to the expansion of the Biafra Atlantic trade compels the examination of the mechanisms of Aro expansion.

ZONING OF THE HINTERLAND

Aro concentration in densely populated central Igboland resulted from its division of the entire Biafra hinterland into spheres of operation among the Aro lineage-groups (Table 3.1). The method by which the hinterland was zoned is also hazy, but it seems that individuals and lineages opened their own spheres and maintained contacts according to familiar lines of trade.[11] Once a family or group of traders from a particular Aro lineage-group had opened up initial contacts at a place, all other Aro traders usually respected it as the sphere of that pioneer family or group, which became the designated Aro link to the host community. By respecting one another's domains, Aro groups were

---

[9] This date is clearly inaccurate, as Dike Oti would have been born about twenty-five years earlier, but this should be offset by other stages in the genealogy that are shorter than forty-five years.

[10] Awa's elder brother was Uche born of Izuogu's senior wife.

[11] E.g. J. O. Dike 1996; Obinani 1996; Michael Ike 1995; Kanu-Igbo 1996b; J.G. Okoro 1996; J.O. Okoro 1996.

TABLE 3.1. *Division of Spheres among Aro Lineage-Groups*

Aro Lineage-Group	Markets
Agbagwu	Item[c], Ohaozara[c], Mgbidi[f], Ose-Moto[f]
Amangwu	Itu[c], Ohaozara[c], Ezza[f], Onueke[f], Affium[6]
Amankwu	Enugu[c], Isuama[b], Nri-Awka[b], Arondizuogu area[f]
Amannagwu	Bonny[a], New Calabar[a,] Oguta[f], Abam[f], Ukwa[f]
Amasu	Calabar via Umom[c], Eki[c], and Uwet[c], Lokpanta[f], Lokpaukwu[c], Ibiasoegbe[f]
Amoba	Afikpo[b], Ohaozara[f], Amasiri[f], Uburu[f]
Amukwa	Uzuakoli[c], Ovim[f]
Amuvi	Ohaozara[c], Enugu[c,e], Igbo hinterland up to Nsukka[a], Awgu[c], Isuochi[f], Ihube[f], Achi[f]
Asaga	Okigwe[c,d], Igbo hinterland up to Nsukka[a], Orlu-Oguta[c], Abakaliki[f], Ikwo[f], Ezaa[f], Izzi[f]
Atani	Bonny,[a,c], Okirika[c], Ngwa[c], & Degema[c], New Calabar[a,h], Ajatakiri[f], Ayama[f], Affium[f,] Ihiala[g,h]
Ibom	Ada[c], Obura[c], nde-Ikelionwu area[f], nde-Owuu area[f], Ogwe[f], Ebijiakara[f], Ihiala[g,h]
Isinkpu	Bonny1,[c], Okirika[c], Ngwa[c], Degema[c], New Calabar[a], Okporo-Enyi[f], Itu-Nta[f], Nkalunta[f]
Obinkita	Ibibio[c],d, Bonny–New Calabar[a], Mbiabong[f], Nturi[f], Ikot-Umossien[f], Ikot-Edet[f]
Oro	Akunakuna[c,d], Aro-Ikpa area[f]
Ugbo	Uburu[c], Igbo hinterland up to Nsukka[a], Amasiri[f]
Ugwuakuma	Ekoi[c], Ewe[f], Ikorokpora[f]
Ugwuavo	Abakaliki[c], Igbo hinterland up to Nsukka[a], Okposi-Akeze[f], Onicha-Isu[f]
Ujari	Enyong[c], Ujari area[f], Ihe[f], Okija[f], nde-Okoroji area[f]
Utughugwu	Akunakuna[c], Nneato[f]

Sources: [a] K. Oji 1972; [b] G.I. Jones 1989:35–36; [c] Anthropologists' Papers 1927:Appendix IV; [d] Grier 1922:34; [e] Kanu-Igbo 1996; [f] Aro-Okeigbo Ancestral Almanac 1996; [g] E. Ike 1985; [h] I. Ugboaja 1985.

able to erect a moral economy of trade and minimize conflict among themselves. The pioneer Aro-community historian Kanu Umo tells us that

> each village or town community in Aro-land had an emissary to different peoples outside. With each of these they had an oath of allegiance in which the Aros swore safe conduct to "Chukwu" whilst, on the other hand, the peoples swore loyalty and staunch reliability to their intermediaries and lords. ... the relative principle between the ... peoples was purely democratic such that any encroachment would be a vital stet – to (sic) the democracy intended. (Umo n.d. [1947]:10)

Just as individual Aro traders knew, and were expected to respect, the boundaries of the zones of influence, their non-Aro suppliers knew their particular Aro men. As one respondent testified:

> It was already recognized at home before they came out. Individuals focused on lines familiar to them. The customers who supplied them with trade goods already knew their [Aro] men. Aro groups never collided over spheres of influence. ... Nobody would move from the Amankwu team to buy captives being supplied to the Ujari; nobody from the Ujari team would buy those being supplied to the Amuvi, and so forth. (Kanu-Igbo 1996)

An Aro person from one lineage-group went into another Aro lineage-group's area of influence only if sponsored by somebody from the group wielding influence (Kanu-Igbo 1996; J.O. Okoro 1996). "In those days, trade through commission agents was part of trade. [Trader A] may find the price of a commodity unfavorable. [He] then decides to shift it to [his friend, trader B] to consider if [B] could cope with the price. [Trader B] may even decide to send it to [trader C]. Buying the commodity did not give [trader C] the right to trade in [trader A's] area of trade" (Kanu-Igbo 1996). One Aro tradition from Ihiala in the southern periphery of the Nri-Awka area relates that an Aro person who scouted for pilgrims to the shrine or for non-Aro caravans in an area controlled by another Aro group forfeited the commission accruing from such a transaction (E. Ike 1985). There can be no doubt that the Aro quarreled among themselves over spheres, but they evidently contained the quarrels sufficiently to prevent such problems from disrupting their activities.

In zoning the region and in forging commercial ties, the Aro capitalized on their multiethnic origins and the strategic location of their homeland.[12]

The zoning of spheres directed the various lineage-groups often to the areas of their ethnic origins. Thus, Arondizuogu, an Amankwu offshoot, controlled much of the Nri-Awka market. Amankwu, in turn,

TABLE 3.2. *Principal Aro Settlements at the Edge of the Igbo Heartland*

Settlement	Parent Arochukwu lineage-group
Arondizuogu	Amankwu
Ndiokwaraeze (Ndieni)	Ujari
Ujari (Ndieni)	Ujari
nde-Owu (Ndieni)	Ibom

[12] Dike and Ekejiuba 1990; Ijoma and Njoku 1991:208; G.I. Jones 1989:35; Northrup 1978:48.

was a branch of the "Igbo" pioneers of Arochukwu. The other major Aro settlements in central Igboland, collectively referred to as Ndieni, were offshoots of an assortment of parent Arochukwu lineage-groups (Table 3.2). In the territory lying between Arondizuogu and the Ndieni group were a group of preexisting clans. Ninety-nine-year-old Jacob Okoro, in 1986, narrated the complicated zoning arrangement as it applied to central Igboland:

There are nineteen "villages" in Aro-Chukwu. ... the Aro "villages" shared out eastern Nigeria into areas of influence. Arondizuogu's share was the region from Uzuakoli to Okigwe up to Akokwa, Uga and the rest of the places. These were the places that this Amankwu dominated. The people whose area of influence bordered that of Arondizuogu was nde-Ikelionwu, the Ibom people here. The Ibom and Amankwu peoples knew their areas and one group would not intrude in another group's domain. A person from one group went into another group's area of influence only through a person of the group responsible for the area. This other person took a cue from the person that brought him. He could secure trade goods only through the person that brought him. So, nde-Ikelionwu and Arondizuogu had a boundary. This was at Ekwuluobia. Nde-Ikelionwu was responsible for one side, including Umunze and Oka. Arondizuogu had Ekwuluobia up to Unu (Orlu). The group with which Arondizuogu shared a boundary there was Atani. Arondizuogu did not go beyond there to buy captives. Arondizuogu people could only go there through the Atani group. Nde-Owu and Ujari (Ajali) were responsible for the area from Umunze. The Ibom group and nde-Ike also shared the area. Ajali, Ibom and nde-Ike were all involved in the same place. Arondizuogu controlled Adazi and Nimo. Nde-Ikelionwu controlled Umuchima, Oko and other places. The Ajali people had a stake in these places too. Beyond these places were places like Eziama, Nokpa and others. ... The peoples of Ugbo and Amoba controlled them. (J.O. Okoro 1996)

Obviously, Arochukwu lineage-groups did not carve out large, neat zones, but respectively controlled small spheres of mostly noncontiguous communities, which were interspersed with communities controlled by other Aro lineage-groups.

The methods employed by various Aro groups to penetrate the different areas depended on local circumstances. One notable local variant – observed in the Nri-Awka region – saw the Aro planting large settlements near the peripheries rather than at the core of the high-density areas, as was done elsewhere. Although major Aro settlements did not pervade the area, the Aro nonetheless formed lineages in many communities there.[13]

---

[13] The settlement in Ihiala in southern Nri-Awka was quite substantial (see I.O. Nwankwo 1986). This evidence shows that, contrary to Northrup's view, Aro settlements do not

To fully understand the character of Aro expansion, one has to come to terms with the changes associated with it.

PRIVATE ENTERPRISE AND ALLIANCES

While the Aro state consciously promoted an expansionist policy, private enterprise increasingly became central to the project. The character of expansion underwent fundamental change in one important respect during the second phase of expansion dating from about 1740 to 1807. While the first phase of Aro expansion witnessed the direct involvement of the Aro state, the second phase rested on private enterprise. The role of *Mazi* (Consul) in the first phase of expansion contrasted sharply with that of the freelancing merchants that held sway from the eighteenth century onward. The appointment of a resident *Mazi*, usually a trusted confidant of the Aro king, for the outlying communities, as far as Afikpo (north of Arochukwu), was perhaps the first act of Aro expansionism during the seventeenth century. The *Mazi* and his retinue of advisers and followers, linked "the local administration ... to the Aro system" (K.O. Dike and Ekejiuba 1990:69). The Aro also constituted themselves into *amadi* (aristocracy), and controlled trade and the Afikpo market.

There is no evidence that the *Mazi* traded on the king's behalf or that the king's trade necessarily preceded that of other traders, as it did in Polanyi's port of trade (Polanyi 1963). Yet, Afikpo at this time seems to resemble the port of trade in that there does not seem to have been a clear-cut distinction between private and state spheres there.[14] However,

---

"halt" at the edge of the Nri-Awka region (Northrup 1978b:131, 134–35). For references to the Aro settlement in Ihiala, see Onwuejeogwu 1987:40; C. Okafor 1986:126; Oriji 1994:39–40, 48, 53, 64, 105.

[14] Polanyi refers to existence in the port of trade of an apparently private trader, who is in reality a state trade and/or financial officer (Polanyi 1963:32). In Robin Law's studies of Dahomey, which raise the usefulness of analyzing precolonial African economy in terms of private/state enterprises, it appears that the functions of the *Mazi* corresponded roughly to Dahomian "Captain of the Market," in a foreign land. The latter's duties "included ... the maintenance of order and the collection of a sales tax on all transactions in the market," and the regulation of the cowry currency and prices (Law 1977, 1978:42–45; Law 1991:51; Law 1996). The rulers of the Malinke and Wolof of Senegambia appointed lieutenants to supervise trade (Aschcroft-Eason 1997). In the mid-seventeenth and early eighteenth centuries Benin, the king's traders were called *Fiadors* – Portuguese for guarantors (see Anonymous Dutch, pp. 50–51; Van Nyendael 1702:434). Falconbridge (1788:8) reports of "officer boys" in Old Calabar during the second half of the eighteenth century. In the Congo River emerged the office of the *Mafouk*, which was "central to the broking systems in the major states along this coast [and] which had emerged during the slave trade as the royal official responsible for regulating trade with Europeans; he appointed

through the *Mazi*, the Aro king seems to have controlled the conditions of trade in an era when the Aro council (Ọkpankpọ) probably had not yet come into existence or was less influential than it later became. The role of the *Mazi* as a state office became less important thereafter, although the freelancing merchants retained the appellation and the term came to apply to virtually every person of achievement and to all well-born male elders sometime in the nineteenth century. The period from the eighteenth century onward was the era of private enterprise.

The ascendancy of private enterprise changed the character of Aro expansion. It was accompanied by the introduction of violence into the process. We do not have any evidence that the Aro resorted to violence before the eighteenth century. The intensifying warfare as groups jostled to take advantage of the slave trade and the need of warring groups for powerful allies called for the services of Aro merchants who built and supported alliances as well as initiated conflicts. Aro wars in the eighteenth century did not involve the entire Aro community; typically merchant-warlords and their followers were involved.

The merchant-warlords were a motley crowd of successful and adventurous merchants. Whatever their backgrounds were, there is sufficient evidence to call into question Dike and Ekejiuba's claim that the merchant-warlords were "acculturated Aro." According to them, the ambitious among the "acculturated Aro", "excluded from politics at Arochukwu could find scope for their energies in the various settlements which the expanding Aro commerce necessitated ... In other words, exclusion from politics at home did not spell doom for the ambitious individual." In fact, Dike and Ekejiuba are explicit in stating that such individuals "were more strongly motivated to pursue risk-taking, and long-distance trading ventures for their survival in the Aro system than the prudent and proud elite and the ruling groups."[15] Of course, the dynamism and risk-taking propensities of certain persons of servile and recent origins are well-known. These characteristics fed on the fact that Aro society honored achievement. Many acculturated Aro contributed

---

the brokers (*maekedores*) who received the caravans bringing produce from the interior" (Lynn 1997:64). In the early nineteenth century, they were referred to as "governors", whose powers were "great and almost uncontrolled" (Bold 1822:72). At Addamugu, immediate south of the Niger-Benue confluence, the office of Nufia or "Captain of the Port" existed by 1841 (see Allen and Thomson 1848a:273). John Adams reports about "the king's trader" in Benin (Adams 1832:31). This phenomenon of African trade should make an interesting study.

[15] Dike and Ekejiuba, 1990:71, 75, 78, 97–98, 99.

significantly to the advancement of Aro cultural and material life (see Nwokeji 1997c). Yet, their exclusion from established elites provides only a part of the explanation for Aro expansion.

The exclusion of certain categories of traders from mainstream Arochukwu politics cannot be used as a basis for generalizing about the settlements. Unlike Ikerionwu the founder of Nde-Ikerionwu, who had entered Aro society as a slave boy, Izuogu Mgbokpo, the founder of the largest Aro diaspora settlement, Arondizuogu, and Oti Emesinwa, who founded the Ndieni settlement of Ujari, were hard-core Aro *amadi*. The *amadi* status was ascriptive, had several gradations, and approximated nobility. Both Oti and Izuogu belonged to *Amadi Nkume Asaa*, the highest order, reserved only for the descendants of the founders of the Aro state.[16] Aro diaspora settlements sprang up in response to opportunities created by the expanding Atlantic slave trade; it was trade, more than political ambition, that originally motivated the establishment of Aro settlements. The merchants did not create political formations initially, but "trading centers." Consequently, they lived in Arochukwu throughout their lifetime; it was their descendants and dependents who settled permanently in the diaspora. The merchant-warlords of the eighteenth century came from various backgrounds – from within Aro ruling groups, recent immigrants, and recently acculturated ex-slaves.

Securing bases did sometimes pose a problem for the Aro. In most situations, they established settlements peacefully (Uku 1993:15). The general pattern is summarized as follows:

Pioneer Aro traders probably shuttled between Arochukwu and their market destinations. In the process, they built up a chain of rest-houses along the routes.

---

[16] For information about Oti Emesinwa, see Eni 1973. Although Dike and Ekejiuba argue that the merchant-warlords were often not free- or well-born, elsewhere in their book, they describe Izuogu, correctly, as the great grandson of Nnachi, "one of the co-founders of Arochukwu" and argue in apparent contradiction of their thesis that "the population of Ndizuogu ... is made up exclusively of people of Aro extraction [and] those who have long associated with them" and that the diaspora settlements "freed the Aro nobility from the strenuous competition for power" (K.O. Dike and Ekejiuba 1990:72, 176, 206, 217). They also note that the "Aro saw the need for colonizing strategic routes in the interests of their trade. Successful Aro traders used their agents[,] who were either sons or trusted household retainees and lieutenants, to pioneer the new settlements and develop an intelligence network over the entire region" (K.O. Dike and Ekejiuba 1990:120). For the record, whereas it may be true that the population of Arondizuogu has a higher proportion of originally Aro people and their long-term associates, the settlement is not composed "exclusively" of these people. In all probability, up to one-third of present-day Arondizuogu families trace the origin of their entry into the society in the second half of the nineteenth century.

The Trade Diaspora in Regional Context

Gradually, the more important of such places developed into trading centers and finally into Aro settlements. The settlements became launching pads for the commercial penetration of the Aro into new areas and for the founding of new settlements, partly through Aro initiative and, partly on the invitation of local people. It was very common for non-Aro communities to invite the Aro to establish in their areas in order that they would benefit from Aro trade and protection. (Ijoma and Njoku 1991:300)

In exchange for their support, merchants exacted tribute or other advantages from preexisting groups (Nwokoye-Emesuo 1996; Uku 1993:14). The Ngwa of southern Igboland had a saying that *Onye Aro Mbi la ke ya whe oma mmera ya* (Harboring the Aro is good fortune) (Onyensoh 1985:17). After the Aro had been established, "chiefs who sought Izuogu's protection against their enemies pledged their land and became his subjects. They paid regular tributes in slaves, labor and food, thus contributing to the economic and manpower needs of the new settlements" (K.O. Dike and Ekejiuba 1990:129n, 165–66). Not only communities in need of protection sought Aro help; communities that threatened others were sometimes Aro allies. Equiano made this observation:

Perhaps [raiders] were incited to this by those traders who brought the European goods ... amongst us. ... When a trader wants slaves, he applies to a chief for them, and tempts him with his wares. It is not extraordinary, if on this occasion he yields to the temptation with as little firmness, and accepts the price of his fellow creature's liberty, with as little reluctance as the enlightened merchant. Accordingly he falls on his neighbors, and a desperate battle ensues. If he prevails and takes prisoners, he gratifies his avarice by selling them; but, if his party be vanquished, and he falls into the hands of the enemy, he is put to death; for, as he has been known to foment their quarrels, it is thought dangerous to let him survive. (Equiano 1995:40)

In this desperate struggle for survival, the Aro would have been "invited" by one side or the other, or by both.

Non-Aro communities also welcomed the Aro because of Aro ability to dispense "justice," including the removal of categorized persons to Atlantic slavery (see J.G.C. Allen n.d.:149; Grier 1922:35). Where the Aro were required to pay rent, it was usually a token amount. The annual tenancy renewal required the presentation of "kola" in Ngwa communities in one of the areas with strong Aro presence. In one community, the "rent" consisted of only two gallons of palm wine, eight manillas, and one cock (Wamuo 1973). In Ibibioland, the acquisition of land required a case of drinks, a piece of cloth, a gun, and some salt (J. Udo 1972). The Aro contracted *igba ndu* (covenant) with their hosts as an instrument of protectionism. Igba ndu often involved mixing protagonists' blood for mutual consumption. This ritual was deemed to carry a spiritual force capable of killing a protagonist who defaulted from the terms of an agreement.[17] Kinship ties were forged and exploited. Marriages figured prominently in these ties. Although this practice creates "the obligation of inlaws," as inlaws and sons of local women, the Aro widened their contacts and increased trade (Levin 1992:103). Kinship ties were reinforced by massive immigration. Immigrants into Aro settlements operated freely in their natal homes under the umbrella of Aro enterprise.

Eighteenth-century merchant-warlords did not negotiate as officials of the Aro state. After reaching an agreement to aid a community or to set up a base in an area, they would display tender palm fronds, which were a central symbol in the Aro national emblem (*Omu Aro*), to signify that the area was under Aro protection (Nwokoye-Emesuo 1996). The merchant-warlords negotiated of their own accord for fighters from Cross River Igbo communities, utilizing blood and marriage bonds.

The role of private enterprise in Aro expansion can, however, be overemphasized. Although it is common for immigrants from a given region of a sending society to cluster in particular locales of the receiving society, the pattern by which Aro lineages controlled certain spheres outside the Arochukwu homeland had institutional underpinnings and was backed by the state. This factor – along with Aro oracular influence – shielded the Aro from the violent victimization that Thomas Sowell has identified as the common lot of trade diasporas (Sowell 1996:5–6, 28–29, 31). Rather than a state program, Aro expansion from the eighteenth century onward was a function of private enterprise, encouraged and regulated by the state.

THE ROLE OF FORCE IN CENTRAL IGBOLAND

In spite of the ties, strategies, and practices that facilitated the establishment of Aro settlements among non-Aro hosts, the Aro deemed force to be particularly effective in the Igbo heartland. Here, the Aro did not always wait for preexisting groups to "invite" them. Their massive and consistent application of force in this region is widely recognized as atypical Aro methods.[18] Wars were not ordinarily in the interests of Aro trade.

---

[17] For details regarding *igba ndu*, see Dike and Ekejiuba (1990:118–19, 163, 164, 198–99, 244–45); Ekejiuba 1972c; Ukwu 1969:127, 131–32.

[18] See Dike and Ekejiuba 1990; Ijoma 1986c, 1994; Ijoma and Njoku 1991; Northrup 1978b:138; C. Okafor 1986.

This seems to have been the key deterrence for wars, not that the Aro made war only on numerically inferior groups instead of such populous groups as Onitsha, Ogidi and Igbo-Ukwu (Northrup 1978:138–139). The view that the presence of populations of potential adversaries was the primary criterion for Aro to make wars gives the impression that the Aro were war-mongers who would make war on any group except those strong enough to give them a good fight.[19] The Aro resorted to wars in central Igboland despite strong opposition from populous societies, including the Nri during the nineteenth century (Chapter 7). There were other reasons the Aro did not make war on certain groups, whether large or small. In the first instance, the Aro would have seen little purpose in making war upon communities with whom they enjoyed peaceful relations. Besides, speculating on the size of the communities which the Aro did not make war against runs the risk of anachronism: present-day populations are not always an accurate measure of the historical strengths of societies. Wars had severe impact on many communities, and subsequent demographic developments have been uneven. Some societies gained from immigration out of devastated areas, while others lost out in the same process (Nwokeji 2000a). In one extreme case, Ora, in the vicinity of Arondizuogu, was completely destroyed during the establishment of the Aro settlement. Present-day population densities reflect, in part, the effect, rather than the cause, of wars. Rather than being a deterrent, the presence of numerically strong groups could have been the very cause of the conflicts in the region.

If the size of potential foes was not necessarily a determinant of Aro invasions, we are still left to explain why warfare prevailed during the mid-eighteenth-century establishment of the principal Aro settlements in the greater upper Imo/Nri-Awka region. The resort to warfare was more likely a consequence of the tighter land-tenure rules that were a corollary of population pressure in the area and that anthropologist Thurstan Shaw attributes to "the antiquity and effectiveness of yam cultivation and the exploitation of the oil palm."[20] The quest for space would likely have increased levels of intransigence in the preexisting societies and led to the breakdown of diplomatic alternatives. The situation was probably helped by Aro's determination to establish themselves strongly in a region that had great potential for them; Aro incursions into the heartland were, in the first instance, a function of the search for captives, and as has been

---

[19] For such a suggestion, see Dike and Ekejiuba 1990:75; 164, 166–67, 177–79; 208.
[20] Cited by Ohadike 1994:2. See also Nwokeji 2000a: 632.

already mentioned, they met with some resistance. This point is important because in pursuing their interests, the Aro generally preferred peace to war. They made war part of their overall strategy in order to dominate trade.

The wars of this period are well documented in Aro historiography.[21] With the use of armed force, each of the principal Aro settlements destroyed or subdued the most important power in its immediate neighborhood. The most spectacular example was Izuogu's destruction of Ora, east of the upper Imo River, in one of the severest acts of violence committed during the Atlantic slave trade era. "What happened to Ikpa-Ora had no parallel in this part of the world. The people were massacred and the entire population was wiped out. The territory was plundered and completely laid waste. [The land has] ever since, remained desolate ... The territory became known as 'the land of blood' " (J.G. Okoro 1985:24). The complete destruction of Ora does not seem to have been necessary for the establishment of Arondizuogu because Arondizuogu was sited thirty kilometers west of the Imo and about forty kilometers west of Ora. Nevertheless, the massacre instilled fear into the communities of the upper Imo River region, leaving them with "awful expectations" (J.G. Okoro 1985:25). Mobilizing warriors for this purpose from the Cross River Igbo community Ohafia was easy for Izuogu, in part, because his mother came from there. The Ohafia people therefore intervened in favor of their *nwadiana* (child of a local woman married to an outside man).[22] Conflicts among the preexisting communities also worked in Izuogu's favor. These conflicts gave him opportunities to increase his influence over the communities. Acting as a broker for the warring groups increased his access to captives, receiving some as gifts from leaders who sought to maintain friendly relations with him and buying war captives from their captors.[23] The traditions of Uruala to the southwest of Arondizuogu report that at one time all

---

[21] Dike and Ekejiuba 1990; Igwegbe 1962; C. Okafor 1986:121–122; J.G. Okoro 1985.
[22] Igwegbe 1962; C. Okoli 1986:121–22; J.G. Okoro 1985:23–24.
[23] Izuogu is said to have attacked Ora because Ora rejected Izuogu's demand for a tribute of 400 captives (see K.O. Dike and Ekejiuba 1990:177). Traditions relate that Okoli Ijoma's forces displaced the present Ugwuoba on the Mamu River from their original site around Enugwu-Ukwu, some sixty kilometers to the south (see Agu 1985). Although Veronica Agu bases her thesis on traditions collected mainly in Awka, I found coroborating evidence in a colonial-era intelligence report, which noted that Ugwuoba (and Amsim) "acknowledge no relationship at all" with the rest of Mbasato-Awka, Amawbia, Ebenebe, Nawgu, Nibo and Nise. See NAE MILGOV – 13/1/17: Mbanasataw-Awka Division, 1936.

the able-bodied men of the community were slaughtered during a conflict with Arondizuogu (Alaka 1984; Ipere 1983). Whatever the specific permutations that helped to cause it, the establishment of strong bases in this region seems to have been critical in Aro operations, and the establishment of Igbo heartland Aro settlements was concurrent with the massive expansion of the Biafra Atlantic slave trade.

MMUBA: EXPANDING THE GROUP

The growth of Aro operations partly depended on Aro strategies for boosting human capital as their commercial network was expanding. But it is important to note that while group expansion resulted from a conscious effort to increase the Aro population, this did not necessarily lead to an increased number of Aro settlements. The proliferation of settlements was largely a function of an inherent motivation for entrepreneurial activity within the Aro system; the system rewarded leaders who created new settlements, which, in turn, advanced the interests of the whole system. As in the Arochukwu metropole, the political economy of the Aro diaspora centered on the slave – as merchandise, for labor, and as a lineage member. As one colonial-era anthropological report puts it, "The original Aro party was not yet very numerous but it quickly collected around it a large number of local followers by purchase of slaves, sheltering of refugees from other villages, and so on."[24] Many of my respondents during 1995 and 1996 explained Aro expansion, especially the phenomenal population increase in the major settlements, by reference to the concept of *mmuba*. As one of the most outstanding elements of Aro expansion, mmuba refers to a range of phenomena that at once embraces human proliferation, prosperity, and even territorial expansion. I have not found an appropriate English synonym, although in some contexts the term *human proliferation* is adequate. Mmuba was not just a practice; it was also a mentality. It encouraged the marrying of numerous wives, the acquisition of slaves, and the aggressive promotion of immigration. Mmuba helps to explain the accelerated manumission processes that characterized the Aro slave system. One Aro elder gave a perspective of how mmuba worked in the Aro slave system.

---

[24] NAE 81/27 – OKIDIST 4/9/70:Anthropological Report of Aros of Ndizuogu and Others," 31 March 1927.

You kept the person as your slave. You brought the person up. When the person grew up and he was a good person, you got a wife for him and he had children. ... After the slave had married and prospered, he could begin to buy his own slaves, and people continued to multiply. In turn, the persons he bought replicated the same pattern. What was important is that people recognized the person under whom they were (J.O. Okoro 1996).

The Aro also boosted their group by promoting a partial exogamy that allowed Aro men to marry non-Aro women without giving out Aro daughters, enabling Aro populations to increase at the expense of other groups (Levin 1992:103).

Of course, other African societies promoted the expansion of their populations, but the Aro raised these efforts to an extraordinary level. Conscious of their small numbers, the Aro drive for proliferation was extremely intense and even programmatic. Their slave-trading role, that is, their role as distributors of human beings, facilitated their drive for proliferation. Different sources have estimated the descendants of originally non-Aro families at ninety percent of the present Arondizuogu population. If this is accurate, the numbers of originally non-Aro who were incorporated by other Aro groups could be even higher, especially in light of the fact that Arondizuogu has the largest concentration of originally Aro groups of all the Aro diaspora settlements.[25] The Arochukwu metropole also incorporated many non-Aro over the centuries. This has also been the case with other Aro settlements about which relevant research has been done.[26]

At the expressive level, at least, the ownership of people was an end in itself among of the Aro. At some point, the people adopted the deity Oda, the icon of the intercessor of proliferation. Most likely of Nri-Awka provenance, Oda served to usher into each household every new baby and every newly acquired person (G. Anyakoha 1996; Igwilo 1996b). Oda was probably borrowed from Amesi on the eastern periphery of the Nri-Akwa region in the general vicinity of Arondizuogu. According to Amesi scholar Bernadette Ezeliora, Oda was the "benevolent mother goddess ... believed to be the giver of children" (Ezeliora 1994:18). A new member of the family was brought before the deity to symbolize his or her entry into the family.

---

[25] For the various estimates, see Dike and Ekejiuba 1990:206, 217; J.O. Dike 1996; M.S. Igwe 1996; T.O. Okereke 1996; Ufere 1996.
[26] Emeruwa 1992; C. Eze 1987; G.C. Mmeregini 1978; I.O. Nwankwo 1986; J.C. Nwankwo 1973.

Medicine men prepared Oda to arrest infant mortality and other forms of premature death.

The practical utility of the compulsive acquisition of people is hard to fathom at first. Anthropologist Claude Meillassoux's view that the channeling of surplus exclusively to reproduction in precolonial African societies meant the "destruction of surplus" might suggest that the Aro penchant for accumulating people was counterproductive and could not have advanced their trade. Reproduction was in fact a form of reinvestment; it entailed such forms of "social insurance" as the accumulation of women; "conspicuous consumption [and] redistribution as gifts."[27] The broad conceptualization of capital as being any resource for future wealth, and not in the restrictive sense of buildings, machinery, and so forth, as has been noted in the West-Central African case, was held by the Aro as well.[28] In a slave-trading group, an increase in population meant an increase in the pool of slave dealers. Partial exogamy carried practical advantages. The marrying of non-Aro women and barely marrying out Aro women, not only aided population increase, but also facilitated the acquisition of the languages and dialects of the groups the Aro wives came from. These "mistresses of language" imparted the necessary linguistic proficiencies to their young Aro children (Umo [1947?] n.d.:18). Some nineteenth-century European visitors to the Biafra hinterland believed that the Aro spoke virtually all the languages in the region (e.g., Baikie 1856:319–40; Burdo 1880:159). In fact, like traders from other trading groups in the region, the Aro trader was often bilingual or multilingual depending on the range of his operations (Afigbo 1981a:20). The enormity of the pool of languages the Aro commanded reflected the range of Aro operations and their incorporation of outsiders, especially women. The wives of Aro traders sometimes accompanied their husbands on trading tours. "The wives helped to supervise their husband's food, [and looked] after the currency and trade goods. They took care of very young slaves between ages ... one and five while they traveled from the market to the settlements" (Ekejiuba 1972a:18). Thus, the Aro channeling of surplus to reproduction was not destructive.

The measure of Aro affluence went beyond the number of slaves one owned or wives one had: it was the total number of dependents, including slaves, ex-slave clients, and all kinds of immigrants that one brought

---

[27] Meillassoux cited by Coquery-Vidrovitch and Lovejoy 1985b:14.
[28] See Miller 1988:42–43 for West-Central Africa.

into the society. The successes of one's dependents in both trade and the acquisition of people enhanced one's status. Having many slaves was esteemed, but it was even better to have many dependents who were themselves prosperous with many dependents of their own. Dependents of one's (ex-)dependents were deemed to be as advantageous, ultimately, as one's dependents within the Aro hierarchical order. This was the key to the accelerated manumission embedded in the Aro slave system. The idea that a slave system could be based on accelerated manumission sounds contradictory, but the Aro slave system did in fact draw strength and sustenance from manumission. This is obviously what one source has referred to as "seemingly contradictory organizing principles of hierarchy and incorporation" (K.O. Dike and Ekejiuba 1990:56, 264–65). In noting the transcendence of slave status in the Biafra region, another source notes:"[t]he designation 'slave' could be little more than a sign of origin and association with the commercial firm of the slave's original master. Once slaves had assumed ... independence and an effective social freedom that placed them in the class of slave owners, emancipation had effectively taken place. Here was a system that promoted slaves as a means of securing strict loyalty and dependence" (Lovejoy 1983:180). The Aro system typifies this model.

The imaginary and real benefits of having many (ex-)dependents encouraged Aro communities to welcome the refugees that violence and famine produced, particularly in the Nri-Awka region. Established members of Aro society often gave asylum to economic and political refugees from other communities, but on the condition of dependency. These refugees boosted the sizes of Aro communities. The refugee factor is so strong that one of my respondents emphasized that most immigrants to Arondizuogu were refugees from war-torn communities of the Nri-Awka region (Nwokoye-Emesuo 1996). This phenomenon seems to have been particularly acute during the period from the second quarter of the eighteenth century to the end of the nineteenth. The most dramatic case uncovered by the present writer during 1995–96 fieldwork concerns Owa, an erstwhile community once located by the Agulu Lake in the Nri-Awka region. Refugees from Owa poured into Arondizuogu, the largest Aro settlement, when an alliance of Owa's four neighbors sacked it during the mid-nineteenth century and divided up its territory among themselves (Maduadichie 1996). Owa has a place in Arondizuogu folklore only because of this tragic event and because it was the ancestral home to many people in Arondizuogu, most of whom are the descendants of the Owa immigrants.²⁹ The massive incorporation of refugees facilitated the rapid increase of Aro population in an era when most African populations were either dwindling in size or stagnating. Reproduction could not have constituted the destruction of surplus under this circumstance, contrary to Meillassoux's claim. Reproduction and surplus coexisted among the Aro. We may now turn attention to the institutions that enabled the Aro to integrate slaves into their society and extend citizenship status to immigrants, ex-slaves, and persons of slave descent on an institutionalized basis, while facilitating the slave trade.

RELEVANT INSTITUTIONS

Aro dominance of the hinterland slave trade rested on identifiable institutions. These institutions defined the means and ways of relating to the non-Aro, the community's modes of expansion, the settlement of civil disputes, and rules of credit, among other functions. Chapter 4 offers a detailed description of linkage institutions that were focused on internal Aro relations; here, it is more useful to examine the institutions that directly promoted Aro influence over the non-Aro because they played a central role in Aro expansion. Such institutions often had political overtones, so that even when they were geared primarily toward intra-Aro relations, they were ultimately a means of dealing with the non-Aro. The Arochukwu metropole alone sponsored these institutions in its capacity as the "central place" in the diaspora: they were the Ọkpankpọ (Aro central council), the Ibiniukpabi oracle, and the Ekpe/Okonko confraternity.

The Aro central council, Ọkpankpọ, the highest level of authority in the Aro system, was the main institution by which the Aro counteracted fissioning. Ọkpankpọ maintained "a structured control of Aro bands in pursuit of military, political and social exploits in South-Eastern Nigeria" (P.C. Dike 1986:15).³⁰ The centralizing function of Ọkpankpọ was evident

---

²⁹ This dimension excited my curiosity about Owa. I had assumed that it must have been an existing small and obscure community, but then I wondered how such a small community could have supplied the large number of people predicted by the frequency with which late twentieth-century Arondizuogu families trace their origin there. When I sought further information and planned to visit the community, I was jarred to learn that it no longer existed. See further details in Chapter 6.

³⁰ Afigbo 1971b:32; Dike and Ekejiuba 1990; Ijoma 1986c:22–24; Lovejoy and Hogendorn 1979:230.

in keeping the diaspora settlements as integral parts of their respective parent Aro lineage-groups. As a result, the settlements were not represented directly in the council, but indirectly through the ọtụsị to which their respective parent Arochuwku lineage-groups ("village") belonged. Every diaspora settlement, regardless of its location, belonged to a parent Aro lineage-group. This way, the diaspora settlements were subject to the authority of Ọkpankpọ through intermediaries – the heads of the respective parent lineage-groups. Sometimes, headship of the parent lineages fell on individuals resident in the Aro diaspora, depending on their ancestral pedigree. This way, coping with the proliferation of diaspora settlements required little adjustment on the part of the Arochukwu.[31] The Ọkpankpọ did not have to control the diaspora settlements by the use of force. The effectiveness of the Aro network and the pride of being Aro helped to ensure that it was in the interest of the Aro diaspora to remain in the Aro system and enabled the Aro state to successfully forestall fissioning.

If the Ọkpankpọ gave the Aro internal cohesion, direction, and political purpose, the Ibiniukpabi, the temple of the universalist Aro God (Chukwu), gave them a spiritual aura and authority in their dealings with the non-Aro. Ibiniukpabi was one of the most effective agencies of Aro domination. It served to siphon captives and maintain Aro influence. Described as the most important agency of Aro influence, the oracle blossomed in the first phase of Aro expansion from its humble beginnings as a medium of "local nature spirits" (K.O. Dike and Ekejiuba 1990:130, 134). Its intelligence network became widespread, and it created and sustained a reputation for clairvoyance among the non-Aro. Through the influence of the oracle, the Aro presented themselves, and were regarded, as the "children of God" (*Umu Chukwu*). The oracle served as an important siphon of captives because litigants were sometimes said to have been "eaten," a euphemism for sale into Atlantic slavery, but more often, they were asked to pay fees and fines in captives. Those unable to pay the requisite fines got sold into slavery (see Ijoma and Njoku 1991:307; S. Ottenberg 1971:24–26, 212). Apart from its judicial function, the oracle was a resort for non-Aro people seeking divine intervention in such existential misfortunes as epidemics, infertility, bad harvests, and serious illnesses. The Ibiniukpabi remained a key

---

[31] Although they do not mention the word "state," Lovejoy and Hogendorn (1979:230) imply this when they note that one of the functions of Okpankpo was to punish those merchants who violated the zoning system.

The Trade Diaspora in Regional Context 77

component of Aro influence throughout the Bight of Biafra until British destroyed it in the beginning of the twentieth century.

The Aro sponsored versions of their institutions in different parts of the region as a way of promoting trade. Thus, the Ibiniukpabi oracle had such localized variants as Kamalu at Ajatakiri, Igwkeala at Umuneoha, Ojukwu at Diobu, and Agbala at Awka.[32] In spite of the existence of these clones, the operation of the Ibiniukpabi was a core function of the metropole. The temple at Arochukwu remained the one of last resort. Second, the Aro settlements and Aro merchants continued to advertize and popularize the Ibiniukpabi itself, which justifies one early twentieth-century British observer's characterization of Aro diaspora settlements as "mission stations" (J.G. Allen n.d.:iii). The Aro diaspora advertised and promoted the oracle, manipulating information and local people's fears. "Over and above their firm grasp of current events, the Aro of the dispersion were consummate students of local institutions, local religion and had the knack of discovering the theoretical basis of many local beliefs and practices. ... It was therefore part of Aro intelligence to see that the verdicts and other interpretations given by the oracle were in line with local beliefs and that they conformed with the idiom and supernatural ideas of the local non-Aro people" (K.O. Dike and Ekejiuba 1990:137–38).

The adjudicative role of the oracle was specifically for the non-Aro (see K. Oji 1972). This is why there was a saying to the effect that *Nwa Aro a nahu a si ib'ye na Ibiniukpabi na-aju ya* (An Aro person does not summon another Aro person on behalf of Ibiniukpabi). This meant, on the one hand, that an Aro person knew better than to expose himself to the Ibiniukpabi ruse and, on the other, that Ibiniukpabi was "a prescription of a code of conduct which specifically means that Aro group identity, internal fidelity, coherence as well as external aggression and imperialism [were] the *raison d'etre*, the lifeblood of Aro hegemony." The second meaning underscores the close relationship that existed between the Ekpe and Ibiniukpabi.[33]

Although the role of the Ekpe should throw light on Aro organization, Ekpe rites are shrouded in secrecy. We know that the Ekpe cult effectively served as a police force and a judicial outfit, and was used to regulate credit. Just as the oracle adjudicated cases among the non-Aro, the Ekpe confraternity regulated and adjudicated disputes among the Aro and

---

[32] Cookey 1974; Mathews 1922:8; Ofonagoro 1972:76, 88.
[33] P.C. Dike 1986:15). The use of Nsibiri, the Ekpe language (see Amankulor and Okafor 1988:40–43; K.O. Dike and Ekejiuba 1990:77, 142, 287–88.

performed a wide range of law enforcement functions. The society thus formed part of the judicial apparatus and it made public the decisions of the lineage-group councils and the Ọkpankpọ. In southern Igboland, where the society was called Okonko or Ekpe Aro (Aro Ekpe), it was the "most powerful administrative organ, especially in Ngwaland." The members of this society, referred to as "friends of the Aro," controlled trade. The establishment of this institution during the eighteenth century in southern Igboland expanded trade (Oriji 1983:315–17). Although several references have been made to the Ekpe and the Nsibiri in the existing literature, these institutions have yet to be studied meaningfully.[34] The Ekpe was shared with the Cross River groups, including Old Calabar, who used it for the same purposes.

The origins of the Ekpe are unclear. If, however, the confraternity and the "trust system" between coastal and European traders had shared origins, as has been suggested, their association goes back to the seventeenth century when the trust system was already in place.[35] As early as 1682, John Barbot (1682:299) reported that some inhabitants of New Calabar and Bonny acted as "factors, or brokers, either for their own countrymen, or for the Europeans; who are often obliged to trust them with their goods, to attend the upper markets, and purchase slaves for them." Perhaps, the dominant view is that the Aro adopted Ekpe from the Efik and/or other Cross River groups.[36] Evidence from Cuba, where the Ekpe offshoot Abakua operated from mid-1830s onward, indicates that Calabar or the Balondo of southwestern Cameroon may have been the original home of Ekpe. Yet, the first language used by the Matanzas, Cuba, cell of Abakua was Isuama Igbo, though the society soon dropped Igbo for a rather obscure language of the Brikamo or Usagare, the place where Ekpe is claimed to be "perfected" (Miller 2009:3, 101–02). Reading Ekpe origins from the evidence of mid-nineteenth-century Cuba is risky, given that Ekpe had already become widespread among various groups in the Bight of Biafra. There are possibilities that the society diffused to the other Cross River groups via the Aro or that it diffused to the Aro independent of the Efik and other Cross River groups. According to an Ibibio respondent that David Northrup

---

[34] Membership of the society is the route to the Nsibiri script, the knowledge of which will enrich our understanding of the history of the Bight of Biafra. The problem is that Ekpe membership prohibits a member from revealing the Nsibiri and other secrets.
[35] The joint origin of the two institutions is implied by Lovejoy and Richardson 1999, although they seem to suggest that this was in the eighteenth century.
[36] For Old Calabar, see Noah 1980:30 and for the Aro, see Dike and Ekejiuba 1990:40, 58, 287.

interviewed in 1972, the Aro gave the Ekpe to certain Ibibio communities. In return, the community gave the Aro "very many slaves" among other gifts (U.U. Obong 1972). One such community became famous for Ekpe and assumed the name Ikot Ibit Ekpe.

The possibility that the society diffused to the Aro independently of other Cross River groups seems more promising. It has recently been argued, based on fieldwork among coastal Cameroonians, that Cross River cultures were enriched by institutions and practices brought by slaves from the grassfields in the north, which "occasionally gave rise to a new cult agency" that their masters "adapted to existing ideas and needs in the forest" (Röschenthaler 2006: 73 n5, 87). Precisely which society/societies the institution diffused from or when are unclear, but the Jukun is among those mentioned. If slaves could disseminate this culture among coastal Cameroonians, nonslave migrants from the north could also have bequeathed the cult to their host societies. The powerful Akpa from the north – who, as suggested in Chapter 2, probably derived from Jukun-related groups – may already have adopted the society at the time of their arrival at Arochukwu in the late sixteenth or early seventeenth century, independent of the Efik and other Cross River groups, and were thus well placed to introduce the cult to other Aro groups. Ekpe or Ekpe-like societies may have existed among the Jukun and other Middle Belt peoples of present-day Nigeria and Cameroon before the Atlantic slave trade era; however, it seems that this cult crystallized in the forest region of the Bight of Biafra when the trade was already underway.

Other strategies aided Aro expansion as well, not least of which was the structure and organization of the market. The Aro rotated the fairs between Bende and Uburu to foster rivalry between the two groups over Aro patronage. This strategy enabled the Aro to maximize its advantages and maintain control of hinterland commerce (see Ekejiuba 1972a, 1972b; Ukwu 1969:135). The four-day fairs were spaced so that each had a cycle of twenty-four days. This system facilitated the participation of suppliers from different parts of the region. Strategically interspersed between the fair sites, Aro diaspora settlements were useful to passing traders from different parts of the region. "The trading settlements … became 'free cities' to which all who wished to 'traffic and exchange' safely repaired, international courts where individuals and clans in conflict sought justice from the undisputed authority of the Oracle" (K.O. Dike 1956:39, 45). As hubs of commercial transactions, the Aro diaspora communities provide a framework for understanding precolonial urbanization. Although some hinterland groups, such as the Awka and the Nkwere, had participated in long-distance trade, Aro incursions stimulated and professionalized trade in predominantly agricultural societies (see, e.g., Isichei 1976:64). According to Ukwu, the presence of Aro diaspora communities boosted commerce in such societies. Some of the inhabitants of the diaspora settlements acted as "trade callers," advisers about Aro relations with the non-Aro and money lenders (Grier 1922:35; G.I. Jones 1989:36; S. Ottenberg 1971). Aro ascendancy was not, however, wholly a direct result of organizational mastery. Soon enough, local myths developed ascribing to the Aro divine rights to trade.

CONCLUSION

To understand expanding trade in the eighteenth century, it is best to see Aro organization in conjunction with other factors at play in central Igboland. In the Nri-Awka region, for example, the impetus for enslavement was a pressure on resources. High population densities in the region had since the time of ancient Igbo-Ukwu been the cause of migrations into less populated areas, such as the west Niger and northern Igboland.[37] Centuries of intensive agriculture seem to have exhausted the soil. Aro traditions regarding the peopling of central Igbo Aro settlements refer frequently to famine in the Nri-Awka region. And warfare, which was a constant experience from the seventeenth century onward, contributed to slaving there as well.[38]

In spite of Aro's role as slaveholders who created institutions that facilitated the slave trade and sometimes employed coercion and violence in their dealings with the non-Aro, there is hardly any evidence of a widespread non-Aro perception that the Aro were exploiters. The Aro were virtually immune from molestation. This is probably because they contracted kinship networks across the region and, perhaps more importantly, because Aro interests were linked closely to those of the influential groups and individuals in other societies. Non-Aro consumers needed the foreign goods that the Aro supplied, and individuals and groups needed the Aro in their struggles among one another over political power and economic opportunities. Moreover, the Aro committed their allies to *igba ndu* (covenant), which deterred the allies from delinquency and apparently justified Aro retribution in the event of a breach of the covenant, saving the Aro from the odium of being perceived as bullies or

---

[37] Afigbo 1981a, 1981b, 1987; G.I. Jones 1963:30; Ohadike 1984.
[38] For references to famine in the Nri-Awka area, see M.S Igwe 1996; Kanu-Igbo 1996a; C. Okoli 1996; G.N. Okoli 1996. For warfare in the region, see Agu 1985; Amaechi 1987; E.O. Okafor 1978; Nkeokelonye 2005:129–31, 181–221.

aggressors. The Ibiniukpabi oracle essentialized these transactions, commending the Aro widely as Umu Chukwu. The seemingly omnipresent Ibiniukpabi was the final resort in the knottiest of cases. As slave dealers, the Aro performed the role of disposing of dissenters, local political rivals, and incriminated persons, who were sold into slavery as punishment or reprisal. Aro expansion was largely instrumental in promoting the Biafra Atlantic trade, not only because of the location and timing of Aro settlements and the strategies, mechanisms and institutions described in this chapter, but also because of the very character of Aro settlements.

4

Culture Formation in the Trading Frontier, c. 1740 to c. 1850

The diasporic character of Aro expansion both facilitated the expansion of Bight of Biafra Atlantic trade, as described in Chapters 2 and 3, and defined the cultural context of Aro commercial and geopolitical expansion. Like other trade diasporas, Aro settlements outside the Arochukwu metropole were sites of cultural exchange. Of necessity, new cultural forms within a diasporic system reflect cultural influences from both the metropole and the natal homes of nonmetropolitan immigrant groups, as well as those of specific host societies. The Aro diaspora scattered throughout western Bight of Biafra reflects these ties, illustrating both how cultural practices shaped the slave trade and how the slave trade reconfigured the cultural landscape of the region.

The idea that the Aro commercial system within Igboland, where most of the settlements were located, was the successor to Nri cultural hegemony places the Aro in the broader context of Igbo cultural evolution.[1] The establishment of Aro diaspora settlements in central Igboland from about 1740 onward promoted contact of unprecedented intensity between the Aro and the Nri "culture area." Nevertheless, the evolving relationship between the Aro and Nri cultures was not a linear progression in which Aro culture replaced the Nri one. Rather, there was an active interaction between Nri and Aro cultural forms, on the one hand, and between these and cultural influences from local groups, on the other. Aro incursions into Igboland and elsewhere involved the "Igboization"

---

[1] For this view, see Afigbo (1991c: 1–2); Dike and Ekejiuba (1990:161–90); Ekejiuba (1991); Ijoma and Njoku (1991).

Culture Formation in the Trading Frontier 83

of the Aro, and the "Aroization" of the non-Aro.[2] Thus, Aro expansion involved trade as much as it involved culture.

The massive incorporation of outsiders into Aro society had implications for culture formation in a manner that was perhaps more intense, or at least different from, what was the norm in, other trade diasporas. Arondizuogu, the largest Aro diaspora settlement, epitomized the incorporation of large numbers of non-Aro groups and the development of a frontier culture during a period of expansion and decline of the slave trade and the unprecedented proliferation of Aro diaspora settlements. Aro tendency to incorporate outsiders was most marked in Arondizuogu (Bentor 1994:120). This settlement offers a useful case study for understanding cultural formation in the Aro diaspora and the role of the Aro diaspora in the expansion of the Biafra Atlantic slave trade.

The problem of locating all of the Aro within existing taxonomies of Igbo subgroups (Chapter 1), calls for a framework that accounts for both the complexities of locating the Aro culturally and the major cultural influences in the Aro diaspora. Although the immediate cultural environment had an impact, Arondizuogu culture developed more from the interaction of the dominant Aro ethos, the cultural input of persons who came into the society through slavery, voluntary immigration, and, least of all, the influence of preexisting groups in the immediate neighborhood of Arondizuogu. Most of the immigrants came from the Nri-Awka region. While resembling Aro ways in some critical respects, Arondizuogu cultural formation also reflected migrant and slave origins of the group.

Distinguishing between the historical Arochukwu in which the founders of the settlements originated and present-day Arochukwu is a prerequisite for any comparison of the latter and the Aro diaspora. The Arochukwu state was less than 300 years old in the 1730s when the first major settlements were founded Arochukwu institutions continued to evolve thereafter. In the frontier environment of the new settlements, some Arochukwu customs became anachronistic and gave way to cultural forms that were attuned to the new realities. By historically examining cultural exchange involving the Aro and other Igbo and non-Igbo groups, we are able to distinguish what actually happened from what might seem apparent to the twentieth-century observer. While the Aro in the Igbo-speaking areas, such as Arondizuogu, have identified themselves as Igbo since the twentieth century, they desisted from identifying themselves with any particular ethnic group in the region during the period of study. They settled among

---

[2] Eli Bentor (1994) also uses the concept of Aroization.

all groups, and consciously promoted a distinct identity and cultural personality. This strategy was characteristic of trade diasporas, which begin and take shape in frontier situations.

The use of the frontier concept to characterize relationships among African groups has gradually gained ground in the past half century.[3] While anthropologist Igor Kopytoff's insight that frontiersmen "came to the frontier with a mental model of what constitutes a good society" is helpful in understanding the Aro experience, his argument that merely "cultural and sociological" reasons drove frontier formation in Africa is less persuasive. According to him, the frontier continually shifted outward as the more established sections of society became "corrupted" (Kopytoff 1987b:13, 17–18). This essentialist model – metropolitan culture mongers immune from instrumental and structural concerns – is inadequate for understanding the Aro frontier. Among the Aro of the upper Imo River, it was not just a commitment to culture that determined the evolution of the new culture; it was also outside influences, not least of which were the consequences of the Atlantic slave trade. The outward growth of the frontier was a product of people's quest for living space, personal and group freedom, and economic opportunities, principally trade. Toward the end of the nineteenth century, the economic impetus for extending the frontier began to also include the quest for agricultural land (Chapter 7). The forces that conditioned the Aro frontier culture included the new environment, the cultural packages that immigrants both from the metropole and other backgrounds brought, as well as the influence of neighbors of the Aro. The Aro did not meet a terra incognita in the diaspora upon which to impress their "mental model"; instead, they encountered terrains with robust social organizations adapted to these terrains.

PREEXISTING SOCIETIES: ECOLOGY, SOCIAL ORGANIZATIONS, AND RELATIONSHIPS

The upper Imo River valley had been settled by four distinct sets of groups before the eighteenth century. The history of these societies is obscure, but colonial intelligence reports of the 1930s, a growing body of published work by nonprofessional historians of the respective

---

[3] De Gregori (1969); Kopytoff (1987a); V.B. Thompson (1995). For the use of "slaving frontier" to refer to the innermost reaches of Atlantic slaving operations, see Miller (1988:148–53); Neumark (1957); Lovejoy and Richardson (1997:3). Slaving frontier has served to describe relationships involving slave-using and slave-supplying societies in the Upper Nile region (James 1988:148–53).

communities, and oral traditions reported in several recent student theses nonetheless provide a partial understanding of the early history of these communities.[4] One way of reconstructing the early history of these autochthonous groups is to relate the available traditions to studies of consanguinous groups and to certain generalizations about this era made in the general context of Igbo history.[5]

The landscape is central to understanding the history of these groups. The British administrator, C.J. Mayne, observed in 1935 that:

> The country is of a broken character throughout and imposing landscapes are general. It would not be out of place, perhaps, to mention that one view particularly impressed the writer by its grandeur, and brought to mind a certain landscape in Scotland, which was represented by Millais in his famous masterpiece "Over the hills and far away". A number of small rivers, tributaries of the Imo river, journey in a southernly direction through the Ndizuogu country and add to the beauty of the scenery. The water supply for Ndizuogu is derived from these sources but numerous springs are available and the supply of water is plentiful (Mayne 1935:3).

Much of the "Sylvan wealth throughout the area and ... the number of iroko trees" survived to impress Mayne. The Umualoma people of the "Isu" group, who largely inhabited the area, were the custodians of this wealth. The many raphia palm trees (*Raphia vinifera*) in the area provided them with plenty of wine (as did oil palm) and the bamboo thatch they made their roofs with. The tradition of tapping palm wine was still strong

---

[4] To the east, northeast and south – east were what are presently referred to as the Otanchara and Otanzu groups, both of which straddled the upper Imo. Umuobom was located to the south of the area that Arondizuogu settled initially – 30 kilometers west of the Imo. Finally, the communities collectively called Mbanasaa (Seven Towns) were located to the west through the north, but, unfortunately, data are scantiest on the older of these communities – Isuokpu (now Umualoma), Uzii, Osina, and Umuobom. Arondizuogu Aro referred to neighboring communities generically as "Isu", but this term seems to have acquired a pejorative quality at some point. A colonial anthropological officer suggested in 1927 that this derogatory term "may have acquired some such meaning as 'peasant'." See NAE 6/1927A – CSE 1/12/1:Anthropological Officer, Owerri, to District Officer, Okigwe, 23 February 1927. Theses dealing with "Isu" groups include Alaka 1984; M.M. Anaedobe 1977; S.O. Eke 1978; F.N. Egbo 1987; P.N. Ogbuozobe 1986; U.E. Ohaegbu 1991; J.C. Okoli 1977; Onyenkpa 1981; Onyiuka 1983; S.I. Uche 1988; C.O. Udeagha 1978; N.N. Udeagha 1980; A.E. Udueze 1982; C.S. Umeh 1984; P.N. Uwazuruike 1987; Nnolim 2007.

[5] The traditions from these groups that I have seen show the same trend (e.g., Alaka 1984; Ipere 1983; Ihimnaegbu 1986; Uwazuruike 1987). The 1930s intelligence report dealing with the "Nkalu" clan (including Akpuru, Obodo – Ukwu, Osina, Uzii, Uruala) reported that "the Nkalu claims to have been where it is now since the beginning of time" (Heslop 1936?:11).

in Umualoma in the late twentieth century. The rich vegetation also contained such semi-domesticated edible plants as castor oil beans (*Ricinus communis*); breadfruit ([*artocarpus?*] *Treculia africana*); ube (*Dacryoides edulis*); starapple (*Chrysophylum albidum*); uchakiri (*Vitex doniana*), and oil bean (*Penthacclettara macrophylla*). There were also edible wild vegetables, fruits, and spices, such as uturukpam (*Pterocarpous mildbraedi*); uziza (*Piper guineense*); utazi (*Gongronema ratifolium*); okazi (*Gnetum africanum*); utu (*Landolphia owariensis*); mkpodu (*Napolenaea imperilis*); oil palm (*Elais guineensis*), and more.[6]

Animal husbandry has considerable antiquity in the Igbo heartland. Oral traditions of the upper Imo valley mention the abundance of domestic animals, a phenomenon that goes back at least to the eighteenth century. Writing about mid-eighteenth-century Igboland, both Oldendorp and Olaudah Equiano give the impression that domestic animals were abundant among the Igbo. Equiano's account is consistent with the oral traditions from central Igbo communities. According Equiano, the "manner of living is entirely plain ... bullocks, goats, and poultry supply the greatest part of their food. These constitute likewise the principal wealth of the country, and the chief articles of commerce." They lived with the relative abundance of agricultural products and poultry (Equiano 1995:35, 36).[7] The share-raising of domestic animals, such as goats, dogs, chicken, and ducks, seems to have become a common part of their social organization.[8] There is, however, no conclusive evidence indicating when it

---

[6] These botanical names are variously from A.O. Anya (1982), Basden (1912) and B.N. Okigbo (1980). I have presented the Igbo and botanical terms where the English translation of any plant is unknown. Zac O. Gile, n.d. "Indigenous and Adapted African Vegetables", International Society for Horticultural Science. http://www.actahort.org/members/showpdf?session=7671 (also see Igbokwe 2001; J. Okafor 1999; and E.C. Okeke 2009).

[7] Relying on enslaved the Igbo in the Americas, Oldendorp was not specific regarding the part of Igboland he was referring to (Oldendorp 2000: ms. 431). The local studies include Maduagwu n.d.; Anaedobe 1977; J.C. okoli 1977; N.N. Udeagha 1980; Udueze 1982; C.S. Umeh 1984; Ogbuozobe 1986; Egbo 1987; C.O. Udeagha 1987; Uwazuruike 1987; S.I. Uche 1988; Onyekwelu 2001:2; Nnolim 2007. The academic theses among these sources are all accompanied by transcripts of the oral traditions the authors collected, so I was able to read the testimonies myself and not rely only on the interpretations these scholars offered.

[8] S.U. Uche (1988:18). Share-raising was a form of accumulation, which is how the principal character in Achebe *Things Fall Apart*, wealthy Okonkwo, got his start in life. It involves an owner giving a female baby animal to another person to raise, so that the owner and the keeper shared the expected offspring that the animal would begin to bear upon maturity. The offspring were shared equally – compensating the owner for his property and rewarding the other party for their effort in raising the parent animal. If the number of any set was odd, the person who had the smaller share would make it up

became an important part of social organization in the area. Possibly the groups practiced domestic slavery, with social rather than occupational differentiation. Oldendorp learned from his Igbo respondents during the late 1760s that Igbo priests held slaves, who had "two free days a week, [were] not treated badly and [had] few beatings" (Oldendorp 2000: ms. 428).[9] The practice, among the Umualoma people especially, which survived into the twentieth century, of keeping numerous dogs for hunting game, may have already started by this time. British colonial officers found that "the ancient Ibo game laws still count[ed] for something" among the preexisting groups (see Heslop 1936:8).

One striking feature of the social organization of the pre-Arondizuogu upper Imo River communities may have been the presence of certain specialists who produced goods for the market. One such group consisted of commercial butchers (*ogbuerighi*, which literally translates as "he that slaugthers but does not consume" – in other words, he who slaughters for the market). Another group of specialists with considerable antiquity in the area consisted of winetappers (*ote mmi*). Winetappers and butchers would likely have combined these activities with some farming. The existence of winetappers provides a framework for understanding precolonial wage labor. The existence of a group of wine owners who were not tappers created a condition for the employment of the professionals, even if most wine owners tapped their own wine.[10] Tappers received their payment in kind. The tapper usually took all the produce until the wine had started to flow freely. This time was

---

during the sharing of the next set of siblings. The sharing lasts the entire child-bearing duration of the animal. Share raising gave the wealthy both help with raising animals and an opportunity to forge and promote social ties. Sometimes, the animals were given to very young children, even babies, who could not themselves look after the animals, in expectation that their parents would raise the animals.

[9] One Akokwa scholar has been suggested that slavery existed among the people before the Atlantic slave trade (S.U. Uche 1988:29). This is improbable, given that the tradition of origin of this society accepted by this and other scholars indicate that Akokwa was founded between the early and mid-eighteenth century, long after the Atlantic slave trade had begun. It does, however, suggest that slavery likely existed among the older preexisting groups of the region. It is perhaps also an indication that slaving for the Atlantic market began effectively in Akokwa after the arrival of Arondizuogu.

[10] The tapper went round the trees routinely three times in a day – at dawn, in the early afternoon, and just before dusk. Each time, he opened up more stem for wine. During the dawn and dusk visits, he also took away the wine that percolated into the calabash. This professional group had been well established among the people that later became Arochukwu. The Ujari lineage-group is said to have descended from professional winetappers (see K.O. Dike and Ekejiuba 1990:60). For a contemporary description of palm wine, see Equiano (1995:37).

usually his discretion. The owner of the palm wine tree received the produce on two days (Eke and Oye) of the four-day market cycle (*izu*) while the tapper took the wine on the other two (Awho and Nkwo).[11] While wine owners could afford to consume their wine and serve it to guests and workers, the tapper could not afford to consume all product of his labor and would have to dispose of the surplus. John Barbot reported as early as the 1680s that palm wine, of which there was a "great plenty," was one of the commodities the Igbo supplied to the coastal peoples (John Barbot 1732:461). This means that by 1866, when W.E. Carew of the Church Missionary Society (CMS) reported the abundance of palm wine in a lower Imo River market, the commercialization of the product was already centuries old in the region.[12]

As an integral part of the Igbo heartland, the preexisting groups had long practiced settled agriculture, cultivating such crops as cowpea *(Vigna unguiculata)*, cococoyam (Colocassia) benniseed (Sesamum Indicum), corn (*Zea mays*), and white yam (*Dioscorea rotundata*).[13] Land use practices before the slave trade era are still unclear, but British colonial officer Heslop, perhaps surmising from oral traditions, observed in the 1930s: "When there was still primeval forest, it was customary that any man farming on the verge of the forest had the right to reclaim part of the forest bordering on his farm" (Heslop 1936:9). Heslop intended to portray a situation of resource abundance, but his comment about the reclamation of virgin forest actually suggests that there was increasing pressure on resources. By the late seventeenth century, as new groups began to arrive in the greater upper Imo, the period of abundance seems to have begun to give way to a period of greater scarcity and intergroup competition for resources. The ecology of the region seems to have been a "pull" factor for streams of migrants. When the Izuogu established a trading center on the elevation in the contested zone, interfacing Umuobom, Uzii and Isuopku, and Akokwa, sometime in the 1730s, (Table 4.1) the Aro were not the only group migrating to

---

[11] There is a tendency to translate *izu* as "native week" or "Igbo week," but this is an awkward and even misleading translation. The two units – izu and week – are incommensurate. The four-day izu has the following cycle: Eke, Oye, Afo and Nkwo. Baikie (1856:316) records this incorrectly as Eke, Oye, Nkwo and Afo.

[12] The Carew report is cited by Isichei (1976:66). Writing about Akokwa before the advent of Arondizuogu, Akokwa scholar, S.U. Uche (1988:2, 7), tells us that Akokwa had practiced farming and hunting; that they also did some blacksmithing and weaving; and that Akokwa began to trade after the arrival of Arondizuogu.

[13] The use of only this species of yam for new yam festivals and other rituals in Igboland underline its antiquity (O.N. Njoku 1991:117).

TABLE 4.1. *Arondizuogu Lineage-Groups before 1890 and the Probable Original Occupiers of the Land*

Lineage-Group	Preexisting Community(ies)
Ndi-Adumoha	Akokwa (initially) Umuduru 2,5,8 (from c. 1850)
Ndi-Akaeme	Umualoma, 2,5,7,8 Umuobom 2,7
Ndi-Ndi-Akunwanta	Umualoma,2,5,8
Ndi-Amazu	Akokwa 2,5,8 Umualoma 4
Ndi-Aniche	Uzii 8
Ndi-Anyake	Umuduru 5,8
Ndi-Awa	Agbobu 1,2,5,8
Ndi-Ejezie	Agbobu 5,8
Ikpa-Eze	Umualoma 2,4,5,8
Ndi-Imoko-na-Onu	Agbobu 2,5,8
Ndi-Nduvwuisi	Umuduru 3
Ndi-Njoku	Agbobu 2,5,8 Umuduru-Okwe 2,5,8
Ndi-Ogbuonyeoma	Umuobom 2,5,7,8 Umualoma 5,8
Ndi-Onuoha	Same territory as Ikpa-Eze
Ndi-Uche	Agbobu & Umuobom (initially) 6 Umuduru-Okwe 2,5,8 (c.1790 –)
Ndi-Ucheagwu	Agbobu
Ndi-Ukwu	Umualoma 2,5
Ndi-Uwaonu	Agbobu

Sources: 1. Eze J.O. Dike (1996); 2. NAE OKIDIST – 19/1/1 1908–25 Intelligence Book, Okigwe Division, 1908–25:21; 3. G.N. Okoli (1996); 4. Kanu-Igbo (1996b); 5. NAE ORLDIST – 14/1/3; 6. J. Uche 1996; 7. NAE 35/1920 – OKIDIST 4/2/32:Land Cases; 8. NAE 38/22 OKIDIST – 4/4/29:Political Report on Ndeziorgu, 14 April 1922:13.

the area.[14] Competition over increasingly scarce resources contributed to the fragmentation of these communities, a situation that began to change in the mid-eighteenth century. Despite traditions attesting to political unity among preexisting groups from the inception of these

[14] Traditions from Umuduru, Umunze, and Akokwa show that these communities had recently migrated into the region – the first from the Nri-Awka region and the last two from the Cross River Igbo area. These groups engaged mainly in occupations similar to those of the preexisting groups, although the newcomers seem to have brought new occupations as well. For instance, Akokwa is said to have come with blacksmithing skills (S.U. Uche 1988:2, 7). Umunze seems to have established itself as the dominant power in the north of the region, probably through the help of Ohafia and Arochukwu (Maduagwu n.d.:12–15, 25). Umunze community historian B.O.J. Maduagwu puts the date of Umunze's arrival in the region at 2000 years ago. This is extremely unlikely because Umunze traditions, which Maduagwu accepts, claim that the group descended from Ohafia, which more estimates to have been established sometime between the fifteenth and sixteenth centuries (see K.O. Dike and Ekejiuba 1990:ch. 2; O.N. Njoku 2000:14). Equally relevant in understanding Umunze's antiquity is the claim that Umunze

communities, there are sufficient indications that it was Aro presence, in particular, that motivated them to amalgamate into towns and town clusters. This did not, however, happen before fragmentation had created opportunities for pre-Aro immigrant groups.[15]

ARO SETTLEMENT AND LINEAGE-GROUP FORMATION

Izuogu's intervention in the area is attributed to a conflict between the Isu group and Ora. The Isu, who were moving toward the Imo River valley from the Awka-Orlu upland, asked Izuogu to intervene in their favor, an opportunity Izuogu exploited to the fullest (K.O. Dike and Ekejiuba 1990:177). Ora was located about seven kilometers east of the Imo and about 40 kilometers from the place in the west Imo area that Izuogu had settled initially. The claim that Izuogu intervened in favor of the Isu groups finds support in Akokwa traditions claiming that relations between Akowkwa and Arondizuogu were cordial (e.g., F.N. Egboh 1987:31, 34–35; S.U. Uche 1988:5, 21, 22, 32, 39–40). The Akokwa, it should be recalled, were recent Cross River Igbo migrants inhabiting the western uplands of the West Imo. Over time, cordial relations sometimes gave way to conflict as the territorial expansion of the Aro population took place at the expense of their neighbors.

As the Arondizuogu population increased, the community fanned out, and more lineage-groups emerged. Each free man needed a homestead, and each lineage-group a hamlet. A complex system of boundaries delineated the territories of the Arondizuogu lineage-groups in the area of the Eke Obinikpa market. Precisely when the different groups arrived is not known. The traditions present their formation synchronically, but certain elements from the same traditions and the genealogies show that the progenitors of the different groups arrived at different times and that the various groups were enfranchised as lineage-groups at different times. For instance, we learn that the mid-nineteenth-century

---

was able to subdue their enemies with the help of Ohafia and the Aro. Maduagwu himself informed me in February 1996 that Umunze pays annual homage to the Cross River warrior group of Ohafia – an indication of Umunze's provenance.

[15] The clearest indication of group consolidation is seen among Umuchu, sandwiched between Arondizuogu and the Ndi – Eni cluster. Umuchu was formed from a number of neighboring small groups for defense purposes (Nnolim 2007:21–23); the same for Amaokpala in the Ndi-Eni area (Onyekwelu 2001:1–2). Seven towns in the immediate surrounding of Arondizuogu, which may each have been originally fragmented formed a cluster known as Mbanasaa (meaning "seven towns").

warrior-merchant, Okoro Udozuka, paid the required enfranchisement fee for his lineage-group, Ndiakunwanta. Before this, the Ndiakunwanta lineage-group had existed in conjunction with another junior lineage-group, Ndiukwu, as one unit (E.N. Okoli 1977:35). This incident underlines the fact that other lineage-groups had already been enfranchised. We learn from another source that the son of the founder of the Ndinduvwuisi lineage-group established the group's present abode in the east Imo at about the turn of the twentieth century. Nwambego Okoli – who was aged more than 100 years when I interviewed her in 1996 – told me that she and her husband, who was Nduvwuisi's dependent's son, partook in this migration (G.N. Okoli 1996). One is therefore able to estimate the entry date of the lineage-group's primal ancestor, Nduvwuisi, at about 1840. The fact that Ndinduvwuisi is ahead of two other lineage-groups, means that the founders of these lineage-groups arrived later than Nduvwiusi.

The lineage organization of the emergent Arondizuogu community was a hierarchy of hegemonies, based on the entry status of early settlers as charter group members, clients, ordinary immigrants, or slaves. The rule of precedence, which guided the order of seniority of the lineage-groups, provides a signpost for sequencing the arrival of the founders of the lineage-groups. When the rule of precedence was waived, as the shunting observed after 1825 (steps 5 and 6 in Table 4.2), this is explicit in the traditions and recognized by all parties. This situation arose from the ability of the formerly junior lineage-group (Ndiakaeme) to pay a certain levy ahead of the formerly senior one (Ndiogbuonyeoma). Although the traditions do not say so, this payment may have been the franchise fee. No other kind of levy could have assumed such importance. The incident led to a civil war between the two lineage-groups, the cause of which virtually everybody still acknowledges. For another example, the traditions hold that Ndiakunwanta is the "youngest" lineage-group. True, Ndiakunwanta was the last to be franchised as a lineage-group, along with the Udozuka transaction related in the previous paragraph. But in fact, Akunwanta made his entry into the society in about 1825, before three other lineage-groups (step 5 in Table 4.2). Prior to enfranchisement, Ndiakunwanta had been remained an integral part of the Iheme lineage-group. We also know that certain lineage-groups themselves were founded by sons of the pioneers, after a first-generation set of lineage-groups had been founded. Based on this kind of information and genealogies, therefore, we can establish a rough chronology using seniority and patterns of settlement.

TABLE 4.2. *Sequence of Nucleation of Arondizuogu Lineage-Groups*

1. c. 1733 Izuougu(a) Amazu(b) Iheme(c) Ejezie(d)
2. c. 1770 Izuougu(a) Amazu(b) Iheme(c) Ejezie(d) Adumoha(e)
3. c. 1790 Uche(a1) Awa(a2) Amazu(b) Aniche(c1) Ejezie(d) Onuoha(c2) Ikpa-Eze(c3) Ogbuonyeoma(c4) Akaeme(c5) Adumoha(e)
4. c. 1815 Uche(a1) Awa(a2) Amazu(b) Aniche(c1) Ejezie(b) Onuoha(c2) Ikpa-Eze(c3)Adumoha(e) Anyake(f)Ogbuonyeoma(c4) Akaeme(c5) Ukwu(c6)
5. c. 1825 Uche(a1) Awa(a2) Amazu(b) Aniche(c1) Ejezie(d) Onuoha(c2) Ikpa-Eze(c3) Adumoha(e) Anyake(f) Ogbuonyeoma(c4) Akaeme(c5) Ukwu(c6) Akunwanta(c7)
6. c. 1840 Uche(a1) Awa(a2) Amazu(b) Aniche(c1) Ejezie(d) Onuoha(c2) Ikpa-Eze(c3) Adumoha(e) Anyake(f) Akaeme(c4) Ogbuonyeoma(c5) Ukwu(c6) Akunwanta(c7) Nduwvuisi(g)
7. c. 1850 Uche(a1) Awa(a2) Amazu(b) Aniche(c1) Ejezie(d) Onuoha(c2) Ikpa-Eze(c3) Adumoha(e) Anyake(f) Akaeme(c4) Ogbuonyeoma(c5) Ukwu(c6) Akunwanta(c7) Nduwvuisi(g) Ucheagwu (h) Uwaonu(i)

Using the sequence of entry into the frontier as an indicator of nucleation, that is, the order by which the various groups actually became lineage-groups, is consistent with what we know of African societies. Kopytoff's observation that "being first" was a critical index of lineage seniority applies in the Arondizuogu case (Kopytoff 1987b:36, 52–61). Therefore, proximity to the original location suggests the sequence of the arrival of their primal ancestors. The cases that seem to deviate from this rule, such as the two lineage-groups originating from Izuogu's sons, Ndiuche (first) and Ndiawa (second), which were now both located away from the original settlement and Ndiamazu, just north of the original area, result from a later migration. Even these anomalies help to periodize the settlement of other lineage-groups. Uche was disinherited and never succeeded Izuogu in the first area of settlement in the Eke region. As a result, Ndiuche was the first to move, after Izuogu's death.[16] The reasons for Uche's disinheritance and its implications for the settlement's geopolitics is analyzed later in this chapter.

The following lineage-groups were established at the initial area of settlement, an indication of their respective progenitors' time and sequence of arrival in Arondizuogu. Eventually, the lineage-groups of Ndi-Iheme, originating from Izuogu's dependent and pioneer, Iheme, came to occupy

[16] This area is the site of the present site of National High School and Ojike Memorial hospital. Thereafter, the lineage-groups relocated to the Umuobom country (B. Asuzu 1992; D. Igwe 1992; E.U. Igwe 1992:4; E. Uche 1992; J.E. Uche 1996).

almost the entire region. Ndi-Iheme later nucleated into seven lineage-groups. Ndiamazu, originating from another of Izuougu's dependent and pioneer, Amazu,[17] settled the region to the immediate north-west of the initial area. Ndiejezie was located on Umualoma land slightly removed from the initial area in the north-easternly direction. Ndiadumoha, originating from Adumoha, who had become Izuogu's direct dependent after Iheme had used him to redeem himself from Izuogu, settled initially by Ndiamazu. Ndiadumoha later moved eastwards into the marshy Umuduru country, in a location removed from the initial area.

Initially, the sequence of nucleation is unclear. The genealogies and the traditions nonetheless permit a more accurate representation of the sequence of entry into Arondizuogu society. The migrations that accompanied lineage-group formation implied continual expansion and the setting up of new frontiers eastwards and northwards in the direction of Umualoma. Given this pattern, it becomes clear why the youngest lineage-groups, whose founders entered the society after 1840 (step six in Table 4.2), did not have a place in the favored upcountry, west of the Imo. Although the founders of these younger lineage-groups had entered Arondizuogu society in the mid-nineteenth century, it was not until very late in that century and early in the twentieth that their descendants could secure settlements of their own. By the time the new arrivals were ready to establish settlements, only the east Imo remained unoccupied by Arondizuogu groups. The Ndi-Ndiakunwanta lineage-group, formed after 1840, was the exception, but this was mainly because of the personal conquests of Okoro Udozuka at the expense of Umualoma. But formation of lineage-groups after the pioneers had been well established was not a free-for-all affair. It must have been sanctioned by the rest of the lineage-groups. Ndiakunwanta had to pay 3,600 "monies"/"markets" (*nnu ahia teghete*, or £180, which is equivalent to £12,800 in 2010 U.K. pound sterling), one barrel of gunpowder, and one cow to secure recognition as an autonomous lineage-group in about the late 1870s (E.N. Okoli 1977:35).[18]

---

[17] Some Ndiamazu traditions claims that Amazu was Izuogu's trading partner (e.g., M.S. Igwe 1996). It is, however, likely that Amazu, who originated from Oro in the Oji River, came as Izuogu's dependent – his first direct dependent. The basis for this assertion is that, though Iheme may have arrived before Amazu, Iheme had come in the first instance as Izuogu's wife's slave boy, whom she later gave to her husband. It is said that the name Iheme derived from the prayer, *ihe emene di m* (let no harm befall my husband) (Kanu-Igbo 1996a).

[18] This value is derived using the Retail Price Index (RPI). Other 2010 values for the same 1870 amount, using other criteria, are £17,600 (GDP deflator), £106,000 (average earnings), £124,000 (per capita GDP), £244,000 (Share GDP) (Economic History Services, http://eh.net/hmit/ukcompare/).

THE FRONTIER AND THE NRI-AWKA REGION

One practice with implication for slaving and culture formation was the specific and consistent interest with which the Aro settlements in central Igboland cultivated people from the Nri-Awka region. The enterprise, resourcefulness, and adaptability that the Aro associated with people from this region recommended them as wives, dependents, and immigrants. A special relationship thus existed between the Aro and the people of the Nri-Awka area. One of my respondents declared that Arondizuogu people "were going to *Nkanu-kwuru-Nkanu* [the length and breath of Nkanu, i.e., Nri-Awka region,]" adding, "Is there any place in this Arondizuogu where you would not find Nkanu people ...?" (Akpu 1996). The mid-nineteenth-century merchant-warrior, Okoro Udozuka, is said to have made the best of these arrangements (Akpu 1996; E.N. Okoli 1977). "He was staying in his mother's land while trading in slaves because his grandfather's relatives were helping him get enough slaves" (Igwegbe 1962:34). Besides his numerous children by an army of wives, Udozuka "was able through the institution of slavery to build a miniature empire for himself." His "subjects" numbered more than 200 and "contributed so much to the increased population of Ndiakunwanta" (E.N. Okoli 1977:35).

It was not only through slavery that people of the Nri-Awka region inundated Arondizuogu; kinship ties also played a large part in the process. Nri-Awka immigrants also often desired to have their relatives join them in Arondizuogu (M.S. Igwe 1996; Kanu-Igbo 1996b). Even the enslaved were generally allowed to maintain noninstitutional, supernumerary kinship affiliations with their natal societies, from which they often took wives. They also introduced other Arondizuogu men to women in their natal homes. As agents of Aro concerns, these Nri-Awka immigrants into Aro society – whether they were originally regular immigrants or enslaved – freely and frequently made business trips to their natal societies, with which they maintained trade links. Apart from bringing in more people, these immigrants routinely adopted shrines from their natal societies. In time, the master class came to subscribe to these shrines, which became the dominant media of worship among the Aro diaspora. The willingness of Aro slave masters to incorporate the enslaved and to embrace aspects of their culture is consistent with the Igbo willingness – noted by anthropologist Simon Ottenberg – to both readily incorporate outsiders and acquire "new religious shrines ... by trade and purchase" (S. Ottenberg 1959: 140). Not surprisingly, immigrants from the Nri-Awka area made lasting impact on Arondizuogu culture.

Culture Formation in the Trading Frontier

The Aro case also raises a point that is often ignored in the analysis of slave incorporation in Africa. The enslaved people's relationship to society was not just characterized by assimilation into a dominant culture. The extension of the aforementioned liberties – though designed to serve Aro interests and not necessarily those of the enslaved – departs from Kopytoff and Miers's assertion that the change in the life of the enslaved "was usually dramatic and total" and that he lost "his social personality, his identity and status [and] suffered a traumatic and sometimes violent withdrawal from kin, neighbors, and community, and often from familiar customs and language." The social experience of people of slave origin was hardly consistent with what Kopytoff and Miers characterize as "playing dead" (I. Kopytoff and Miers 1977:14–15). Enslaved people in Aro settlements did actually influence the culture of host societies, contrary to the phenomenon of "social death" advanced by Orlando Patterson in his monumental *Slavery and Social Death* (1982). Despite this formulation, however, Patterson sees "absolutely no evidence from the long and dismal annals of slavery to suggest that any group of slaves ever internalized the conception of degradation held by their masters," and that enslaved people never lost "the quintessential human urge to participate and want a place" (Patterson 1982:97). But his argument that all slavery is an alternative to death – as apt as it is in many historical instances – is too rigid to accommodate the Aro experience. The enslaved in Aro society certainly were not usually – if ever – "denied all claims … on his more remote ancestors" and disallowed from freely integrating "the experience of their ancestors into their lives," as Patterson has asserted (Patterson 1982:5). Aro masters and their societies did under several significant circumstances – probably even routinely – encourage and enable slaves to reach back to their ancestors. It must be conceded though that these privileges presupposed certain codes of conformity on the part of the enslaved that sustained and reproduced the Aro slave system. Except for "free" migrants, the incoming people did not bring shrines or deities upon arrival; they did so after they had earned the confidence of their owners.

Apart from the Aro's special interest in Nri-Awka people, the social and economic conditions in the Nri-Awka region exposed its people to enslavement and emigration. Needy parents often sold their children. Igbudu and Ebuteilo of Ndiakunwanta in Arondizuogu were brothers by the same mother in Nimo. Ebuteilo, in particular, later acquired many people from the region (Maduadichie 1996). Similarly, the Ndieni Aro heavily acquired people from non-Aro communities in their immediate neighborhood.[19] The present Arondizuogu people take this dimension of their history for granted. The following is typical of the kind of explanations that I got during fieldwork.

The Anambra [Nri-Awka] people ... were more prudent than the people from many communities in our immediate neighborhood. And they did not have food ... At that time, there were no cities. Many people arrived here due to yam cultivation possibilities.[20] These people multiplied in the process. At that time too, Mazi Izuogu Mgbokpo traversed that country in his slave dealing business. After he had settled here, he got his own people from the same place that he got trade slaves. He retained those with good character. Those retained in this process may have come overwhelmingly from Anambra. (M.S. Igwe 1996)[21]

The presence of a large group of immigrants from the Nri-Awka region had a foundational impact upon the Aro diaspora in central Igboland. A review of the workings of pan-Aro institutions in the diaspora places this impact in its true context.

LINKAGES

An analysis of the Aro cultural network is an analysis of linkage institutions, rites, or practices in both the metropole and the diaspora and of those that linked them. In addition to the formal institutions through which the metropole regulated the operation of the diaspora – the Aro central council (Ọkpankpọ), the Ekpe secret society, and the Ibiniukpabi oracle – already discussed in Chapter 3, there were those that governed conventions and rites. Linkage institutions maintained political precedence and routine contact within the diaspora populations and between the metropole and the diaspora. The Aro diaspora paid regular visits to Arochukwu to conduct and discuss trade, take the non-Aro to Ibiniukpabi, receive advice from oracular priests, partake in the annual Ikeji festival, join the Ekpe society or partake in its rites, and visit kin members.[22]

[19] Chinyele 1972; J. Ike 1972; Iloha 1972; C. Kanu 1972; J, Kanu 1972; Ngene 1972; Nwene 1972; F. Obi 1972; N. Okoli 1972.

[20] Only those arriving in the last decade of the nineteenth century onward did so for the purposes of farming because farming became important only at that time. This claim exemplifies telescoping in the traditions. "Anambra" is the present state in Nigeria dominated by the Nri-Awka.

[21] The traditions of the Nri-Awka communities recognize these movements into Arondizuogu as well. Among the traditions that I have seen, the ones from Awka seem most explicit on this matter. They mention large-scale "migrations" to Arondizuogu (Agu 1985; I. Oguocha 1996).

[22] N.A. Anyakoha (1996); Chinyele (1972); Dike and Ekejiuba (1990); C. Okafor (1986:124–25); J.G. Okoro (1985).

Aro settlers abroad also attended town or clan councils in Arochukwu "and 'gave advice' which was invariably taken" (Grier 1922:35). In 1973, one Aro respondent told the historian Northrup, in an Aro settlement of Nung Okoro in Ibibioland where the respondent had been born: "Every year we would return home [to Arochukwu] for the New Yam Festival. Other meetings would be held among the Nung Okoro settlers to discuss trade matters and aid traders who had ill luck" (F.E.S. Okoro 1973).[23] This practice appears to have been widespread in Aro diaspora settlements.

The Aro of Arochukwu (metropole) are reluctant to see Aro people visiting Arochukwu from the various diaspora settlements as visitors, and this attitude implies a reluctance on the part of metropolitan Aro to promote the idea of the people of the diaspora building institutions of their own and/or developing alternative identities. The Aro made it a point to call these visits "returning home," and this practice survives today. During my fieldwork in 1995 and 1996, the elders quickly corrected me each time I referred to my trip to Arochukwu as a visit. Many persons from the diaspora have remigrated back to Arochukwu and integrated into the lineages that their sojourning ancestors left behind in Arochukwu. Many others maintain dual residences in the metropole and the diaspora. The *Eze-Ogo* (ruler) of Amankwu in Arochukwu during my fieldwork was an Arondizuogu man whose ancestors left Arochukwu in the eighteenth century. He left his Ndi-Njoku lineage-group in Arondizuogu to assume that role (Obinani 1996).

These linkages did not result from later developments. Izuogu Mkpokpo himself, who set up Arondizuogu, never resided there permanently. Tradition is unanimous that he participated regularly in Arochukwu council meetings. Most Aro in the diaspora maintained residences in Arochukwu, and many were buried there. In early 1996, the Ndiamazu lineage-group of Arondizuogu won a major court case over the house that their primal ancestor, Amazu, had retained in Arochukwu. One Arochukwu man had attempted to claim the property. Ndiamazu won this case with the help of Jacob Ogbonna Okoro (c. 1897–2001) who maintained double residence in Arondizuogu and Arochukwu since 1927.[24] Ndiamazu people collected rent on this property and put it in

---

[23] The festival originated in pre-trade Arochukwu, to mark the harvest of the new yam, but it came to lose its agricultural purchase over time as the Aro became traders, to the extent that homeland and some diaspora Aro had come to mark it at the opposite ends of the agricultural season by the nineteenth century.

[24] Because I was on my way to Arondizuogu, Okoro requested me to, and I did personally convey letters from him to some Ndiamazu leaders, in which he reported the end of the case.

their common fund. As late as 1900, Okoroji, the founder of Ndikoroji, an Aro settlement near Arondizuogu, was buried in his home at Ujari in Arochukwu (Okoroji 1996; K.O. Dike and Ekejiuba 1990:308). Even people who became Aro in their lifetime or first-generation Aro born in the diaspora often wished to be either buried in the metropole or that some of their funeral rites be performed there. The practice of burying diaspora Aro in Arochukwu continued until the imposition of British colonial rule.[25]

The best example of the institutions that linked the Aro metropole and its diaspora is, perhaps, the Ihu rite. In this rite, every adult free male regularly renewed obeisance to his oldest male relative (in the immediate family), ex-master, patron, or host. Ihu was specifically tied to the annual cycle of the Ikeji festival, and the rite of passage. The physical embodiment of Ihu consisted of a particular assortment of seven meat parts of the ritual beast, usually a goat or a cow.[26] Ihu was tied specifically to two occasions: death and the annual Ikeji festival, described as the "annual festival of thanksgiving and propitiation" (C. Okafor 1986:124). Ikeji marked an annual renewal of loyalty to masters and seniors in the lineages. As the renowned Arondizuogu folklorist and singer, Azubuike Nkemakonam Nwokoye-Emesuo (alias Perricomo) told me, Ihu was a "census" of surviving dependents (Nwokoye-Emesuo 1996). Ihu celebrated interpersonal and group hierarchy. Each free adult male took Ihu to his immediate male superior. The superior could be the oldest relative in the immediate family, ex-master, patron, or host – depending on individual circumstances. According to one of my respondents:

The system of this person acquiring that person and that person acquiring yet another was quite complicated. The way that people clarified who was who was the ihu, observed during the Ikeji festival in Arondizuogu. For instance, my father came to Arondizuogu [from Arochukwu] through Anumba. When he celebrated the Ikeji, he gave *ose ihe* to Anumba as ihu. For his part, Anumba gave to Mazi

---

[25] Arochukwu elder Kanu-Onuoha (1996) recalled the 1928 second burial at Arochukwu of Okoro Udozuka of Arondizuogu. Such funerals would have involved considerable material cost, but before the late nineteenth century, the diaspora people were generally affluent enough to support this important rite of passage or to have that financed by relatives.

[26] These parts are rib cage (with seven ribs on each side) (*ose anu*), chest (*ntinana*), upper bowel (*isi akpakwuru*), a tiny portion of the liver (*umeji*), a small portion of the spleen (*anyinya*), a small piece of flesh from the upper abdomen (*ofufe enu*), and a small part of the lower abdomen (*ofufe ana*). I am grateful to the late Orizu Nwokeji (1996) for this information. The meat parts were also accompanied by "five big yams", one keg of palm wine and four kolanuts (Muotoh 2000:43–44).

Ufere [of Ndiamazu] because it was Ufere who had brought Mazi Anumba. He, Mazi Ufere himself, had an elder/superior under whom he was. That person was a descendant of Mazi Izuogu Obunukpo Akuma Nnachi. Mazi Izuogu was the person who left this Arochukwu to open up the way up to Arondizuogu to establish a settlement. (J.O. Okoro 1996)

By clarifying relationships within and among kin groups, and routinizing precedence and seniority, Ihu tied all Aro, both in the homeland and diaspora, to a standardized system of identifying, acknowledging, and legitimizing Aro authority structures. Ihu from all the Aro lineage-groups, including their offshoots in the diaspora, flowed ultimately to Eze Aro at Arochukwu. The system served to perpetuate ex-slaves as political and social juniors after their emancipation at the level of production. This junior status also applied to clients and guests. The system encouraged ex-slaves and immigrants to acquire wealth and dependents, but routinized precedence based on charter status, heredity, and age.

As a gesture of gratitude, Ihu was obligatory; but, as a measure of precedence, it was also compulsory. What would happen if a person refused to give Ihu? One respondent echoed many others when he answered: "A human being could not even discuss that ... failure to give Ihu amounted to rebellion. The punishment was removal from society – *mmevu* (wasting) – which could be sale or execution. Did he who refuses to observe Ihu fall from heaven?" (Arodiogbu 1996). Unlike the feudal tithe, Ihu was not economically exploitative in any significant sense for men, but was designed as a ceremonial observance to essentialize access to productive resources in past and present relationships. The Ihu system exploited women directly. The women of a household were required to make fixed annual contributions from proceeds from the economic trees they controlled. The household head used these proceeds, and added to it when necessary, to buy the sacrificial beast. In short, women may have borne the economic brunt of Ihu, although the demands seem hardly significant – given the material requirements for the annual sacrifice vis à vis the possible number of women in a household.

The Ihu rite was central to a system that required every male entrant to have either a master or patron. The system secured for the guest, client or ex-slave a permanent place in the lineage hierarchy, thus making belonging to Aro society a cardinal condition for belonging in it. It encouraged slaves to work toward their emancipation and to acquire wealth and dependents. Although many societies exact tribute from incoming elements, Ihu stands out because its observance was not restricted to any single status group but was incumbent on all. It also encouraged deference based on age within all status groups.[27]

In the face of these relationships, British colonial anthropologists noted the following. "The Aros were clan-conscious rather than town-conscious, and today the average man will declare with pride that he is an Aro before he gives the name of his town, recalling the spirit of St. Paul triumphantly declaring 'Civis Romanus sum', followed by the information 'I come from Tarsus, no mean city'" (Anthropologists' Papers 1927:16). Later, a colonial officer reported that the people of Arondizuogu had "retained their Aro customs."[28] While these realities demonstrate strong linkages, they also mask the deviations from the Aro cultural grid.

DEVIATIONS IN THE FRONTIER

The Aro diaspora also showed signs of separate patterns of cultural evolution. It bears noting that many milestone events and developments that shaped and reshaped Arochukwu institutions had not yet occurred when Arondizuogu and the other major Aro diaspora settlements were being formed. For example, the ascendancy of the "Igbo" faction of Arochukwu had not yet happened when Izuogu founded the upper Imo River valley settlement in the 1730s.[29] The ascendancy of the Igbo faction marked a watershed in the Arochukwu political culture. Also, status groups that were identified in the nineteenth-century Arochukwu had not yet crystallized in the middle of the eighteenth century. The *amadi nkume asaa* (literally, the amadi of the seven stones – euphemism for the founding lineage-groups), the upper-crust amadi (nobility), derived from the number of the Arochukwu lineage-groups (otusi, or "stones") which reached *asaa* (seven) only after 1850 (K.O. Dike and Ekejiuba 1990:68, 71, 91). In Arochukwu symbolism, one stone denoted one lineage-group cluster. As a result of these historical developments, the following simple, three-class structure had developed in Arochukwu by the nineteenth century. The highest echelon was the amadi, which "was rigid enough to amount to caste." This group consisted of the direct descendants of the foundation

---

[27] Only two recent studies have mentioned Ihu – although they do not analyze it in detail (see Bentor 1994:167; K.O. Dike and Ekejiuba 1990:210, 274).

[28] NAE EP 12481 – MINLOC 6:1. 306: Intelligence Report on the Ndizuogu Village Area, Orlu District, Okigwe Division, Owerri Province: Resident's Covering Report.

[29] For this development, see Dike and Ekejiuba (1990:63, 67).

Culture Formation in the Trading Frontier 101

families of Arochukwu society. The second group was the *amuda*, consisting of immigrants, their descendants, and those of slaves. The *ohu*, the first-generation slaves, were the lowest group (K.O. Dike and Ekejiuba 1990:79, 284; Uku 1993:3, 18–20). The status hierarchy in the different diaspora settlements was bound to take different courses, reflecting the specific circumstances of each settlement.

The starting point of the status distinction in Arochukwu, then, was the foundation families. All nineteen Arochukwu lineage-groups were either foundation communities or direct offshoots of these.[30] Consequently, all the lineage-groups had their amadi and corresponding lower orders. Not surprisingly, therefore, status formation in Arondizuogu took a different turn where the history-specific phenomenon of the seven stones was absent. The differences in status formation between Arondizuogu and Arochukwu reflected their differing circumstances of societal formation and the fact that the Arochukwu institutions continued to undergo transformations after the establishment of Arondizuogu. The Arondizuogu case was more complicated. Arondizuogu was formed with just Izuogu's family and the persons of his household (Table 4.2). Of the resulting original nine lineage-groups, eight were founded by persons of Izuogu's household. After the increase of the lineage-groups to sixteen in the course of the nineteenth century, Izuogu's direct descendants came to compose the ruling minority of only two lineage-groups, Ndiawa and Ndiuche, while the ruling minorities of all fourteen other lineage-groups descended from Izuogu's dependents. The ruling groups of the remaining two of the present eighteen lineage-groups of Arondizuogu come from the descendants of Izuogu's brothers, Njoku and Udensi. These last groups, Ndinjoku and Ndimoko, migrated late into the region during the 1850s and 1870s, respectively, as separate and autonomous Aro settlements (see T.O. Okereke 1996). Izuogu's direct descendants constituted minority ruling elites in Ndiawa and Ndiuche. By virtue of their position, these elites also exercised authority over the rest of the lineage-groups, forming the amadi both in these lineage-groups and over Arondizuogu at large. The direct descendants of the other lineage-group founders, for their part, constituted the minority amadi within the respective lineage-groups, as they also massively incorporated outsiders through slavery and other forms of immigration. These incorporated outsiders formed subordinate lineages within the lineage-groups, and

---

[30] The best informed discussions of this subject are Dike and Ekejiuba (1990) and J.O. Ijoma (1986c).

those acquired by the subordinate lineages formed sub-subordinate lineages, and so forth. The outstanding feature of this system is that while the original non-Aro founding lineages were subject to the authority of lineages that descended directly from Izuogu, the non-Aro founding lineages constituted the amadi within their lineage-groups because they had enfranchised lineage-groups, in contrast to later-arriving lineages in Arochukwu. In contrast to the simple three-class hierarchy described above for Arochukwu, Arondizuogu had a complex hierarchy of hegemonies, or a "hierarchy of hierarchies." The Arondizuogu structure reflected conditions peculiar to the diaspora.

Changes in such a key area as class structure between the metropole and the diaspora foreshadowed other cultural changes. One such change was in the Ikeji festival, where the diaspora introduced new elements, and even changed the season for holding it. At the formative stages of the Aro diaspora, the Aro everywhere returned to Arochukwu to celebrate the annual festival. At one point that is not yet clear, the diaspora communities began to celebrate theirs at different times that did not conflict with the Aro general Ikeji as well. In Arondizuogu, the season changed from August, when the metropole celebrated it, to April.[31] August generally coincided with the beginning of the harvest season, while April generally coincided with the beginning of the planting season. The literary translation of Ikeji-yam – "staking" (for preservation) – suggests strongly that the original purpose of the festival was to usher in the harvest season. Some Arondizuogu elders have speculated that the reason for the change was to ensure that the rain did not interfere with the masquerade performance, the hallmark of the Ikeji festival in Arondizuogu: the drier month of April provided better weather for masquerade performance than did rainy August. But the change of the Ikeji season to April brought home the fact that agriculture had little clout in a trading society. Change was possible only because yam agriculture was not central to the spiritual life of Arondizuogu at the time. Otherwise, not even the likelihood that rain would ruin the event could have occasioned a change. If the festival had originated in an early agricultural era, before the Aro became a predominantly trading community, agriculture did not become important again

---

[31] Initially, after the change in seasons, the different Arondizuogu lineage-groups had celebrated Ikeji variously, but consecutively during the long season from March to April. Since the emergence of the Arondizuogu Patriotic Union (APU) in the 1930s, the whole of Arondizuogu have celebrated the festival on the same dates in April. For a comprehensive history of this union and informative details of Ikeji and its evolution, see Ohia 2007.

among the Aro until the last decade of the nineteenth century, after the festival had been in existence for centuries. The shift of the Ikeji season from August to April not only marked a shift in season but also the separation of Ikeji and the new yam festival. The new yam festival, which in late twentieth-century Arondizuogu was celebrated in September, when the rest of the Igbo and Arochukwu celebrated it (the latter calling it "Ikeji"), was most probably (re-)introduced or revived when yam agriculture became important in Arondizuogu. Yam agriculture did not become important in Arondizuogu until the final decade of the nineteenth century, when the people began to establish settlements in areas east of the original Arondizuogu site. This (re-)introduction of the new yam festival should explain why Arondizuogu celebrates in September today, to avoid a conflict with the Arochukwu event in August.

The domestication of the Ikeji festival in the diaspora served practical and symbolic purposes. The need to protect the settlements and to legitimize them in the eyes of the preexisting societies called for a more demonstrative presence that Ikeji provided. Since the frontierspeople were always concerned with security against the occasional hostile neighbor, it would not have been in their interest to embark on a predictable annual mass trip to the distant metropole. Simultaneously, Ikeji provided opportunities for diplomacy. As Chinyere Okafor has pointed out, people in the diaspora and in the preexisting communities exchanged visits during festivals. Ikeji gave the Aro the opportunity to reciprocate these invitations (C. Okafor 1986:124). Internally, the festival offered the ruling members of the diaspora a regular opportunity to renew and routinize their hegemony over their wards through the Ihu institution. Such symbolisms were essential to maintaining order and control in the dynamic diaspora environment. The festival was remarkable for its blend of metropolitan and frontier practices. The rituals were metropolitan, while the entertainment aspects bore the signature of preexisting and Nri-Awka groups.

The Aro diaspora deviated more completely regarding incest rules. In the Aro metropole, loose incest rules permitted marriage between second cousins. But in the central Igboland frontiers, rigid incest rules prevailed. Among the all Aro, women could only marry men of the same or a higher status – never below. These practices implied the social isolation of unmarried women among the original Aro migrants to the frontier, who could not marry the majority of men in society because these men came from lower status groups. Because the original Aro in these settlements often descended from one person or, sometimes, from a few close blood relatives, creating a scarcity of eligible men for the original Aro women. The impact of this restrictive marriage practice on the marriageability of high-status Aro women would have been great. It also created an artificial scarcity of women for men of slave origin, who either had to secure wives from non-Aro groups or remained unmarried. This partial exogamy, by which Aro men married outside women without giving out any of their own, as mentioned in Chapter 3, ruled out the rest of Igboland as a source of spouses for high-status unmarried women. In Arondizuogu, as in the other Aro frontier settlements, men outside Izuogu's pedigree were outside the eligible pool, as were comparable classes in both Arochukwu and in the diaspora. High-status women were left to marry only men from the amadi nkume asaa, but this was a small and very exclusive group found only in Arochukwu and those diaspora settlements whose founders were Aro amadi. The adoption of strict incest rules in the diaspora resulted from the influence of Igbo norms, especially those of Nri-Awka.

Yet, in one important respect, Arondizuogu deviated, not only from Arochukwu, but also from the rest of the Igbo world, notably the Nri-Awka culture area from which most of the frontier populations were drawn. Both Arochukwu and the rest of the Igbo observed the "twin taboo," which was based on the belief that twins were spiritually unclean and purveyors of communal misfortune. The Igbo are known to have thrown twins into the "bad bush" (unused bush, often a virgin forest, where all things considered sacrilege and evil were thrown). The involvement of Arochukwu in the twin taboo is ironic, given the people's emphasis on group expansion. Perhaps because their slave trading activities made them more likely to see human beings as commodities, the Aro tended to eschew Igbo practices that wasted human lives. For example, while the Igbo normally threw into the bad bush children who cut their upper teeth first, the Aro diaspora in the perimeters of central Igboland preserved them. Despite the varying attitudes of Arochukwu and the Aro diaspora toward the twin taboo, however, Arochukwu shared the Igbo world's perception of twin birth as a major abomination and both Aro groups considered twins sellable commodities.[32] Given the twin taboo prevailing in much of Igboland, the Aro tendency to buy and sell twins and the apparent absence of a similar practice elsewhere in Atlantic Africa, the

---

[32] The taboo against twins in Arochukwu is so strong that it survives to date. For instance, it was first ascertained that I was not a twin during my fieldwork in February 1996 before I was admitted to a historical site, *Oghuti Okoroji* (the house of the late nineteenth-century slave trader, Okoroji), even though the Nigerian government had declared it a national monument in 1972.

Bight of Biafra would have sent a relatively significant number of twins into the slave trade. The members of the British Niger Expedition of 1841 give us a view of this practice among the Igbo.

> The little victims are no sooner born than one or both are taken away, placed in the neighboring thicket in earthen pots or baskets, and left there to become the food of hyenas or other wild beasts. The unfortunate mother is separated for ever from her conjugal alliance; she is obliged to pass a long period or repentance and purification, in a rude hut some distance from the town; and if she outlives all these trials, mental and physical, and returns once more to society, she is regarded as an especial object of Fetish wrath, and no woman will knowingly sit in her company, or hold communion with her. (Capt. W. Allen and Thomson 1848a:243)

Arondizuogu oral traditions reveal the community's deviation from Igbo and Arochukwu twin discrimination. Sometime in the 1820s, a woman from Abatete in the Nri-Awka area, fleeing the consequences of having given birth to twins, found her way to Arondizuogu. With her were her male twin children, Achusim and Onyevwuchi, whom she concealed in a long basket covered with fresh leaves. Uchendu, the ex-dependent of Akaeme, the founder of the Ndiakeme lineage-group, granted asylum to the woman and her children, under the usual condition of dependency.[33] Today, Ndi-Achusim and Ndi-Onyevwuchi, descendants of these twins are principal lineages in the Ndiakeme lineage-group. As this story demonstrates, immigrants from the Nri-Awka and other areas did not wholly transpose their cultures in Arondizuogu. Arondizuogu deviated not only from Arochukwu but also from the Nri-Awka region.

Still, Aro influences and practices remained. For instance, in spite of the massive immigration of originally non-Aro elements, Arondizuogu did not adopt a specialist shrine for agriculture. A colonial officer interpreted the nonexistence of the Ana shrine (the shrine of land and agriculture) to be evidence of Arondizuogu "stranger" status in the area (see Mayne 1935:8). If what "strangers" means is that Arondizuogu was comparatively recent in the region, many other Igbo communities were also of

---

[33] This date is an estimate from genealogies. Traditions related by various respondents in different lineage-groups show the same basic pattern (Arodiogbu 1996; Ekwobi 1996; Igwegbe 1962:30–31; Igwilo 1996a; C. Okoli 1996). Whatever truth there may be to this story, it suggests to me that the idea of accepting twins has been entrenched in Arondizuogu folklore since the early nineteenth century. None of my respondents seemed aware that this act deviated from the Aro norm. They simply used the incident to illustrate the principle of *mmuba*. Igwegbe (1962) renders the traditions in the same manner.

recent origin and were the results of migration, and recent migration to the area did not prevent these communities from invariably adopting the Ana, or analogous agrarian-oriented cults. Residency status did not determine the adoption of the earth shrine. Arondizuogu did not adopt it only because agriculture was, until a decade before British colonial conquest, marginal to the trade-based political economy. Up to the 1890s, the community depended on its neighbors for the supply of provisions. Although oral traditions often tout the "strangers" idea, the term is not useful in the Igbo historical context. As part of a strategy of colonial domination, the British played up the idea to help intimidate the intractable Arondizuogu community and to isolate it from neighboring non-Aro communities. In itself, the stranger status is not useful in understanding the prevalence or otherwise of the Ana cult. The cult's diffusion was not coterminous with the series of migrations that mark the histories of many Igbo groups. After all, most of Arondizuogu peoples originated from areas in which the Ana cult prevailed.[34] They could have brought it with them, but, as already mentioned, the cult had little reason to exist in a trading frontier. Instead, ancestral cults were, according to Dike and Ekejiuba, often central among trading groups, such as the Aro (K.O. Dike and Ekejiuba 1990:132). As with the adopted shrines, these ancestral cults were important in Arondizuogu – even among immigrants.

However, evidence from the Ndieni, a commonwealth of other major Aro communities in central Igboland, complicates the trade-based explanation for the absence of agricultural shrines in a trading frontier. Up to the 1920s, these Aro groups still subscribed to Ajana, the earth deity of the respective preexisting groups amid whom their ancestors had settled a century and a half earlier.[35] The reason for this difference between Arondizuogu and Ndieni may lie in Arondizuogu's more thorough subjection and its greater displacement of preexisting groups than Ndieni experienced with its neighbors. In the Ujari case, according to an Ujari historian, the preexisting community of Akpu offered Ujari people land that "was near the grove around the shrine of a local deity called Ajana."[36] Like the Ujari, other Ndieni communities generally settled in close proximity to preexisting societies, establishing Aro dominance over time, often by

---

[34] For the centrality of the Ana cult, see Meek (1937:Ch. 2; Green 1964:26–28, 100). In Arochukwu, the trade cult, *Inyamavia*, prevailed.

[35] NAE ONPROF – 7/16/150:Awka Division Intelligence Notes on the Towns of Ajalli Native Court Area 1929. See abstract of file, p. 2.

[36] The Ujari community had just been harried out of their original place of settlement at Uvume by the hosts (Eni 1973:12).

Culture Formation in the Trading Frontier 107

war. Arondizuogu, on the contrary, made war at the outset. Although they sometimes married women and acquired people from neighboring communities, Arondizuogu maintained some spatial and social distance from the preexisting groups; thus, it was people from the Nri-Awka area who had significant influence on the evolution of Arondizuogu culture. Yet, the Nri-Awka influence did not lead to the emergence of the Ana cult there. Although all cultures evolve from interaction with other cultures, and each is, therefore, a synthesis, Arondizuogu and the Ndieni cluster showed the marked influence of their immediate neighbors, and this seems to have been especially true of the Ndieni cluster. The specific situation of the Aro diaspora settlements made them not only distinct communities in their neighborhoods, but also distinguished them from metropolitan Arochukwu and from other Aro diaspora communities, each of which had its own distinguishing characteristics.

DIALECT FORMATION

Language is an important distinguishing characteristic of the Aro diaspora. The Aro dialect of Igbo in the upper Imo River region is a reflection of the historical interactions of religion, commerce, the large-scale incorporation of elements from other societies, and marriage. One way to measure the distinctness or otherwise of any Aro diaspora community is to compare its dialect to those of its immediate neighbors, metropolitan Arochukwu, and the major source of originally non-Aro immigrants. The task is best accomplished by comparing vocabularies – the basic methodology of lexicostatistics, which establishes the relationship between two or more languages, including how long ago they separated from a single, common language. However, the task in this case is primarily to determine the extent to which each of three major dialectal areas influenced the dialect of a fourth group – Arondizuogu.

Unfortunately, however, the Igbo orthography does not capture some basic phonemes in Igbo dialects, a limitation that is striking in the case.[37] Such a limited orthography forecloses any necessity, or even the possibility,

---

[37] John McCall encountered the same problem with respect to his work among the Ohafia (McCall 2000:161). Although interested in the historical development of language, both traditional and modern linguistics ignore the sociocultural contexts in which languages emerge. Yet patterns of speech shape and are shaped by "dominance and exchange patterns of kinship and other idioms of speech" (H.C. White 1995:5, 41). To be sure, the Igbo orthography ignores sociocultural realities. When I once raised this matter on the electronic interactive medium, Igbonet, early in 1995, the views of the other contributors,

of interdialectical comparisons. To carry out the historically significant task of comparing the Arondizuogu dialect with the dialects of its population sources, therefore, it is necessary to transcend the existing orthography. Historian Elizabeth Isichei apparently had to employ a unique consonant (*wh*, pronounced like the English word "who") to represent a word from the Awka dialect (*whum*) (Isichei 1978:67). I have adopted the consonants *wh* and *vw* (both as in the Urhobo orthography) to represent the Arondizuogu phonemes not otherwise represented. Also adopted is "rl" to represent a sound in eastern Nri-Awka Igbo that seem to combine "r" and "l," with the "r" sound predominating (Table 4.3).[38] The rl sound resembles is identical to the sound of the single "r" in Spanish.

Another complicating factor in the lexicostatistics of the Aro diaspora is that the derivative dialects are not homogenous. Arochukwu comes closest to homogeneity; yet, different Arochukwu lineage-groups speak slightly varying dialects. Ibom, Ujari, Amankwu and especially Amannagwu speak something closest to the quintessence of Aro dialect, while the rest are, to widely varying degrees, influenced by the dialects of different Igbo groups and Ibibio.

Adopting the lexicostatistical approach and an appropriate orthography with which to execute it place the ethnolinguistic history of the Aro diaspora in clear relief. Fifty-five randomly selected words show the diverse origins of Arondizuogu dialects, with the Nri-Awka dialects dominating. While eleven words are all used in Arochukwu, preexisting communities and the Nri-Awka region, two words originate from both from Arochukwu and preexisting communities, two from both Arochukwu and Nri-Awka, and four from both Nri-Awka and preexisting communities. Four originate exclusively from Arochukwu and one exclusively from the dialects of the preexisting communities, but as high as nineteen words

---

including one Igbo linguist, favored the existing orthography. They rested their case on the political imperative of Igbo integration, a view that illustrates the connection between language and politics and sacrificing cultural interaction and historical context. This view is not only at variance with the postmodernist sensibility to the multiplicity of identities but it also certainly hampers the historical understanding of Igbo societies.

[38] Such nuances in Igbo phonemes complicate scholars' efforts to transliterate names of enslaved people in the Americas because the people who first transcribed the names approximated the sounds with the orthographic traditions the transcribers were familiar, regardless of whether Igbo orthography would later incorporate the sounds. Maureen Warner-Lewis uses "rl" to throw light on "Durl," the name of the father of the Igbo Archibald Monteith, who was enslaved in Jamaica, as transcribed by Europeans. Warner Lewis suggests that this name represents the name that appears in standard Igbo as "Duru," observing that despite the apparent strangeness of "rl" in Durl, "erery Igbo speaker recognizes this word to have been Duru" (Warner-Lewis 2007: 28).

Culture Formation in the Trading Frontier 109

TABLE 4.3. *Lexicostatistics of Arochukwu, Arondizuogu, Nri-Awka, and Non-Aro Communities Around Arondizuogu*

	English	Arọndizuogu	Arọchukwu	Nri – Awka	Preexisting Communities
1	Market/Trade	ahịa	avịa	afịa/avịa/afịa	ahyịa
2	Big	Nnukwu	ukwuu	Nnekwu/nnukwu	Ukwu
3	Small/Little	Oberle	Nta	ọbele/oberle	ntakịrị
4	Male	nwoke/oke	ikom/oke	Nwoke	Nwoke/oke
5	Female	nwanyị	Inyom/nwanyị	Nwanyị/nwanya	nwanyị
6	Elder	Okoha	ochie-ochie	okenye/ichie	Okenye
7	Child	nwata, nwatakịrlị	nwanta	nwata, nwatakịlị, nwatakịrlị	nwata/nwatakịrị
8	Children	ụmụazị	ụmụrịma	ụmụaka	ụmụazhị
9	Body	ahụ	Azị	Arụ	ahụ
10	Land	Ana	Ala	Anị/Ana	Ala
11	Shrine, Temple	arlụsị	arụsị	alụsị, arlụsị	arushị
12	Afternoon	Ukorli	Ukori	efifie, evivie	Ehihie
13	Morning	ụtụtụ	ụtụtụ	ụtụtụ	ụkụtụ
14	Night	Abani	Abani	Anyasi	abali, anyashi
15	Patron Deity of Trade	ịnyamahịa	ịnyamavịa	NA	NA
16	To Waste, to Eliminate	mmewhu/imewhu	mmevu/imevu	mmefu/mmewhu	mmefu, nlalu
17	To Spoil	mmevwi	mmebi/mbibi	Mmebi	mmebi, mmeghi
18	To Oppress	mmewu	mmegbu	mmegbu	Mmegbu
19	Stone, Rock	Nkume	nkume	Okwute	Okwute
20	Money	Ego	ikpeghe/okpogho	Ego	Ego
21	Leg	ọkpa	ọkpa	Ukwu	ọkpa
22	Take	ngaa/werlụ	were	nnaa/welụ/werlụ	were
23	Ancestral Wand	ọwhọ	ọvọ	ọfọ, ọvọ, ọwhọ	ọfọ
24	House	uno	ụlọ	ụnọ	uluo, ulo
25	Welcome	nnọ/neekwaa	neekwaa	nnọ	ilọ/ilọla
26	Food	Nni	Ndi	Nni	Iri
27	Meat	anụ	anị	anụ	anụ
28	Here	ịbaa/nọọnwa	ịbaa, ebonwa/eb ọọwanani	ebaa/nọọnwa	Ngaa
29	There	ibeahụ	ibeọhụ/ibeohụnanị	Ebanwa	ebeahụ

(continued)

TABLE 4.3 (continued)

	English	Arọndizuogu	Arọchukwu	Nri – Awka	Preexisting Communities
30	Water	mmirli	Mmini	mmili/mmirli	Mmiri
31	Now	Ha	ugbue	ugbua/kịtaa	Ugbua
32	Then/ That Time	mgbeahụ	mgbeọhụ	ogeanwa/ ogeafụ	eshiahụ
33	When	Mgbe	mgbe	Oge/mgbe	Eshi
34	Friend	Enyi	Enyi	oyi/enyi	enyi
35	Play	egwu/ egwurlegwu	egwu/ egwuregwu	egwu/ egwuliegwu/ egwurliegwu	egwu/ egwuregwu
36	Dance	Egwu	Uri	Egwu	uri
37	Love, Likeness	ịwhụnaya	ịvụnanya	ịfụnanya/ ịwhụnaya	ịhụnaya
38	Work	ọrlụ	ọrụ	ọlụ/ọrlụ	ọrụ
39	No	Mba	ọdighi	Mba/waa	oolo
40	Hate	asị	Iro/asị	asị	ashị
41	War	Agha	Aha	Agha	agha
42	Sun	anyanwụ/ anwụ	anyanwụ/ anwụ	anyanwụ/ anwụ	anyanwụ/anwụ
43	Star	Kpakpando	kpakpandụ	Kpakpando	kpakpando
44	Moon/Lunar Month	ọnwa	ọnwa	ọnwa	ọnwa
45	Dry Season	okochi	okochi	okochi	okochi
46	Wet Season	Udummirli	udummiri	Udummili/ Udummirli	udummiri
47	Stomach	awhọ	Avọ	afọ/avọ/awhọ	afọ
48	Head	Isi	Isi	Isi	ishi
49	Leg	ọkpa	ọkpa	ụkwụ	ọkpa
50	Show	Gosi	Zi	Gosi	Zhi
51	Senerosity/gift	amarla	amara	Amala/ amarla	Amara
52	First Day in the Market Cycle	Eke	Eke	Eke	Eke
53	Second Day in the Market Cycle	Oye	Orie	Oye	Orie
54	third day in the market cycle	Awhọ	Avọ	Afọ/Avọ/ Awhọ	Afọ
55	Fourth Day in the Market Cycle	Nkwọ	Nkwọ	Nkwọ	Nkwọ

originate exclusively from Nri-Awka dialect(s). Arondizuogu developed twelve unique words and word forms. (Table 4.3).[39] Overwhelmingly, however, the version of the Nri-Awka dialect adopted by Arondizuogu is the one spoken by the people of eastern Nri-Awka, in the Ekwuluobia – Igbo-Ukwu – Nanka Area. Arondizuogu shares many words with preexisting groups, but this is not always the case with the pronunciations. People in the preexisting groups nasalize most of their sounds. The Arondizuogu pronunciation of the letter "r" is identical to that of preexisting communities and the communities of eastern Nri-Awka region, where the "r" rolls, as in Portuguese and Spanish "r" when it does not begin an Iberian word. Among the Arondizuogu and the communities of eastern Nri-Awka region, "r" takes the latter form in every case, while it varies among preexisting communities. The Arochukwu pronunciation always takes the regular "r" (as in English), identical to much of southern Igbo pronunciation.

Language mutation has continued since the establishment of Arondizuogu. The process and pattern of immigration that produced the frontier culture continued in the nineteenth century but were, of course, altered following the imposition of British colonialism very early in the twentieth century. As a result, there is often the possibility that, wherever the Arondizuogu word is unique, it is an archaic variant of the Nri-Awa, especially eastern Nri-Awka, and, rarely an archaic variant of Arochukwu word. Since colonial times, eastern Nri-Awka speech has come under the influence of western Nri-Awka dialect(s), especially Onitsha (Onicha). While the possibility of borrowing from archaic Arochukwu or preexisting dialects is there, it is by far less. As Arondizuogu people turned greater attention to new economic and political centers that emerged under the colonial and postcolonial political economies than they once did to Arochukwu, the Arondizuogu dialect moved much farther from that of Arochukwu during the twentieth century. In spite of the non-Aro influences on Arondizuogu dialect, however, "pure" Arochukwu dialect remained the one of wisdom and for philosophical reflections, to be invoked on appropriate occasions. The elderly population of Arondizuogu in the late twentieth century tended to switch to archaic Aro when they wanted to sound astute, cerebral, or to command respect. Despite the linguistic changes they encountered, the Aro diaspora still retained a special place in the language for the homeland dialect.

[39] Wherever there are two variants of an Arondizuogu word, I have placed the western Nri-Awka version first. When there is a northern Nri-Awka variant, the alternatives appear in the following order: western, northern, and eastern.

The scenario was different in one section of Arondizuogu. Ndiuche, one of the two lineage-groups that descended directly from Izuogu's own children, developed along separate cultural lines, in ways that this chapter has not captured. Although Ndiuche is contiguous to Arondizuogu territories, Ndiuche dialect today reflects a mixture of Arochukwu dialect and those of the preexisting societies. This situation is in turn a reflection of their history of alienation and separate development.

Although he was the eldest son to survive Izuogu, Uche was prevented from exercising his primogeniture right of inheriting the bulk of his father's estate and suzerainty over his dependents. Various versions of Arondizuogu traditions have sought to explain this anomaly. One version holds that Izuogu faced execution for the murder of a fellow Aro amadi but that the Arochukwu community was prepared to execute one of Izuogu's sons in lieu of his father. Uche lost his primogeniture rights after his mother failed to produce him to ransom Izuogu, and it was Awa's mother who presented her son instead. Luckily for Izuogu, the Arochukwu community had a change of heart and allowed Izuogu to present a slave instead. But because of the disloyalty of Uche and his mother, Izuogu named Awa as his inheritor (Igwilo 1996a; C. Okoli 1996). Another version claims that Uche lost his primogeniture rights because he refused to give the head of his mother Eriaba (Mpi) for the burial of Izuogu and that Awa gained such rights because he gave up his mother Egbocha. This tradition claims that it was customary for the first son to give up his mother for human sacrifice, and that Uche reneged on this obligation (J.G. Okoro 1996). Ndiuche tradition dismisses these versions, suggesting instead that Izuogu's well-established dependents and henchmen supported Awa over Uche as inheritor because Awa's mother, like them, came from the Nri-Awka region (J.G. Okoro; Jonas Uche 1996).

While the first story expressly claims that Izuogu decided in his lifetime that Awa would inherit his estate (Arodiogbu 1996; J.O. Dike 1996; M.S. Igwe 1996), the two other versions imply that the matter was decided after Izuogu's death. Only the first story seems plausible, even if it does not satisfactorily explain Awa's ascendancy. Aro law did indeed stipulate the execution of an amadi who murdered another amadi. What is unclear is how Izuogu apparently got himself a waiver. Even more problematic is the claim that Izuogu's dependents backed Awa because they shared affinity with Awa through his mother. There is no evidence to suggest that people from the greater Nri-Awka felt a particular affinity with a person from Umuchu, the natal home of Awa's mother. In spite of Izuogu's marriage to a woman from Umuchu, Arondizuogu did not see this society as an integral part of Nri-Awka; instead they deemed it to have had a close affinity with other preexisting groups from whom Arondizuogu did not usually draw dependents. The most problematic version is the one that claims that the head of Izuogu's wife was needed for Izuogu's burial. If such a request was made, it must have been without precedent, and there is no evidence – not even a claim – that anybody after Awa was required to sacrifice his mother for the burial of his father. Although Oldendorp was told by his American-based Igbo respondents in the 1760s that in an unspecified part of Igboland "with every notable man who died his first wife and various servants were buried with him, to serve him in the other world," no such custom has been uncovered in Arochukwu or any other Aro community (see Oldendorp 2000: ms. 468). Possible explanations for Awa's supersession of Uche include that Izuogu may have had special affection for Awa; Awa had the personal qualities and ability to rally Izuogu's dependents to his cause, and then they rationalized the unusual development to legitimate Awa's authority; Or, as explored below, that Awa's mother, Egbocha, was the principal influence in inheritance dispute.

This development had enduring implications for the settlement. First, it demonstrates the great influence of ex-slaves from the Nri-Awka region in shaping the course and structure of Arondizuogu geopolitics. Second, the exceptional power that one of these dependents, Iheme, and his descendants came to acquire in the Arondizuogu politics seems to have originated in his role in Awa's emergence as Izuogu's heir. If any Izuogu dependent was predisposed to support Awa, as the Ndiuche claim, it would have been Iheme. Unlike other dependents, who were acquired directly by Izuogu, Iheme is said to have come into Izuogu society as the dependent of Awa's mother, Egbocha. Indeed, Iheme's full name is claimed to be Ihemenedim, meaning, "let my husband be safe," and was given to him when Egbocha transferred Iheme to her husband Izuogu. Egbocha could have influenced Iheme to support young Awa in his dispute with Uche. In all likelihood, Iheme came to influence the victorious Awa more than any other dependent of Izuogu because of this special relationship. Another indication of Iheme's critical role in this development and the influence he gained from it is that Iheme and his descendants – as opposed to Awa and his descendants, who were the inheritors of Izuogu's estate – came to occupy the Eke Obinikpa region where Arondizuogu had settled originally, Ndiawa. It seems that Ndiawa did indeed settle in this location at one point. One rivulet at the north end of the Eke Obinikpa market is named after Ndiawa (*Mmiri*

Ndiawa, meaning "Ndiawa water"), suggesting that Ndiawa was specifically located by it at some point. Today, that rivulet marks the boundary between two Ndi-Iheme lineage-groups. It is otherwise odd that the rivulet should bear this name, which it retains to the present day. The reason for this seeming abrasion is unclear. It should be noted that Izuogu and his sons – who from all indications were minors when their father died – did not permanently settle at Arondizuogu. Izuogu operated from Arochukwu while his people were settled at Arondizuogu. It seems that Ndiawa later secured their current space about sixteen kilometers to the east with the help of Ndi-Iheme and other loyal lineage-groups. The apparent oddity of Ndiawa being many kilometers away from *Ndiawa Water* has escaped the attention of local historians, and its implications have thus been left unexplored until this book. Yet, this tiny and otherwise insignificant rivulet bears loud witness to a crucial power shift in Arondizuogu history. The rise to prominence of Iheme from a lowly to the most powerful dependent and the triumph of Awa over Uche illustrate the power and influence that Aro women wielded in shaping power structures and outcomes of political disputes. Much of the power Iheme came to wield derived from his relationship with Izuogu's wife Egbocha, whose dependent he was.

In spite of their alienation, Ndiuche developed along similar lines to the rest of Arondizuogu. Just as Arondizuogu people overwhelmingly married women, acquired slaves, and welcomed immigrants from the Nri-Awka area, Ndiuche's populations derived mainly from preexisting communities. Ndiuche went as far as incorporating preexisting groups, such as Umuago, unlike the rest of Arondizuogu. In part, the Ndiuche's focus on establishing relationships with and incorporating preexisting groups reflected its inability to compete with Arondizuogu for trade with the densely populated communities of the Nri-Awka region. On the other hand, Ndiuche may have developed a bias against persons from that area, given the indictment that Ndiuche traditions heap upon them for Ndiuche's marginalization in Arondizuogu. The lineage-group also assimilated mercenaries who had come to the society with their families. Today, Ndiuche, along with the two settlements formed by the later-arriving descendants of Izuogu's half-brothers, Ndinjoku and Ndi-Imoko, is essentially an integral part of Arondizuogu. At the same time, Ndiuche maintained kinship ties with the preexisting society from which Uche's mother had been drawn in the eighteenth century. These ties seem to have been made even stronger as a result of Ndiuche's alienation from the rest of Arondizuogu. This chapter has not captured the cultural developments

Culture Formation in the Trading Frontier

of these late arrivals, who came to the area in c. 1850s and c. 1860s, respectively, but it should be noted that, in spite of their incorporation of significant numbers of non-Aro, their dialects are closer to the dialect of Arochukwu than to Arondizuogu. They must have found the multicultural character of Arondizuogu remarkable.[40]

CONCLUSIONS

Far from severing regular ties with the Arochukwu metropole from the onset, the Aro diaspora settlements and the metropole were linked, and this linkage can only be understood as a historical process. One must separate earlier periods from later ones, when host and immigrant cultures (and in the twentieth century, colonial, capitalist, and Christian presence) had made their marks on the diaspora settlements. Aro diaspora perceptions of the settlements in the mid-eighteenth century had changed somewhat in the mid-twentieth century when Kanu Umo remarked that: "Ndizuogu settlers are naturalized or, in other words have become planted in the settlement that the average medial Settler (sic) is not very much interested in home Aro and her ways" (Umo n.d.:21). Still, the severance of relations had not even by the mid-twentieth century gone as far as is claimed in the recent literature for much earlier periods (e.g., Northrup 1978). As Umo himself – despite his synchronic tendencies – points out for the first half of the twentieth century, "an infinitestimal minority in cursory comparison with the block population, are being deadly concerned with home affairs. During the '*Ikeji*' annual festival some outside settlers ... usually go home to enjoy the '*Ekpe*' and '*Ayanma*' displays" (Umo n.d.:22). When these pan-Aro observances are considered together, it is clear that the Aro maintained what one can call a system. In this way, they differed from the Hausa diaspora in mid-1960s Ibadan, which apparently did not feel the pull of home. Many new migrants into the Hausa diaspora came to look for a relative who had left and never visited home (A. Cohen 1969:39–42). The far greater geographic range of the Hausa diaspora was, of course, a major reason for their less frequent trips to their homeland. Although many Aro, to a lesser degree, also did not opt to return home permanently, they nevertheless always retained that option, were always welcome back in Arochukwu, and often maintained dual residences. The examination of Aro organization as a trade diaspora explains

---

[40] In an implied comparison with Arondizuogu, Thomas Okereke of Ndi-Imoko told me early in 1996: Ndi-Imoko "tradition and customs are purely Aro" (T. Okereke 1996).

the ways by which cultural processes, commercial politics, and institutional change shaped the Biafra Atlantic trade, and vice versa, during the era of Aro expansion. As an increasing number of captives came to be retained in the region, the Aro diaspora facilitated the process by which some captives were sent overseas and others retained within the region, illustrating the interaction between the overseas slave trade and slavery within the Bight of Biafra. This process is the subject of Chapter 5.

5

Household and Market Persons
Deportees and Society, c. 1740–c. 1850

The rise of the Atlantic slave trade increased not only the number of captives exported to the Americas but also the number who were retained in the region. The increasing importance of slave use in African political economies during the Atlantic slave trade era had implications for the trade in quite material terms: it implied a relationship between indigenous slavery and the Atlantic slave trade, which raises two inversely related central questions about Aro political economy. Why did the Aro retain people when the trade in people was the basis of their wealth and power? And why did the Aro and other slaveholders sell people when their social organization was based on group expansion?

In the Angolan case, Joseph Miller has asked and persuasively answered the second question. According to him, West-Central African entrepreneurs, who calculated their advantages based on the number of dependents that remained with them and the degree of their dependency, became slave traders reluctantly. They released "a portion of their hard-won dependents" to Euro-American slave traders as a last resort in order to acquire the imported goods that were necessary to attract dependents, even if the foreign slave traders came across as agents of a bad spirit and harbingers of death for those they took with them (Miller 1988:40, 105). Biafran entrepreneurs shared with their West-Central African counterparts a tendency to retain large numbers of dependents, especially from the mid-eighteenth century onward, but unlike the West-Central African entrepreneurs, they neither intended nor hoped to retain all the captives that came into their possession; instead, the Biafran entrepreneurs – particularly professional Aro and coastal traders – had by the mid-eighteenth century often come make a sharp distinction between captives they intended to keep and those they intended to sell.

Notwithstanding the existence of specialist slave traders who sought profit in every transaction, some people were destined for the overseas market, not because of the proceeds that accrued from their sale, but for the simple reason that their natal communities wanted to get rid of them. Thus the trade complied with, not only economic and political imperatives and choices, but also social, cultural, and ideological ones. The slave question involved the pecuniary choice between selling people for material proceeds or retaining them for labor purposes; the juridical choice of imposing enslavement or another form of punishment; the social and ideological choice of whom to sell and whom to retain; and the cultural choice of which group or gender to incorporate and which to sell. For better or for worse, some indigenous people had the power to make these choices and exercised it over others, leaving an imprint on the composition of the export captives. Slave traders, who were often slave owners as well, mediated these transactions. Just as Euro-American planters gave shopping lists of preferred captives to slavers' captains, slave owners and prospective slave owners in Biafra had "mental models" of good and bad captives. Slavery's special function of group expansion makes the Aro case especially provocative. Local Aro literature and, particularly, the traditions acknowledge that slavers had predetermined destinations for the victims. Equally important, the circumstances of a captive's enslavement figured prominently in their choices of whom to retain and whom to send into Atlantic slavery.

The circumstances of enslavement have thus far figured little into discussions about the structure of the Atlantic slave trade, where any attempts have been made at all to analyze these circumstances. The scholarship has relied almost exclusively on export-captive samples for evidence. The sample most often cited comprises Africans whom the British Anti-Slavery Squadron rescued and resettled in Sierra Leone and who were interviewed by the German-born missionary linguist Sigmund Koelle of the CMS in the late 1840s or early 1850s. As analyzed by historian Paul Hair, the overwhelming majority of captives in this sample were enslaved through warfare or kidnapping[1]. The recently released collection of Oldendorp's diaries suggest that the dynamics had not changed

---

[1] Hair (1965:196–97). The sample is from Koelle (1963).

much since the second half of the eighteenth century (Oldendorp 2000). Although scholars have relied heavily on the Kolle sample, as they will likely now also rely on the Oldendorp data, both sources actually tell us only about those captives who were exported to the Americas during the respective periods; they do not necessarily offer great insights into the general nature of slaving in Atlantic Africa. To rely on such data in assessing the general character of slaving in Africa is to ignore the bias inherent in them and to assume that hinterland slave users did not discriminate between the people they retained and those they sold away. It is also unclear how much can be extrapolated from the general Atlantic-African information to explain the situation in the Bight of Biafra. We must therefore analyze these sources in conjunction with the pertinent ethnographic evidence and historical evidence from the Bight of Biafra.

The nature and scope of Aro operations permit the use of evidence from across the region to understand the means of enslavement. In outline, the slave systems of the Aro and coastal city-states were similar, and both differed from the systems found in most parts of the Biafra hinterland. This distinction has been made clear in the Aro case, where slavery emphasized incorporation based on acculturation and accumulation. "In contrast, Igbo and Ibibio patrilineages and village heads continued to be ascriptively filled and were respected not because of achieved position but as the link between the villages and ancestral spirit" (K.O. Dike and Ekejiuba 1990:209). Nonetheless, the rest of the Igbo and Ibibio groups do not seem to have become significant holders of slaves until after the suppression of the Atlantic slave trade in the nineteenth century.

Two further reasons justify the emphasis on the Aro and the coastal states instead of other groups in the region. First, slavery existed among the Aro in the heyday of the Atlantic slave trade. Second, the incorporative nature of these systems warranted the careful selection of household persons (domestic slaves), which impinged on the composition of captives for export overseas. The preferences of indigenous slave users and the way modes of enslavement influenced these preferences determined the composition of slavery on both sides of the Atlantic and thus throw light on slavery in both regions. As historian Herbert Klein has noted, "since African slavery was quite dissimilar from the American chattel plantation variety, its demands for slaves were quite distinct as well" (H. Klein 1978:241).

It is appropriate to begin by distinguishing between the household and market categories of captives. Understanding the meaning of the term *slave* in its historical context clarifies our understanding of why people wanted to keep enslaved persons in the household. In the postslavery era, this approach also seeks the original meanings of approximate African terms, which seem to have changed, at least in Igboland, from what they were in the days of slavery. Such changes in meaning are common to slavery, not only in Igboland but elsewhere. The metamorphosis of the meaning of slavery in the Western world has influenced present-day conceptions of slavery as well. In classical Latin, the word was *servitus*, but because slaves came to be mainly slaves from the Caucasus, the reference metamorphosed to *sclavus*, or "slave" in English beginning in the ninth century. It was in plantation America during the seventeenth century that the term "slave" came to refer to a person without rights.[2] Because of the differences between American plantation slavery and African slavery, on the one hand, and differences between African slave systems on the other, Igor Kopytoff and Suzanne Miers have recommended the use of local vernacular terms in characterizing slavery in African societies (Kopytoff and Miers 1977). In spite of the heuristic value of this idea, local terms might serve either to obfuscate kinship idioms designed to whitewash slavery or to convey a sense that the master class had more power over slaves than the reality would suggest. In this manner, a local term might function as an ideological tool for controlling the slave population. The Igbo term *ohu* usually equated with slave, referred to inferiority or inauthentic status. It hardly referred to a person without rights. Yet, postslavery era descendants of the master class have used ohu to mean a person without rights when it has been politically advantageous to do so. How do we find a term that captures a historical relationship?

Choosing a label is complicated, but it does provide an opportunity to offer a much-needed corrective in the conception of ideology of slavery in African studies. Anthropologist Jack Goody suggests a distinction between "the label 'slave' (or its local equivalent) as a statement of origin and as a statement about present status. ... We can best understand the problem if we think of the double meaning that occurs in our use of labels for nationality or classes; sometimes we refer to origin; sometimes to present position, though less confusion arises when we know the context" (Goody 1980:16). In Aro slavery, we have not just double, but triple, meaning – acknowledgment of present reality, denial of present reality, and essentialization of past reality. The term "slave" acknowledges reality when the real slave is referred to as slave; it denies present reality when the slave is glorified as kin; and essentializes past reality when one group

---

[2] Curtin (1971a:81–82; 1990:29); Davidson (1971:61–62).

labels as slaves people of slave origin who are no longer slaves. Because colonial reports tended to focus on the slave – versus-free differentiation, modern scholars of slavery in Africa have tended to dismiss the contrary indications that are found in the oral traditions as strands of apologist ideology. Ironically, however, those who stress the prevalence of a more rigid regimen claim that colonial reports whitewashed slavery and utilized information that was collected when the institution was already in decline. This view that the ideology of slavery promotes the kinship idiom is one-sided; the ideology of slavery does more than simply give a benign veneer to a harsh system, by, for example, attempting to essentialize slavery where masters' control over slaves was tenuous or where slavery had effectively ended. When early ethnographers and modern scholars talk about a "slave" owning a slave, they may actually be referring to a former slave owning a slave. A broader view of ideology allows us to transcend the mainstream ideology of slavery, which essentializes slavery with regard to people who were no longer slaves. Contrary to the prevailing tendency in African studies to see only the side of dominant ideology that expressed the kinship idiom that was used to whitewash slavery, charter groups often denied kinship and free status to *previously* enslaved groups, after they had earned full citizenship status, or after the charter groups had lost their ability to enforce the servile subordination of the ex-slaves. Rather than simply deemphasizing the oppressive character of slavery, colonial reports sometimes also ignored or understated "the degree of assimilation which wealth or the kinship idiom could produce" (Northrup 1981:118–19). The key parameters that figured in the consideration of who became a household or a market person throw light on indigenous slavery and its relationship with the overseas human traffic.

HOUSEHOLD AND MARKET TYPES

A "person of the household" meant more than simply a person of the house or a house slave or domestic slave. The household was the unit of production and the locus of exchange and trade. It incorporated the nuclear family, the polygynous family, and other persons or families, who could be slaves, refugees, long-term guests, or clients. Most importantly, a person of the household did not need to live within the spatial confines of the household. He or she could live in separate or outlying compounds within the same community or away in noncontiguous settlements or distant diaspora communities. A rite of passage marked the conversion of an outsider – including a slave – into a person of the household. The cornerstone of this ritual was an invocation for the multiplication of household members. By contrast, market persons were treated like commodities or, otherwise, as something that must be dispensed with. In spite of his more favorable placing, a person of the household could be killed or, as more often happened, resold if he was lazy, rebellious, or committed any malfeasance, according to accounts of nineteenth-century Aro and coastal city-states (Uku 1993:19, Waddell 1970:318–21). Novelist Buchi Emecheta's lucid portrayal of early-twentieth-century Igbo slavery – that the best chance for a person of the household was to be "docile and trouble-free" – also reflected the nineteenth-century situation (Emecheta 1977:63). A household person that satisfied these conditions was not sold merely because the price was right. It was in the interest of the master or mistress to treat the household person humanely. Oppressed slaves often ran to other masters, usually in rival communities, who were glad to have them. This kind of situation routinely "produced winners and losers of people" (Martina Ike 1996b). Rather than maximizing profits, the sale of a household person served immediate needs – when it happened at all. As will be clarified in the following pages of this chapter, the nature of these transactions warranted that buyers understood both the circumstances leading to a sale and the attributes of individual captives. These circumstances and attributes modulated an indigenous user's choice to retain a particular person or sell him into Atlantic slavery. Decisions about captives' fates were often a function of established criteria, principally the captives' skills, region of origin, and means of enslavement.

PREFERENCES I: SKILLS

The incorporation of skilled outsiders was important in Aro society. There is some evidence that the Aro began to do this during their formation in the early seventeenth century. Other Igbo evidence shows the continuing importance of craftsmen. Oral traditions inform us that the upper Imo River Aro settlement Arondizuogu harbored skilled dissidents from non-Aro societies and other skilled immigrants during the eighteenth and nineteenth centuries.[3] One of my Arondizuogu respondents, in 1996, referred to such acquisitions and showed me some apparently slave-produced archaic works of art, including a special war drum called

---

[3] See Dike and Ekejiuba (1990:58; 73), C. Iroh (1991); O. Mgbemena (1991); Okorie (1991); O. Udensi (1991); T.O. Okereke (1996); J.E. Uche (1996) for the Aro, and Equiano (1995:42–43) and Uchendu (1977:123) for Igboland.

Ikperikpe and some religious icons dating to about the mid-nineteenth century (Igwilo 1996a, 1996b). Another source of information indicating the deliberate retention of skilled captives comes from the home of the nineteenth-century Arochukwu merchant-warrior Okoroji, which has been a Nigerian national monument since 1972. The custodian of this structure, Emmanuel Okoroji, a descendant of the merchant warrior and Eze-Ogo (king) of the Ujari lineage-group in Arochukwu told me in 1996 that one of the platforms in the building was used for questioning new captives about their occupation (Okoroji 1996). If, for instance, a captive was a skilled or talented hunter, he was retained and given a gun and shown a gaming domain. The animal skulls contributed by the enslaved hunters hung from the building's ceiling in neat symmetries, according to animal species. This finding parallels an account from Dahomey wherein, as in the Aro case, the direct evidence comes from the nineteenth century, but family genealogies suggest that the phenomenon of slave dealers retaining captives who were highly skilled in craft or specially talented in artistic performance goes back further – to the heyday of the Atlantic slave trade. The families concerned retained their skills and peculiar dance forms into the twentieth century (see Adandé 1997). Given the tendency of the African slave-owning elites to retain skilled artisans and talented artists, it is plausible that a greater proportion of these categories of captives were retained than were exported, at least in the bight of Biafra and Dahomey.

PREFERENCES 2: REGIONAL

Region played no less a role than skills in determining the fate of a captive. Based on positive stereotypes, indigenous slave holders preferred captives from certain sections of the region to others. Again, the evidence of this is clearest among the Aro. For reasons explicated in Chapter 4, the Aro had an ongoing interest in cultivating persons from the Nri-Awka region. This means that even when every other factor that could determine the fate of a captive was taken into consideration, a captive from outside the Nri-Awka region was more likely to end in the market than an Nri-Awka counterpart. Aro preference for Nri-Awka people went beyond captives. In fact, the Aro, especially the diaspora in central Igboland, incorporated huge numbers of Nri-Awka people as refugees and voluntary immigrant[s], and seldom incorporated non-Nri-Awka for these purposes. This process gained momentum in the mid-eighteenth century, following the foundation of the major

Aro settlements in central Igboland at the southeastern edge of the Nri-Awka region.

An analysis of the regional patterns of the Aro incorporation of outsiders and the sub-ethnic composition of the captives exported to the Americas indicate that Aro preferences affected the composition of captives exported from the Bight of Biafra. Such an indication emerges from a detailed study of the sub-ethnic composition of the Aro diaspora within the Bight of Biafra. The Aro preference for Nri-Awka seems to have been established early in the history of the Aro diaspora settlements of central Igboland. Of the three principal dependents of Izuogu, the founder of Arondizuogu, only one, Iheme, came from the Nri-Awka region. By contrast, the Nri-Awka group provided the progenitors of virtually all the later lineage-groups formed from about 1770 onward – seven out of nine, or 78 percent (Table 4.2). Even when incorporated groups did not originate in the Nri-Awka area, they followed the tradition of acquiring people from Nri-Awka region as slaves, clients, wives, and guest immigrants. This was also true of other Aro settlements in the vicinity of the Nri-Awka region, whether their founders were originally Aro or non-Aro. It is therefore not accurate to suggest, as has been done recently, that the Aro took care to incorporate slaves from faraway areas rather than areas in close proximity.[4] While it was essential to enslave deportees, such as dissidents, other "trouble makers," and kidnaping victims, in communities far from their natal homes, the Aro did not draw most of the people they enslaved from faraway. The Aro settlements in the Igbo heartland drew an overwhelming majority of their slaves from a 70-kilometer perimeter to their west and northwest. People from this region, even when they were slaves, maintained kinship ties with the people they had left behind in their natal homes. In fact, men of slave origin often obtained spouses from the communities in which they themselves originated.[5] Although it has become an orthodoxy in African slave studies, the idea that slaves were of necessity procured from far away ultimately derives from observations of slave systems elsewhere. Thus, the Aro pattern controverts the widespread view that kinlessness was a necessary condition for slavery.[6]

It appears that from the mid-eighteenth century onward, the sub-ethnic composition of the outsiders incorporated into Aro society differed from

---

[4] For the suggestion that the Aro deliberately incorporated people from far away places, see Dike and Ekejiuba (1990:74).

[5] Igwegbe (1962:12); Dike and Ekejiuba (1990:206); Kanu-Igbo (1996).

[6] The most forceful idea statement about kinlessness as a necessary condition of slavery is perhaps in Moses Finley (1968:308–09).

the composition of the captives the Bight of Biafra sent to the Americas. While captives from the Nri-Awka region dominated the enslaved Igbo population in the Americas up to the early eighteenth century (Chapter 3), their numbers had declined substantially by the nineteenth century. The sub-ethnic breakdown of the Sierra Leone sample makes this point. The sample is small, but, significantly, none of the five Igbo respondents comes from the Nri-Awka region, and only one of the fifteen Igbo "countries" represented in Sierra Leone, "Mudioka" (Umudioka), falls in within the Nri-Awka area (the present Anambra State), a region of sixty odd claus or towns.[7] Even then, it is equally possible that this was another Umudioka, the one located outside of the Nri-Awka area, near Orlu. Most of the Sierra Leone Igbo respondents have been traced to Isuama in south-central Igboland (including the Orlu area) and Agbaja in present Enugu State in northern Igboland.[8] Although we have little information about the sub-ethnic composition of Igbo captives sent to the Americas during the second half of the eighteenth century, the massive Aro incorporation of Nri-Awka people suggests that it was likely to have been closer to the nineteenth-century pattern in which captives from the Nri-Awka region accounted for a relatively small proportion of those exported. While this dimension of the geography of regional slaving calls out for further research, it is reasonable to hypothesize that Aro expansion and the concomitant rise of the Biafra Atlantic slave trade corresponded with increasing proportions of southern Igbo people and declining proportions of Nri-Awka people arriving the Americas from the mid-eighteenth century onward.

OTHER PREFERENCES

Social and religious taboos also affected preferences. Individuals categorized as abnormal were likely exported overseas, as long as their abnormalities would not discourage Euro-American buyers. As many of those who were deemed abnormal in the Bight of Biafra would have passed Euro-American standards of normality when measured principally in labor worth and potential, the presence of the Aro in the region made it easier

---

[7] This evidence is from Koelle (1963:8).
[8] Northrup 1978b:62; Oriji 1981:318. Among these subgroups, Isuama is the reference least used in the twentieth and twenty-first centuries was the most populous and it was actually a cluster of several major Igbo subgroups, such as Mba-Ano, Mbanasaa, Mbaise, Orlu area (including Nkwere) and the Owerri area. It is home to virtually all the autochtonous Igbo communities. For an outline of Isuama's boundaries, see Ojiaku (2008:5).

for the other communities to dispose of certain categories of individuals who would otherwise have been killed or consigned to the "bad bush." "Before the arrival of the Aro[,] people who committed 'abomination', eg, possessed 6 fingers, were twins, girls who menstruated prematurely, children with extra teeth or [who] cut the upper teeth first were thrown into the bad bush. With the Aro, they became merchandize."[9] Although the Aro adopted many individuals who fell into these categories, they would have shipped the vast majority of them to the Americas. It is unlikely that Aro communities could have absorbed the large numbers of people who had been routinely consigned to a state of abnormality by the societies of the region. Even physically deformed captives sometimes found their way to slave ships. Of the 67,000 captives freed from Americas-bound vessels intercepted by the British navy between 1819 and 1850, thirty-one were identified as physically disabled. Unfortunately, we cannot draw major conclusions from this small number, but it is notable that captives leaving Bight of Biafra ports accounted for as many as twenty-two of the thirty-one captives with disabilities, or 71 percent.

MEANS OF SLAVING I: WAR AND KIDNAPPING

Without question, therefore, warfare was an important source of captives everywhere. Warfare and other kinds of violence occurred with such a high during the slave trade era that they are said to have permanently changed the political sociology of Africa (Ekeh 1990). Euro-American slavers on the Biafra coast in the eighteenth century routinely told war stories. Between 1788 and 1790, a few slave traders admitted the importance of wars in generating captives when questioned by a British parliamentary committee that was investigating the slave trade. The most graphic account from Biafra comes from one Isaac Parker. A ship's mate, Parker had in 1765 deserted his cruel captain at Old Calabar, where he lived for five months with a local chieftain, Dick Ebro of New Town. Parker testified in 1790 that Dick Ebro organized routine captive raids on unsuspecting communities, in which Parker had participated (Parker 1790:126–27). Wars remained an important source of captives until the end of the overseas slave trade in the mid-nineteenth century, according to the accounts of contemporary British visitors and African missionaries (Laird and Oldfield 1837:106; Crowther and Taylor 1859). As will be

---

[9] Meek (1937:31, 224–25); Goodlife (1952:6); Onyiukah (1983:27). "Bad bush" refers to the sacred forest, which was never cut and into which repugnant items were thrown.

shown in Chapter 7, the Aro themselves fought wars in many parts of the region up to the end of the nineteenth century, as opposed to simply relying on the Cross River Igbo warrior groups, contrary to what scholars have thought until the present study (see especially K.O. Dike and Ekejiuba 1990:161–95).

But a comparison of the Bight of Biafra with other regions shows that wars had differential impact on the composition of captives. In the Gold and Slave Coasts, where the evolution of professional armies has been analyzed, states also employed raiders by the seventeenth century. William Bosman reported that "Prisoners and Ornaments of Gold" formed the booty there. By the eighteenth century, captives became the region's principal export. Although wars did not always primarily aim to capture people, captives taken in war accounted for the single largest category of the captives sold into the Atlantic market. These captives would have been mostly combatants in regions that supplied mostly females and children to the Saharan and domestic markets. The same was true for the Upper Guinea Coast and eighteenth-century West Central Africa.[10] War captives were always likely to be exported, and even militarized states tended to send prisoners of war into the external slave trade.

For its part, kidnapping was so widespread and obvious that slave-ship surgeon Alexander Falconbridge thought, in 1788, that most captives from Africa entered the slave trade in this way (Falconbridge 1788:13). Kidnapping was common enough; Igbo victims in Sierra Leone and at least two New World locations recorded their ordeals (Equiano 1995; Monteith 1966). The manner in which they were harried to the coast is akin to real life stories from oral traditions (e.g., E. Okoli 1996). The Igbo association of kidnapping with *panyaring*, a term used by European slave traders in the Bight of Biafra to describe seizure of person, often to recoup debts from their Biafra suppliers, points to the close relation between kidnapping and the Atlantic slave trade slave suppliers. Up to today, the word *panya* in Igbo folklore refers to forceful removal to the unknown.[11]

The pervasiveness of kidnapping evinces pressured social relations at the interpersonal and intergroup levels and highlights some of the contradictions of slave-trade-era Africa. Generally, reaction to kidnapping varied with the victim's relationship to the society. As among the

---

[10] Bosman (1705:182). For the Gold Coast, see Reynolds (1974:9–15); Kea (1982: ch. 4). For the Slave Coast, see Law (1992:103–26); and for Upper Guinea Coast, Thornton (1983:42, 45).

[11] For descriptions of *panyaring*, see Blake (1861:112); G. Williams (1897:584).

Diola of Senegambia, the people of the Bight of Biafra vehemently disapproved of the practice if the victim was an insider – usually conceived as a resident of a village or member of a lineage-group, or a person from another village or lineage-group closely related to them by blood, marriage, or occasionally, by historical friendships or alliances.[12] Among the Aro, the culprit (kidnapper) was either killed or sold away. The punishment was invariably more severe if the victim was an amadi. If at all, only extremely powerful persons might conceivably get away with kidnapping. The King of Old Calabar "was a partner with the manstealers of other countries, while punishing a manstealer with death in his own [country]." In the Bight of Biafra, as in the Diola case, people from other communities – in other words, outsiders – were often fair game.[13] In the Bight of Biafra, protagonists in internecine conflicts often sought to reduce the populations of rival units by kidnapping and selling off the members of those groups to the Aro (K.O. Dike and Ekejiuba 1990:248). Evidently conceptions of insider and outsider statuses promoted kidnapping.

The salience of warfare and kidnapping is further highlighted by the Oldendorp and Koelle data, but of which show the two processes as the dominant sources of enslavement. As broken down by Hair, the Koelle sample shows war captives to be the largest group making up 34 percent of all the exslaves Koelle interviewed, and captives who had been kidnapped came in a close second at 30 percent. Oldendorp found from the enslaved Africans in the Caribbean and North America, about whose mode of enslavement he gathered information in the second half of the eighteenth century, that the kidnapped victims were the largest single group among the African captives sent to the Americas, followed by war captives: "One can see from their own testimony that the slaves were for the most part guiltless and without issue taken by slave chasers and high[way] robbers, captured and sold to the European. Following these stolen people were those taken in war, as the majority of wars are actually just invasions for the simple purpose of capturing people ... Then come those who were either given as debt or were given as pawn

---

[12] For what it worth, Equiano recalled a case in which a man was arraigned for kidnapping a boy. "[A]lthough he was the son of a chief or senator, he was condemned to make recompense by a ... slave." Equiano (1995:35).

[13] See also Anyakoha (1996); J.O. Dike (1996); Kanu-Igbo (1996b); M.S. Igwe (1996); Igwilo (1996a); Maduadichie (1996); Muotoh (1996); E. Nwankwo (1996); E. Okoro (1996); J.G. Okoro (1996). For the Old Calabar case, see Waddell (1970:429). See Baum (1999:114–17) for the Diola case.

at some point but were never redeemed" (Oldendorp 2000: ms. 489). Oldendorp also reported that the enslavement of people in lieu of the death penalty was rare. Both the Oldendorp and the Koelle data show war and kidnapping to be the two most important sources of the captives they interviewed. But Oldendorp and Koelle differ on the relative importance of the two modes of enslavement, with Oldendorp assigning greater importance to kidnapping.

Can we then infer that kidnapping was the most important single source of enslavement among Atlantic-bound captives in the late eighteenth century, and wars the most important in the early nineteenth? This is quite possible. It could also mean that the greater importance of warfare in producing captives during the nineteenth century reflected the increased incidence of warfare during that century. If we factor in the greater exponential potential of incidents of war because of the relatively large numbers of captives usually involved, however, war captives may account for a greater share of the sample than the nominal figures suggest.

On the average, an incident of war or raiding was likely to yield more captives than an incident of kidnapping. On the one hand, Oldendorp referred to thirteen people who became captives in only twelve incidents of kidnapping. On the other, he referred to twenty-four who became captives in only fifteen incidents of war or raiding. Apart from this twenty-four captives, in five of the war/raiding incidents he described, Oldendorp makes references to unspecified numbers of "children," as well as "many," "many others," "several others," and "a number of others" captives, respectively, were also being taken. Oldendorp's interpretations of some incidents may differ from those of this writer. He notes, for example, the overlap between invasions and "slave chasers' robberies" and that they differed "only in regard to their method of catching people" (Oldendorp 2000: ms. 489). His conclusion was clearly informed more by his own ethnographic observations than the actual data he presented. This exponential factor and the lack of information about the destinations of the "many other" captives suggest that wars and raiding may have yielded more captives than can be derived from the information collected from individual captives in the Americas. The exponential factor also certainly underlines the importance of warfare as source of captives during the eighteenth century.

It would be a stretch to read too much from the few specific descriptions Oldendorp and Koelle give about captives from the Bight of Biafra, but the picture that emerges bucked the general African trends suggested by the data. Oldendorp's specific descriptions of captives from the Bight of Biafra seem to show a lower incidence of enslavement by warfare and kidnapping and a higher incidence of enslavement by indebtedness than appear to have been the African norm. For their part, Koelle's specific descriptions of ex-slaves from the Bight of Biafra reveal a higher incidence of enslavement by kidnapping and a lower incidence of enslavement by warfare than was the norm. Indeed, a face-value reading of this sample and of the experiences of certain individuals sent to New World slavery have led to an emphasis on kidnapping in explaining modes of enslavement in the Biafra hinterland. Yet, the data do not account for the individuals who were retained as slaves within the region.

To be useful in understanding enslavement as a whole, including the enslavement of those enslaved internally within the region, the export samples need to be "unpacked." The difference between Atlantic-bound captives and those retained in the region is crucial to this study. Indigenous slave users discriminated between whom they kept and whom they sold to Atlantic slavery. Accordingly, reliable conclusions on the general character of enslavement must incorporate the character of both export captives and of internal slavery. The composition of captives and means of enslavement were related. One respondent of Oldendorp from the coastal city state of Kalabari (New Calabar) told him that prisoners of war were sold, "who are then passed from one master to another in such a way that one of them might have half a hundred masters before being sold to the Europeans on the coast" (Oldendorp 1987: 167). That these captives passed through 50 masters being sold is most likely an exaggeration, but this testimony does suggest not simply that most captives were enslaved through warfare – which is how historians have interpreted the samples drawn from America-bound captives – but that the vast majority of war captives invariably ended in the Atlantic trade among the Kalabari. The limitations of the Oldendorp and Koelle sources include also the fact that they derived their data virtually exclusively from males. There is no reason to think that Oldendorp interviewed women, and only two of the 177 excaptives in Koelle's data were women.

Quite apart of the differential impact of warfare and kidnapping by regionn, the importance of both in slaving can be overemphasized. First, as historian John Thornton has reminded us, slave-trade-era African warfare is not reducible to slave capture or disputes directly related to the slave trade; Africans fought wars for myriad other reasons. Second,

Household and Market Persons

the role of warfare varied from region to region.[14] The Aro relied heavily on Cross River Igbo warrior groups to fight Aro wars, which were often reprisals against communities that had offended the Aro or resisted their trading overtures. Headhunting rather than slave-catching was the primary motivation of the warriors, and so warfare was not a major source of captives in the Bight of Biafra, although captives inevitably were taken.[15] In contrast to the Western Sudan, where warfare as a means of procuring captives was institutionalized, cutting human heads was an avenue for attaining full citizenship status and prestige within the warrior communities throughout the eighteenth and nineteenth centuries. The killing of war prisoners by the militarist states of Senegambia became widespread only following the decline of the Atlantic slave trade and as a security measure because they could no longer dispose of captives at Atlantic markets (Klein 1983:72; Meillassoux 1982:89, 90).

As common as kidnapping was during the slave trade era, however, it was, like warfare, less important for enslavement as a whole than the export samples suggest. The exclusive reliance on these samples in transatlantic scholarship tends to exaggerate the importance of kidnapping, but most regional specialists working with other evidence deemphasize it, which suggests that the means of enslavement were highly varied.[16] Kidnappers knew that they were often breaking the law and that the punishment for this was often harsh; they often had to carry their victims far away from the place of capture to prevent them from escaping and to avoid discovery. Kidnapping was a risky venture – riskier if the intended victim was a man, who was more likely to escape and expose the kidnapper's identity if known. An attempt to kidnap a man could result in the kidnapper himself being seized and sold. Children were easier to capture, subdue, confine, or to trick than adults. Logically, a lot of kidnapping efforts targeted children.[17] But one can deemphasize warfare and kidnapping without necessarily denying that "any of these sources was. ...

---

[14] For accounts showing that sale into Atlantic slavery was deemed extreme punishment, see Lovejoy (1983:56, 61, 68–78); Curtin (1990:37–38, 119); Thornton (1992:99, 110).

[15] This conclusion has been anticipated by K.O. Dike (1956:40); Northrup (1978b:65–69); Afigbo (1981a, 1981b).

[16] K.O. Dike (1956:40); Afigbo (1980:86; 1981a:21; 1981b:267); Ijoma (1986a); Dike and Ekejiuba (1990).

[17] In the late eighteenth century, Aniaso, or Archibald Monteith, was tricked by a young prospective suitor of his sister, who asked the unsuspecting ten-year-old boy to accompany him to the market, where Aniaso was sold into slavery (Monteith [1853] 1966: 30–31). Equiano also claims that kidnappers were themselves sold into slavery when caught (Equiano 1995:38).

disruptive to society," contrary to what one source has suggested.[18] The activities of Cross River Igbo warriors were disruptive enough, but they produced fewer captives than did warfare in which securing human heads was not the primary purpose of fighting. The capacity for disruptiveness and the capacity for generating captives are two different issues. It is equally important to note that even enslavers had an interest in law and order as well, no matter how imperfect and self-serving such interest may have been. The means by which a person became a captive was sometimes more important than his or her market value in determining where that person was sold.[19]

MEANS OF SLAVING 2: THE POLITICS OF LAW AND ORDER

The interaction of politics, economic practices, and legal and belief systems in African societies suggests that ideas of law and order would have been central in enslavement. Sale into Atlantic slavery was widely deemed an extreme form of punishment in Atlantic Africa, and so was – at least in theory – reserved for those who committed serious offenses or who challenged the existing political and social order.[20] Captain William Snelgrave's observation that "the Negroes ... dread foreign slavery above all things" sums it up. This dread was particularly acute in Biafra (Snelgrave 1730:506). The zeal and determination with which captives from the Bight of Biafra revolted and, especially, escaped captivity even by taking their own lives, often confounded their Euro-American captors. Asked pointedly by a British parliamentary committee in January 1790 whether captives from Calabar and Bonny "shew reluctance at being carried off the coast," Captain James Fraser, who had twenty years experience in the slave trade and had since 1772 been commanding ships to Biafra and Angola answered: "They shew more reluctance than the Angolan slaves. They are too often of the opinion that the White men intend to eat them" (Fraser 1790:34, 38). This is consistent with what Alexander Falconbridge, as a slaver's surgeon who made several trips to the African coast in the same period, reported (Falconbridge

---

[18] For such a suggestion, see Noah (1980:74–75).
[19] It nevertheless is unlikely that kidnapping was the predominant means of enslavement in the region as some scholars have maintained. See Isichei (1976:45–47); Northrup (1978b:77–80); Oriji (1987:161–63); Geggus (1989:40). For examples of kidnapping see Equiano (1995); Monteith (1853:29–52).
[20] Davidson (1971:65); Miller (1988:116, 128); Thornton (1991); Lovejoy (1994a); Bay (1997).

1788:30–32). At Old Calabar, captives dreaded being "sold over the great waters, or eaten at sea" (Waddell 1970:321). Until the 1840s, the Igbo still widely believed that the captives sold to the New World "were killed and eaten, and that their bodies were used to make red cloth" (Niger Expedition 1842:56). Equiano's mid-eighteenth century experience tallies with these assessments. Because "there was much dread and trembling ... and bitter cries" among Equiano and his fellow Biafra captives when they arrived in Barbados in 1756, the planters got experienced slaves to assure the newly arrived that they would not appear on the menu (Equiano 1995:57). If indeed Equiano did not witness this experience firsthand, as has been recently suggested, his account does at least indicate that this assessment was spreadwide among contemporary mariners. The members of the 1841 Niger Expedition made sure to inform King Osai of Abo in August 1841 that "wicked white men come and buy slaves; not to eat them as your people believe, but to work them harder than they can bear, by flogging and ill-using them" (Allen and Thomson 1848a:221).

Extreme fear of the Atlantic world, coupled with indigenous religious ideas, would likely have played a part in the well-known suicidal tendencies of New World–based enslaved Igbo. Igbo belief in transmigration was deep (Equiano 1995:41). Oldendorp writes that belief in the migration of souls and reincarnation by the Kalabari and "several other black nations," which would no doubt have included the Igbo, caused many a suicide in the West Indies on the part of enslaved Africans, who imagined resurrecting in their homelands (Oldendorp 1987: 199). William Baikie, who commanded the British Niger Expedition of 1854, reports from Abo that Igbo people believed "that after death, those who have been good on earth may either go to Orisa and abide with him, or they may, if they like, visit any country on earth; and so slaves often, when dying, say they will go and revisit their land; if, on the other hand a wicked man dies, it is understood that he is driven to *O'komo*."[21] Given that it was deemed a taboo in contemporary Igboland, this interpretation might well provide a clue on the appeal of suicide among the enslaved Igbo.

The idea that captives were to be eaten in the Americas probably took root in the early years of the slave trade when individuals who would normally have been put to death – because of still-limited use for them in the domestic economy – made up higher proportions of overseas-bound captives than they did in later years. The development of the

---

[21] Baikie (1856:312). *Oku muo* refers to hell.

slave trade into a well-established business and the corruption of African institutions for the sake of that traffic cheapened the standards of justice and decreased the proportion of hardcore criminals and other locally unwanted elements among captives sent to the Americas. While these captives continued to be routinely sent to the Americas, nonoffenders and individuals guilty of simple malfeasance came to preponderate. In spite of this change, early images of the Atlantic slave trade as the lot of dispensable elements died hard.

The Aro equated sale to the Atlantic market with being used for human sacrifice (see J.G. Okoro 1996). To "take away" (*mmevu*) was the idiom for sale into Atlantic slavery, invoked primarily in questions of intra-Aro social control.[22] One respondent captured this practice in a popular saying meant for the purpose: *Onye umunna ya si na o ye-eje, o ye-eje* (N.A. Anyakoha 1996). This statement literally translates as "he whose kinsmen have decided would embark on a journey must travel," meaning that if a person's kinsmen decided to sell a person, that person must be sold. But in the Bight of Biafra the practice of punishing people by selling them was not restricted to the Aro; it was widespread indeed. The Aro are, however, of interest, not simply because they sold off their own undesirables as well, but also because they mediated such transactions in the hinterland. Colonial anthropologists of the early twentieth century viewed the Aro as having performed the function of removing convicted persons.

Persistent troublemakers were not tolerated. The simple village code only permitted execution of thieves and witches: other minor offences were punished by the enforced payment of a fine or compensation to the victim. But if these penalties proved insufficient to control the more intransigent characters the ultimate punishment was to be sold into slavery, and the Aro "missionaries" waxed fat on these sales, whereby the villagers effectually disposed of their incorrigibles and the slave dealers profited by the transaction.[23]

Respondents from different parts of Igboland and Ibibioland attest to the practice of selling away "evil doers," "trouble makers," adulterers, criminals, or "stubborn children."[24] Among Koelle's Sierra Leone–based

---

[22] N.A. Anyakoha (1996); J.O. Dike (1996); Echemazi (1996); Kanu-Igbo (1996); Nwaokoye (1996); Ufere (1996).

[23] This quotation is from J.G.C. Allen (n.d.:149), but also see Grier (1922:35).

[24] E. Akpan (1972); L.U. Akpan (1972); Ebu (1972); J. Inokun (1972); S. Isangedighi, et al. (1973); U.U. Obong (1972); I.A. Odung (1972); A. Okori (1972); Russell (1972); J. Udo (1972); Udonyah (1972); D.K. Eshiet (1973); Ibok (1973); Wamuo (1973).

respondents was one Okon (or John Thomas, as they called him in Sierra Leone) from the Igbo warrior community of Ohafia, northwest of Arochukwu, who was sold at Bonny for adultery in about 1820. He was married to two women and had a ten-year-old child (Koelle 1963:8).[25] Apparently, whether adultery was deemed a criminal or a lesser offense depended on the status and gender of the perpetrator. It was unlikely that a wealthy man or some other member of the elite would be sold as punishment for committing adultery with the wife of a dependent or some other low-status woman. On the contrary, selling away was usually the fate of a man who committed adultery with the wife of a man of superior standing.

The judicial role of the Aro oracle, Ibiniukpabi, reinforced the Aro role as disposers of people who had been incriminated in their communities. As agents of the oracle, the Aro paraded themselves as harbingers of "peace" and "truth" who mediated disputes and disposed of "bad" people, even though their main interest was in the human traffic. Baikie recorded in 1854 that one unidentified informant had alone located up to twenty Ibiniukpabi victims in Cuba. Another informant had bumped into several in Sierra Leone (Baikie 1856:313). The role of the oracle in procuring captives seems to have been unique in the Biafra case, but while earlier studies portrayed the oracle as *the* major direct source of captives, recent studies have correctly deemphasized it.[26] The oracle nevertheless played an important role in dealing with dissidence and criminality. Faced with the choice between owning up to a crime and being sent to

---

[25] Although Koelle mentioned "Mbofia" instead of "Ohafia," there can be little doubt that he meant Ohafia. His location of Mbofia south of Ebiriba (Abiriba) is imprecise (Ohafia is located east of Abiriba, not south), but it is as close as a description can be without reference to maps. Even then, he correctly locates Ohafia east of Bende and roughly north of Otutu (Ututu). The fact that Okon spoke a language "similar to that of Aro" suggests Koelle meant to reference to Ohafia. The term "Mbofia" does not specific to any particular locale or community. It is a generic reference – meaning "bush country" – to the uncouth, badly behaved. The pronunciation of the term varied in dialectical areas. The variant "Mbofia" was used by the Cross River Igbo, exclusive of Arochukwu, and by northern Igbo, most of the Nri-Awka area, and the Niger riverine and west Niger communities. The Isuama area and southern Igboland pronounced it "Mbohia." The Aro and the Awka pronounced it "Mbovia." From all indications, however, the Aro do not refer as such to Ohafia, who were one of the most reliable allies of the Aro. Mbohia, as recorded by Baikie during 1854, lay "north or north-northwest of O'zuzu," which in turn lay northwest of Ngwa, close to Ogoni (Baikie 1856:309). Ozuzu was located northwest of Ngwa (p. 308); it would not have been close to Ogoni, which lies southeast of Ngwa, beyond the Ikwerre. "Ozuzu" is a term Koelle used to refer to yet another Igbo group in Sierra Leone. It is actually a community, west of Ngwa.
[26] Afigbo (1980:86; 1981b:267); Ijoma (1986a); Dike and Ekejiuba (1990).

be "eaten" overseas or denying and, therefore, risking being "eaten" by the oracle, the mental state of an accused or guilty person must have been one of extreme fear and anxiety. In spite of the profit that ultimately accrued to the Aro, the initial sale by the non-Aro to the Aro of captives in this category was not always the result of pecuniary considerations on the part of the sellers. In Ibibio communities, the handling of proceeds from such sales ranged from burial under a plantain tree (and, therefore, not used) to deposit in a common fund (see Ebu 1972; J. Inokun 1972; Udonyah 1972). In some Igbo communities, "those people who were not wanted, such as trouble makers, would be handed over to the Aro free of charge" (Mefo and Ibe 1972).

There was a thin line between criminality and dissidence. Both offenses often concerned men of prime age and resulted in their sale into the Atlantic market, but the procedures for adjudicating the offenses differed. Once an individual had been identified as a dissident, people who had been deemed competent to take such summary measures sold him immediately. In the case of a loser in a political contest, the victorious party did the selling. Such an action did not require elaborate consultations or ceremonies (see, e.g., Igwilo 1996a). "The Aro buyer came as a casual visitor to the house of the seller and both of them began to negotiate for the Aro's walking stick as if it was the article to be sold. When the price was settled, the person to be sold was called in and suddenly grabbed" (O. Okoroafor 1972). Similar tricks were employed in the open market (Igwilo 1996a; Okoli 1996). The procedure for adjudicating criminal cases was different. But while dissidents were sold summarily, persons convicted of a crime would first go through some form of legal procedure before competent authorities. Criminality included not only the commission of theft and murder but also witchcraft and adultery (see Akpabio 1936:47). Enforcement of criminal sanction was not always fair, especially when a suspect was an outsider. For instance, on August 9, 1786, the Old Calabar chiefs put on board a slaver one "gentleman" from neighboring Bakasi on the apparently baseless suspicion that he had killed their ruler, Duke Ephraim, presumably by witchcraft (Duke 1956:47, 98). In this case, the procedure for punishment for alleged criminality was the same as with dissidence.

Summary sale into the Atlantic market was also common in cases where a master no longer wanted a slave. Many of these resales had been enslaved internally at a more amenable age. Having been rejected, these captives had little chance of being retained in the region during the Atlantic slave trade era. It is evident from the diary entries of the prominent late-eighteenth-century Old Calabar merchant, Antera Duke, that one slave, named Toother, was earmarked for exportation. Toother was put on the Liverpool ship *Gascoyne*, captained by Peter Comberbach, that sailed from Old Calabar to Dominica on February 8, 1786.[27] Resale appears to be the most common punishment for slaves, at least among the Aro. In about 1805, an Igbo boy, Adibe (or George Rose, as he later became known in Sierra Leone) was kidnapped and sold. He lived with an Arochukwu master and spoke the Arochukwu dialect, but in 1826 his master sold him into Atlantic slavery. The British navy intercepted the Portuguese ship that was carrying him to the New World. Freed from captivity, Adibe told his story to Koelle in Sierra Leone.[28] There must have been strong reasons for his master to resell him *specifically* to the Portuguese at Bonny, as opposed to selling him to other Aro traders or to Bonny middlemen.

The practice of reselling insubordinate slaves to the Atlantic extended far into the hinterland. The story of a slave called Macaulay is similar to Adibe's. Macaulay had been born in Mamagi (Nufi) just south of the Niger-Benue confluence where, as a boy, he was "stolen by the Filatahs." His kidnappers sold him to a Muslim mallam at Egga, who sold him again to a Buddu woman. At some point, the woman's husband insisted that Macaulay be sold off. As in Adibe's case, there would have been compelling reasons for Macauly's mistress' husband to insist on the sale of Macauly. She sold him to the king of Abo, who soon resold him to King Pepple of Bonny, who in turn sold him to Spanish slavers, from whom he was rescued after the British captured their Americas-bound vessel (Allen and Thomson 1848b:118). In Bonny, recalcitrant slaves – who could include the likes of Toother, Adibe, and Macauly – were sold into New World slavery, even if they were hardworking (Hargreaves 1987:101, 108). This practice was indeed widespread within the Bight of Biafra.

Historian Walter Rodney's depiction of legal and religious power as the "greatest weapon in the hands of the African ruling class" underscores

---

[27] Duke (1956:43, 75, 94). Duke's diary has the ship as *Combesboch*, but a search of the DuBois Database strongly suggests that this is the *Gascoyne*, captained by Peter Comberbach. No ship in the database is named *Combesboch*. The spelling discrepancy between Comberbach and Combesboh is probably a mistaken reading of Duke's diary, which was originally handwritten by those who prepared the manuscript for printing.

[28] Koelle (1963:8). Most of my Aro respondents, at least, implied that resale was common.

the importance of the judicial process in generating captives (Rodney 1967:10). Eighteenth-century European observers reported that a conviction on trumped-up charges led to the sale of many captives. This pattern, apparent in many other parts of Africa, also held in the Bight of Biafra (see e.g., Blake 1861:113, 114–15, 118). If the Atlantic slave trade served African rulers as an avenue for punishing offenders, it also served as a way of getting rid of political enemies at little or no cost (Curtin 1990:119, 120; 1993:177). In the Bight of Biafra, many victims of the slave trade were known dissidents in their communities. The practice of sending dissidents into the Atlantic slave trade was distinct in the Bight of Biafra, according to two Liverpool ship's masters, Captains John Adams and Hugh Crow, both of whom specialized in the Biafra trade in the late eighteenth and early nineteenth centuries. They both identify a group of high-born Igbo whose members were regularly sent into the overseas traffic, despite their tendency to revolt and to incite revolt, and the ships' masters' aversion to taking them aboard.[29] This category of captives were the victims of what has been described as the Aro power of "removing any one opposing or 'even desirous of opposing' [Aro] authority" (Steel 1908:7). The summary nature of dealing with dissidence suggests that political deportees would have made up large number of the captives exported to the Americas from the Bight of Biafra.

Common people may have feared that deportation to the Americas put them into the hands of voracious cannibals, but merchants and other prominent individuals who regularly sent people into Atlantic slavery were sufficiently informed about what happened to captives in the New World. By the 1720s, the ruling groups of Dahomey were sending into overseas slavery convicts who had been sentenced to capital punishment in the 1680s (Law 1991b:184). The ruling groups viewed the sale into Atlantic slavery as a punishment worse than execution, which was reserved for the bitterest rivals of the princes who triumphed in struggles for succession (Bay 1997a). Unlike in Dahomey and Senegambia, where people traveled forth and back to the Americas, better informing the local populations about conditions there, the Bight of Biafra seems to have lacked a significant number of resident European traders and African

---

[29] Captain John Adams, who carried captives from the Bight of Biafra between 1786 and 1800, noticed "a class of Heebos [whom] masters of slave-ships have always had a strong aversion to purchase." These captives had enjoyed an "exalted rank ... in their own country" (Crow 1830:199; Adams 1832:41). These were *ozo* men, holders of the highest social rank in the Nri-Awka area.

returnees from America. Information about the outside world nevertheless did reach the Bight of Biafra.[30] For instance, the early-nineteenth-century Muslim jihadist of the Sokoto Caliphate, Mohammed Bello, discussed the characteristics of individual European and American countries. In the Bight of Biafra, Old Calabar merchants were in personal contact with correspondents in Europe by the 1770s at the latest. The king's advisers in Bonny styled themselves "parliament gentlemen" during the eighteenth century. Even the hometowns of European sailors, however remote, were known to coastal merchants. For instance, in 1804, King Pepple of Bonny teased Captain Hugh Crow of Liverpool about the smallness of the Isle of Man, Crow's natal home. It is no surprise then that, decades later, at Fernando Po, Pepple's exiled son stunned William Baikie by reciting the names of all the British ministers and describing the exploits of Napoleon Bonaparte and Wellington in great detail.[31] To this example must be added a sensational case in which two Old Calabar princes returned to their home in 1774 after years of enslavement in the Caribbean and a short spell of freedom in England. They had been seized in 1767 during a violent internecine conflict in Old Calabar in which European slave traders had actively participated. The princes were able to secure their freedom and to return to Old Calabar on the strength of the transatlantic network they had become part of while growing up in the Bight of Biafra (Sparks 2002). This shows that movement back and forth the Bight of Biafra, on the one hand, and Europe and the Americas, on the other, was more widespread than is usually assumed. There is no doubt, then, that the ruling groups, especially on the coast, had a good idea of the use Biafra captives were put to in the Americas.

That there was awareness of the outside world in the Bight of Biafra means that such information likely filtered to the hinterland through the Aro. Throughout their participation in the slave trade, the Aro were regular visitors to the coastal states, and they maintained temporary settlements there. In turn, coastal elites regularly visited the Aro oracle to settle criminal cases and rulership contests. Baikie reports King Pepple of Bonny as saying that he (Pepple) and his people made "pilgrimages"

---

[30] Captain Hugh Crow reports taking a 15-year-old boy, Finebone, who was travelling from Bonny to England in early 1793 (Crow 1830:45). Also, John Africa, a Bonny courtier, "had been several times in England" by 1807 (Crow 1830:139). For the Senegambian case, see Ashcroft-Eason (1997); Law and Lovejoy (1996:14–16).

[31] Baikie (1856:333). About Mohammed Bello, see Lovejoy (1994b); Old Calabar merchants, see Lovejoy and Richardson (1996); G. Williams (1897:543); and for Bonny, see Falconbridge (1788:8) Crow (1830:87).

to Aro.³² Indeed, there was more than the direct cross-fertilization of information involved in the Aro relationships with the coastal groups. The oracle was able to bamboozle its coastal customers with the knowledge of "everything – the names of all ships trading in the river, of the [overseas-based] merchants to whom they belong, and of the supercargoes" (Hutchinson 1861:53). If coastal merchants knew about Europe and the Americas, so did the Aro who dealt with them on a regular basis. Thus, sending away people or retaining them within the Bight of Biafra did not always happen at random; deportation would have been the lot of individuals meant to be punished severely, as in the Dahomian case.

Social scientists have begun to realize that much-vaunted Igbo egalitarian norms often lent themselves to abuse and that certain individuals held far more power in slave trade-era Igboland than is usually assumed. A specialized political class that exacted tribute and labor had the resources and the time to engage in "political manipulation."³³ Sometimes, individuals fell victim simply by crossing the paths of powerful men, sometimes over competition for women (Maduadichie 1996; J.G. Okoro 1996). That people were sold by "great men, who hated them" – or feared them – had been known widely among nineteenth-century Old Calabar people (see Waddell 1970:429). Among the Efik, Ibibio, and Aro as well as the Cross River and southern Igbo, powerful men were invariably members of the powerful Ekpe or Okonko society.³⁴ The key point here is that, whether sold on trumped-up or real charges, people were disposed of for reasons other than their market value. Many were forced into the trade for reasons relating to conceptions of the political and social order.³⁵

---

³² Baikie (1856:336); Hutchinson (1861:46–47, 54); G.I. Jones (1963:69, 87, 147, 152, 210); A.G. Leonard (1906:486, 254). For Aro settlements in coastal societies, see Anthropologists' Papers (1927:Appendix 1V); K. Oji (1972); G.I. Jones (1989:35–36); Aro-Okeigbo Ancestral Almanac (1996); Kanu-Igbo (1996).

³³ Anikpo (1985:35–38); P.C. Dike (1986); Ahajioku Lecture (1986:iii). Okonko is the reference for Ekpe in southern Igbo communities.

³⁴ Membership did not, however, mean immunity to sale. An Ekpe member could be seized and sold in a foreign community whose people might not have known or cared about his Ekpe status. Also, an Ekpe member could be sold officially as punishment for serious malfeasance. At any rate, seizing a person for sale was stealing, and thieves did not discriminate, except if they could foresee severe repercussions (Igwe 1996; Kanu-Igbo 1996; C. Okoli 1996).

³⁵ There may be exceptions to the rule of selling people as punishment. Traditions of Oron on the west bank of the lower Cross River claim that the sale of a community member was taboo and that the people never participated in the slave trade. Here, "a person who constituted a nuisance to the community" is said to have been "buried alive with common consent." The claim that community did not participate in the slave trade is doubtful; the same traditions acknowledge that slavery was practiced among the people

Household and Market Persons 141

MEANS OF SLAVING 3: ECONOMIC NECESSITY

Other captives were victims of economic necessity. Because these people were often reluctantly sold by their families and not usually stigmatized as violent or malevolent, they were popular with indigenous slaveholders. Once agreed, a ritual was performed to separate the person from his kin (Uchendu 1977:125). The probability that such people would be sold to Europeans declined over time as domestic slavery expanded and absorbed this category of captives. The intended victim rarely participated in the discussions leading to his sale. Often, he or she did not know about it and would unsuspectingly follow the would-be seller to the market (Nwokoye-Emesuo 1996). One of my respondents told me that his own uncle used the respondent's father, an Arochukwu free person, to settle a bet he lost at the Bende fair with a trader from Arondizuogu, in what I estimate to be about 1870. The uncle promised to return on the next fair day (in 24 days' time) to redeem the respondent's father, but he never did return until he, the uncle, died (J.O. Okoro 1996). While it is not clear that the respondent's uncle intended to sell his younger brother, camouflaging the sale of relatives and wards as temporary means of resolving financial emergencies seems to have been common. In the 1880s, Arondizuogu merchant Igwegbe Odum (alias Omenuko) sold his apprentices, some porters, and a relative in the Bende market to another Aro merchant named Oji, after Omenuko had lost his wares to an overflown river. Omenuko told them:

This man, named Mazi Oji, is kind to me because of the disaster that has hit me on this trip. He has therefore told me that it is a shame that I have lost all my wares, and for me and all my porters to go back to our land empty-handed. Because of this, he has suggested that I and some of my porters return home today so that this my relative and some of my other porters [go with him] for three days to enable him to give you things to carry back to me. I will depend on these things to survive. (quoted by Nwana 1950:7)[36]

Omenuko's sale of his apprentices may have been a result of a business misadventure, but social practices fostered economic conditions that routinely ensured the flow of captives. The experience of Ofodobendu Nwaoma (Ofodobendo Wooma) or Andrew the Moor, an Igbo who

---

by the late nineteenth century (see Uya 1984:79, 112–13). There is no indication that the practice of slavery among the Oron was more recent than in other communities.

[36] The text was translated by the author.

enslaved in Pennsylvania between 1746 and his death in 1779, points to a relationship between enslavement and share-raising. His needy elder brother pawned him to secure two goats from another man for a two-year term, but the creditor sold Ofodobendu before the end of the term. Ofodobendu then passed through a chain of slave traders before reaching the coast, ending up first in Antigua in 1741 and was quickly transshipped to New York when he was 12 (Thorp 1988: 447–51). Whether Ofodobendu's brother gave him temporarily as a pawn or had actually sold him by subterfuge, using share-raising as a smokescreen, Ofodobendu's experience demonstrates how intricately linked share-raising could be with enslavement.

Owerre-Ezukala, north of the major Aro settlements in central Igboland, provides a model by which the interaction of religion, marriage, work, and credit effectively facilitated enslavement in the nineteenth century. Men were expected to marry, and an unmarried man was the object of derision. Even upon death, the leaders of *umuada* (the women born in the extended family), cursed his body and forbade him from reincarnating. Men were under great pressure to marry; yet, bridewealth included as many as two heads of cattle (Ukonu 1979:17). Suitors often had to borrow money to meet this requirement, and their creditors sold them or exact other usurious compensation when they were unable to repay. The following describes how unpaid debt might be settled: "The council [of elders] might choose youngmen randomly to accompany the plaintiff in order to seize property to the value of the debt or the compensation from the defendant. If a large amount was involved, the plaintiff might be authorized to sell the defendant, or to take him over for a specified period to repay the debt by ... labor" (Eni 1973:36–37). In a society in which marriage was so important and men paid excessive bridewealth, sellable debtors were in plentiful supply. The system obviously also produced a small class of lenders who doubled as slave dealers. Thus, the institution of marriage routinely forced men into production relations that led to their enslavement and the reproduction of a creditor-enslaver class.

While those who became slaves this way were many, they were seldom among those sent to the Americas. John Barbot, who made trips to the Bight of Biafra in the late seventeenth century, reports that only "a very few [are] sold to us by their own kindred, or parents" (John Barbot 1732:352). For his part, Captain Snelgrave, who visited the region many times during the first three decades of eighteenth century, reports that the people sold their own only in times of extreme need (Snelgrave 1730:505; 1734:159). This information accords with what we know about the Biafra hinterland during the eighteenth and nineteenth centuries (K.O. Dike and Ekejiuba 1990:249, 255; Isichei 1976:46–47).

CONCLUSIONS

The relationship between the means of enslavement and the composition of captives exported from the Bight of Biafra shows that cultural factors shaped the structure of the slave trade there just as much as market forces did. The deportation element, that is, the sale of people into Atlantic slavery for judicial and political reasons, for instance, does not lend itself to cost-benefit analysis. Market forces had a rather limited role to play in the decision to retain a person in the region or to sell him to Euro-American slave buyers. Internal slave users did not bid for captives in the categories that were considered undesirable, who were rarely available on the local market anyway. The deportation element and the role of persons of the household in lineage expansion (especially among the Aro) transcends conceptions of people merely as commodities or even as units of labor. Market forces were not the primary determinant of whether dangerous war captives, kidnapping victims (who could find their way back home), rebellious slaves, incriminated persons, or rivals ended up in the Atlantic market. Quite apart from economics, the choices slave holders made reflected their idea of the ideal society, even though such an idea was manifestly unjust, and the means of achieving it inherently violent. Some palpably nonmarket circumstances limited their choices, compelling them to choose not to choose certain categories of captives, irrespective of region.

6

The Slave Trade, Gender, and Culture

Whether a captive ended up in the Americas or was retained in the region was not only a function of his or her origin, skills, or means of enslavement but also of indigenous conceptions of gender. This chapter shows that constructions of gender roles helped to shape the age and sex structure of the Atlantic slave trade. Understanding the gender structure of the transatlantic slave trade is critical to understanding the societies of the Bight of Biafra and the rest of the Atlantic world. Considering the issue from the broad perspective of contact between the Old World and the New, two salient characteristics of that structure have emerged in the literature. First, as is now well known, males predominated in the Atlantic slave trade, though compared to other branches of pre-nineteenth-century migration, both coerced and free, females and children were well represented. Second, the proportion of African women and children carried across the Atlantic was far from constant or uniform; sex and age ratios varied strongly by region and over time (Eltis and Engerman 1993:308; Eltis and Richardson 1995a). Attempts to explain these broad patterns have generally focused on the economic functions of slaves on both sides of the Atlantic, and especially, on the requirements of the plantation complexes of the Americas, without which a transatlantic slave trade would not have existed. Even though New World planters demanded men, they quickly discovered that enslaved African women had a high work rate.[1] Planters forced black men and women alike to

---

[1] Fogel and Engerman 1974:75–77; D. G. White 1985:67–68, 98–105; Beckles 1989:7–23; Higman 1976:194; Craton 1978:142–47; Walvin 1992:119–21; Moitt 1989; Berlin 1998:111.

labor in the fields, and the price differential between males and females was generally much lower in the Americas than on the African coast (Eltis and Engerman 1992:253).

The labor needs of New World planters were articulated in the categorical instructions Euro-American shipowners gave to West Africa–bound agents. Let us consider just two examples of these instructions from the peak years of the Atlantic slave trade. On October 7, 1725, a group of Bristol merchants, who then dominated the Biafra trade, directed Captain William Barry of the *Dispatch* to buy 240 "Choice slaves" from the obscure port of Andoni. None of these should "exceed the years of 25 or under 10 if possible, among which so many men, and stout men boys as can be had seeing such are most Valuable at the Plantations" (Hobhouse et al. 1725:327). Although plantation America and the organization of the slave trade had undergone important changes, due partly to major wars, rising shipping costs (Eltis and Engerman 1993:314–15), and a substantial drop in the male/female price differential in Biafra ports (Inikori 1992a:137–38), Africa-bound ship captains continued to receive similar instructions. On July 18, 1803, seventy-eight years after Captain Barry's instructions, Thomas Leyland (1803:651), owner of the *Enterprise* and a member of the Liverpool merchant community that had since the 1740s assumed the helm of the British slave trade, charged Bonny-bound Captain Caesar Lawson with the following instruction:

By Law this vessel is allowed to carry 400 Negroes, and we request that they may all be males, if possible to get them, at any rate buy as few females as in your power, because we look to a Spanish market for the disposal of your cargo, where Females are a very tedious sale. In the choice of the Negroes be very particular, select those that are well formed and strong; and do not buy any above 24 years of Age, as it may happen that you will have to go to Jamaica, where you know any exceeding that age would be liable to a Duty of £10 per head.

Some Americanists have supplied details about how New World planters chose the sex configuration of captives, but the gender structure of the slave trade reflected African choices as well.[2]

African gender studies, on the other hand, have rarely focused on the era of the Atlantic slave trade. Economic historians have generally avoided gender questions, and historical demographers who address the issue have usually assumed uniform sex and age ratios for all African regions.

---

[2] For the American angle, see Littlefield 1981:56–73; Sheridan 1994:241–42, 253; Wax 1973.

To the historical demographers, the main question to be resolved was why males were preponderant among those forced to leave Africa.[3] The few historians who have explored the gender structure of the slave trade see the predominance of males in overseas export as more a function of supply than of demand. For them, African suppliers of captives channeled women and children away from the Atlantic and men toward it. Women could be sold for more in domestic African slave markets, whereas men commanded higher prices in markets supplying the Atlantic.[4] Women thus constituted a large majority of slaves within Africa. A survey of available price data in African regional markets seem to confirm this hypothesis (Lovejoy and Richardson 1995a). The discovery of the high value that Africans placed on women is especially useful in suggesting that African conceptions of gender helped to shape the structure of the Atlantic slave trade. But this new emphasis on the ability of Africa to shape the pattern of coerced migration still means that it is the economic function of slaves and market forces that receive the most attention. Although social processes are acknowledged, the emphasis remains on market forces, which crystallized in three overlapping markets – Atlantic, Saharan, and

[3] African gender studies have been the subject of special issues of three major Africanist journals since the early 1970s (Wipper 1972; Bay and Hafkin 1975; Marks and Rathbone 1983). Only the last has contributions (Donald Crummey, "Family and Property amongst the Arnhara Nobility," pp. 207–20, and Anne Hilton, "Family and Kinship among the Kongo South of the Zaire River from the Sixteenth to the Nineteenth Centuries," pp. 189–206) dealing with the era covered in this chapter, and only Hilton's deals with Atlantic Africa. Most other historical works on this sphere have concentrated on the nineteenth-century transition from the Atlantic slave trade to other economic activities, made most explicit in Roberts 1984. See also Coquery-Vidrovitch 1997; Robertson and Martin A. Klein 1983a; Robertson 1984; Martin 1988. Other exceptions include Bay 1977, 1998; Alpers 1984; Greene 1996; Ogbomo 1997. The interdisciplinary volume edited by Flora Kaplan provides the widest range of precolonial case studies about gender, overwhelmingly from West Africa. These case studies provide a window into the intricacies of gendered power structures, allowing us to discern that rather than all African women simply being objects of gender constructions, some were actually players whose power helped to shape the slave trade (Kaplan 1997). Sandra Barnes's contribution makes a vigorous case for the focus on elite women power, mostly in terms of its role in shaping political conflict; Edna Bay grounds some of the key themes of elite women with an empirical analysis of their power Dahomey; Sabine Jell-Bahlsen, Flora Nwapa and Helen Henderson provide useful analyses of elite women in Igbo communities, mainly post-eighteenth century (Barnes 1997; Bay 1997; Jell-Bahlsen 1997; Nwapa 1997; H. Henderson 1997). However, the volume's focus on elite women is of necessity a limited view of how gender constructions – particularly with regard to labor – affected the slave trade, and try as one may, several of the contributions cannot be read backward beyond the mid-nineteenth century. For historical demography, see Thornton 1980, 1981; Inikori 1981; Manning 1981; 1990:61.
[4] Robertson and Klein 1983; Manning 1990:42; Lovejoy and Richardson 1995a, 1995b.

domestic – and which generated significant price differentials between males and females.

Even the few studies to take up interregional variations in the age and sex of captives follow a similar tack. One view suggests that women were sold in inland markets because they attracted higher prices there and men were moved to the coast for the same reason. Women and children were important in overseas markets only where the major provenance areas were near the coast. Transportation costs are deemed the critical factor in such decisions. If Atlantic markets put a lower value on women and children than on men, then it was not worth the expense to move women and children long distances to reach those markets (Hogendorn 1996; Manning 1998a). This argument makes sense, but it is more useful for explaining the differences between inland and coastal markets than between one part of the coast and another. Different coastal regions with nearby provenance zones still exhibited marked differences in the age and sex patterns of those sent into the trade. Strikingly, West-Central Africa, the region with the longest supply lines in Africa, had one of the largest ratios of children entering the trade. Transportation cost thus did not play as significant a role in shaping the gender structure of the slave trade as often assumed.

The proportion of women who entered the transatlantic slave trade was higher at the Bight of Biafra than at any other coastal region of Africa. Here, too, the market approach dominates attempts to account for this exception. For economic historian Joseph Inikori, outside forces – specifically, planters in the Americas – overwhelmed the impact of trans-Saharan and internal markets. Inikori explains the large proportion of females leaving the Bight of Biafra by suggesting, first, that African suppliers moved male captives to ports in adjacent regions where prices were higher, and, second, that Euro-American buyers were prepared to accept females only in this region (Inikori 1992:141–43). While letters of instruction to Africa-bound supercargoes and captains confirm that buyers predominantly demanded men, Euro-Americans sometimes made favorable comments on Biafra women.[5] But neither merchants nor planters expressed a consistent preference for Biafra women, nor did the occasional favorable comment translate into effective demand. Males typically outnumbered females from the Bight of Biafra, and after 1730, as the region grew in importance to the Americas, the proportion of males increased.

---

[5] Edwards 1793:74; Adams 1832:41; Crow 1830:198; Lander and Lander 1832:240–41; Leonard 1898:207.

The present study does not reject outright the conclusions of any of the recent work on age and gender in the slave trade. It does, however, attempt to recast the question of gender by taking into account African factors to explain not only the overall demographic structure of the trade but also interregional differences.[6] In particular, it draws on the insights of the historian Sandra Greene, even though her work has been chiefly concerned with the impact of the slave trade on Africa, whereas the present study examines how African constructions of gender interacted with and shaped the Atlantic slave trade. For the Ewe group on the both Gold Coast and the Slave Coasts, Greene links demographic pressures on land arising from conflict to the evolution of a culture of conspicuous consumption, both of which stemmed ultimately from the slave trade. She traces the impact of this process on constructions of gender and gives a central role to ethnicity in her analysis. In short, she recognizes that gender relations often varied from group to group (Greene 1996). Differing conceptions of gender among African peoples are central to explaining the structure of the slave trade as well as its impact.

While markets mediate both economic and noneconomic values, economic behavior has many cultural determinants. As was made clear in Chapter 5, there are some obvious patterns of behavior in the Bight of Biafra (and no doubt elsewhere) that are difficult to account for in terms of maximizing profits. It seems unlikely that economics will explain why, for example, the region's specialized warriors decapitated the men they captured in warfare instead of selling them, especially when Europeans went to the coast looking first and foremost for men. Profit maximization was only one factor that shaped African conceptions of gender. Of the three slave markets known to have coexisted in Africa during the Atlantic slave trade era, the Saharan market was generally female oriented, whereas both females and children predominated in the domestic market. The Atlantic market concentrated on dealing in males, preferably adult males. The specific configuration of any of these markets in a particular region, as well as the nature and local uses of other commodities produced there, might be expected to have some impact on the gender structure of export captives. In the Bight of Biafra, the institution of female slavery was marginal and the influence of the Saharan market was remote.

The role of two agricultural products – yam (ji) and kolanut (oji) – distinguished the Igbo from their neighbors and was also a major factor

---

[6] Significant steps have already been taken in this direction. See Eltis 1986:257–72; Eltis and Engerman 1992:237–57, 1993:308–23; Eltis and Richardson 1997:29–33; Geggus 1989:23–44; Nwokeji 1997b.

The Slave Trade, Gender, and Culture 149

in these outcomes. Kolanuts are produced by trees of the *Sterculiaceae* family, which are native to Atlantic Africa's tropical forest. The fruit consists of two to twelve nuts (seeds) enclosed in an apple-sized, oblong-shaped carpel, depending on the size of a carpel and/or of the nuts (Hutchinson and Dalziel 1928:247, 253–56). While yam and kolanut were known to Igbo neighbors, such as the Ibibio, Anang, and Oron, the Igbo were unique in the high degree of social and spiritual importance they attached to such products, and this, in turn, determined their social and economic value among the Igbo. As a well-educated Igbo elder put it recently, the Igbo accord the kolanut and the yam "special recognition" and handle them in a "reverential manner."[7] Probably because of their centrality in Igbo spirituality in which men played an authoritative role, the use of these products reinforced male domination in the starkest of ways. But the kolanut and yam did also shape the gender structure of captives sent to the Americas from Bight of Biafra ports. As will be made clear in the discussion of gender division of labor in agriculture that follows, yam production was partly the reason for the relatively high female ratio of captives leaving the region.

For its part, the significance of the connection – or the lack thereof – between the kolanut and the trans-Saharan trade lies in its role in shaping the gender structure of the slave trade in three regions – the Bights of Biafra and Benin, and the Gold Coast. Kolanut reverence among the Igbo partly accounted for the virtual absence of the trans-Saharan trade in the Bight of Biafra's forest region, which would have absorbed many female captives that ended up in the Americas. Interaction between the domestic and Atlantic markets, on the one hand, and the virtual absence of interaction between the domestic and trans-Saharan markets, on the other, resulted in a higher proportion of females leaving the Bight of Biafra – and to a lesser extent the Bight Benin – than from regions that were more susceptible to trans-Saharan influences and put a different value on female labor. Effectively, therefore, this chapter compares the patterns in the Bight of Biafra with other regions of Atlantic Africa with a focus on trading patterns, consumption patterns, social structure, and ideology, including the gender division of labor.

---

[7] Ojiaku 2008:14. Ojiaku places palm oil on the same level of importance among the Igbo. Though this may have been the case before palm oil was heavily commercialized in the nineteenth century and even though the product continues to have use value, it is no longer handled reverentially if it ever was. Although the Oron and Anang – as well as the Efik and Ibono – see themselves as different peoples, historical and linguistic evidence strongly suggests that they are subgroups of the Ibibio (Essien 1991:48; E.A. Udo 1983).

AN OVERVIEW OF KEY QUANTITATIVE DATA

The Trans-Atlantic Slave Trade Database is an invaluable resource when probing these issues. Information on the sex and age composition of captives is available for 656 voyages from the Bight of Biafra, which were perhaps up to 20 percent of all the slaving voyages that left the region after 1600. More important than the size of the sample, however, is the ability to examine the shares of men, women, and boys and girls. For the centuries between 1601 and 1864 for which adequate data are available, ratios of females in the transatlantic trade are higher than for those leaving other regions of Atlantic Africa. In the second half of the seventeenth century, when the traffic from the Bight first became significant, females were consistently in the majority. The region was the only large provenance zone in Atlantic Africa, or any part of the Old World from which people sailed for the New, for which this was the case.[8] If more than half the deportees in the seventeenth century were female, it was only 42.5 percent and 35.5 percent in the eighteenth and nineteenth centuries, respectively (Table 6.1). The above eighteenth-century figure is deceptive. The 1726–50 quarter suffers from insufficient sample size; sex and age information is available on only two vessels in the Bight of Biafra, compared to 156 vessels for all African regions. When we exclude the data from this period, the female ratio of captives leaving the Bight of Biafra increases to 43.7 percent, compared to 32.6 percent for all other African regions combined.

The female ratio does, however, disguise a dramatic change in the distribution of women and girls. Whereas women had constituted nearly half of those forced to leave the Bight of Biafra in the seventeenth century, fewer than one in six captives leaving Biafra ports in the final quarter century of the trade (1826–50) were adult females. Girls, who had made up less than 10 percent of females in the Biafra traffic before 1700, came to outnumber women by the third quarter of the eighteenth century. In other provenance zones the proportion of girls also increased over time, but women always remained more numerous than girls outside the Bight of Biafra. Among males, the percentage of men had remained relatively stable before, during, and after the rapid increase in the trade. It was 46 percent in the seventeenth century, dipping to just under 40 percent in the eighteenth century, then recovering to its earlier level after 1775 and until 1850. Most of the increasing male ratio in the trade during the first three

---

[8] This was the case in the Gold Coast before the seventeenth century, a phenomenon explained below.

TABLE 6.1. *Proportion of Females Leaving the Gold Coast, the Bight of Benin, and the Bight of Biafra, 1601–1864*

Period	Gold Coast	Bight of Benin	Bight of Biafra and Gulf of Guinea Islands	All African Regions Combined
1601–1700	43.70%	40.60%	50.60%	41.50%
1701–1800	32.80%	38.50%	42.50%	36.40%
1801–1864	33.00%	33.30%	35.50%	32.40%
Averages	33.90%	37.70%	41.50%	36.10%

Source: slavevoyages.org

quarters of the eighteenth century came from increased numbers of boys, whose share overall doubled between the seventeenth and eighteenth centuries. This pattern again differentiates the Bight of Biafra from the rest of Africa, where men consistently made up more than half of those entering the trade before 1800 and where, in the nineteenth century, their ratio slipped somewhat. Boys were thus proportionately more important in the Bight of Biafra than elsewhere in sustaining and, indeed, driving upward the high male ratios before the nineteenth century.

MARKET FORCES, DIVISION OF LABOR, AND CULTURE

These intriguing differences between the Bight of Biafra and the rest of Atlantic Africa are best understood in terms of interactions of indigenous conceptions of gender and the process of Atlantic slave trading. The gender division of labor is often at the core of constructions of gender. It is in this division that productive roles of gendered persons in freedom and slavery are located and defined. Women likely did have a larger economic role in sub-Saharan Africa than they did in most other continental groupings of societies. In all African societies, women's and men's "spheres" were separate but interrelated and complementary.

Given the preponderance of men sent into the slave trade, women probably formed the majority of the population of many African societies during the era of the overseas slave trade. In one region in Angola, which seems to be the only place where a census count was taken before the nineteenth century, there were 70.9 male slaves and 81.8 free males to every 100 women.[9] During the late seventeenth and early eighteenth centuries, Benin women

---

[9] Manning 1981:501, 1990:42; Thornton 1977, 1980; Miller 1988:159–67.

were said to "have so much Employment, that they ought not to sit still." In the same period in Whydah in Dahomey, women "Till[ed] the Ground, for their Husbands only." In West-Central Africa, the Capuchin priest Denis de Carli reported that, while seventeenth-century Kongo men served in large armies and carried "great Logs of wood of a Vast weight," they nevertheless enjoyed considerable leisure time. Women, on the other hand, worked from morning to evening tilling the ground, sowing all crops, cultivating, and harvesting in addition to their family and household duties. The same was true of contemporaneous coastal societies of the Upper Guinea Coast, a region that also exported small proportions of females, according to reports written in both halves of the seventeenth century. In southern Mozambique, men were said to have done next to nothing.[10] The foregoing situations reflected the immediate agricultural needs in many African societies in which women performed the bulk of agricultural labor.

Yet do all these indications of a major economic role for women mean that the cultural determinants of unbalanced sex ratios were the same in all sub-Saharan societies and remained constant over time? For historian Catherine Coquery-Vidrovitch, the pattern that held in most of West Africa was also valid in the Bight of Biafra. She claims that among the Igbo "it was women who worked in the fields" (Coquery-Vidrovitch 1997:11). But if the economic role of women was so great, why was a higher proportion of females sent into the trade from this region than from elsewhere in Atlantic Africa? Interregional differences in the gender division of labor suggest interregional differences in conceptions of gender that may have affected the sex ratios in both the slave trade and in societies supplying that trade, at least as much as did the requirements of planters in the Americas.

Enough is known about women's work in the Bight of Biafra to question Coquery-Vidrovitch's observations (Ekechi 1981:41; Hargreaves 1987:94). In this region, both males and females contributed significantly to agriculture. The hoe per se has never been, as Coquery-Vidrovitch claims, principally a women's tool among the peoples of the Bight of Biafra. Generally, men used the big hoe to till the ground, and women and children used the small one for weeding.[11]

The division of labor was particularly clear-cut among the two groups that supplied the overwhelming majority of the region's captives – the

---

[10] For Dahomey, see Bosman 1705:344; for Benin, Van Nyendael 1702:463; for Kongo, de Carli:622, 629, 630–31; for southern Mozambique, Alpers 1984:39–40; and for Upper Guinea Coast, Rodney 1970:103, and Thornton 1983:44, 1992:107.

[11] Leith-Ross 1939:89–92; Forde and Jones 1950:13, 70; Uchendu 1965:24; Paul Bohannan and Laura Bohannan 1968:66; Njoku 1991:120.

The Slave Trade, Gender, and Culture

Igbo and the Ibibio. Females performed a wide range of tasks, such as weeding and planting vegetables and other crops – pumpkins, maize, okra, beans, pepper, and cocoyam (Colocassia). Tilling the ground, planting and stemming yam, building, and climbing trees were exclusively male tasks. Both men and women were involved in clearing, but it was nevertheless a predominantly male activity.[12] In several Igbo communities, the historical agricultural role of men was such that women assumed a major role only in the twentieth century largely because men were at the time diverting their labor to the new opportunities created by the colonial economy (Chuku 2005:88). In the coastal societies, male slaves dominated the market for manual labor related to trade and did the same when agriculture became important. Most women performed "non-slave, low-status" domestic, agricultural, and commercial activities. Captain Hugh Crow, in his regular visits to the region from the late eighteenth century to 1807, observed that in Bonny it was the women who fetched condiments for the kitchens of European ships.[13] So unimportant was women's role in agriculture made to seem in the patriarchal order that even in the second quarter of the twentieth century the missionary G.T. Basden omitted it altogether in his otherwise informative chapter on "women's work" (Basden 1966:325–33). The major role of males in the agriculture of the Bight of Biafra–Igbo societies, in particular, is not replicated in other African regions that supplied captives to the Americas. The one place where a similar phenomenon has been observed is a small part of Senegambia – the Balanta country. Here, as in the Bight of Biafra, men, rather than women, dominated agriculture, and, again, as in the Bight of Biafra, the societies he studied supplied a higher proportion of female captives to the Atlantic trade than was the norm (see Hawthorne 2003:14–15, 137–39).

It is not always easy to determine how much of the gender division of labor antedated the slave trade and shaped its gender structure or how much of this division was a direct result of the trade. Historian John Thornton presents a useful method for measuring change during the Atlantic slave trade. He assumes that the preponderantly male exports affected the women the transatlantic traffic left behind in two major ways. First, the export slave trade depleted the size of the working population

---

[12] In the twentieth century, these crops included the new varieties of yams, which were considered as inferior: Forde and Jones 1950:13, 70; Green 1947:170–71; Uchendu 1965:24–25; Ifemesia 1979:62; Mba 1982:29–30; Nwala 1985:178.

[13] Crow 1830:44; Nair 1972:37, 42–43; Latham 1973:91–96. The quotation is from Hargreaves 1997:95–97.

and by so doing increased the dependency ratio. Since the remaining working population was mostly women, the burden of providing subsistence to the dependent population fell heavily on women. Second, with about 20 percent fewer males to perform male roles, women had to step into the breach or leave such tasks undone. Invariably, this situation resulted in lower production and lower quantities of high-protein food because women did not take over hunting (Thornton 1983:41). Thus the division of labor was altered, and females increasingly assumed tasks and responsibilities hitherto performed by men.

If Thornton's model holds for regions throughout Atlantic Africa, then Biafra societies, which sent significantly higher proportions of females and children overseas and so must have had more balanced population pyramids, would have escaped some of the ruptures that the model predicts. The African regions where women have been found to constitute the majority of the slave populations were also areas where women cost more, performed the bulk of agricultural labor and were recognized as doing so. Slavery in those regions centered on women. The Capuchin missionary Michael Angelo reports that, in seventeenth-century Kongo, "Young Women [were] of the same Value as Men" (Angelo 1704:620). Unlike in these regions, Biafra slavery did not rest on women. It is most interesting that research on Bonny, the populous Ngwa of southern Igboland, and the Aro indicates that female slavery for domestic purposes was marginal.[14]

To better understand these intriguing differences between the Bight of Biafra and other regions, it will be useful to evaluate the differences in the sex ratios between captives leaving different Bight of Biafra ports. The evidence here is rather more limited than it is at the regional level. Not only is the sample smaller (544 voyages for all identified ports), but the distribution over time is uneven (Table 6.2). Of the three major ports Bonny, Old Calabar, and New Calabar, few observations exist for Bonny before 1776. Further, information on New Calabar is totally lacking for the period between 1700 and 1776 and is meager for the nineteenth century. A continuous series is thus possible only for Old Calabar, which overall embarked far fewer captives into the Atlantic trade than did Bonny. This discrepancy is unfortunate because the dramatic increase in the volume of the trade from the Bight of Biafra is associated with the rise of the port of Bonny to predominance. Bonny surpassed the other ports

---

[14] For the entire Igbo, Nwokeji 1998b:325–26; for the entire Biafra, Nwokeji 1997b; for southern Igboland, Martin 1988:25; for Bonny, Hargreaves 1987:94–97.

TABLE 6.2. *Women, Girls, Men, and Boys Leaving Major Embarkation Points in the Bight of Biafra, Selected Quarters, 1651–1850 (in percents)*

Period	Women		Girls		Men		Boys	
	Bonny/New Calabar	Old Calabar	Bonny/New Calabar	Old Calabar	Bonny/New Calabar	Old Calabar	Bonny/New Calabar	Old Calabar
1651–1675	46.3	45.7	4.2	3.7	39.2	43.7	10.4	6.9
1676–1700	45.4	50.5	3.9	3.2	44.2	39.8	6	6.4
1776–1800	37.8	30.7	8.2	10.5	46.8	46.8	6.8	12
1801–1825	21.3	19.7	17.9	13.4	49.6	53	11.2	14
1826–1850	13.7	15.9	17.8	19.2	51.3	42.8	17.2	22.1
1651–1850	31.2	30.9	11	12.4	47.3	42.6	10.3	14.3

The quarters 1701–1725, 1726–1750, and 1751–1775 are omitted because of a lack of data. For a full representation of the data for 1651–1850, including measures of variance and tests of significance, see http://www.wm.edu/oieahc. Rows do not always total 100 percent owing to varying sample sizes for each demographic group.

in numbers of captives dispatched in the third quarter of the eighteenth century, and between 1776 and 1825, it sent between three and four captives to the Americas for every one captive who left from Old Calabar and New Calabar combined.

In the earliest years of significant slave trading in the Niger Delta–Cross River region, no significant differences occurred in the demographic structures of the traffic from New Calabar and Old Calabar, despite the distance between the two ports and the reputedly different hinterlands on which they drew. Statistically significant differences among major ports emerge only in the later period, although there are large gaps in the data for the crucial middle half century of the eighteenth century when the Bight of Biafra trade was increasing so rapidly. From 1776 onward, the flow of captives from Bonny, by now the dominant port of departure, had captives with a different mix of sex and age from those leaving Old Calabar, and New Calabar's profile was closer to that of the geographically adjacent Bonny than to the more distant Old Calabar. More females, in particular, more women, left Bonny and New Calabar than left Old Calabar, and among males, the increasing share of boys, a striking feature of the nineteenth-century trade, had become salient in the last quarter of the eighteenth century. If patterns observed in the nineteenth century had also held in the eighteenth, a significant proportion of captives leaving Old Calabar would have originated in western Cameroon, especially the highland grassfields, where women dominated agriculture as in the rest of African supply regions.[15] After 1800, most of the statistically significant differences between the major ports of Bonny and Old Calabar (once more the New Calabar data are inadequate) disappear, except for the last quarter century of the trade, when the age profiles of departing males are different – more men leaving Bonny and more boys leaving Old Calabar.

In summary, flows of captives departing from the major ports in the Bight of Biafra generally show little difference in age and sex mix, with all

---

[15] A database of Africans on board recaptured Americas-bound vessels in the nineteenth century shows that no less than 10 percent of captives leaving Old Calabar between 1822 and 1837 came from western Cameroon (Nwokeji and Eltis 2002b:204). The proportion of Cameroonians among captives leaving Old Calabar in the eighteenth century would have been much smaller than is suggested by the nineteenth-century sample; above all, the Cameroons slave trade did not come into its own until after the mid-eighteenth century. Information about the gender division of labor in western Cameroons comes from historian Fritz-Canute Ngwa and his students at University of Beua, Cameroon, on October 26, 2002.

The Slave Trade, Gender, and Culture

three ports (together accounting for 85 percent of all departures from the Bight of Biafra) deviating from other African regions, though the Bight of Biafra, in common with most other African regions, sent increasing proportions of males and children into the Atlantic slave trade over time. To the extent that there were differences among ports in the Bight of Biafra (and readers should keep in mind the gaps in the data in the important mid-eighteenth-century period), they show up in the last quarter of the eighteenth century when the slave trade from the Bight of Biafra was at its peak. Bonny in these years (and possibly, too, in the preceding two quarters when data are lacking) sent more females into the trade than did the Cross River port of Old Calabar, probably due to the presence of western Cameroonians among captives leaving Old Calabar.

Fieldwork among the Aro supports the argument that female slavery was marginal in the region. Asked whether men routinely acquired slave women, respondents indicated that even if a man retained a female trade captive in his household, the relationship invariably changed to that of husband and wife. Alternatively, the man might give her to his wife as a slave or to one of his sons or dependents as a wife. One respondent reported that, among the Aro, women were a small part of slaveholding: "There were [women slaves], but not so many. A female slave would be given to a slave man because a woman could not establish an *ama* [lineage]."[16] Moreover, as one elder noted, an important reason for the accumulation of male slaves is that they could be used in fighting wars (M.S. Igwe 1996). According to another elder, the Aro believed that

> Women were difficult. Their mobility was minimal. It was only practical to buy a woman and she became your wife or that of your son, or she became a fellow woman's slave. Except if she was sold to a far away place or overseas, it was not very practical. In certain circumstances, people bought female slaves, but they invariably ended as wives. I do not think, however, that a person set out to buy a woman so that she would become his wife. What I am sure of is that women bought women slave. (N.A. Anyakoha 1996)

Whether women were significantly less mobile or not, the attitude reflected in this comment seems to have affected the choice of enslavers. Another respondent explained how slave women became wives: "A man could buy a woman from the market and bring her home. You

---

[16] Kanu-Igbo 1996. See also Akpu 1996; Anyakoha 1996; M. S. Igwe 1996; Maduadichie 1996; E. Nwankwo 1996; C. Okoli 1996; Elizabeth Okoro 1996; J. G. Okoro 1996; J. O. Okoro 1996; J. E. Uche 1996.

know that man-woman matters are complicated. ... If he was the sort that had a soft spot for women, he might decide to keep her longer and might marry her. ... A woman who came as a slave was effectively the man's wife once she got pregnant and bore children for him" (M.S. Igwe 1996). Historian Susan Martin has observed a similar phenomenon with respect to southern Igboland (S. Martin 1988:25). Female slaves usually belonged to females, whom feminist anthropologist Ifi Amadiume has misidentified as "female husbands."[17] Although present in modern-day Igboland, this form of slavery – considered as marriage – likely evolved in the twentieth century and incorporates the basic slave/mistress relation of earlier times.[18]

After the 1771–75 period, when the slave traffic from Biafra peaked, Bonny sent more females into the trade than did other ports. The rise of Bonny probably meant that the long-term trend toward fewer females entering the trade slowed down due to the relatively high female ratio among captives departing from there, mitigating a precipitous decrease

---

[17] Amadiume 1987. Contrary to Amadiume's claim, many of my respondents indicated that slave women were eventually labeled "wives" (Akpu 1996; Anyakoha 1996; M.S. Igwe 1996; Maduadichie 1996; C. Okoli 1996; E. Okoro 1996; E. Nwankwo 1996; Igwilo 1996; Martina Ike 1995; Aloy Nwankwo 1996; M. N. Okoli 1996; Umunnakwe 1996).

[18] The change must be associated with slavers' response to the antislavery efforts of the British colonial administration, which peaked in the 1930s. This was when child dealing, especially in girls, became endemic. Most of the transactions were cloaked as "marriage," confusing the colonial administrators who came to regard all bridewealth payment as slave dealing (Nwokeji 1998b:337). Buchi Emecheta's novel *Slave Girl*, set in the 1900s through the 1920s, confirms that these marriages were indeed slavery: "Many of the market women had slaves in great number." The female slaves referred to in the novel are all owned by mistresses. Even Chiago, who was sold by her father and purchased by another man, is presented to her buyer's wife. Yet selling girls to mistresses is actually expressed in terms of "marry[ing] her away" (Emecheta 1977:50, 58, 60–61). When it did not involve slavery, it was probably proxy marriage contracted by the first wives of male Christian converts who sought to maintain Christian status while being polygynous, as Oliver Akamnonu's novel, *Taste of the West*, makes clear (Akamnonu 2008: 99–102). Marriage differed from slavery because, unlike a slave, a married woman and her total labor power were not alienated from her lineage (Kilkenny 1981: 158–59). In her important biography of the wealthy, late-nineteenth, early-twentieth-century Onitsha market woman Omu Okwei, Felicia Ekejiuba writes that Okwei "acquired beautiful girls mostly 'adopted' children or children pawned to her by her debtors." In 1921, Okwei admitted that one Uyanwa was her slave as Okwei struggled to retain the right of inheriting the property that Uyanwa's husband, a European United African Company manager to whom Okwei had given her in "marriage," would leave behind (Ekejiuba (1967: 633–46). As in Emecheta's novel, the story revolves around girls. The idea that the "female husband" relationship is an ancient institution seems to have sprung from the unfortunate tendency of much existing literature to view Igbo women as unchanging.

The Slave Trade, Gender, and Culture

in the proportion of the overall females entering the Bight of Biafra slave trade. Bonny was the main outlet for captives from central Igboland. The expansion of the Biafra trade, the rise of the Aro network, the shift of trade from Old Calabar to Bonny, and changes in gender ratios were correlated developments. In the Bight of Biafra, then, unlike in other African regions, preexisting gender constructions seem to account for the export of a high proportion of females.

The objective here is to recognize, first, that men played an important role in agriculture, second, that scholars of the slave trade have given this male role insufficient attention in the recent literature, and third, that the gender ideology that emerged (or was "constructed") in some societies in the Bight of Biafra had more to do with preexisting cultural norms than with the reality of what women could or could not do. On this last point, among the Tiv of the Middle Belt in the hinterland of the Niger Delta, male and female roles in agriculture were initially carefully defined and to a large extent, separated. The Tiv explained this division as a function of the physical inequality of men and women and the need for females to be modest, even though the differentials in the strength requirements of tasks on either side of the divide are not obvious and modesty is culturally determined (Bohannan and Bohannan 1968:66).

Cultural, as opposed to biological, factors were important in the allocation of crops and crop tasks in most of Igboland and had important implications for the slave trade. Although yam was the staple food in many societies bordering on both the Bight of Benin and the Bight of Biafra, including the adjacent Middle Belt, only among the Igbo and the Ibibio of Biafra was it regarded as the king of crops and cultivated exclusively by men. Among the Igbo and Ibibio, yam, if available, would be eaten before anything else, but the significance of yam was more far-reaching among the former. As anthropologist Charles Meek put it, "all other crops [were] merely subsidiary" to the yam among the Igbo. Alexander Falconbridge observed that "Yams are the favorite food of the Eboe." This preference remained constant into the twentieth century, which cannot be said of their neighbors. While ownership of a large yam barn was also a mark of high status among the Oron on the Cross River for the known precolonial period, cultivation of the most valued species quickly "petered out" during the colonial period (Uya 1984:61), which was when Basden observed that yam "stands to [the Igbo] as the potato does to the typical Irishman. A shortage of the yam supply is a cause of genuine distress, for no substitute gives the same sense of satisfaction." More important, the amount of yam a person possessed was a key measure of his wealth, and yam had varied ritual functions as well. Women's role in yam cultivation was restricted to weeding. The so-called subsidiary crops such as maize, cocoyam, okra, and beans surpassed the yam in both nutritional quality and yield, but yam was considered supreme because it was in the male domain. Literary luminary Chinua Achebe calls yam "a very exacting king" and writes that "for three or four moons it demanded hard work and constant attention from cock-crow till the chickens went back to roost." Basden further assessed the cost effectiveness of yam cultivation:

From an agricultural point of view, the yam is a very extravagant vegetable to grow. Each tuber requires a full square yard of land which, in itself, is a big demand. For seven or eight months of the year, regular attention must be given to its care, absorbing much time and labor. If wages had to be paid, it is doubtful whether a yam farm would pay its way, let alone yield profit.

Although Basden's observation reveals the Igbo and the Ibibio fixation on the yam, perhaps beyond the point of economic rationality, the crop did yield reasonable economic returns (Achebe 1996:33; Basden 1966:389–90, 394; Falconbridge 1788:21; Meek 1937:16–17, 32–35, 49, 168, 188, 215, 238; Onyekwelu 2001:82–84).

Yam production owed something to women's input, but females occupied a lesser agricultural role in the Bight of Biafra compared to other African coastal regions. In Biafra, anthropologist Victor Uchendu writes, "women's crops follow the men's." Apart from symbolizing the degradation of women's role in agriculture, this statement indicates that part of women's labor (principally weeding) went to yam production. Women were made to plant their crops, in Uchendu's words, "between the spaces provided by the yam hills."[19] Yams occupied the central point of the hill or mound of earth, while women's crops were planted around its base, a symbolic representation of perceived inferiority of women's crops and women's labor. This mentality affected day-to-day decisions and food-preference patterns. Because women did not primarily work yam and were not acknowledged as important in its production, this region's leaders, it would seem, were more willing to countenance the forced migration of females. By contrast, in the Gold Coast, Upper Guinea Coast, and West-Central Africa, females were vital to the production of rice or corn, and, as a result, smaller proportions of females were sent

---

[19] Uchendu 1965:24–25; P. Ottenberg 1959:207; Ifemesia 1979:62; Amadiume 1987:28–30, 37–38. Among the Owan, northwest of the Igbo, where yam was also gendered, men and women appeared more powerful in localities where they respectively controlled this crop (Ogbomo, 1997:97).

The Slave Trade, Gender, and Culture 161

into the Atlantic traffic from these regions. Interestingly, in Yorubaland, where men also had a major agricultural role (at least, in the nineteenth century), the proportion of women sent into the trade from the eighteenth century onward is closer to that in the Bight of Biafra than in the Gold Coast, Upper Guinea Coast, and West-Central Africa.[20] Was the gender division of labor in agriculture alone responsible for the relatively high proportion of females among the captives that left Bight of Biafra ports?

MEANS OF ENSLAVEMENT

If, as was shown in Chapter 5, the means of enslavement shaped the composition of captives exported overseas, it would have had an impact on the gender and age composition as well. Although enslavement strategies might be expected to have adjusted to whatever means supplied the market best, some practices in the Bight of Biafra are hard to explain in those terms. Male captives were more valuable than their female counterparts in Atlantic markets, but instead of Bight of Biafra warriors targeting male captives, they cut off heads as a matter of honor – provided the victims were men. Surviving prisoners tended to be women and children (Nwokeji 1997b). The fact that the Upper Guinea Coast, through which the Western Sudan supplied captives to the Atlantic, recorded the highest proportion of men, and the Bight of Biafra, the lowest indicates significant differences in social processes, including enslavement mechanisms. In the Senegambia section of the Upper Guinea Coast, where the economies of the Bambara and Tukolor states – particularly the resources needed to socially reproduce their warrior class – were heavily dependent on slaving during the eighteenth and nineteenth centuries, warfare was so central to slave procurement that it assumed the proportions of a means of production (Roberts 1980). All kinds of war

---

[20] For gender division and specialization among the Yoruba, see Belasco (1980:7, 59, 68), Toyin Falola (1984:54), Coquery – Vidrovitch (1997:11). It is important to note that recent studies of the Yoruba have suggested the fluidity of gender (Matory 1994). Oyeronke Oyewumi has gone as far as denying any notions of the gender division of labor and suggests that the concept of gender is alien to Yoruba culture (Oyewumi 1997, esp. 64–77). Even Jane I. Guyer (1980:362), who deals specifically with gender division of labor in Yorubaland, notes in a comparative context that the notion was "phrased in terms of pragmatism rather than metaphysics." These are useful pointers. Nevertheless, we must still come to terms with why one sex was over-represented in some activities and not in others, and why the sexes were sent into the Atlantic traffic in a significantly unequal distribution.

wasted lives, but a model geared to the procurement or "production" of captives mostly by a professional warrior class like that of Senegambia would likely "produce" more captives, including males, than the model practiced by the warrior groups of the Bight of Biafra, which revolved around part-time, albeit skillful, headhunters. Both were destructive, but one was primarily a "productive" activity and the other primarily a destructive one. The pressure on the Cross River Igbo warrior to produce men's heads could be expected to result in large numbers of women and children being forced into the slave trade in the Bight of Biafra. Kidnapping, judicial processes, and specifically, political struggles guaranteed that men were well represented (Nwokeji 1997a, 1997b). Those sent away on account of rivalry, dissent, or other acts considered deviant were usually men.

GENDER, KOLANUTS, AND THE REGIONAL MARKET STRUCTURE

The aforementioned social and cultural forces combined with the peculiar market structure of the Bight of Biafra to shape the unusual sex ratio of the region's slave trade. Both the Saharan and domestics markets placed a premium on female captives (Lovejoy 1983; Robertson and Klein 1983b). The focus of the domestic market in the Bight of Biafra was male rather than female, but more relevant to the point at hand, the Saharan market was virtually nonexistent in the Bight of Biafra during the Atlantic slave trade era, effectively leaving the region with a two- rather than three-market structure. Not even the relentless pursuit of kolanuts by Hausa traders – the great purveyors of trans-Saharan commodities – could bring the trade to the forest region of the Bight of Biafra during the overseas slave trade era. The kolanut trade would have facilitated trans-Saharan commerce, which in turn would have impacted the gender composition of captives leaving the Bight of Biafra.

It is a puzzle that Hausa traders did not go to Igboland in search of kolanuts. The Igbo did produce kolanuts, and the Hausa were the most voracious consumers of the product, which they used in a wide variety of ways that ranged from stimulant to snack. Before their mass consumption by the Hausa, kolanuts were a luxury item limited to royalty (Lovejoy 1980:2). With mass consumption, kolanuts became probably the single most important Hausa import from the forest belt by the eighteenth century, when trade in the commodity began to support a vast commercial system in which Hausa trade diasporas played a pivotal role.[21] The nuts remained so valuable into the nineteenth century that Hausa caravan traders en route to Asante still used them to pay tolls to local authorities because they were "much relished and not easy to get" (Herskovits 1936:18). Given the proximity of kolanut-producing Igboland to Hausaland, a trade in kolanut between the two regions should have resulted as, according to Onuora Nzekwu (1961:305), it did between the Cameroon section of Bight of Biafra's forest region and Bornu in present-day northeastern Nigeria. Why, then, did the kolanut not support the trans-Saharan trade in the Igbo-dominated part of the Bight of Biafra, in spite of its potential to generate substantial demand among the Hausa majority of the savanna?

The special significance of kolanut in Igbo life is one important factor. Much of the information we have about the kolanut in the Bight of Biafra comes from twentieth-century sources, but since there is no hint in Igbo oral traditions, or in the relevant historical and ethnographic studies, that the significance of the kolanut has changed significantly since the days of the slave trade, this evidence is valuable in understanding the role of kolanut in Igbo life before the twentieth century. As has been mentioned, several West African groups used kolanut, but none – certainly in the Bight of Biafra – seems to have attached to it as much social and ritual significance as did the Igbo.[22] The special niche that kolanut had occupied in Igbo life is well stated by one character in Achebe's storied novel *Things Fall Apart*: "He who brings kola brings life" (Achebe 1996:6). Kolanut served as the mandatory focus of prayers; its rites invoked *ndi-ichie* (the ancestors) at the commencement of any significant occasion, such as festivals, contracts, covenants, adjudication of cases, asking for important favors, and rites of passage. During festivals, women of the household, extended family, or town – depending on the level at which the particular rite was celebrated – usually supplied the kolanuts. Women presented kolanuts to men as special gifts in appreciation for a favor done or simply to demonstrate obeisance. The kolanut also had immeasurable quotidian uses. It was the first thing a host was expected to present to a visitor.[23] Individuals

---

[21] Lovejoy has observed that kolanuts have "been singled out as the commodity of most interest" in the trade between the Hausa of Nigeria and the Asante in today's Ghana (Lovejoy 1980:1).

[22] One other group among whom kolanut meant more than mere stimulant and/or snack were the Ibibio. Anthropologist P. Amaury Talbot has described how kolanut was used welcome guests and for divination (Talbot 1967:238).

[23] The presentation of kolanut by a woman to a man required no ceremony; the man would simply accept the kolanuts, thank the woman and keep them for future

who could afford kolanut beyond the aforementioned uses also used it as a stimulant or snack, but social and spiritual uses predominated. The ritual of "breaking" kolanut was an elaborate four-step process, with minor local variations.²⁴ The fact that kolanut and yam were among the earliest Igbo crops seems to account for the spiritual and social importance they acquired in Igbo culture.²⁵

> occasions. If, however, the kolanuts were presented at the beginning of an occasion, the kolanuts or some of them were utilized for the prayers. Both men and women ate kolanut among the Igbo, but it was taboo for women to break kolanut except in the absence of a male. As long as a male is old enough to break kolanut, which could be as young as 4, he was his responsibility to do so. For the ritual and social aspects of kolanut, see Talbot 1926b:316; Meek 1937:21, 22, 32, 62, 151, 167, 168–69, 170, 174, 194, 205, 239, 241, 245; Nzekwu 1961; Uchendu 1965:84–85; Ezeliora 1994:43, 60–61; Muotoh 2000:44–46; Ohia 2007:25–26; Achebe 1996:18–19; Metuh 1973:5; H.A.P. Nwana n.d.: 34–36; Onwuka Njoku 2000:70; Alisa 2003. Igbo Catholic priest Asonye Ihenacho has likened the ritual around kolanut with the Christian Holy Eucharist (Ihenacho 2004:106, 160–65). Oral tradition from Amaokpala in the Ndi-Eni area asserts that dispute over kolanut protocol was the immediate cause of one war between Amaokpala and Aro Ndikelionwu in the second half of the nineteenth century (Onyekwelu 2001:4–7).

²⁴ The first step involved the relay presentation of the kolanut(s) (icho oji) that recognized every person present in the order of their relationship to the host, representing the symbolic "travel" of the kolanut to the respective hometowns of all adult males present, with the kolanut ultimately "returning" to the host. The second step consisted in the offer of prayers to the ancestors, usually by the oldest male present. The third act consisted in the actual breaking of the kolanut(s) by the oldest male present (or his delegate), who would give one cotyledon to the ancestors by throwing it on a shrine or the ground as may be deemed appropriate, take one cotyledon or a piece of it for himself. Finally, the youngest male present passed the remaining pieces to all present. The remainder was then returned to the host as *aka oji*, which literally translates as "hand of kolanut" but actually refers to the share of the person (hand) who had brought the kolanut.

²⁵ Following the theory advanced by Russian botanist and geneticist Nikolai Vavilov that the region of the greatest diversity of species of any plant is likely to be the location where the plant was first domesticated, life scientist A.O. Anya has significantly argued that what we know today as Igboland was the center where these two particular plants were first domesticated (Anya 1982). Although Anya did not analyze the implications of kolanut and yam in terms of gender, slavery or interregional trade specifically, he did stress a relationship among the economy and ecology and social organization.

> What is clear is that even the cosmological and religious constructs of a society – the way it sees the world around it and the forces which shape its world are functional derivatives of the ecological and economic situation. The Igbo polity must, therefore, be understood against the background of its evolution and stability through the millennia: it was a viable organism designed to mediate and conserve relations in a sophisticated and successful but nevertheless predominantly sedentary agricultural economy. Even the religious and moral attributes which are associated with this culture bear the imprint of its ecological and thus agricultural origin (Anya 1982).

Whether or not Igboland was where the kolanut was first domesticated, as Anya has suggested, the antiquity of the use of kolanut (and yam) in Igbo life is beyond doubt.

There are several other reasons that long-distance trade in kolanut did not develop in the north. The Igbo preferred a different species of kolanu from the one preferred by the Hausa. To the Igbo, *Cola nitida* – the species preferred by the Hausa – was grossly inferior to *Cola acuminata* and was unsuitable for ritual and social purposes. The Igbo placed much value on the multiplicity of cotyledons or segments of a kolanut – the greater number of cotyledons the better and the fewer, the worse. A monocotyledon kolanut was deemed taboo and discarded as *oji ogbu* (dumb kolanut). The preferred C. *acuminita* typically had a minimum of three but often several more. Yet, the much-desired C. *acuminata* had a poor yield relative to C. *nitida*, taking upward of ten years to produce its first fruits, and the yield was thereafter agonizingly slow. Mature C. *acuminata* trees do not produce any fruits at all in some years.[26] C. *acuminata* is also more perishable, requiring more elaborate preservation arrangements than C. *nitida*. Even if the Igbo had tried, it was unlikely that they could have developed an export trade based on C. *acuminata*. The combination of relatively poor yield, higher perishability rate, and robust domestic demand would have made C. *acuminata* too expensive to compete with products from elsewhere. On the other hand, the Asante, who produced the more prolific C. *nitida*, were not significant consumers, nor did kolanuts have social or spiritual purchase among them, a fact that enabled them to supply vast quantities of the product at competitive prices. For the Igbo to compete with the Asante for the Hausa kolanut market, they had to produce C. *nitida*, quite apart from surmounting the other obstacles to the north-south trade with the Hausa.[27] There are also indications that the Hausa preferred C. *nitida* to C. *auminata* (Dickson 1969:72–73, 103; Abaka 2005:19, 20). Hausa traders could thus afford to bypass the region throughout the Atlantic slave trade era, channeling captives, mainly from the Middle Belt, and trade goods from across the Sahara toward the Gold Coast.

[26] With modern agricultural methods, C. *acuminata* bears fruits in seven to eight years, but it needs to be watered regularly (www.tradewindsfruit.com). Since the Igbo did not water fruit trees regularly, their kolanut trees would have taken somewhat longer to yield fruits.

[27] Despite the impression given by Anya that the Igbo have produced multiple varieties kolanut for centuries, however, it is unclear that C. *nitida* was among their products before the twentieth century. One strong indication of this is that the twentieth-century Igbo identified C. *nitida* specifically with the Hausa, referring to it as *oji Ausa* (Hausa kolanut) or "gworo," which is the generic Hausa reference for all kolanut. Hausa traders in the late nineteenth and early twentieth centuries may in fact have given C. *nitida* the little popularity it gained in Igboland, if they did not introduce it in there in the first place.

While there is evidence of goods entering the region from Asia and the Middle East as early as the ninth century and probably considerably before, suggesting long-standing trade links with regions across the Sahara, nothing shows that such trade contacts survived into the slave trade era. The religion of Islam, which usually accompanied the trans-Saharan trade in West Africa, was lacking in the Bight of Biafra because trade contacts with the north were made before Islam became a significant force in West Africa. One other indication of the marginality of the trans-Saharan trade in the region is that the Middle Belt does not appear to have accounted for a large share of the captives exported through Bight of Biafra ports in the period up to 1700, even though the Hausa and the Bornu raided the Middle Belt for captives as early as the early sixteenth century.[28] After the seventeenth century, Hausa traders drew from the Middle Belt most of the captives they sold in Gold Coast markets, where they were valued as *ndonko* (foreigner slaves) (Herskovits 1926:20; Lovejoy 1982, 271; Reynolds 1974, 12). This practice escalated in the nineteenth century and the Hausa continued to send many of the victims to Gold Coast markets (Herskovits 1936:17, 20, 22; Mason 1969). Based on his frequent slaving voyages to the Bight of Biafra in the last twenty years of the eighteenth century, Captain John Adams confirmed that captives leaving the Bonny port rarely included people from north of the Igbo. No evidence of trade from across the Sahara exists for this period for the forest region of the Bight of Biafra. Certainly, there were no horses, and in spite of all the talk about their high mortality rates in forest conditions, horses became an instant attraction when they eventually reached the forest region of the Bight of Biafra during the nineteenth century. It is true that several crops – such as bananas, plantains, cocoyam (or *Colocassia esculata*) and even the *Dioscorea* species of yam – and domestic animals such as goat and fowl that have long been considered basic items in the diet of people of the Bight of Biafra are said to have derived from South Asia sometime in the distant past. Other than these artifacts of the Igbo-Ukwu vintage, dating back to the ninth century, are the only goods from the Indian Ocean commerce known to have traveled into the region from across the Sahara.[29] Other

---

[28] In the 1520s, Leo Africanus reported of Hausa raiding their neighbors and Hausa merchants being involved in trade with distant lands, principally "the Region abounding in Gold" (Africanus 1896:831, 832). Raymond Mauny is of the view that the raids were directed against against southern groups (Middle Belt) (Mauny 1961:190). See also Barbour and Jacobs 1985: 127.

[29] Adams (1832:33). See Hair (1967:262–64) for ethnolinguistic distribution of Americas – bound captives up to 1700, Sargent (1999:8, 9, 13, 106–31) for Benin expansion

items that may have continued to enter the Bight of Biafra from the Indian Ocean during the Atlantic slave trade era were more likely to have done so via east-west routes through Central and East Africa in the east and Benin in the west. The four-day market cycle, which Central African communities as eastward as the Kongo shared with groups in the Bight of Biafra, is probably an indication of long-standing commercial interactions between this part of West and Central Africa.[30] Clearly, there were important structural reasons for the failure or virtual absence of the trans-Saharan trade in the Bight of Biafra during the centuries of the overseas slave trade. These reasons go beyond the simple idea that the forest is a great impediment to the horse- and camel-driven caravan trade. Hausa traders did, after all, trade as far as Kumasi in the Gold Coast, a trade which Leo Africanus informs us was well in place by the 1520s when he visited West Africa (Africanus 1896:831, 832).

The isolation of the forest region of the Bight of Biafra from the trans-Saharan trade during the Atlantic slave trade era seems to have also been associated with the rise and special circumstances of the state of Kwararafa in northeastern Middle Belt by the fourteenth century. Incessant conflicts with neighboring Muslim Hausa states, including the trans-Saharan commercial powerhouses Kano and Borno, forced Kwararafa southward, transforming it "from a Sudanic state with limited access to the trans-Saharan commercial system to a troubled middle belt polity competing for Benue commerce and overland trade to [Old] Calabar in the south." Kwararafa then clashed perennially with the Middle Belt polities, until its demise and supersession by non-Islamic states in the seventeenth century (Sargent 1999:8, 211–40). These conflicts in both the north and south disrupted the trans-Saharan trade in the Middle Belt, especially in the eastern axis adjacent to the Bight of Biafra, a process that culminated in the decimation of the Kwararafa successor state Jukun by the Tiv and Igala by the eighteenth century. The westward and northward expansion of Benin after 1500 enabled the kingdom to link the transatlantic trade to northerners, who increasingly desired goods from the trade, but no comparable process promoted

---

and northern states' development of interest in transatlantic trade goods, Lovejoy (1994: Appendix) for a nineteenth-century sample, Herskovits (1936) and Adamu (1979). For the importance of the horse in West African history, see Law (1980:23), and for the provenance of key crops and domestic animals from South Asia, see Forde 1953: 210–11.

[30] For a suggestion of east-west routes, see Afigbo 1977:119; and for Central African market cycle, see Vansina 1961:100.

north-south exchange in the Bight of Biafra.[31] The trade that resulted was significant only in comparison with the Bight of Biafra; Benin influence apparently did not sustain a large volume of trade between the Hausa and the greater Bight of Benin. The region, like the Bight of Biafra, did not have kolanuts for export, but here it was due to lack of significant production. It also appears that the instability in the Middle Belt worked to discourage Hausa traders from nurturing a kolanut trade with the Bight of Benin, leaving Gold Coast kolanuts as the cost-effective option. Given the influence of trans-Saharan demand in influencing low female ratios among captives sent to the Americas via West African ports, the kolanut, by its failure to generate the trans-Saharan trade in the Bight of Biafra, is implicated in the gender structure of the region's overseas slave trade.

If the absence of the kolanut trade in the Bight of Biafra was somehow linked with the relatively high female ratio among captives exported from there, some correlation between the kolanut trade, on the one hand, and the gender structure of the Atlantic slave trade in both the Bight of Benin and the Gold Coast, on the other, is also to be expected. As Table 6.1 shows, the Bight of Benin has the highest female ratio after the Bight of Biafra. After the seventeenth century, when the female ratio of captives sent to the Atlantic from this region had parity with the African mean, the region sent a higher proportion of females than was the norm, except for the Bight of Biafra. Significantly, the kolanut trade did not take off in the Bight of Benin until the overseas slave trade had ended, toward the end of the nineteenth century, after liberated Africans from Sierra Leone and, more important, Hausa merchants had begun importing kolanuts to Lagos from Sierra Leone and the Gold Coast, respectively (Dickson 1969:150–53; Lovejoy 1980:6, 94, 114–17, 145).[32] The late development

---

[31] See Lovejoy and Hogendorn 1979:225 for the decimation of the Jukun trade, and Sargent 1999:93, 191, 194 for the role of Benin in facilitating north–south trade in the seventh century.

[32] This import would have catered, in part, to the needs of the Lagos Afro-Brazilian community, among whom Kristin Mann found kolanut to be of some economic and cultural significance during the second half of the nineteenth century (Mann 2007:127). It was also around this time that the Egba Yoruba of Abeokuta joined the kolanut trade (Biobaku 1965:10). Evidence from the nineteenth century suggests that the Yoruba used kolanut in divination and as can be gleaned from the work of Saburi Biobaku also as status symbol and the symbolic "breaking kola together" (sharing a kolanut) was used to mark the settlement of disputes (see Biobaku 1965:14–15 n1, 28, 106n; Ojo 1966:53). No doubt, kolanut was important among the Yoruba, but Afolabi Ojo appears to have exaggerated its historical, social and spiritual significance among them when he stated in the 1960s: "Kolanuts remains the choicest present and offering on all occasions: no

of the kolanut trade between Bight of Benin's forest belt and Hausaland during the eighteenth and nineteenth centuries reflects the fact that trade between the two regions was not as robust as is usually assumed and pales in comparison to contemporary trade between Hausaland and the Gold Coast. When in the first half of the twentieth century anthropologist Melville Herskovits asked Hausa elders who had participated in the caravan trade late in the previous century, "whether or not trading was carried on to the south into the territory of the Yoruban peoples of Southern Nigeria, or into Dahomey, the reply was negative – for both countries it was said that 'the donkey doesn't go there'" (Herskovits 1936:19). Had this trade been robust and had production of kolanut resulted as expected in Bight of Benin's forest belt, more Hausa traders would have traded in this region and likely would have bought more female captives from there than they did, reducing the pool of female captives available for overseas export through Bight of Benin ports.

The Gold Coast provides perhaps the starkest example of the kolanut trade impacting the gender structure of the slave trade. The proportion of females sent overseas from the region was noticeably higher than the African mean during the late seventeenth century, but their numbers declined drastically in the eighteenth century, suggesting changes in the pattern of demand for female captives in the hinterland (Table 6.1). Evidence from the nineteenth century, which in all likelihood held for the eighteenth century as well, shows that female captives were sold at a premium in inland Gold Coast, where Hausa traders operated (Herskovits 1936:20). This trend suggests the existence of a virile northbound export market for female captives in the Gold Coast. Since we know that the Atlantic market placed a higher value on males, this export market would have seen the trans-Saharan sector featuring Hausa buyers, who resold the bulk of the female captives to buyers from across the Sahara. The sharp decline seen in the female proportion of Atlantic-bound Gold Coast captives has recently been attributed to the decline of the male labor-intensive gold economy and the rise of nonmining sectors, principally agriculture (Nwokeji, forthcoming). To this must be added the kolanut trade

---

ceremony or function, ancient or modern, is complete without it. Its antiquity and usefulness are further attested to in its being entrenched in the life and thought of the people" (Ojo 1966:52–53). These comments effectively place kolanut among the Yoruba on the same pedestal as among the Igbo, but the ubiquity of kolanuts in historical and anthropological studies of the Igbo appears to be unmatched in Yoruba studies, and the kolanut ritual is not as prominent in Yoruba life as Igbo. In fact, the only source Ojo cites in support of his comments is Igbo scholar Onuora Nzekwu (1961).

which, as Kwamina Dickson and Lovejoy have shown, crystallized in the late seventeenth and early eighteenth centuries (see Dickson 1969:72–73, 103; Lovejoy 1980). The increased male ratio of captives leaving Gold Coast ports after the seventeenth century was – even if in a small way – also reinforced by the aforementioned supply of male captives by Hausa caravan traders. The surplus male captives from the north – that is, those not enslaved by Gold Coast masters – ended in the Atlantic markets. The kolanut trade was not the only explanation for the gender structure of the slave trade as a whole, but it does need to be taken into consideration in assessing the impact of trans-Saharan demand on the structure of the overseas slave trade.

The kolanut also invokes the role of culture in shaping markets as well as the relation of culture to economics in shaping the overseas slave trade. It is suggested here that, while economic considerations motivated Gold Coast producers to take advantage of Hausa demand, the role of the kolanut in Igbo culture acted as an impediment to the development of trade with the Hausa, even if we exclude the other identified obstacles to that trade. Because of the marginality of the Saharan market in the overseas slave trade era in the Bight of Biafra and to a lesser extent, in the Bight of Benin, effective demand for female captives from the Saharan market did not exist in the former and seems not to have been as robust in the latter as is usually supposed. Saharan demand had little influence on the Atlantic and domestic markets for captives in the Bights, particularly the Bight of Biafra, in comparison to what happened elsewhere in West Africa, a compelling factor in the relative high female ratios among captives sent into the Atlantic from the two regions.

CHANGES IN GENDER STRUCTURE OVER TIME

If the share of females entering the trade in the Bight of Biafra was apparently always larger than that of other major African regions, why did it decrease over time? In Niger Delta and Cross River ports, the percentage of females remained near parity until the first quarter of the eighteenth century, fell to about 41 percent in the third quarter, when it stabilized, and fell again in the fourth quarter to just above one-third, a figure that held for as long as the trade lasted in the nineteenth century. The second-quarter plateau between these downward shifts coincides with the rise of Bonny to its position as a major departure point. The decline in the share of females is apparent in all African regions, but in the Bight of Biafra it appears to be associated with Igbo lineage practices and the character of Aro expansion. This development – though perhaps not decisive – would have left fewer females for the Atlantic traffic.

The central importance of reproducing the lineage in most African societies accounts for this behavior. Association with large groups of people through kinship networks conferred a prestige separate from the economic rewards that the labor of those people generated. Lineages could expand through the addition of outsiders or through natural increase. In most parts of Atlantic Africa, procreation was the primary means of expansion, a phenomenon that placed a premium on fecundity. In late seventeenth-century Benin, the Dutch witness David Van Nyendael observed that "the fruitful Woman is highly valued, whilst the Barren is despised" (Van Nyendael 1702:447, 462, 463). Similarly, according to Coquery-Vidrovitch, the African "woman's value and status depended first on her fertility and second on her cooperativeness, initiative, and ability to work" (Coquery-Vidrovitch 1997:16). Among Igbo women, bearing children was a source of joy; daughters would strengthen existing ties and create new ones, and sons would consolidate a woman's place in her husband's lineage. Not having children often led to a miserable life, and Igbo folk tales suggest that infertile women were often objects of mockery and victimization.

Within the context of the value of children in Biafra societies, the rise in child ratios – which with the decline in male ratios were major distinguishing features of nineteenth-century Biafra Atlantic captive exports – is initially puzzling. Increased child ratios, however, reflected the increased proportion of girls sent into the overseas traffic, not of boys. Similarly, increased female ratios derived in part from the greater increase in girl ratios. These are clear indications of the region's greater readiness to export females, and especially girls, than was found in other regions.

The increase in girl and decrease in boy ratios reflected the male (especially boy) bias of the indigenous institutions of the family and slavery. Boys were so important that a man "must have a son or be written off the dynasty" (Ojike 1946:6). The preference for boys seems to have taken roots in Biafra societies before the Atlantic slave trade, and we see evidence of the incorporation of boys acquired from outside to boost lineage-groups. The founders of at least two major Aro settlements are known to have entered Aro society in this way from communities in the Nri-Awka area sometime in the first half of the eighteenth century (K.O. Dike and Ekejiuba 1990:178–79, 181, 208). These boy slaves,

Ikelionwu Ufere and Owuu Mgboli, grew up, became free, rich, and famous, and established Ndikelionwu and Ndiowuu, respectively, in the eastern Nri-Awka area. The higher numbers of children and young adolescents sold in the internal markets suggest that indigenous slavery focused on increasing the existing population by integrating outsiders (K.O. Dike and Ekejiuba 1990:74, 250–51; Ekejiuba 1972b:12). The basic reason for slaveholders' preference for children within the Bight of Biafra was the ease of assimilating children into kin groups in most societies. This calculation remained important even in the late nineteenth century when the labor consideration seems to have been predominant. Adults might pose social problems if incorporated into the household. Although the price data are sketchy and they do not distinguish between boys and girls, we might still ask what implication this trend would have had on prices in the hinterland. In contrast to the assumption that girls fetched higher prices than boys in African markets (e.g., Galenson 1986:107–10), ceteris paribus, a higher cost of boys (relative to girls) in the Biafra hinterland should be assumed.[33]

Although such values are scarcely unique to the Igbo, the extension of Aro influence had some exceptional features that have implications for the falling female ratios in the Bight of Biafra. The Aro network was the only non-Muslim trade diaspora and a large African organization espousing what Uchendu describes as "big compound" ideals to acquire slaves primarily by trade (Uchendu 1965:54–56). Military activity was probably

[33] Most available prices are quoted in different currencies and exchange rates are not available. Moreover, sources are often vague in describing the categories of captives whose prices they quote. For example, although British observers in Abo tell us that a sixteen-year-old cost sixty shillings in 1832 and a woman "something more," the age of the woman and sex of the sixteen-year-old are unclear (Laird and Oldfield 1837:103, 106). Another Abo price in 1854, is quoted at one pair of ivory for three captives (Baikie 1856:56). In about 1855, four to six adult captives exchanged for one horse in the major fairs of the hinterland. Whatever may be the specific value of ivory or horses, the sizes of which could vary significantly, it is clear that these prices were very low, at least in part, a reflection of the ending of the slave trade. These low prices for adults are consistent with contemporaneous information on the hinterland fairs, where an adult sold for one bullock (Ekejiuba 1972a:21). Late nineteenth-century information shows that adults above twenty-six years old, disparagingly called *otankwu* (s/he who consumes palm nuts), were the least expensive. They sold for only 40 *mkpona* (brass rods) or £3, compared with £5 to £10 for *apapa* and 400 *mkpona* or £30 for *asamiri* (Fox 1964:23). Although Fox gives the exchange rate at 1 *mkpona* = 1s. 6d, the conversion of the figures results in rates drastically different from his £30 = 400 *mkpona*. This works out at 13.33 *mkpona* = £1. The low prices offered for the *otankwu* not only reflects low desirability for them but also the effect of the elimination of the overseas market. For the complexity of African price data, see Law (1991a).

a less important means of getting captives in the Bight of Biafra than in other regions. The Aro did not rule directly over the source populations, and their influence spread primarily through trade, cultural prestige, and religious clout, not conquest. They augmented their own population through the massive incorporation of people as immigrants, refugees, clients, and slaves. The Aro acquired women principally as wives and overall absorbed more females from central Igboland than males. Those men they did take in – by whatever means – invariably found wives from elsewhere (Chapter 4). In other words, for each new male entrant, there was at least one female entrant as a wife. A principal mechanism ensuring this practice was that immigrants, including ex-slaves, could not normally marry Aro women, and they often chose to marry from their natal homes. In this, they were encouraged by Aro men who also saw the region as a prime reservoir of wives. The preference for Nri-Awka women derived from the Aro drive to expand business ties and a belief, firmly entrenched by the nineteenth century, that Nri-Awka women made good wives. Since most marriages originated from third-party introductions, commercial and nuptial ties reinforced each other. Many Aro from the central Igbo settlements were the sons or grandsons of Nri-Awka women. It is difficult to find a man who did not marry from the Nri-Awka region.

The Aro tendency to accumulate women and the rising influence of the Aro network – though not decisive – would have contributed to the decline in the ratio of women leaving the Bight of Biafra. Women accounted for 46 percent of the total 51 percent of female departures between 1650 and 1700 but a mere 15 percent of the total 35.3 percent of females in the last quarter of the trade.[34] Thus, while the proportion of women decreased radically over these periods, the proportion of girls increased sharply as well. While the girl share of the trade moved erratically, about a third of the increase occurred in the nineteenth century. The increased shares of men and girls reflected a short-term need for women in the Bight of Biafra in the nineteenth century and the premium placed on boys as instruments of the lineage.

SEX RATIO AND POLYGYNY

Despite the dramatic fall in the portion of women, polygyny – an institution that both fascinated and remained largely beyond the comprehension of European visitors to Atlantic Africa – does not appear to have either

[34] The female ratio is drawn from www.Slavevoyages.org.

shaped or been shaped by the demographic composition of the slave trade, notwithstanding the strong opinions of some modern scholars.[35] There is no evidence in the Bight of Biafra of a rising incidence of polygyny during or after the expansion of captive departures from the region. If the decreasing female ratio of export captives is an indication of increasing incidence of polygyny, this would have been more because there was an increasing need for women's labor than, as has been suggested in recent literature, the mere abundance of women in the population, caused partly by the increasing share of men sent into the Atlantic trade. If the abundance of women in populations left behind by the overseas slave trade had been the cause of polygyny, then the ending of that traffic would have reduced the incidence of polygyny.

But this is not the case; the incidence of polygyny instead rose in the Bight of Biafra and elsewhere following the suppression of the overseas traffic in the mid-nineteenth century, a phenomenon historian Nakanyike Musisi in another context calls "elite polygyny" – defined as marrying more than four wives (Musisi 1991:757–86). By this time, the palm oil trade had become more valuable than the slave trade. In the slave trade era, dramatic examples of polygyny tend to come from the Slave Coast and West-Central Africa rather than from the Bight of Biafra and the Gold Coast. Bosman reported that in the late seventeenth and early eighteenth centuries Gold Coast men "content[ed] themselves with one, two, three, and the most considerable Men, with eight, ten or twenty Wives," while men in the Bight of Benin port town of Whydah had "forty or fifty, and their chief Captains three or four Hundred, some one Thousand, and the King betwixt four and five Thousand." Joseph Miller documents that "the numbers of young wives surrounding older males ... astonished visitors to the interior of Angola" in West–Central Africa.[36] This difference between the Bight of Biafra and the Gold Coast, on the one hand, and the Slave Coast and West-Central Africa, on the other, could be either the cause or effect of

---

[35] Philip Curtin (1964:252) has observed that "polygyny stood out as a special evil" to Europeans of the Enlightenment. The British slave trader John Hippisley pointed to the gender imbalance of export captives and men lost in wars. But the tendency for the richest men to have many wives "does not prevent the poorest from having one or two .... The number of women must, therefore, exceed that of men" (Hippisley 1764: 14–16, 16n). For a modern opinion that the trade encouraged polygyny, see Manning 1990:41; 1981:501, 503.

[36] Bosman 1705:344. The importance of sex ratios in polygyny is well recognized by modern scholars, for example, Manning 1990:42; 1981:501, 503; Miller 1988:163; Thornton 1980:425.

the higher proportions of females among the captives sent from these regions.

The sex ratio does not, however, appear to be the principal factor driving polygyny. In one region in Kongo (West-Central Africa), for instance, a baptismal register for the years 1774 and 1775 reveals that only fifty-four (10.6 percent) of the 507 recorded families were polygynous. Among this polygynous group, perhaps forty-six (9.2 percent of all the families in the register) had only two wives. Only one man, described as "the lord of the area," had as many as four. As John Thornton notes, "the majority of marriages were monogamous" (Thornton 1977:411–12). His conclusion accords with what we know of the conditions in the vast majority of Bight of Biafra societies, beyond the trading states, and likely also for much of Atlantic Africa, at least up to the early nineteenth century. Of the fifty-six ex-slaves in the Koelle Sierra Leone sample who were married at the time of enslavement, only ten (18 percent) were polygynous – four of them had only two wives each; only two had three wives; there was one each with four, five and seven wives, and another (an Ewe) had married two wives and inherited twenty-two or more wives from his father (Hair 1965:194). How representative were these statistics? Because the ex-slaves in Koelle's sample were mostly young at the time of enslavement – only nine or 5 percent were more than forty years old – the rate of polygyny among them appears to be considerably less than in the general African population. But if, as Hair has observed, the average age of marriage for the contemporaneous African male population was twenty-five, and 53 percent of the male respondents was aged twenty-five or more, with more than half of these being over thirty years old at the time of enslavement, then the Koelle sample is more representative of the general population than appears to be the case at first. In light of low life-expectancy rates in precolonial Africa, the ex-slaves who were married at the time of enslavement would have been closer in age to the average age of married men in the general population because they were likely drawn overwhelmingly from the ones who were older at the time of enslavement. Yet, while West-Central Africa, with a similar rate of polygyny with the Bight of Biafra and indeed much of Atlantic Africa, sent into the Atlantic slave trade the lowest proportion of females after the Upper Guinea Coast, the Bight of Biafra sent the highest. This comparison suggests that polygyny was not universal in Africa and that men married women, not simply because of the abundance of women, but also because men needed women's labor and reproductive resources.

In the final decades of the slave trade from the Bight of Biafra, the declining female ratio was reinforced by a change in the economic role of women in the Niger Delta and Cross River areas. Palm oil production became a major activity in the region. Because palm oil was a labor-intensive industry in which the Aro had a major role (though less so than the slave trade) and because by the late 1830s the value of palm oil exports surpassed those of captives sent to the Americas, the pressures on the Aro to hold women at home are evident. Less easy is a quantitative assessment of this effect.

CONCLUSION

African conceptions of gender shaped the sex and age structure of the overseas slave trade. These constructs emerged from factors altogether more profound than the merely economic. The unusual pattern in the sex ratio of captives exported from the Bight of Biafra is perhaps best explained by the cultural determinants of the male and female roles in agriculture, the virtual absence of the trans-Saharan market, and by enslavement methods in an environment of decentralized political power. The convergence of these factors resulted in large numbers of women being sent into the overseas trade. The region with female ratios closer to those of the Bight of Biafra is the Bight of Benin. This is because the gender division of labor in the Yoruba region of the Bight of Benin and the region's involvement in the trans-Saharan trade were more similar to those of the Igbo in the Bight of Biafra than is often recognized. Though the influence of the trans-Saharan trade seems to have been considerable in the Bight Benin during the early stages of the transatlantic slave trade era, the former trade seems to have waned after the seventeenth century, following the rise of the kolanut trade between the Hausa and the Asante of the Gold Coast. The kolanut trade seems to have diverted trans-Saharan trade from the Bight of Benin to the Gold Coast.

This proposition is indicated in fluctuations in the female proportions of captives exported through both the Bight of Benin and the Gold Coast. While the female ratio declined sharply in the Gold Coast with the rise of trans-Saharan demand via Hausa traders between the seventeenth and eighteenth centuries, it increased appreciably in the Bight of Benin during the same period with what appears to have been a decline in trade with the Hausa. While females accounted for 40.6 percent of captives exported through Bight of Benin ports and 50.6 in the Bight of Biafra during the seventeenth century; the corresponding figures were 38.5 percent and 42.5 percent in the eighteenth century; and 33.3 percent and 35.5 percent in the nineteenth century (Table 6.1). The continuing lag in the Bight of Benin female ratio in comparison to the Bight of Biafra may have reflected a greater role of warfare in the procurement of captives in the Bight of Benin. The gradual decrease in the female ratio over time may have resulted from both the peculiar nature of Aro expansion and the drive to incorporate new members into the lineage in the Bight of Biafra, where this trend was steepest. Across the board, however, the Atlantic slave trade intensified gender inequality everywhere, creating a wider role for women (and therefore an increased demand for women in the domestic economies) so that this process may have been self-correcting in the long run.

7

Cultural and Economic Aftershocks

Cultural transformations of the Atlantic slave trade era and the aftershocks of the traffic conspired to promote new value systems in the second half of the nineteenth century that were markedly different from earlier times. These changes occurred in the production and marketing of the commodities that had replaced captives in the overseas trade. The Bight of Biafra dominated the production of palm oil, which had become the key commodity in West African trade. This fact bespeaks an intensive economic activity in the region that had far-reaching implications for the social structure, understood as an identifiable pattern of social relationships among the principal groups and institutions in society over the long term. Profound cultural, demographic, and economic changes deriving from the Atlantic slave trade and the increasing involvement of the British in the internal affairs of the region converged in a maelstrom of violence. This process is consistent with the violence that pervaded Africa during the nineteenth century.

Nowhere in Atlantic Africa, however, was this violence as intense and widespread as in the Bight of Biafra. The impact of external trade had been perhaps more far-reaching here than in any region in Africa during the period. The slave trade era had witnessed continuing Aro expansion and its consolidation of existing diaspora settlements. Although trade remained a significant part of Aro life, the Aro trading economy entered a terminal crisis. The nature and intensity of warfare changed, and agriculture became a significant part of the equation in Aro life. Particularly striking was the Aro's development of a martial ethos – militarization and its representations as an integral part of its value system – personified in the proliferation of the merchant-warriors that increasingly controlled bands of Aro fighters. In a milieu and time in which the most successful slave traders were the most respected, and the most ruthless were the most feared and even revered, this fueled a state of instability rarely witnessed even during the long centuries of the overseas slave trade. The emergence and valorization of the merchant-warrior increased the incidence of Aro wars against non-Aro groups, of Aro civil wars, and of violent rivalries among the major Aro merchant-warriors as the clash of colossal egos mixed with competition for spheres, clients, fame, and – from the 1890s – land, straining and reshaping intergroup relations in the region. This constituted a profound cultural shift because before the mid-nineteenth century the Aro had been averse to directly partaking in martial activities. In fact, they had taken pride in not being warriors themselves.

The perception of the Aro as a people disinclined to martial activities endured long after the group had embraced a martial ethos. European observers, especially in the wake of the British Aro Expedition of 1901–02, held this view, and modern scholars have accepted it as a permanent characterization of the Aro value system up to British conquest. In fact, the Aro attitude to martial activities began to change in the second quarter of the nineteenth century. There is thus a perplexing disconnect in the literature between the well-known Aro military activities of the second half of the nineteenth century and perceptions of the Aro as nonmartial. The change in Aro attitude to fighting became conspicuous in the second half of the century, making it the most violent era in Aro history. Centuries of slaving fostered institutions and practices that had escalated both organized and random violence. The fact that the Aro, who were slave dealers, now spent their time and energy destroying life suggests a significant change in their value system. Why, then, did militarization take root among the Aro? Answers to this question lie not only in the emergence of martial ethos among the Aro but also in the macroeconomic and structural implications of the transition from slave to palm produce exports, as well as of British imperialist maneuvers.

ATLANTIC ECONOMIC CONTEXT

Dramatic changes in the structure and volume of the external trade had far-reaching political and social consequences for all West African societies, but this transformation was bound to be extraordinary in the Bight of Biafra. The circumstances of the region were peculiar.[1] For much of the century, the Biafra economy was the most dynamic in Atlantic Africa. Palm oil, which perhaps accounted for three-quarters of the total value of all African exports in the 1860s, was almost all produced in the forest-belt hinterlands of the Bight of Biafra and Bight of Benin, and the Bight of Biafra was in pole position and the largest producer worldwide. So central was the palm-oil trade that it was reportedly of greater value in this period than the slave trade ever was.[2] The development of the palm-oil trade was accompanied by substantial economic growth, the greatest in all of West Africa (Northrup 1979:5). Since the region accounted for a substantial share of the value of African exports, it is safe to assume even in the absence of comprehensive import data that it would have dominated imports as well.

The economic and social change in the mid-nineteenth century that resulted from trade expansion and the transition from slave to nonslave exports also involved transformations in the organization of trade that resulted from technological changes associated mainly with the advent of the steamship. The introduction of the commercial cargo steamer obviated the huge capital outlay that was needed to operate a ship, just as the use of currency obviated the need for buyers to be importers as well. These changes opened the African trade to the small-scale European trader, who was able to penetrate inland markets, ultimately dislodging local middlemen.[3] According to British trader Harry Cotterell, who pioneered the new system in the Bight of Biafra and was active in the delta trade from 1863 onward:

We found that our system of working the trade by steamers answered well, as compared with the old-fashioned way followed by other Merchants of sending sailing ships out with full cargoes, and keeping them waiting for months in the River until they were loaded, as in addition to our advantage of getting out fresh goods by each steamer, we also had the advantage of sending our Produce home by them, thus getting it to the market, and the proceeds converted into the goods

---

[1] Various studies have detailed the local effects of this change. Davidson (1961); M. Klein (1968, 1971, 1972); Newbury (1969); Hopkins (1973:125–35); Reynolds (1974); Inikori (1979, 1986, 1994a, 1994b); Noah (1980); Lovejoy (1983:159–83; 1989); Manning (1986, 1988, 1990:140–47); Eltis (1987:223–42); Eltis and Jennings (1988); Becker (1988); Law (1993, 1995b); Zeleza (1994:370–89); Sundiata (1996). For work dealing with nineteenth-century changes in the region in the Bight of Biafra, see Dike (1956); Northrup (1976, 1978, 1979); Noah (1980); Lynn (1981, 1997); Martin (1988); Oriji (1982, 1983).

[2] Hartley (1977:8); Eltis and Jennings (1988:946).

[3] Lynn 1997:5, 7, ch. 6. See also P.N. Davies 1976:89n; Zeleza 1993.

Cultural and Economic Aftershocks 181

two or three times, while other Merchants had theirs waiting until their ships arrived, when the same process was again repeated. (Cotterell n.d.:38)

Dramatic economic change was also caused by the imperialist activities of the British, who happened to be seeking to suppress the overseas slave trade as well as their imperial designs. But the successful ending of the overseas slave trade in the region did not end British meddling in regional affairs. To justify their imperialist agenda, the British articulated a connection between imperialist encroachment on African societies and the ending of the overseas slave trade, but the two were not necessarily connected. True, the British were committed to ending the overseas slave trade, but their intervention in the region drew its impetus from economic self-interest. In their bid to displace local traders, European traders enlisted official support of the British, who had already been flexing their muscles for decades, in trying to curtail the independence of coastal states. The overbearing presence of the British, highlighted by a series of bombardments and sponsored expeditions against certain key indigenous traders, mainly along the Niger waterway, tangled the imperial power with many local ruling elites.[4] The European presence also incited and emboldened weak indigenous groups to stand up to oppressor groups, escalating existing rivalries and creating new ones as rival power groups sought to renegotiate existing arrangements to their advantage. These developments posed a serious challenge to Aro dominance, forcing the group to change its methods.

CONTINUING IMPORTANCE OF THE SLAVE TRADE

It is a well-acknowledged paradox of nineteenth-century West African history that the suppression of the overseas slave trade and the rise of the export commodity trade led to increased slaveholding in the region. The British primary goal of controlling the new trade in the Bight of Biafra at the expense of the indigenous middlemen was a palpable source of tension. If the importance of ending the slave trade was secondary to efforts to dominate trade in British calculations, ending domestic slavery hardly figured in at all until the twentieth century (Brown 1996; Ohadike 1988; Nwokeji 1998b). The goal of the British was the uninterrupted production of palm produce and European traders' displacement of inland middlemen in the name of "free trade." Eager to promote the commodity trade,

---

[4] For a documentation of these invasions, see J.U.J. Asiegbu 1984.

the British in the Bight of Biafra welcomed and even advocated the use of slave labor in the production of export commodities. This was evident in discussions British officials and traders had among themselves and with the regional rulers with whom they came in contact (T.J. Hutchinson 1858:113, 264; Whitford [1877] 1967;163). In 1858, British governor of Fernando P$_o$ and former consul in the Bight of Biafra Thomas Hutchinson praised Kings Eyo and Eyamba of Old Calabar for having in 1842 sought technical assistance in exploiting slave labor in the cultivation of coffee and cotton and in the manufacture of sugar. "These men, with a sagacity which did them much credit, saw that the slave population, becoming superabundant by the forbiddal of their exportation, would require employment to keep them from mischief, as well as to contribute to their daily sustenance." Apparently, Commander Raymond of Royal Navy's *Spy*, with whom coastal kings had made an antislave trade treaty, was equally impressed (see T.J. Hutchinson 1858:113). In fact, Hutchinson saw the enslavement of people within the region not only as a source of labor for producing export staples but also as a direct solution to the Atlantic slave trade. He argued that

> the external as well as internal slave trade will only be effectually put an end to when the chiefs and masters in Africa are taught, and understand, how far more profitably to themselves they can exercise slave labor in the cultivation of their soil, than by selling it. They will then be brought to see, that it is not consistent with common sense, transporting away the native Africans to Brazil to cultivate and manufacture sugar, to America to grow and pick cotton, to Cuba to aid in the tilling of tobacco, when the very same products can be obtained from their own ground at home. (Hutchinson 1858:264)

In about 1875, a British trading agent on the Niger, John Whitford ([1877] 1967:163), urged an Abo prince to "make your slaves collect palm-oil to exchange for those desirable things" – a sure reference to European products. British policy of promoting commodity production as an alternative employer of slave labor formerly exported to the Americas fueled the domestic slave market.

Demand for labor in the region sustained a sizeable slave market. Although the use of slave labor in palm produce production was minimal, the extreme labor intensity and inefficiency of the industry stretched household labor to the limit and indirectly encouraged the growth of slavery in other industries. With much woman and child labor occupied by working in aspects of the multifaceted palm produce production process, particularly the tedium of cracking palm kernels, entrepreneurs in other industries looked to the slave market for the recruitment of labor.⁵ The interactions of the three economic zones – coastal, palm belt, and the northeastern – which Northrup argues emerged during the nineteenth century, casts light on the expansion of slavery (Northrup 1979:5–11). The labor needs in all three regions were directly or indirectly related to the palm-oil trade. In the coastal zone, traders utilized manpower as assistants and porters and to man the canoes that the traders used for transporting their wares (Northrup 1979:6–7, 12). King William Dappa Pepple of Bonny accepted captives in liquidation of debts owed him, and increased his own slaveholding (Hargreaves 1987:222). Virtually everywhere in the zone, wealthy merchants established food producing, slave-worked "plantations" of mainly yams and plantains.⁶ The second zone consisted of the densely populated central Igboland, which formed a part of the palm belt, and the more stratified inland trading communities.⁷ Given that women did much of the oil extraction work, the cessation of the overseas traffic would have had a salutary effect on labor in a region that exported by far the highest proportion of females in the heyday of the Atlantic slave trade.⁸ Significantly the demand for captives in the palm belt and among the trading groups of the zone appears to have been on the increase in the 1860s (Northrup 1979:8; Oriji 1981:318). The third zone, according to Northrup, was the area north and east of the palm belt, the slave-dependent food basket of the region. Low population densities had characterized this region at the beginning of the nineteenth century, but settlements here spread and expanded as the century wore on.⁹ Complementing the significant natural population increase was the addition of "large numbers of slaves" bought from Aro traders.¹⁰

Although the palm produce industry was a minor direct employer of slave labor, agriculture and trade depended heavily on slave labor, and

---

⁵ For details, see Nwokeji 1999:201; Hartley 1977:716–18; A. Martin 1956:12; S. Martin 1988:33; R.K. Udo 1970:73.
⁶ Becroft, et al. 1844:268, 271; Cookey 1974:15, 63; Dike and Ekejiuba 1990:252; Ekejiuba 1972b:14; Latham 1973:91–96; Lovejoy 1983:178; Nair 1972:37, 42–43; Walker 1875.
⁷ The palm belt also encompassed the entire Ngwa and Isuama as well as much of the Cross River areas, especially Ibibioland.
⁸ For the role of women in palm produce production, see Becroft et al. 1844:274; S. Martin 1988:32; R.K. Udo 1970:73.
⁹ Also Floyd 1969:50–51. These processes were a source of bloody conflicts among groups in this region, such that were still prevalent in the early colonial period (see Bridges n.d.:68–69).
¹⁰ Northrup 1979:9–10; W.R.G. Horton 1954:311; G.I. Jones 1961.

British policy promoted massive slaveholding. The Aro controlled a thriving domestic slave market as they had controlled its overseas-oriented counterpart, and were thus able to continue to maintain some influence throughout the region.

Continuing Aro influence drew also on the ongoing expansion of their diaspora communities and markets, as well as the establishment of new ones. This expansion had three dimensions. First, existing diaspora groups expanded through addition of new lineage-groups. For example, three new lineage-groups emerged in Arondizuogu between 1840 and 1850 (see Table 4.2 in Chapter 4), and the Ndieni cluster added new lineage-groups from migrants from the Nri-Awka area, assimilating some of their neighbors in the process.[11] Second, the diaspora settlements themselves established diaspora settlements of their own. For example, between the 1850s and 1870s, the Ndieni settlement Ndeikelionwu and sections of Arondizuogu established settlements in the southwestern Nri-Awka region and northeastern Imo River region, respectively (Umo n.d.:57; I.O. Nwankwo 1986). Third, more Aro from the homeland poured into existing diaspora settlements, as when the merchant-warrior from Arochukwu, Okoroji, founded a settlement immediately northeast of Arondizuogu (G.C. Mmeregini 1978; Okoroji 1996), and two Aro groups, Ndinjoku and Ndimoko, moved into the upper Imo River, just east of Arondizuogu (see Umo n.d.:57). This expansion explains the obvious increase in Aro activities in northeastern Igboland in the second half of the nineteenth century, which resulted in some of the many Aro settlements in that region.[12]

Existing slave marts continued to wax and new ones seem to have been opened in the Middle Belt and along the Niger into west Niger.[13] Apart from local traditions, reports of African repatriate missionaries and of European officials, missionaries, explorers, and traders, have described numerous Niger slave markets and Aro role in the second half of the century.[14] The Ibiniukpabi oracle remained a major instrument

---

[11] Agu (1985:17); Chinyele (1972); Dike and Ekejiuba (1990:180–81); J. Ike (1972); M. Iloha (1972); J. Kanu (1972); Ngene (1972); Nwene (1972); C. Okafor (1986:122); N. Okoli (1972).

[12] For Aro activity in late nineteenth-century northern Igboland, see W.R.G. Horton (1954:311); G.I. Jones (1961); Northrup (1979:10).

[13] It was in the nineteenth century that the Aro became truly influential in the Middle Belt (Ijoma and Njoku 1991:208). For Aro settlements and markets in this region, see Mathews 1922:9.

[14] Baikie (1856:308); Crowther and Taylor (1859:23, 256, 288); Moor (1902:1). For relevant traditions, see Mefo and Ibe (1972); Chukwura (1977); Kwentoh (1977).

Cultural and Economic Aftershocks

of Aro influence. European visitors during the second half of the nineteenth century frequently reported on this influence.[15] The new state of Opobo established in 1869 made trade with the Aro the cornerstone of its economic policy. King Jaja, whom A.A. Cowan described as "the most powerful potentate the Oil Rivers ever produced," was desirous to court and protect Aro trade (Cowan 1935:400; Johnston 1923:178). He "made certain that those within his sphere of influence respected the authority of the Aro oracle." In one instance, he had a leading citizen of Ndoki, north of Opobo, flayed alive for ignoring the oracle's injunction (Cookey 1974:90). The Obi of Abo named one of his sons Chukwuma, signifying a person whose birth was connected with the Aro oracle, Chukwu (Ibiniukpabi).[16] In the 1890s, as many as 800 persons from the Niger communities visited the oracle yearly, according to British High Commissioner Ralph Moor in 1902.[17] The influence of the oracle reinforced the domestic slave trade.

While the internal slave trade continued, Aro society and economy began to change fundamentally in the late nineteenth century. The catalyst was not Aro an inability to compete in the produce trade, but the consequences of production and marketing – the same forces that sustained the internal slave trade. Thus, the main problem that confronted the Aro was not the end of the Atlantic slave trade per se, but the response of non-Aro groups to the palm-oil trade, the macroeconomic consequences of palm produce production, and British imperialist maneuvers. Aro influence worried the British, who took care to monitor Aro activities, especially in the Niger riverine states of Oguta, Atani, and Assay (Anene 1959:22–23). The Aro were an obvious target for British imperialists, who could justify their actions by citing the Aro role as the principal slave traders.

It was not until the 1890s, however, that the Aro came under the direct searchlight of the British. Why did it take the British so long after the onset of European commercial encroachment on the interests of coastal middlemen to encroach on Aro commercial spheres in the hinterland? The coastal traders' success, up to the 1880s, in holding their own against British maneuvers accounts for the time lag. Until this time, the British were still "pacifying" coastal middlemen and had

---

[15] Baikie (1856:336); J.A.B. Horton (1868:183–85); Hutchinson (1861:46–47, 54); Moor 1902:1–2; ; A.G. Leonard (1906:486, 254); G.I. Jones (1963:69, 87, 147, 152, 210).
[16] Names of persons born after consulting *Chuwku* were Chukwuma, Uzoaru, Ukpabi, Chukwu (K.O. Dike and Ekejiuba 1990:150).
[17] CO 520/14: "Memorandum Concerning the Aro Expedition," April 24, 1902, p.10; Moor (1908:22).

not yet decided to rule them directly or to turn on the Aro. With the establishment of the Oil Rivers Protectorate in 1891, the British formally declared their rule over the Niger Delta and explicitly set about establishing "control over the tribes of the coast who acted in all cases as middlemen or carriers for the transport of trade goods to the interior and that of the produce factories of the [European] merchants which were all situated on the coast line at the mouths of the various rivers." British planners also realized that "the Government of the territories could not be regarded as in any sense established" until the "country of the producers," specifically, "this Ibo country dominated by the Aros was dealt with." The British reckoned that the Aro "could practically cause almost cessation of trade by stopping production."[18] Fearing that the Aro were expressly misrepresenting "the Government and the whiteman," the British began to send officials to assess the Aro, beginning in 1892 when they made "overtures" to Aro traders on the Cross River and explained "the aims and objectives of the Government." Aro responses developed from "tolerant contempt" for the British, as Moor put it, to angst that the British were scheming to encroach on their turf. British affirmations of good intentions did nothing to assuage Aro fears and anxiety.[19]

These pressures were building against the backdrop of dwindling world commodity prices. A major international economic depression seems to have driven British moves to subjugate inland traders, given that successful subjugation would increase the profit margins of the European traders and cushion them from the depression. By the 1890s, the British had also inched closer to ending slaveholding, and their intervention in the inland trade and the fall in world commodity prices had begun to impact Aro interests adversely. British forays into inland markets, suppression of coastal middlemen and dwindling world commodity market prices all converged in the 1890s to push the Aro over the edge.

---

[18] CO 520/14: "Memorandum Concerning the Aro Expedition," pp. 4–5, 6, 12–13.
[19] They continued along these lines through such emissaries as Roger Casement in 1894, Captain A. Turner in 1896, as well as the party of Major Leonard and F.S. James. Further attempts in 1897 culminated in a meeting in the Cross town of Itu between Aro representatives and British Consul General Major Gallwey in March 1898. The Aro thwarted these attempts, but the encounters had given the British much valuable intelligence on the Aro. CO 520/14: "Memorandum Concerning the Aro Expedition," pp. 6, 7–8, 9; Leonard 1898.

MILITARIZATION AND VIOLENCE

The Aro understood that the British had begun a policy of undermining Aro influence by playing other groups against them. They witnessed hostile British actions, such as persuading the coastal communities to stop patronizing the Aro oracle and banning the importation of rifles and even cap guns. Not only did the firearms embargo reduce the amount of firepower at Aro disposal, the British also intended it to increase Aro cost of doing business, calculating the Aro would purchase captives and commodities at higher prices with alternative imported items, such as cloth, tobacco, and spirits.[20] The embargo also increased the premium for firearms, illustrating not only the heavy militarization of the region but also the urgency of British threat.

For their part, the beleaguered Aro interpreted any local resistance to their influence as a manifestation of British machinations and perceived resisting groups as collaborators with the British. They were determined to resist British encroachment, which they did with considerable success (Lynn 1997:167).[21] By 1899, however, their exasperation came to a head; they abandoned diplomacy as a way of dealing with the British, resorting to force in communities friendly with the British (Gallwey 1902). When in 1899 the Aro "proclaimed a *Ju Ju* [curse] of barrenness on all women who should crack palm nuts and deal in kernels ... the kernel trade in some localities fell off 50 per cent or more."[22] In the same year, the Aro incited and assisted the Ibibio, certain communities on the upper Cross River, in the delta and along the Niger to oppose the British.[23] On November 21, 1900, the Aro invaded the town of Obegu in southern Igboland as a punitive action for its friendship with the British, and, by British account, massacred some 400 people.[24] Similarly, "under a shallow pretext," they attacked in May 1901 several Ibibio communities which were friendly to the British, "killing large numbers, in one case wiping out a whole

---

[20] CO 520/14: "Memorandum Concerning the Aro Expedition," pp. 8–9, 12.
[21] Anthony Nwabughuogu (1982) has argued that penetration into the interior by European traders and, therefore, the displacement of African middlemen in the lower Niger did not start until 1905. While this may be true for the Cross River region, where Nwabughuogu draws his data exclusively from, the Niger delta was different. In the Niger, unlike the Cross River region, European traders and firms had been a common feature since the mid-nineteenth century, evidenced by the activities of William Cole (1862), Harry Cotterell, John Whitford (1877) and Harold Blindloss (1898).
[22] CO 520/6/33280: More to Secretary of State, October 11, 1900.
[23] CO 520/14: "Memorandum Concerning the Aro Expedition," pp. 9–11.
[24] CO 520/14: "Memorandum Concerning the Aro Expedition," pp. 14–15.

village, and carrying off all they could seize to sell as slaves."[25] No doubt, the British viewed such incidents as hostile acts, and they were inclined to blame the Aro for any obstacle they faced. Their reports were not simply exaggerations by British officials intent on justifying their colonial project. Traditions from among the Aro and other groups in the region confirm the trend reflected in the reports. The wars of the era are fresh in the memory of Aro people, and they reflected the changed Aro perceptions of violence and its place in their relationships.[26]

OTHER CAUSES OF MILITARIZATION

Aro militarization also drew from economic and cultural changes within Aro society. By the 1890s, intensifying competition from non-Aro traders, an increase in the regional population, and the involvement in palm-oil production of hitherto food-producing groups, which resulted in dwindling food supplies, compelled the Aro virtually everywhere to embark on food production on a large scale. Faced with a food shortage, which was bound to affect a nonfood producing group severely, the Aro saw food production not only as a way of resolving the food shortage but also as a commercial opportunity. The palm-producing groups provided markets for Aro agricultural surplus. Agriculture on a large scale required a massive labor supply and abundance of arable land, but as a trading group, the Aro had settled in small, semi-urbanized compact settlements without considering agricultural suitability.[27] The Aro thus had to acquire both labor and land, a need that fueled militarization. One might expect that as slave traders with ready access to people and with whom the non-Aro often desired to be associated, the Aro would easily be able to increase their labor pool in a period of expansion, but this was not to be.

[25] CO 520/12/25807: Moor to Secretary of State, July 7, 1901, p. 3.
[26] Mbonu Ojike, born in the 1900s in the Aro diaspora settlement of Arondizuogu, recalled his father and his father's friend "talk invariably ... about wars" they had witnessed in "the good old days" (Ojike 1946:9). Missionaries in the Okigwe area, near Arondizuogu, in 1910 reported about the impact of "continual wars" and slave raiding (Isichei 1976:85). I was informed that merchant-warriors from late-nineteenth-century Arondizuogu carried out operations in northern Igboland (Maduadichie 1996).
[27] "The trading settlements ... became 'free cities' to which all who wished to 'traffic and exchange' safely repaired, international courts where individuals and clans in conflict sought justice from the undisputed authority of the Oracle" (K.O. Dike 1956:39, 45). A British observer in the early twentieth century described them as "mission stations" (J.G. Allen n.d.:iii). Some of their inhabitants acted as "trade callers" and some others as money lenders (G.I. Jones 1989:36; Ottenberg 1971).

The very process of acquiring people fomented friction and civil crisis; wars arose, among other reasons, as a means of acquiring and retaining dependents. One of the most frequent causes of conflicts among the merchant-warriors was the granting of asylum to (or the acquisition of) disgruntled slaves by "powerful nobles" from groups competing with the ones the dependents defected from (K.O. Dike and Ekejiuba 1990:180; Igwegbe 1962:114). This was the case in the skirmishes involving rival merchant-warlords Okoro Idozuka of Arondizuogu and Okoli Ijeoma of Ndeikelionwu. Okoro Idozuka's internal enemy, Ozigbo Okereke of Ndiogbuonyeoma, also called Itejirisinkakwu (a pot used to cook bush rat, meaning "atrocious" pot), allied with Okoli Ijeoma. Okoro Idozuka was in the habit of making punitive expeditions against those who "kidnapped" his men (E.N. Okoli 1977:31, 33). In spite of the violence that accompanied this activity, these disputes did nothing to stop the massive expansion of the Aro populations that was observed during the period.

The acquisition of land was even more contentious. Struggles over land gave free reign to the martial ethos among the Aro. Arondizuogu groups, in particular, fought against one another in the scramble for land seized from non-Aro groups. As one of my respondents put it, "we first opened up the place and later began to quarrel over boundaries" (Maduadichie 1996). Eastward migrations to the Imo River and other areas from the last years of the nineteenth century onward resolved the crisis of agricultural space among the Aro, but it increased Aro conflicts with their non-Aro neighbors. Land grabbing placed a higher premium on having dependents than ever before, and at the same time presented the dependents with the opportunity to raise their economic and social standing through acts of valor.

The Nri-Awka cultural influence was a major agent of militarization and increased violence among the Aro. Nri-Awka traditions often refer to the Aro as predators, but martial ethos probably diffused to the Aro diaspora from the Nri-Awka area. The contemporary history of the Nri-Awka region is replete with wars and violence, and their repercussions, as the region's oral traditions and numerous undergraduate theses in Nigerian universities and colleges testify.[28] Since these wars often involved struggles over arable land and living space, which had been scarce in Igboland for at least the previous century, militarization would have taken root in the region before it diffused to the Aro. One warrior from a nearby war-like community in eastern Nri-Awka reportedly founded one of the

---

[28] Amaechi 1987; Anaedobe 1977; Ezenibe 1977; Ifediora 1987; Ogbuozobe 1986; E.O. Okafor 1978; J.C. Okoli 1977; C.S. Umeh 1984.

quarters of the Ndieni Aro settlement of Ndikelionwu (J. Ezeilo 1980). The Nri-Awka cultural influence accounts for the regional variations in Aro attitudes to warfare. Whereas the Aro who were operating out of Arochukwu, Ibibioland, and southern Igboland continued to rely heavily on Cross River Igbo fighters, their counterparts in close proximity to the Nri-Awka region increasingly organized and fought their own wars. The brand of warfare that the Aro came to adopt differed from that of their machete-wielding, surprise-invading Cross River Igbo allies, whose primary war objective was to decapitate as many people as possible; rather, it resembled that of the Nri-Awka region. The Nri-Awka model of warfare had in the nineteenth century come to be marked by giving advance warning to the enemy and the use of overwhelming force and a wider array of weaponry, ranging from charms to firearms, with occasional raiding, plundering, and as has happened to Owa, often land grabbing as a major objective. Meek has observed that although the use of firearms in wars was forbidden, this rule "was frequently broken." Even though he does not pinpoint Aro merchant-warriors, we have already seen that they relished pushing the boundaries (Meek 1937:243). Nri-Awka was also invariably organized around what Onwuejeogwu (1981:49–50) has described as the "personality cult," a phenomenon that combined strong character, drive, entrepreneurship and big ego in a "big man" (Talbot 1926c:838, 844; Eni 1972:15–17; Nnolim 2007:35–36; Onwuejeogwu 1975:51; Onwuejeogwu 1981:28, 61, 170; Onyekwelu 2001:5–7). The Aro merchant-warrior of this era embodied the personality cult. With the direct participation of the Aro in wars, the hitherto localized destabilizing influence of martial ethos among small, fragmented Nri-Awka polities became more systematic in the hands of an ambitious, networked trading group backed by widespread oracular influence and commercial power.

FEATURES OF MILITARIZATION

In addition to the increased incidence of Aro wars during the second half of the nineteenth century was the phenomenon of Aro civil wars, which had been extremely rare in Aro history up to this point. The earliest incidence of Aro civil wars of the nineteenth century was perhaps the Ogu Amakoba (Allied War), between Ndieni groups of Ndikelionwu and Ujari in what appears to have been the 1820s.[29] Such conflicts became more

---

[29] The date of this war is inferred from genealogy. Ijeoma was the fifth son of Ikerionwu, the mid-eighteenth-century progenitor of Ndeikelionwu. Ijeoma died shortly after the

frequent in the second half of the century, as Aro groups feuded over spheres of influence and agricultural space. British Major A.G. Leonard, who had ventured into Igboland as far as the main Aro market town of Bende in 1896, reported that the Aro traders had split into rival factions (Leonard 1898:205). Another British observer, Roger Casement, had reported in 1894 that two Arochukwu lineage-groups were at war with one another (see Northrup 1978b:141). One such conflict had occurred in about 1862 between Arondizuogu and the Ndieni cluster.[30] In fact, each Arondizuogu lineage-group at one time or another engaged another in a war that involved "a significant element of firearms."[31]

Not only did militarization increase friction among Aro groups, it also promoted reliance on external alliances in intra-Aro disputes. During the Allied War of about the 1820s, for example, Ndeikelionwu under the leadership of Ijeoma relied on an alliance that included several non-Aro communities in the vicinity of Ndieni to make a protracted war on fellow Ndieni group Ujari.[32] These alliances developed at the same time the Aro civil wars became frequent.

Defensive requirements against invasions and raids facilitated the evolution of new residential structures. Up to second half of the nineteenth century, the Aro maintained a compact residential structure, reminiscent of what Equiano describes for the eighteenth century.

Each master of a family has a large square piece of ground, surrounded with a moat or fence, or enclosed with a wall made of red earth tampered, which, when dry is as hard as brick. Within this, are his houses to accommodate his family and slaves, which, if numerous, frequently present the appearance of a village. In the middle, stands the principal building appropriated to the sole use of the master and consisting of two apartments; one in which he sits in the day with his family, the other is left apart for the reception of his friends. ... These houses never exceed one story in height. (Equiano 1995:37)

While this compact residential structure survived in Arochukwu and, to a lesser extent, in Ujari, it broke down in many Aro settlements in the 1890s, notably in Arondizuogu. This was when many people migrated to outlying low-density regions in pursuit of agricultural land, a process

---

Allied War, suggesting that he was probably advanced in years at the time of the war (Eni 1973:15–17).
[30] This date is provided by Dike and Ekejiuba (1990:180).
[31] M.S. Igwe (1996); Igwegbe (1962); Maduadichie (1996); E.N. Okoli (1977:34). The quotation is from Igwe.
[32] For details of these alliances, see Eni (1973:15–17).

that produced highly dispersed settlements in the new areas. At the same time, Aro architecture changed in response to the defense requirements of the period. Architectural change was marked in Aro settlements in central Igboland, where some merchant-warriors built two-storey structures; the upper floor served as a guard post, while the base housed the cannons and other ordnance.[33] One of these structures was still intact in Arondizuogu in 1996.

The frequency of wars inevitably led to specialization in different facets of war-making. Specialized strategists and tacticians, generically called ọkpa ịta, got credit for valor (M.S. Igwe 1996). Men who bestrode the commercial and military life of the time emerged in all the central Igbo Aro settlements. Perhaps the two most prominent merchant-warriors of this period were Okoro Udozuka of Arondizuogu and Okoli Ijeoma of Ndieni. These merchant-warriors were sometimes generally known as *agawhu* (bandit, outlaw, crook, hero). Depending on the context, this awe-inspiring term evoked abhorrence and contempt or endearment and reverence. Men of valor generally enjoyed high status as heroes or, at least, were feared. Nicknames like Ogburie (may the conqueror appropriate the booty), Ụgbọgụ (war chest/war vessel), and Ọsụachara (grass terminator/general terminator) gained currency. Some of those names, such as Nkpụñụghụñụ, Ogbujingidi, Otirigidi, and Ogbunyịvwa, have no definite meanings outside their onomatopoeic value, which at any rate is suggestive of ruthlessness and inspires awe. Okoro Idozuka, also called Agadagbachiriụzọ (the pillar that blocks the way), took an additional awe-inspiring alias after every major triumph (Igwegbe 1962; E.N. Okoli 1977:33–34).

The moral economy of the region all but broke down. The Aro had had merchant-warriors before this time, including men like Izuogu Mgbokpo of Arondizuogu, Ikelionwu Mgboro of Ndikelionwu and Oti Emesinwa of Ujari (Ajali). These merchant-warriors were primarily entrepreneurs, but they commanded respect by virtue of their wealth in trade goods and people and their ability to influence non-Aro using tact and diplomacy, while not hesitating to mobilize the Cross River Igbo warriors when this approach

---

[33] Information about Aro architecture is based on fieldwork observation and interviews with respondents in Arochukwu, Arondizuogu and Ujari. Information from Ndeikelionwu comes from N. Okoli (1972). I am particularly indebted to Ezumoha Okoroji 1996; Igwilo (1996b); Mgbemene (1996); Okoro Ndubisi (1996); J.G. Okoro (1986). I first became interested in the towers after reading J.G. Okoro's (1985) concern about their disappearance. There is also detailed information in Ojike (1946:21–25). Some of these structures are now disappearing.

failed. Taking part in fighting was beneath him. The merchant-warrior of the second half of the nineteenth century was also an entrepreneur, but he thrived on ruthlessness, craved to be feared, and was willing to demonstrate his military prowess. It was not just how the merchant-warriors saw themselves; being a warmonger and a war maker became respectable. There were few taboos in the eyes of the merchant-warriors, who seemed to relish their guts and ability to perpetrate outrage. The merchant-warriors upset what appears to have been a mutually respectful relationship between the Aro and scared Nri. As Onwuejeogwu reports, for example, Eze Nri Ezenwali spent considerable time in the second half of the century trying – ultimately unsuccessfully – to check the activities of Aro merchant-warrior Okoli Ijeoma of Ndikelionwu through war and diplomacy (Onwuejeogwu 1975:51; 1981:28, 61, 170). Ironically, most of the Aro merchant-warriors now harassing the communities of the Nri-Awka region were descendants of men and women from that region, a fact that also underscores the provenance of Aro warrior ethos of the nineteenth century.

As in life, the warriors received great honor and reverence in death. Typically, during the funeral of a late-nineteenth-century Ndieni merchant-warrior, a cock "was torn mouthwise" and its blood spilled in the eyes of the man. "The heart of a live ram (emblem of fortitude) was dug out and placed on the [dead] warrior's chest. His spirit was prayed to reincarnate with the fortitude of a ram and the bravery of a lion."[34] In Arondizuogu, ogbugba, a war dance that only the strongest men dared to participate in, followed at the central market, Eke Obinikpa, the last act in the funeral of a great man. The dancers dressed up in war gear, danced to the tune of the *ikperikpe* (war drum) and dared anyone to challenge them for a duel. Ikperikpe specialists used the instrument to glorify the feats the dancers had performed in battle and to inspire future exploits. A sample of a lyric used on these occasions rendered to me in 1996 is instructive in understanding the mentality that prevailed in the period (Igwilo 1996a). Only those with the will and resources mobilized a sufficient following of agile youths that attempted to perform it. The performers received congratulations after a successful outing (Ojike 1946). Okoro Idozuka demonstrated his mettle with an impressive performance of this dance during the funeral of his brother-in-law, the founder of an Arondizuogu lineage-group (E.N. Okoli 1977:36). *Ogbugba* illustrates how much warrior ethos had penetrated even the artistic life of the Aro diaspora.

---

[34] Eni (1973:42). Parentheses are Eni's.

The emergence of agawhu among central Igbo Aro was consistent with the culture of violence of nineteenth-century West Africa. Daryll Forde noted the rise of "petty war leaders" across the region (Forde 1953:218). Elizabeth Isichei identifies "New Men" whose emergence generally characterized nineteenth-century Igbo history (Isichei 1976:104–07). These men were invariably Aro allies, and in Awka, they used their profits to build flamboyant houses and to take prestigious titles (N. Nworji 1986). One such man, Ejiofo of Oba, a returnee from Arochukwu, settled on the eastern flank of the town in the direction of Ichi. He "became so powerful ... encroached into and seized many people's lands (sic). He kidnapped and sold into slavery everybody who dared to question his authority" (Obi-Buenyi 1986:5–6). According to one northern Igbo tradition, people from those communities visited Aro settlements to trade and returned to sell their people (Nwamba 1973). The late-nineteenth-century trader Onyeama of Eke in northern Igboland fits this description (see Onyeama 1982:21). Given that similar characters and the conflicts they inspired sprouted in coastal societies as well, Aro merchant-warriors and militarization were a conspicuous extension of region-wide escalation of violence.

CONSEQUENCES OF MILITARIZATION

Not surprisingly, the wars of the nineteenth century left permanent scars on the region. Owa in the Nri-Awka axis is one of the communities known to have disappeared completely during the mid-nineteenth century. Oral traditions of the area attribute Owa's destruction to its neighbor Nimo, which was joined in an alliance by Adazi-Nnukwu and Oraukwu. These towns shared the despoiled Owa territory. Two other towns, Umu-Ori and Ozu, are said to have also been destroyed in that part of the Nri-Awka region during the same era (Ogbukagu 1997: 323, 330, 331–33). As noted in Chapter 3, Owa exists in Arondizuogu folklore only because many of its inhabitants descended from Owa refugees, including the founder of a major lineage-group, transferred to Arondizuogu. Traditions relate that an Aro merchant-warrior displaced the present-day Ugwuoba on the Mamu River from their original site around Enugwu-Ukwu (Agu 1985).[35] Many of the people of Amaokpala, a preexisting group

---

[35] Indeed, Ugwuoba people were reported in the 1930s to have acknowledged "no relationship at all" with the rest of Mbasato – Awka, Amawbia, Ebenebe, Nawgu, Nibo and Nise. See NAE MILGOV. 13/1/17: Mbanasataw-Awka Division, 1936. Agu attributes

in the Ndieni area, "were scattered in many places," including Nkwere, Ekwulobia, and Ihiala. Perhaps, the largest concentration of these refugees were in Nkwere, where they cloned Amaokpala deities (Onyekwelu 2001:2–3, 7).

The following incident illustrates the close relationship between firearms, violence, slavery, displacement and general insecurity in the Nri-Awka region in the late nineteenth century. After Ezenne Ezeanakwe, a prominent person in Adazi-Nnukwu in the Nri-Awka region, shot and killed his friend – apparently inadvertently during a funeral gun salute – he was required to proceed on a seven-year exile, in addition to three of his five children being sold into slavery as a reprisal and the two others going into hiding. While his son Anaeto who was sold to Arondizuogu was later redeemed and returned to Adazi-Nnukwu by Ezeanakwe's other son Ojiako, his two unidentified daughters never returned, though her family suspected that one of them ended up being "married" into the prominent Bob-Manuel of the coastal city-state of Degema. Ezeanakwe was himself later killed while fighting in one of the wars involving his town (Ojiako 2010; "Genealogy"). Indeed, Ezeanakwe's life and experience sum up the violence and insecurity that pervaded nineteenth-century Nri-Awka. Displacement often came with destruction and transplantation.

The rise of martial ethos among the Aro overheated the social and political landscape to the extent that it strained relations between the Aro and the Cross River Igbo warrior groups that had fought Aro wars. Growing Aro pugnaciousness and belligerence tested the limits of the moral economy that governed the warriors' participation in wars. "These warriors would ... be satisfied that there was really an injury that warranted reparation or enforcement of a mutually agreed contract which had been broken. Contrary to the received notion, they were not at the beck and call of the Aro." Traditions of the "Abam" recount occasional refusal to fight for the Aro if they were not satisfied with the cause.[36] The breakdown of this alliance was felt most in central Igboland; some of it was probably connected to aggression against Nri by the Aro merchant-warriors. As the warrior communities increasingly grew unwilling to tangle with ever-increasing Aro conflicts, the Aro took war matters into their own hands, and established their own fighting units and traditions.

---

the displacement of Ugwuoba to Okoli Ijeoma of Arondizuogu, but the antecedents of his Ndieni namesake suggests to the present author that the latter was the culprit.

[36] J. Okoro Ijoma (1994:43); Isichei (1976). The quotation is from Ijoma. For more on the nature of this relationship, see Onwuka Njoku 2000:61–72.

Apart from the strain in the Aro relations with the warriors, the declining relevance of the machete-wielding head hunters was also a consequence of the proliferation of firearms. Firearms were by far more effective offensive weapons than machetes, and the British embargo in the 1890s did not change that. The spread of firearms was a key development of nineteenth-century West African history. Not only had the weaponry stock of African societies increased over time, principally from the exchange of captives for guns and gunpowder, but importation of weapons increased during the nineteenth century. Imports into Africa increased most dramatically between the 1820s and 1860, from £10.6 million to £41.3 million (in 1988 British sterling). The value of British exports to Africa increased tenfold between 1817 and 1820 and 1846 and 1849 (Eltis and Jennings 1988:940, 941). Per capita gun imports into Africa were probably highest in the 1860s.[37] Because the elite groups of this region had the most purchasing power in western Africa, they were the ones who would have acquired much of the weaponry imported before the ban took effect. The likely existence of a weapons stockpile in the Bight of Biafra would have been enough to stimulate militarization, and increased importation in the second half of the century made such a prospect even more likely – a fact that prompted the British to suspend imports of this item. More than simply increasing the frequency of warfare, however, the increasing influx of firearms changed its character and the structure of relationships and alliances. As Cross River Igbo fighters did not significantly modernize their tactics and, certainly, did not modernize their arms, the Aro invariably relied less on them over time. The increasing participation of the Aro in fighting wars was therefore also consequence of changes in the structure of warfare in the region. Faltering alliances with Cross River Igbo neighbors, the accumulation of firearms, and the rise of martial ethos among the Aro reinforced one another in a vicious cycle of violence.

DECADENCE

Violence during the second half of the nineteenth century symptomized deeper systemic malaise than had originated in the slave trade and its

---

[37] European and American exports to Africa are estimated as follows: one gun per 118 persons in the 1780s, one gun per 145 persons in the 1820s, and one gun per 103 persons in the 1860s (Eltis and Jennings 1988:954). The quantities could be higher; guns were recorded under "iron wrought" (p. 361). Except for ordinance, firearms were not normally recorded separately in British Customs figures (Johnson 1984:364).

Cultural and Economic Aftershocks

ending. The effective ending of the Atlantic slave trade in the 1840s occasioned major changes in economic and social practices. For example, those deemed as miscreants and political enemies and had typically been exported overseas in the heyday of the Atlantic slave trade now ended up in the hands of indigenous slave owners, creating problems of social control. Sale to Euro-American buyers had given the authorities a way of dealing with these individuals. Their sale raised revenues and made expenditure on prisons unnecessary (Curtin 1990:119, 120; 1993:177). One respondent, who lived long enough to have witnessed the immediate post–slave trade era, recalled in 1996 that the Aro bought two dissenting Ọzọ titled men from leaders of their communities in about 1900 (G.N. Okoli 1996). Her description of their Ọzọ marks and the circumstances of their sale recall the image of rebellious captives that Captain John Adams carried regularly to the Americas in the late eighteenth century (Adams 1832:41). The acquisition and retention of such individuals added to the tensions and violence of the period. This category of people would often have been killed during the second half of the nineteenth century, or their incorporation into their owners' societies would have been a potential source of violence.

Of importance in understanding these tensions is the fact that the reckless oppression of dependents on the part of Aro notables breached the moral economy of slavery. The remnants of late-nineteenth-century architecture eloquently testify to increasing oppression. A dark, windowless room that served as a detention chamber (*mkpuruisi*) became an indispensable part of the homes of late-nineteenth-century Aro slave owners. Torture platforms, such as the one observed in the residence of late-nineteenth-century merchant-warrior Okoroji, seem to have been widespread as well. These structures were necessary to control recalcitrant captives now employed domestically. If the ideology of slavery emphasizing the social mobility of acquired persons and their assimilation into Aro society had seemed realistic and facilitated acquired people's embrace of Aro society before the mid-nineteenth century, such an ideology was harder to sustain in the face of the systematic and routine oppression that prevailed in the second half of the century. Increased oppression was the necessary consequence of the insecurities of a master class threatened by the presence of large slave populations.

Dependents and subordinate groups did not always choose to remain victims. For example, two large subordinate groups in Arondizuogu formed a "grand alliance" against the local amadi group sometime in the second half of the nineteenth century, and won a "decisive victory" (see Igwegbe 1962:15–16). Other oppressed people embarked on solo and unorthodox forms to resistance. The story of Ogbuofelu, acquired from Nnobi in the Nri-Awka region in the 1890s, recurred during fieldwork in Arondizuogu. One respondent said in a rueful tone shared by Ogbuofelu's owner's grandson that "no one died naturally among us. The cause [of the unnatural death of many in the lineage] was this idiot that they brought from Nnobi called Ogbuofelu."[38] Clearly, increased oppression contributed to the tensions of the period.

The deepening sense of oppression associated with late-nineteenth-century transitions also affected the social order and had implications on the spiritual life of the Aro diaspora. It led to the emergence in the largest Aro diaspora settlement, Arondizuogu, of the *osu*, an Igbo caste system that deemed some individuals and families to "belong" to particular deities. Forbidden all social contact with the regular community, these people lived by, and performed custodial services for, the shrines of the specific deities they supposedly belonged to. People who became osu remained so along with their descendants in perpetuity (see Nwokeji 1998b:323n; 2000b). Unlike Senegambia where castes were occupational groups and interacted with the general population, however, the osu were outcastes, whom others consigned to cater to the shrines or who placed themselves in the services of those shrines.[39] The *osu* were an occupational group only to the extent that they tended to the shrines and received part of the sacrifice made to the shrines. They also did subsistence farming. Oldendorp was clearly referring to the *osu* when he noted from his interview of Igbo-area respondents: "There are various people under him, which can be called living sacrifices. No shears come to them, no hair of theirs can be cut. They do not marry, do not have their own house, rather they are always with others, they eat and drink by themselves, take what they will and no one prevents them. The priests are named from among these people" (Oldendorp 2000: ms. 466). The *osu* responsibility for tending shrines supports the suggestion that the institution represented a priestly function before the Atlantic slave trade, but that the trade changed its character (J.G. Okoro 1996; Umo n.d.:20). Every market had a priest who was also called osu, after the name of the market that he served. Thus, there were Osueke (for the Eke market), Osuawho (Awho market), Osunkwo (Nkwo market), and Osuoye (Oye Market). In other words, Aro people used the term osu to designate the priest. Just "like pastor means servant of God,

---

[38] C. Okoli (1996). Ogbuofelu's owner's grandson is Igwilo (1996a).
[39] For the Senegambia case, see M. Klein 1968:10; Tamari (1991).

osu means servant of a shrine" (J.G. Okoro 1996). Although these names are common among the Aro, it is unclear that all or even most of the bearers of the names were priests.

While the institution seems to have been well-established among the Igbo by the nineteenth century, the Aro did not discriminate against the osu, and their society did not develop the institution, except in Arondizuogu in the late nineteenth century. When, for example, Oti Emesinwa made his early trips to the Nri-Awka region from his Arochukwu base in the mid-eighteenth century, outcasts (presumably osu) were among the individuals he "gathered around" him, showing that the Aro were willing to incorporate the osu. Later, he and his Ujari group settled among the Umu-Ajana (people of the earth shrine) of preexisting Akpu, on whose land the Ujari settled (Eni 1973:9, 15). This location was reminiscent of an osu quarter, but there is not even a hint that the Ujari were bothered by such an arrangement. Thus, the Aro embraced a group which central Igbo people rejected. Why then did the institution emerge in Arondizuogu toward the end of the century?

If the Atlantic slave trade changed the character of the institution in other parts of Igboland, it was the ending of the trade that generated these changes in Arondizuogu.[40] Flight from the oppression that hallmarked the tensive transition of the late nineteenth century was the immediate cause of the osu institution in Arondizuogu. Aggrieved Mgbawho Ogirisi, a slave of Okoro Udozuka's wife, fled to the Ududonka shrine with her children during a time that would have been the 1890s, becoming perhaps the first osu family in the town. One free family, running away from their creditor, sought refuge in the Haba deity in another lineage-group.[41] At the destination deity, the refugee would say the ritual:"*Arusi, mbaa*!" (Shrine, I submit myself to your protection).[42]

The Arondizuogu version of the osu institution differed in character from that of the rest of Igboland in other ways. Some of my respondents

---

[40] Kanu Umo (n.d.:19) has claimed that the shrines that produced the institution became part of Arondizuogu "after the decline of 'Chuku'" (i.e., the *Ibiniukpabi* oracle). *Ibiniukpabi* did not decline until after the British Aro Expedition of 1901–02. As late as 1878, the Belgian mariner Adolphe Burdo had noted *Ibiniukpabi*'s influence as far as the Niger River (see Burdo 1880:159–61). The shrines in Arondizuogu coexisted with *Ibiniukpabi*. *Ibiniukpabi*'s main function was judicial, for the non-Aro. The Aro, both in the metropole and in the diaspora, had the shrines they worshipped.

[41] M.S. Igwe (1996); Kanu-Igbo (1996b); Maduadichie (1996); A. Muotoh (1996); J.G. Okoro (1996).

[42] This particular dimension was given by Kanu-Igbo (1996b). He could not tell the meaning of the word *mbaa*. It is probably not an Igbo word.

stressed that, unlike in other parts of Igboland, nobody sacrificed to the shrines persons who became osu; the victims themselves chose to become osu, albeit under indirect duress.[43] Also, contrary to the situation in most Igbo societies, all of my respondents stressed the fluidity of the osu institution in Arondizuogu. They also stressed that it no longer existed by the late twentieth century. This difference touches at the core of the osu system – the immutability of the osu condition elsewhere in Igboland. While the osu condition was (and still is) immutable in other places, it may be nullified in Arondizuogu with the simple performance of the appropriate rites of passage.[44]

While the transitions of the late nineteenth century created the material conditions for the emergence of the osu institution in Arondizuogu, the broader cultural impact of people from the Nri-Awka axis created the ideological environment. Individuals – whether slaves, ordinary immigrants, or refugees – came to Arondizuogu with various cultural packages. The historian J.G. Okoro told me in English that "Arondizuogu did not result from the migration of one race. People came with different kinds of manners and customs. There is no single way of shrine worshipping in Arondizuogu" (J.G. Okoro 1996). The result is that every lineage-group has shrines that reflect the provenance of its population or sections of it. Among the myriad shrines that sprang up in Arondizuogu, only the Ngene Okwe at nde-Awa has Arochukwu provenance. These various shrines were adaptations of the parent shrines of the same names in various parts of the Biafra hinterland.[45] The idea of seeking refuge in shrines as an escape from oppression emanated from the shrines, beliefs, social constructions, fears and myths of immigrants from other parts of Igboland, particularly those from Nri-Awka.

---

[43] For *osu* as a priestly function originally, see R. Okeke (1986); Isichei (1976). For the sacredness of the *osu*, see M.S. Igwe (1996); Igwegbe (1962:102); J.G. Okoro (1996).
[44] M.S. Igwe (1996); Kanu-Igbo (1996b); Muotoh (1996); C. Okoli (1996); J.G. Okoro (1996). The fluidity of the Arondizuogu variant of the institution probably led the historian J. Okoro Ijoma (1994:41) to deny that the *osu* institution even existed among the Aro.
[45] For example, a pioneer member of Arondizuogu and founder of the Ndiamazu lineage-group, Amazu, came from Oro in the Oji River region of today's Enugu State with *Iyi-Ogba*. Another, Iheme from Nise near Awka, came with Ajagu. *Udogwugwu* of nde-Ejezie came from Eziama, the original home of Ejezie, the founder of the lineage-group. Nde-Ukwu has Ochichi from Achi. Many subordinate groups within these lineages also brought shrines corresponding to their original homes. For example, *Nkwo Adazi* of Ndiamazu was brought by the section that immigrated to nde-Amazu from Adazi near Nri. The same was the story of *Haba* in nde-Aniche. *Haba* was adopted from Agulu.

The pursuit of conspicuous consumption promoted greed, impoverished people and rendered them vulnerable to enslavement by their creditors. A growing culture of conspicuous consumption ensured the extremely high cost of funerals, marriages, and other ceremonies. "Gun salutes," or multiple firing of canon, as well as human sacrifices – practices that developed during the overseas slave trade era – became regular features of the funerals of the rich. Slave-ship captains ordered gun salutes when coastal kings boarded newly arrived ships to collect customs, and human sacrifice developed as the overseas trade cheapened human life.[46] Even though the sale of human beings generated revenues, diminished value for human life was an inevitable consequence of a culture of violence and death that resulted from slave capture, warfare, raiding, and resistance. Although slave traders calculated the value of their captives in terms of profits, nothing would stop them sacrificing the captives if they calculated that such sacrifice would replenish their cost in manifold proportions. The primary focus of their interest was not human life but profit, which they could apparently achieve through either destruction or preservation, as they might calculate in any given circumstance. Economic and spiritual considerations were linked. These extremely expensive, decadent and sometimes gruesome undertakings deepened stratification. Human sacrifice also fed on and promoted the domestic slave trade, as perpetrators had first to acquire the individuals needed for the purpose. Even head hunting is associated with the late-nineteenth-century history of Arondizuogu.[47] These untoward practices represented cultural changes that were the consequences of either the overseas slave trade or of its suppression.

How can one argue that the slave trade was socially malevolent and at the same time argue that its ending made the situation worse? Indeed, in spite of significant increases in population and material conditions, the ending of the slave trade and the corresponding growth of the commodity export trade failed to relieve the affected societies of violence

---

[46] The practice of "gun salutes" had developed by the end of seventeenth century when European slave traders used it to entertain and honor both themselves and prominent Africans they dealt with. For example, on or about May 1, 1699, the slaver *Albion-Frigate* fired seven-gun salute for King William of New Calabar when he went aboard to collect duties. In late June of the same year, King William and master of another English ship at the port were also each recipients of a seven-gun salute; later, Captain Edwards of the *Albion-Frigate* received another seven rounds, when "he returned ashore" (James Barbot).

[47] Dike and Ekejiuba (1990:252–53); Ekejiuba (1972b:14); Ofonagoro (1972:80). For head hunting, see Maduadichie (1996).

and insecurity. The ending of overseas slave export did not end the slave trade. Human sacrifice escalated as stratification deepened. Warfare became more frequent and more deadly as, among other factors, old slave trading elites resisted the challenge of powerful groups that emerged from the new economy. Finally, increased slaveholdings and inability to export recalcitrant slaves increased social problems and oppression. In the case of the Aro, the development of the warrior ethos and militarization added to the conundrum of violence.

A COMPARATIVE PERSPECTIVE

The extent of the region's involvement in the broader Atlantic and global contexts bespeaks not only the impact of external trade on these changes but also how these changes compared with changes elsewhere in Atlantic Africa. Nowhere else in Atlantic Africa, except perhaps Senegambia, did the ending of the overseas slave trade provoke as much tension as in the Bight of Biafra. The crisis that led to the eventual disintegration of the Oyo Empire had originated in the dynamics of the overseas traffic itself, rather than its ending, a process that was completed during the slave trade era.[48] In the Gold Coast, rather than disintegrate under the weight of the ending of the traffic, Asante expanded and consolidated its hegemony. In fact, the Gold Coast had witnessed its own crisis in the seventeenth century, when gold export plummeted and thereafter trade in captives lagged, which drastically reduced the region's stature in Atlantic Africa's economy. The Islamic jihads that contributed so much to the pressures of the nineteenth century in much of West Africa had nothing to do with the ending of the slave trade; they had been in progress well before. One fact that escapes the notice of historians is that, in comparison to earlier periods, most regions outside the Bight of Biafra witnessed political stability in the immediate aftermath of the ending of the transatlantic slave trade. In West-Central Africa, the effect of the ending of the overseas traffic also differed from the Biafra case. To start with, unlike in the Bight of Biafra, where the trade ended quickly (by the late 1830s), captive exportation lasted the longest in West-Central Africa, which in the nineteenth century exported more captives than it did in any previous century, and did so until as late as the 1860s.

---

[48] For the Oyo Empire, see Law 1977:245–99, esp. 255, 268, 274–75.

CONCLUSION

This chapter has highlighted the impact of the Atlantic slave trade not already anticipated in earlier chapters, as well as the impact of the ending of the traffic. The political, social, and ideological developments of the nineteenth century received impetus from the expanded internal slave trade and ongoing cultural transformations that resulted from the massive incorporation of non-Aro. The developments also resulted from Aro attempts to continue their dominance of trade against the backdrop of challenge from many other groups, often with British encouragement. The widening of the commercial sector encouraged other hinterland groups to become heavily involved in trade and in palm-oil production, at the same time that coastal traders were moving inland to trade rather than continue to depend entirely on the Aro as intermediaries between the hinterland and the coast. Extensive economic activities in the region, highlighted by its role as the center of palm produce production worldwide, accounted for the attention the British paid the region as the imperial power sought to influence affairs here. As traders and an influential group, the Aro drew much of this attention. The intensification of militarization and violence among the Aro must be understood in the contexts of long-term cultural evolution among the Aro and the nineteenth-century regional political economy of the Bight of Biafra.

8

Summary and Conclusions

In this book, I have departed from the sharp distinction that is often made between the roles of internal and external agencies in bringing about change in African history. Rather than seeing agency and causation in terms of these binary opposites, the book acknowledges the collaborative relevance of African and external agencies in shaping the transatlantic slave trade and its impact. Central to this approach is an emphasis on the interactions between slaving and culture and between the Bight of Biafra and the rest of the Atlantic world. Such a perspective has shaped the five main questions that have underpinned this study. These questions have implications for both the history of the region and the Atlantic system at large.

The first question concerns the dramatic rise of the Biafra Atlantic trade during the mid-eighteenth century. The emergence of the Aro in the early seventeenth century and their expansion that gathered momentum in the second quarter of the eighteenth century, facilitated the expansion of the Biafra Atlantic slave trade and shaped its character. Although this study has emphasized that Aro organization rested on identifiable institutions that had both state and diaspora characteristics, an Atlantic perspective is key to an understanding of the slave trade and its aftermath. The region responded to escalating labor demand in the Americas, and it was the Aro organization that ensured the gathering, bulking, transportation, and delivery of huge numbers of captives to the coast. The cultural corollary of this economic process was that, while captives from the region embarked on their forced journey to various American destinations with their experiences, including those relating to their deportation, the slave trade reconfigured the cultural landscape of the region, including the culture of the Aro who orchestrated the traffic in the hinterland.

An Atlantic perspective also throws light on a second question addressed in this study, namely, why there was a relatively high proportion of females in the Bight of Biafra slave trade. The gender structure of the slave trade provides a window for a more thorough understanding of transatlantic interactions involving African patterns of supply, American patterns of demand, and the sociocultural processes underpinning them. By focusing on the region's institutions and sociocultural processes – including the spiritual and social importance the Igbo attached to yam and kolanut – comparing them with other African regions, and relating them to developments elsewhere in the Atlantic region, the study has explained the unusual gender structure of the region's slave trade. Gender is part of a third, larger question about the means by which individuals became slaves or captives and why some were sent overseas and others were retained in the region. For example, while warfare in the region produced large numbers of women and children, it reduced the numbers of men because the region's principal warriors fought for men's heads, creating the possibility that war captives would be, overwhelmingly, women and children. At the same time, captives convicted of various criminal offences or classified as dissidents were overwhelmingly men. Dissidents, incriminated persons, and kidnap victims were sent into Atlantic slavery, while individuals who were enslaved out of economic necessity were mostly enslaved locally in the region, illustrating that the means of enslavement was a key determinant of where a captive served as slave. I have used both export samples and local sources to derive reliable information on the general character of enslavement, including the difference between those forced into Atlantic slavery and those who remained within the region. Until this study, scholars have relied exclusively on export samples in explaining the composition of the slave trade, an approach that distorted the reality of enslavement in Africa during the centuries of the Atlantic slave trade.

The fourth question with which this study was concerned is how the Aro coped with the suppression of the Atlantic slave trade in the nineteenth century and the long-term impact the export slave trade had on indigenous value systems. Many decades of significant integration of people from the war-ridden Nri-Awka region and the violence inherent in a slaving culture had resulted in a definite change in the Aro value system by 1850, specifically, the embrace of warrior ethos. Previous studies either ignored or glossed over these developments and have failed to link them to the impact of the Atlantic slave trade. Consequently, the irony in stories of the ravages of nineteenth-century Aro merchant-warriors, who commanded forces equipped with firearms, existing alongside a widespread belief that the Aro never took part in war but completely relied on the machete-wielding Cross River Igbo fighters to prosecute their wars remained unresolved.

A final central question that spurred this study is how such a large-scale commercial complex flourished in the Bight of Biafra, a region apparently characterized by segmentary political organization. This study has identified the evolving role of the state in Aro expansion, in particular the shift by the second quarter of the eighteenth century from state-sponsored expansion to expansion driven by state-supported private enterprise. Rather than emphasize either the presence of state or its absence as the key factor, however, this study has emphasized that the role of a trade diaspora is distinct from that of centralized state systems. The social organization of a trade diaspora enabled the Aro to establish and control a vast and sophisticated trading network and to preserve their identity and unity in the face of radical developments, especially during the nineteenth century. In contrast to explanations of Aro expansion that stress predilections and attributes of individual Aro, this study has pointed to identifiable institutions that had both state and diaspora characteristics.

Given their political and judicial influence, one might wonder if the Aro did not constitute an imperialism rather than a trade diaspora. After all, commerce was an important component of British imperialism – perhaps the best example of imperialism in modern history. The existence of a range of specialized political institutions in Aro organization supports such a proposition. At the apex of Aro organization was the Nna Ato (Three Fathers) chaired by Eze Aro (Aro King). Ọkpankpọ (Aro central council) was the most important of these institutions. The relevance of Ọkpankpọ to the present question of imperialism has been noted by the anthropologists P.C. Dike and Simon Ottenberg, who use the term "imperialism" to characterize Aro influence. As discussed below, the Aro promoted clones of some of their institutions in areas that were within the Aro network.

In spite of these imperial characteristics, the Aro are best seen as a trade diaspora. Unlike the British, for example, who often (although not always) maintained specialized sections of imperial agents (traders, soldiers, administrators, and missionaries), every male Aro was, at least until the 1890s, primarily involved in trade. Up until the mid-nineteenth century, their fighters were exclusively non-Aro. These Aro communities were involved in trade, and they incorporated significant numbers of non-Aro elements.

The cultural developments recounted in the foregoing pages shaped economic change and the structure of the Atlantic slave trade. I make no attempt to deny the economic basis of Aro slaving. As anthropologist Peter Gose has noted, culture itself is played out in the understanding and practice of the economic process (Gose 1994:xii). In this respect, the claims made in this study that demand conditions and prices encouraged the expansion of the Biafra trade, on the one hand, and that cultural elements shaped the categories of export captives, on the other, are compatible. The first claim touches on quantity, and the second on composition – two complementary, rather than contradictory, variables. Two implications may be drawn from this interplay of supply and demand dynamics. First, while slave dealers decided on whom they sold to Euro-American buyers (in this case, mainly kidnap victims, war captives, deviants, and incriminated persons), they directed most of these to the most profitable market, except when it was too dangerous to do so. Bonny had become this market by the mid-eighteenth century. Second, the demand pull affected the composition of export captives, just as the supply conditions affected quantity. Without Euro-American demand for captives, fewer persons would have been kidnapped, captured in war, or fallen victim to judicial processes. The heavy presence of captives from these categories, procured in response to demand, defined the composition of export captives. Aro exploitation of the hinterland, in particular the densely populated Igbo heartland, made captives available in large numbers and assured buyers reduced docking periods at Bonny. The fast turnaround rate reduced buyers' contact with the Biafra disease environment that was so inhospitable to Europeans. In short, Aro trade as an economic enterprise thrived as much as it did in part because of effective economic decisions; however, slaving among them and other groups in the Bight of Biafra was not a purely economic phenomenon.

Fundamentally, the study has thrown new light on Africa's role in shaping the Atlantic system and highlighted the ways one African region shaped the Atlantic slave trade. But the impact of external processes remained important throughout the era. In the first instance, the trade expanded in response to the expanding plantation complexes of the Americas. While forces within the Bight of Biafra shaped the trade, it was also subject to influences from Atlantic-wide processes. For example, the War of Jenkin's Ear, 1739–48, and the Seven Years' War, 1756–63, impacted the trade by disrupting shipping. In the end, too, external developments played the prominent role in ending the traffic. The slave trade involved African patterns of supply, American patterns of demand, and a whole range of processes underpinning them. Thus, a study of this kind also highlights the interaction of regional developments with those in the rest of the Atlantic world. The internal developments included macroeconomic processes, demographic trends, institutional development, and political and ideological change. On the other side of the Atlantic were mines and plantations that depended on African slave labor. In European cities, such as Bordeaux, Bristol, Liverpool, and Nantes, were financiers and merchants who organized the trade. These are well-known developments, but the interactive approach allows us to appreciate the extent to which African history helped to shape Euro-American processes.

Notes on Sources

Besides the scholarly literature, other kinds of sources inform the present study – export figures, memoirs, mariners' journals, archival material, missionary records, and oral data – each with its peculiar strengths, problems, and context. The overwhelming majority of the quantitative data for captive exports comes from the Trans-Atlantic Slave Trade Database. The present study initially used the first edition on CD-ROM (1999), but the database has since been revised and expanded in an online version (www.slavevoyaes.org). Wherever needed figures could not be generated from database, David Eltis always kindly provided them. Ironically, estimates for exports from the Bight of Biafra have been revised downward in the new Trans-Atlantic Slave Trade Database, meaning that the share of the slave trade for other regions, principally West-Central Africa, increased proportionately. The data used here were revised accordingly. Despite the changes, however, the basic trends in the volume and age and sex ratios of captives exported from the region remain virtually intact. The basic arguments, therefore, remain unaltered, although the changes inspired recalibrations in some interregional comparisons presented in the study, such as the rate at which slave ships loaded in African ports and the gender structure of the trade.

The archival material used in the study contains mostly concrete, dateable information. Still, several caveats about the use of these sources are necessary. First, the archival sources are strong only for the early twentieth century. Second, tracking down the relevant material was a tedious process. Many files that came under the slavery label contained unrelated material,[1] much of which tells us more about general social trends than slavery per se. For example, the reports of the commanders of the antislavery task force that began its work in 1933 and other reports and items of correspondence, often produced undifferentiated slavery-related data. The colonial intelligence and anthropological reports conform to Patrick Manning's characterization of them: they reflect "the political objectives of the administration [and] the social realities of the early twentieth century better than ... the history of slavery in Africa" (Manning 1990:16). In a moment of introspection, one colonial officer wrote that, in place of an "organized judicial and administrative system" for the Aro, "so great was the desire to destroy Aro power that little of the indigenous system was permitted to survive" (Shankland 1933:3). Court records, especially those relating to land cases, illuminate changes that followed the suppression of the Atlantic slave trade. Finally, concerning archival sources, a marriage register kept in 1919 and 1920 by the officer in charge of the Okigwe District, which included the largest Aro settlement, helps to reconstruct changes in marriage practices and occupational trends in the aftermath of the overseas slave trade. The occupations of the parents of the couples found in the register enable us to push the chronology of occupational changes one generation back.

The missionary records used here are from the Holy Ghost Fathers in Dublin, Republic of Ireland, the Church Missionary Society in Birmingham, England, and the Primitive Methodists in London. However, the actual use of these records in this study belies the effort put into sourcing and collating them, and the gracious support I received from the Holy Ghost Fathers in Dublin. First of all, the records are strongest on the Niger riverine communities where Christianity arrived earlier – in the mid-nineteenth century. Second, many of the records of the missionary societies that operated in Igboland have only contextual relevance. The missions have rich documentation on such issues as female circumcision, polygyny, and even fattening. I found no files on slavery. In 1995, in Dublin, when I asked why, Rev. Fr. Duignan, a Holy Ghost priest who spent his active service in Igboland from the late 1930s onward, told me that by the time he began his missionary work, the missions had already made their contacts – principally through the schools. Besides, the Igbo,

---

[1] For example, the Enugu archives file, "Cases of Slave Dealing," includes all manner of cases such as petty theft, marital squabbles, and land disputes that say little about slaving. NAE 1/1920 – OKIDIST 4/2/1:"Cases of Slave Dealing."

according to the retired pastor, had not been forthcoming on the question of slavery (Duignan 1995).

Although the Aro were a literate group, I have not been able to master their script enough to benefit from the information embedded in it. Together with the Cross River Igbo warrior groups and the Ibibio, the Aro had a script called *nsibiri* (or *nsibidi* in the Ibibio language).[2] This study could have benefited from the script, but literacy in it is restricted to the Ekpe confraternity.

These problems reinforce the role of oral tradition in this research, despite its many pitfalls. I formally interviewed forty-five respondents and discussed Aro slavery and slave trade with many more people, mainly in Arondizuogu and Arochukwu. I also studied hundreds of other traditions collected by such illustrious earlier researchers as David Northrup, Elizabeth Isichei, and the various authors of undergraduate theses in Nigerian universities. The purpose of this effort was threefold: to interrogate and buttress my evidence, infuse non-Aro perspectives into the study, and situate the Aro in the regional context.

Given that oral traditions constitute a significant part of the material utilized in this study and given their rather controversial reputation, it is necessary to clarify related methodological issues. My understanding of oral tradition is broad and consistent with the ideas of Jan Vansina and E.J. Alagoa, to whom oral tradition refers to all orally transmitted testimonies about the past, especially those passed from generation to generation, as well as a people's folklore (Alagoa 1966, 1968; Vansina 1961:142–64; 1985:25–27). But given that traditions tend to appear in synchronic form when cast in the *longue durée*, how does one deal with the important question of chronology? By posing this question, I do not mean that indigenous groups lacked a sense of chronology, that is, about what happened before or after, or the coincidences of events. They did, by and large.

Conscious of the established standards of my discipline, I urged respondents to endeavor to cite concrete examples of the issues and events they discussed and to indicate when they occurred. They did not always do so, leaving me to devise remedial strategies in my conceptualizations, data collection, and analysis. This is one reason that I, unlike some scholars, prefer to use the term "respondents" to "informants" for people interviewed. Many of them not only resisted my attempt to hedge them in through my professionally informed prescriptions, but they also taught

---

[2] For details about *Nsibiri*, see Dayrell 1911; Macgregor 1909; Talbot 1912: Appendix G.

me a lot about their history while relying on their own devises.³ From this, I learned like a critical student. While traditions may not refer to specific or actual events, they embody the cosmogony of a people and indicate historical trends. They also express abstract and real possibilities, as well as limitations, in such a people's society. As Afigbo has observed,

> the functions of oral tradition in a preliterate society go beyond the need to validate social structures, groups or institutions. They also serve as ideologies as well as represent a genuine attempt to reconstruct a meaningful story of the past. The interpretation of the past in the light of the present and vice versa is not peculiar to oral tradition. It is also characteristic of history in the best tradition of the word. It is this fact that makes Groce's famous dictum that all history is contemporary meaningful and valid. (Afigbo 1981b: 233n)

There is no one word that means "history" in the Igbo language. My Aro respondents referred to it as *akuko mgbe ochie* (story of old times). It seems that most other Igbo societies refer to it as *akuko-ala* (society's story). As literary critic Emmanuel Obiechina elaborated, the latter term encompasses history in the Western sense, plus a corpus of morals (see Obiechina 1994). Most of my respondents preferred to use the English word – history – including those whose knowledge of English was slight. It was clear that the people did not conceptualize history simply as charter narrative to validate the present, and they *did not* always tell charter. This observation departs from the widespread impression that oral traditions are invariably apologies for present politics.

Everyone that I spoke to – not just interviewed – conceptualized history as a distinct and knowable body of knowledge. One of my more helpful respondents said the following about Eze Izuogu, the ruler of Arondizuogu: "Go to him. He is a nice man. He might not know it all, but he will not tell you lies" (Michael Ike 1996). Many people lamented that, had I done my research a few years earlier when this or that man or the occasional woman was living, she or he "would have told you all about it." There was remarkable consistency in the mention of particular names, such as the late Obasi Bassey Igbo of Ikpaeze and late Udoji Mmeruonye of Ndiakunwanta. The social backgrounds of these persons varied widely, but they were united in their acclaimed knowledge

---

³ Bentor reports of a similar experience in Arondizuogu. "I began to feel irritated. Things were not working the way they should. ... My hosts resisted the division of labor. I had to rethink my relationship with them. My own response was to abandon terms such as informant and field research" (Bentor 1994:3, 4).

of "history." Yet, this kind of recognition implies that a historian could interview one person and find out all there is to historical knowledge! The essential point here, however, is that history for the Aro people is, above all, a body of knowledge and truth, of which there are pundits and which should not be contaminated with falsehood. One of the men that I interviewed was recommended widely by persons from various backgrounds, but, in almost every case, I was warned to beware of his lies! This means that there is an objective body of historical knowledge –not simply group charter – which even the enemy (or one who is known for telling lies sometimes) alone might posses.[4]

Due to the sensitive nature of the subject of slavery, an overwhelming majority of the respondents with whom I had lengthy interviews reached a point where they refused to answer certain questions. Such questions as whose ancestors were slaves and how the Aro came to occupy certain regions were often sensitive. Some respondents preferred to refer me to particular individuals to answer such questions. In some cases, the reason for not discussing given issues was that a particular respondent was afraid of misrepresenting history; at least I was given that impression. Women often hesitated to discuss matters concerning their husband's lineages, always pointing out that "*a biaru m abia*" ("I came here [from elsewhere]"). Depending on circumstances, this response grew out of apprehensions over the prospect of appearing impertinent to male elders of her husband's lineage or was simply an inoffensive way of withholding information for unstated reasons. Several respondents decided to involve other individuals in their interviews. In other instances, male and female respondents refused pointedly to answer particular questions, insisting that answering those questions was inimical to present relations. For the same reason, a respondent often told me something but charged me emphatically never to "write it down." One is thus caught in the tension between research ethics and analytical rigor, both of which I have strived to satisfy.

Given that this view of history – as something some people are skilled in, the sanctity of which should be vigilantly protected, even from the acclaimed experts – I cannot insist on regarding the traditions that arose from this experience as mere charters. Charters are disseminated as widely as possible because they are meant to serve group interests. Neither

---

[4] The reputation as a knowledgeable historian is obviously a cherished one. To maintain or claim it, some respondents in the diaspora communities switched to archaic Aro dialect, or resort to theatrics or other antics.

should one insist on calling these persons "informants," implying non-creative, passive suppliers of data. Far from it, the people I interviewed did not simply supply with me data but instead sometimes dictated the pace and direction of the discussion. Besides, to describe these people merely as informants implicates the researcher in the implied passivity. On the contrary, the researcher plays an active role in teasing out historical data. Thus, the appellation "informants" is appropriately reserved for providers of folkloric data, such as relevant proverbs, idioms, and folk tales.

In my experience, charters are more likely to result from group interviews. Group interviews were not part of my original plan for fieldwork, but circumstances forced them on me. Such circumstances arose when a potential respondent decided to include lineage members, often their seniors, for unknown reasons or because those members were visiting for a weekend from a city. In other instances, people intruded in the interviews, sometimes by accident, other times deliberately. Group interviews generally failed to yield much reliable information. In one interview in an Arondizuogu lineage-group, one lineage-level amadi (aristocracy) intruded when I was interviewing a man of humbler origins. After listening for a while, the intruder began vigorously to urge my respondent to stop answering my questions. The intruder charged that I was asking questions like a "trained person," asserting that my method was uncannily similar to that of dynamic radio anchor the late Chima Eze. It should be observed that I knew nothing about the family origin of my respondent beforehand, but his submission to the intruder's authority came across to me as reluctance on his part to seem to be speaking for his lineage-group. Even though I was not seeking a spokesperson for the lineage-group, he had nevertheless feared the intruder might interpret it that way. The intruder's presence ruined the remainder of the interview. Unfortunately, I could not return to this respondent because the incident occurred toward the end of my fieldwork. But this encounter also revealed the current class situation. Despite his humble origins in terms of lineage, the respondent would have been more confident in his participation in the discussion had he been richer and/or more educated than the intruder, in which case, he could have felt confident speaking for himself, while the intruder would have shown him more respect. In another lineage-group, one intruder insisted that I should see their "chief" and other elders. Defensively, this respondent explained to the intruder that we were discussing procedural matters and "minor issues," and that he had already advised me and my company on how best to approach the elders.

Notes on Sources

I have found genealogies to be particularly useful in sorting out the problem of chronology. This process opens doors to other historical issues. Until very recently, *itu eye* (genealogical recitation), was required of every male Aro in public deliberations. The possibility of distortion was remote in a society where everyone knew almost everyone else and where ancestral claims were verifiable. Thus, genealogy plays a major role in Aro life. A point that has been missed so far in the historiography of the dispute over Aro warrant chieftaincy during the early colonial period is that the main issue was not the antiquity that contestants claimed for their lineages; false claims hardly ever stood. It was about statuses of ancestors at the point of entry and the nature of their relations to other groups. Because those who got appointed as warrant chiefs during the early colonial period were descendants of relatively recent entrants, colonial anthropologists constructed a genealogical chart that dated Aro formation wrongly at "most probably around 1750" (Anthropologists' Papers 1927).

The issues that were, and still are, often vigorously contested in Aro traditions concern who achieved what and, especially, the specific status (i.e., slave, client, or immigrant) of an ancestor at the point of his entry into Aro society. It was not, and still is not, through whom he came. The annual Ihu rite (homage) takes care of these issues. As detailed in Chapter 4, this rite routinized ties among individual males in a hierarchical order defined by social origins, age, and kinship affiliation. It is rare, if at all, for an Aro to deny the provenance of his or her ancestors. Also, disputes regarding who came into the society before another or who came later are extremely rare, if they exist at all. I wish to observe in this connection that even in the long-standing dispute over the Arondizuogu throne, dominant ndiawa have never claimed seniority over Ndiuche; its claim of precedence is based on Uche's alleged disinheritance by Izuogu.[5]

---

[5] There are contesting traditions regarding Uche's supersession by Awa. The popular version relates that Izuogu disinherited Uche, his first son, in favor of Awa, during Izuogu's lifetime. It is claimed that Izuogu had inadvertently killed a fellow Aro *amadi* (aristocrat) over a disagreement in an Aro council meeting. In the last analysis, Izuogu was asked to present one of his sons. Failing to do this, Izuogu would pay with his own head. Uche's mother, Mpi, took her son away in order to protect him. By contrast, Awa's mother, Egbocha, offered her young son. As luck would have it, Izuogu was spared the ordeal when, either he was pardoned or a slave was accepted in his son's stead. Consequent upon this experience, Izuogu made Awa his heir. But the tradition put forward by nde-Uche does not acknowledge this incident, claiming instead that Izuogu's dependents used their matriclan

The implication of the foregoing for oral tradition is the minimization of one of its central defects, that is, the confusion often associated with lineal precedence. A colonial anthropological report of 1927 noted that the Aro had "an undimmed recollection of their past history" (see Anthropologists' Papers 1927:2). Another, in 1935, observed that Arondizuogu did not have any legends (see Mayne 1935). In spite of twentieth-century manipulations, these observations are consistent with those of modern scholars who have done fieldwork among the Aro (Bentor 1994; K.O. Dike and Ekejiuba 1990; Northrup 1978:34). As a result, one does not start to reconstruct Aro history from "time immemorial." While debates about entry statuses still create problems, Aro genealogies are reliable enough for establishing rough chronologies.

I have compared the results of my calculations with the dates given by other researchers.[6] In some cases, as in the formation of Arondizuogu, my calculations correspond with other estimates. Where comparative chronologies are absent in the literature, for example, the entry points of Arondizuogu lineage-groups, I have relied solely on my own. In analyzing the genealogies, for example, the formation of individual lineages, which appeared in the traditions to be separated only by a few years, turns out to have spanned a century and a half. Also, the movement of two Aro groups into the upper Imo River, said to have been made by Izuogu's brothers, and by implication to have happened in the same generation as the formation of Arondizuogu, actually took place more than one century later (in the late 1850s and early 1870s), and it involved the *descendants* of the supposed pioneers.[7] Having put the chronologies in a chart, as was done in Chapter 4, a pattern emerges regarding the physical location of the lineage-groups. Also, the dates established in these chronologies help us to learn about what was happening in those other societies from where the Aro recruited immigrants. For instance, the time

---

connections with Awa to support Awa in Awa's wrongful bid for power. Whatever be the case, both traditions affirm the fact that Uche was Izuogu's first son and that Izuogu's dependents determined the outcome of the succession dispute between the two princes.

[6] Bentor 1994; Dike and Ekejiuba 1990; Ekejiuba 1972a; Eni 1973; Ijoma and Njoku 1991; Isichei 1976; G.I. Jones 1963; Latham 1973; Northrup 1978; Nwuauwa 1990, 1991; J.G. Okoro 1985; Oriji 1994.

[7] Following the tradition, J.G. Okoro writes: "The success of [Izuogu's] business adventures soon attracted his brothers Njoku and Imoko, to the commercial centers. They also joined in the business and later founded their own colonies which, with time, became merged with that of Mazi Izuogu under one name by mutual consent" (J.G. Okoro (1985:12). The dates for Ndinjoku's and Ndimoko's arrivals are my estimates, working from the genealogies of the settlements concerned.

of refugee influx from Owa in the Nri-Awka axis helps us to estimate a date for the catastrophic obliteration of that society.

Genealogies are, however, more complicated than the foregoing may suggest. For example, a slave acquisition or immigration that a tradition may connect to a particular name within a lineage may actually have been associated with another person within that same lineage at an earlier or a later period. Lineage members of different generations are sometimes related to one another in a synchronic form. Thus, it is not enough to focus on one lineage in establishing chronologies on cross-lineal matters.

Material culture found during fieldwork also helped me a great deal in understanding Aro history. Architectural structures and their components are living contemporaries of the past. They tell lively stories about settlement patterns, occupations, warfare and other processes. Religious icons go very far in unknotting important aspects of the people's cosmogony. On a final note, although I owe much of my understanding of the subject to my encounter with traditions, it seems that I learn a new thing each time I re-read the published eyewitness sources, especially mariners' journals. John Thornton translated Oldendorp (2000) from German, and Heike Raphael-Hernandez helped with one passage of this source. Victor Madeira translated all relevant sections of Sandoval ([1627] 1956).

The authority of one prominent eyewitness has become a subject of contestation during the preparation of this study. Olaudah Equiano's widely read autobiography, *Interesting Narrative*, has long been regarded as the quintessential slave narrative globally, and Equiano's claim to having been born and raised in Igboland had since the 1960s bestowed on his comments a prominent niche in the reconstruction of the hazy history of eighteenth-century Igboland. Equiano's testimony seemed to receive a boost in the 1980s from the research of Catherine Acholonu, whose analysis of the linguistic and ethnographic information gleaned from Equiano's narrative led her to narrow the searchlight to a small area on the western periphery of the Igbo heartland. There, she found a town called Isieke, where some of the key ethnographic and historical facts mentioned by Equiano seem to check impeccably. She also located an Ekwealuo family, whose living members remembered a story of a boy who went missing long ago (Acholonu 1987, 1989). Even if we rule out the several other Isiekes in Igboland on the basis of Acholonu's linguistic claims, several aspects of her findings are questionable.[8] It suffices to

---

[8] Since Chinua Achebe had in article published in 1978 identified Iseke as Equiano's natal home, it is unclear that Isieke resulted wholly from Acholonu's linguistic analysis (Achebe's

point out that Acholonu's work did not assuage the skepticism about Equiano's account that has been raised by such scholars as S.E. Ogude and Afigbo. Both noted that Equiano quarried large portions of his account of Igboland from contemporary descriptions of Africa authored by others as well as indulged in fiction and embellishment. Nonetheless, these critics attributed these shortcomings to natural lapses in memory that should be expected in a story told by an adult who was removed at a tender age from the context he was describing. They did not question Equiano's claim to have been born in Igboland (Afigbo 1981:147–84; Ogude 1982).

The landscape of the Equiano discourse has shifted entirely in the past ten years. Preoccupation with where in Igboland Equiano originated and which elements of his descriptions of the Igbo country are accurate and which are not has given way to whether Equiano was born in Africa at all and, ipso facto, whether his descriptions of Igboland can be relied upon as an eyewitness account. The literary scholar Vincent Carretta has uncovered evidence that suggests that Equiano was probably born in South Carolina rather than Igboland, which Equiano purported to write about in parts of his *Interesting Narrative* (Carretta 1999, 2005). Central to Carretta's work are two documents – a record of Equiano's baptism at St. Mary's Church in the then London suburb of Westminster in January 1759 and one of his service on the *Racehorse* during the Arctic expedition of 1773 (Carretta 1999, 2005). Carretta deserves a lot of credit for his startling discoveries, not only of the documents that cast doubt on Equiano's nativity, but also of related information that strengthens our hands in scrutinizing Carretta's own inferences

---

article is cited by Ogude 1982:34). Acholonu's interprets "Oye-Eboe," the name Equiano claimed his people called red-colored slave traders, as Oyibo, claiming it is the term the Igbo used to refer to light-kinned people rather than Europeans. It is unclear when the Igbo began to make such a distinction, if they did at all. The Igbo referred to White people/Europeans as *Bekée*. It is likely that late-nineteenth- and early-twentieth-century Igbo may have borrowed "Oyibo" from the Yoruba, who used (and still use) it to refer to Europeans or White people, which is probably why that reference is more current among the western Igbo who had greater intercourse with the Yoruba. Perhaps, the most curious aspect of Acholonu's findings is that Equiano's family name Ekwealuo has survived since the eighteenth century and continues to be used as surname by the family. In the actual fact, the Igbo practice of surnames prescribed the use of the name of somebody's immediate ancestor, usually father, as surname. The practice of static surnames – a European rather than precolonial Igbo practice – was adopted with Christianity and colonialism in the late nineteenth and early twentieth centuries, so that family names of the eighteenth century did not survive into the twentieth century. Also, the name Ekweanua/Ekweanuo is more plausible as Equiano's last name than Ekwealuo.

and conclusions. Without question, information about a Carolina birth in the two documents, which Equiano used over the years and never confronted directly, even in his autobiography, places a question mark on his nativity.

The question then is whether the newly discovered records should be treated as sacrosanct and Equiano's affirmation of his nativity considered a falsehood. Carretta claims that Equiano fabricated his African nativity claims, to boost the abolitionist movement with a much-needed voice of an African who witnessed traumatic capture into slavery and the horrendous Middle Passage. Many scholars, however, think that the Equiano evidence can be interpreted in different ways (see Blackburn 2005:37; Bugg 2006:572; Lovejoy 2006; Nwokeji 2006:840–41; 2009:7; Torrington 2005). Whether Equiano's claim to African birth is true or not may never be established beyond reasonable doubt; by the same token, the baptismal register and the muster lists do not provide conclusive evidence that he was born in the carolinas.

The specific situation of Equiano, first as a slave boy and later as a free man in eighteenth-century Britain, during the years his apparent Carolina nativity was documented should be taken into account. Carretta does not give much weight to the probability that Equiano may have had little to do with the birth place that appears in his baptismal record. Equiano's baptism was sponsored by the relatives of his master Michael Henry Paschal, an officer in the British Royal Navy, probably at Paschal's behest. It should be borne in mind that as somebody who concealed Equiano's slave status from the British naval authorities and illegally took Equiano's salary, Paschal had an interest in how Equiano's identity was represented. It was in Paschal's interest to represent Equiano's birthplace as America rather than Africa. A young African-born boy in eighteenth-century Royal Navy as an officer's servant was more likely to draw attention to slavery than a boy born in the Americas. By failing to report that Equiano was his slave, Paschal did actually falsify the record of Equiano's real status or, at the very least, demonstrated his willingness to do so (Nwokeji 2006; 2009). Under these circumstances, therefore, we must allow for the possibility that Equiano – a young slave boy – was not the original source of that information. Paul Lovejoy has compellingly asserted that the very fact that Paschal's cousin Mary Guerin, who had acted as Equiano's godmother, later attested – alongside respected members of the British public – that Equiano spoke only an African language at the time he arrived in England blights the information in the baptismal record (Lovejoy 2006:336).

Carretta suggests that Equiano giving South Carolina as his birth place for the Arctic expedition of 1773 rather than Africa, despite being a free man, shows he was not born in Africa. But as literary critic Bryan Carrey has observed, it was indeed uncommon for former slaves to use their African names.[9] As we learn from Carretta's own work, Equiano did even more than this when he identified himself as Africa-born while applying for employment with the bishop of London in 1779, before the take-off of the abolitionist movement he was supposed to boost by allegedly falsely claiming he was born in Africa. Equiano using his slave name Vassa for the most part until publishing his autobiography does not carry the evidential weight assigned to it by Carretta.

Questions about the newly discovered documents counsel against a rush to discard Equiano's own claim that he was born in Igboland. Some scholars – notably Lovejoy – have insisted that the nativity testimony that Equiano supplied in his autobiography is at least as good as the information in his baptismal record and the muster list of the *Racehorse*. According to these scholars, Equiano's thorough embodiment of Igbo values and command of historically accurate descriptions of Igboland demonstrate that he lived the Igbo experience (Byrd 2006:124–26; Kroll 2007; Lovejoy 2006:325, 331, 336; Nwokeji 2001:10; Ogude 2003).[10] For Angelo Constazo, Equiano, rather than misrepresent his nativity in his autobiography, had vested interest in being truthful about it. He would probably have known that misrepresenting his nativity would destroy the credibility of his narrative and undermine the abolitionist movement (Constanzo 2003). And Robin Blackburn has noted that the image of a conniving fabricator does not fit the character of Equiano that emerges in the *Narrative* (Blackburn 2005:37). Alexander Byrd takes it for granted that Equiano came from the hinterland of the Bight of Biafra (Byrd 2008:21–27, 42–43;159, 249).

The evolution of this discourse has caused a continual reassessment in the use of the Equiano source as this study progressed. I have always treated Equiano's work with a measure of skepticism because of his very young age at the time of initial enslavement to the time he made the

---

[9] www.brycchancarey.com/equiano/nativity.htm.
[10] At the conference "Olaudah Equiano: Representation and Reality," conference held at Kingston University-upon-Thames on March 22, 2003, Ogude who first raised serious questions about Equiano's work in modern times, argued that his reading of the autobiography left him in no doubt that Equinao was born in Igboland. I have not read this paper, but I heard Ogude's presentation at the conference and had a conversation with him afterward.

forced Atlantic crossing (Nwokeji 2001:9–10). We cannot however discard entirely Equiano's comments about the eighteenth-century Biafra hinterland for the following reasons. To do so is to treat the newly discovered documents as sacrosanct in the face of lingering questions about them and the fact that other claims in Equiano's narrative tend to check well wherever they can be verified. Further, many of his comments about Igboland have been widely acknowledged as historically accurate, including by Carretta himself. If we can use other New World sources of the slave trade era who never visited Africa, such as Sandoval and Oldendorp, we can use Equiano's as well, knowing that he probably actually lived the experiences he related. If, however, he did not, his account would be rendered less reliable because, unlike the other writers who mentioned their sources, Equiano would have falsely claimed to have witnessed what he reported. I have got rid of the Equiano's evidence entirely in at least one instance and toned down my reliance, including corroborating his account with other sources. As the Equaino controversy shows, different sources often enough tell different stories – sometimes different angles to the same story – and each kind of source places all the others in perspective.

Sources Cited

Abaka, Edmund 2005. *Kola is God's Gift: Agricultural Production, Export Initiatives and the Kola Industry of Asante and the Gold Coast c. 1820–1950*. Athens, OH: Ohio University Press.
Achebe, Chinua 1996. *Things Fall Apart*. New York: Anchor Books.
Acholonu, Catherine Obianuju. 1987. "The Home of Olaudah Equiano – A Linguistic and Anthropological Search." *The Journal of Commonwealth Literature*, Vol. 22, No. 5:5–16.
  1989. *The Igbo Roots of Olaudah Equiano: An Anthropological Research*. Owerri: Afa Publications.
Adams, Capt. John 1832. *Sketches Taken during Ten Voyages to Africa, between the Years 1786 and 1800; including Observation on the Country between Cape Palmas and the River Congo; and Cursory Remarks on the Physical and Moral Character of the Inhabitants*. London: Hurst, Robinson, and Co.
Adamu, Mahdi 1979. "The Delivery of Slaves from the Central Sudan to the Bight of Benin in the Eighteenth and Nineteenth Centuries." In *The Uncommon Market*. See Gemery and Hogendorn 1979.
Adande, Joseph 1997. "Traite Négrière et Art dans le Royaume du Dahomé (xviiiè – xixè Siècle)." In *Identifying Enslaved Africans*. See Lovejoy 1997.
Adderley, Roseanne M. 2006. *"New Negroes from Africa": Slave Trade Abolition and Free African Settlement in the Nineteenth-Century Caribbean*. Bloomington, IN: Indiana University Press.
Afigbo, Adiele E. 1966. "Chief Igwegbe Odum: The Omenuko of History." *Nigeria Magazine*, Vol. 90: 222–31.
  1971a. "The Eclipse of the Aro Slaving Oligarchy of South-Eastern Nigeria, 1901–1927." *Journal of Historical Society of Nigeria*, Vol. 4, No 1: 3–24.
  1971b. "The Aro of Southern Nigeria: A Socio-History Analysis of Legends of their Origin – Part I." *African Notes*, Vol. 6, No. 2: 31–46.
  1972a. "The Aro of Southern Nigeria: A Socio-History Analysis of Legends of their Origin – Part II." *African Notes*, Vol. 7, No. 1: 91–106.

1972b. "Igbo Historians and Igbo History." *Workshop on the Peoples of South-Eastern Nigeria*, December 5–8, 1972, University of Nigeria, Nsukka.

1972c. *The Warrant Chiefs: Indirect Rule in South-Eastern Nigeria, 1891–1929*. London: Longman.

1973a. "The Indigenous Political Systems of the Igbo." *Tarikh*, Vol. 4, No. 2: 13–23.

1973b. "Trade and Trade Routes in Nineteenth Century Nsukka." *Journal of the Historical Society of Nigeria*, Vol. 7, No. 1: 77–90.

1974. "The 19th Century Crisis of the Aro Slaving Oligarchy of South-Eastern." *Journal of the Historical Society of Nigeria*, Nos. 110–112: 66–73

1977. "Precolonial Trade Links between Southeastern Nigeria and the Benue Valley." *Journal of African Studies*, Vol. 4: 119–39.

1980. "Igboland Before 1800." In *Groundwork of Nigerian History*. See Ikime 1980.

1981a. "The Age of Innocence: The Igbo and their Neighbours in Pre-Colonial Times." 1981 Ahiajoku Lecture, Owerri, Ministry of Information, Culture, Youth and Sports.

1981b. *Ropes of Sand: Studies in Igbo History and Culture*, Ibadan, Nigeria: Ibadan University Press.

1987. *The Igbo and their Neighbours*, Ibadan, Nigeria: Ibadan University Press.

Afigbo, A.E. (editor) 1991a. *The Image of the Igbo*. Lagos: Vista Books.

1991b. *Groundwork of Igbo History*. Lagos: Vista Books.

Afigbo, A.E. 1991c. "General Introduction." In *Groundwork of Igbo*. See Afigbo 1991b.

1991d. "Igbo Cultural Sub-Areas: Their Rise and Development." In *Groundwork of Igbo*. See Afigbo 1991b.

1992. "The Spell of the Master Being a Review of Onwuka Dike and Felicia Ekejiuba: The Aro of South-eastern Nigeria 1650–1980." *Ikoro*, Vol. 7, Nos. 1 and 2: 108–13.

1996. "The Anthropology and Historiography of Central-South Nigeria before and since Igbo-Ukwu." *History in Africa*, Vol. 23: 1–15.

African Historical Demography, Volume II. Proceedings of a Seminar held in the Centre of African Studies, University of Edinburgh, April 24–25, 1981.

Africanus, Leo [1526] 1896. *The History and Description of Africa and on the Notable Things Therein Contained Written by Al-Hassan Ibn-Mohammed Al-Wezaz Al-Fasi, a Moor Baptized as Giovanni Leone, But Better Known as Leo Africanus. Done Into English in the Year 1600 by John Pory, and Now Edited with Introduction and Notes, by Dr. Robert Brown in Three Volumes* – Vol. III, London: Hakluyt Society.

1738. "Of the Province of Cano," Moore, Francis 1738. *Travels into the Inland Parts of Africa Containing a Description of the Several Nations ... Also Extracts from the Nubian Geographer, Leo the African, and Other Authors Ancient and Modern*. London: Edward Cave, pp. 74–79.

Agu, N.V. 1985. "The Role of Okoli Ijeoma in the 19th Century Slave Trade in the Old Awka District." NCE project (History), Alvan Ikoku College of Education, Owerri.

Sources Cited

Ahiajoku Lecture (Onugaotu) Colloquium 1986. *Igbo Jurisprudence: Law and Order in Traditional Igbo Society.* Owerri, Government Printer.
Akamnonu, Oliver 2008: *Taste of the West.* Xlibris.
Akang, J.U. et al. 1972. Transcripts of oral interview. See Northrup 1972–1973.
Akpabio, U. 1936. "The Story of Udo Akpbio of the Anang Tribe, Southern Nigeria recorded by the Rev. W. Groves." *Ten Africans*, edited by M. Perham. London: Faber and Faber Ltd.
Akpan, E. 1972. Transcripts of oral interview. See Northtrup 1972–1973.
Akpan, L.U. 1972. Transcripts of oral interview. See Northrup 1972–1973.
Akpu, Eneanya 1996. Interview Ndikunwanta-Uno, Arondizuogu, 10 March (Eke).
Alaka, E. 1984. "A Historical Survey of Urualla in the Pre-Colonial Period." BA thesis, History Department, University of Nigeria, Nsukka.
Alagoa, E.J. 1964. *The Small Brave City-State: A History of Nembe-Brass in the Niger Delta.* Ibadan, Nigeria: Ibadan University Press.
  1966. "Oral Tradition among the Ijo of the Niger Delta." *Journal of African History*, Vol. 7, No. 3: 405–19.
  1968. "The Use of Oral Literary Data for History: Examples from Niger Delta Proverbs." *Journal of American Folklore*, Vol. 81: 235–42.
  1970. "Long-Distance Trade and States in the Niger Delta." *Journal of African History*, Vol. 11, No. 3: 319–29.
  1971a. "The Development of Institutions in the States of the Eastern Niger Delta." *Journal of African History*, Vol. 12, No. 2: 269–78.
  1971b. "Nineteenth Century Revolutions in the Eastern Niger Delta States and Calabar." *Journal of the Historical Society of Nigeria*, Vol. 5, No. 4: 565–73.
  1972. *History of the Niger Delta.* Ibadan, Nigeria: Ibadan University Press.
Alagoa, E.J. and A. Fombo 1972. *A Chronicle of Grand Bonny.* Ibadan, Nigeria: Ibadan University Press.
  1986. "The Slave Trade in Niger Delta Oral Tradition and History." In *Africans in Bondage*. See Lovejoy 1986.
Alagoa, E.J. and A.M. Okorobia 1994. "Pawnship in Nembe, Niger Delta." In *Pawnship in Africa*. See Falola and Lovejoy 1994.
Alisa, Larry 2003. "The Function and Significance of Kola Nut (Oji) in Igboland." *APU Newsletter*, Special Edition, APU National Congress of North America 4th Annual Convention, New York: June.
Allen, J.G.C. n.d. *Nigerian Panorama – 1926–1966 (A District Officer from Eastern Nigeria Looks Back.* Rhodes House MSS. Afr. s. 1551: "Allen Papers."
Allen, Capt. William 1837. "Is the Old Calabar a Branch of the River Quorra?" *Journal of the Royal Geographical Society*, Vol. 7: 198–203.
Allen, Capt. William and T.R.H. Thomson 1848a. *A Narrative of the Expedition Sent by Her Majesty's Governement to the River Niger in 1841 under the Command of Captain H.D. Trotter, R.N.*, Vol. 1. London: Richard Bentley.
  1848b. *A Narrative of the Expedition Sent by Her Majesty's Governement to the River Niger in 1841 under the Command of Captain H.D. Trotter, R.N.*, Vol. 2. London: Richard Bentley.

Allison, Robert J. 1995. "Introduction: Equiano's Worlds." In *The Interesting Narrative*. See Equiano 1995.
Alpers, Edward A. 1984. "State, Merchant Capital, and Gender Relations in Southern Mozambique to the End of the Nineteenth Century: Some Tentative Hypotheses." *African Economic History*, No. 13: 23–55.
Amadiume, Ifi 1987. *Male Daughters, Female Husbands: Gender and Sex in African Society*. London: Zed Books.
Amaechi, W.C. 1987. "Warfare in Umudioka, from Pre-Colonial Times to the British Conquest." BA thesis, History Department, Abia State University.
Amankulor, J.N. and C. Okafor 1988. "Continuity and Change in Traditional Nigerian Theatre among the Igbo in the Era of Colonial Politics." *Ufahamu*, Vol. 16, No. 3: 35–50.
Anaba, E.C. 1988. "Aro/Ngwa Relationship: A Case of Mutual Interaction." NCE thesis, Alvan Ikoku College of Education, Owerri.
Anaedobe, M.M. 1977. "Uga from the Earliest Times to 1916." BA thesis, History Department, University of Nigeria, Nsukka.
Anene, J.C. 1959. "The Protectorate Government of Southern Nigeria and the Aros 1900–1902." *Journal of the Historical Society of Nigeria*, Vol. 1, No. 1: 20–26.
  1966. *Southern Nigeria in Transition*. Cambridge: Cambridge University Press.
Angelo, Michael 1704. "Voyage to the Congo." In *A Collection of Voyages and Travels, Volume One*, compiled by Awnsham Churchill and John Churchill. London: Thomas Astley.
Anikpo, Mark 1985. "Nigeria's Evolving Class Structure." In *Political Economy of Nigeria* edited by C. Ake. Lagos: Longman.
Anonymous Dutch Manuscript 1995. *West Africa in the Mid-Seventeenth Century* (Transcribed, translated and edited by Adam Jones), United States of America, African Studies Association Press.
Anthropologists' Paper 1927. NAE ARODIV 20/1/15 "Anthropologists Papers on Aro Origin: Discussion and the Basis of the Widespread of Aro Influence, 1927."
Anstey, R. 1975. *The Atlantic Slave Trade and British Abolition, 1760–1810*. London: Macmillan Press Ltd.
Anstey, R. and P.E.H. Hair (editors) 1976. *Liverpool, the African Slave Trade and Abolition: Essays to Illustrate Current Knowledge and Research*, Great Britain, Historical Society of Lancashire and Cheshire Occasional Series, Vol. 2.
Anya, A.O. 1982. "The Environment of Isolation or the Ecology and Sociobiology of Igbo Cultural and Political Development." *1982 Ahiajoku Lecture*, Owerri, Imo State Ministry of Information, Culture, Youth and Sport.
Anyakoha, Godwin 1996. Interview, Ndiamazu-Ikpa-Akaputa, Arondizuogu, 3 March (Oye).
Anyakoha, Nwankwo Anicho 1996. Interview, Amankwu, Arochukwu, 24 February (Oye).
Anyanwu, U.D. 1993a. "*Erima*: Towards a Theory of Igbo Tradition of Politics." In *The Igbo and the Tradition*. See Anyanwu and Aguwa 1993.

1993b. "Gender Question in Igbo Politics." In *The Igbo and the Tradition*. See Anyanwu and Aguwa 1993.
Anyanwu, U.D. and J.C.U. Aguwa (editors) 1993. *The Igbo and the Tradition of Politics*, Abia State University, Uturu, Centre for Igbo Studies.
Anyoha, A.O. 1977. "The Role of Masquerades in Arondizuogu with Special Emphasis on Onyekurum." *S.U.A. Education Week*. See Students' Union Arondizuogu 1977.
Arodiogbu, Alexander Obinani 1996. Interview, Ndadumoha, Arondizuogu, April 11 (Eke-Odu).
Aro-Okeigbo Ancestral Almanac 1996.
Aschcroft-Eason, Lillian 1997. "She 'Voluntarily Hati Come to ... [the Georgia Province]': A Gambian-Woman Trader among the Enslaved." In *Identifying Enslaved Africans*. See Lovejoy, 1997.
Asiegbu, E. 1985. Transcripts of oral interview. See P.N. Ogbuozobe 1986.
Asiegbu, Johnson U.J. (editor) 1984. *Nigeria and Its British Invaders 1851-1920: A Thematic Documentary*. Lagos, Nigeria: NOK.
Asiegbu, R.N. 1973. Transcripts of oral interview. See Northrup 1972–1973.
Asuzu, B. 1992. Transcripts of oral interview. See C.E. Igwe 1992.
Austen, Ralph A. 1970. "The Abolition of the Overseas Slave Trade: A Distorted Theme in West African History." *Journal of the Historical Society of Nigeria*, Vol. 5, No. 2: 257–74.
    1987. *African Economic History: Internal Development and External Dependency*. London: James Currey.
Aye, Efiong U. 1967. *Old Calabar through the Centuries*. Calabar: Hope Waddell Press.
Baier, Stephen 1980. *An Economic History of Central Niger*. Oxford: Clarendon Press.
Baikie, William B. 1856. *Narrative of an Exploring Voyage up the Rivers Kwora and Binue (Commonly Known as the Niger and Tsadda) in 1854*. London: John Murray.
Baillie, Capt. 1757. "Captain Baillie to the Owners of the Carter," 31 January. In *Documents Illustrative*. See Donnan 1931:511–12.
Balogun, K. 1991. "Preface." See *Rebirth of a Nation*.
Barbot, James 1699. "A Voyage to New Calabar, 1699." In *Documents Illustrative*. See Donnan 1930: 430–35.
Barbot, James, Jr. 1705. "The Slave Trade at Calabar, 1700–1705." In *Documents Illustrative*. See Donnan 1931: 14–15.
Barbot, James and J. Grazilhier 1699. "Abstract of a Voyage to New Kalabar, Bandi, and Doni Rivers, in 1699." *Collection of Voyages and Travels*, Vol. 3. London: Thomas Astley: 105–18.
Barbot, John 1682. "John Barbot's Description of Guinea." In *Documents Illustrative*. See Donnan 1930: 282–301.
    1698. "At Old Calabar, in 1698." In *Documents Illustrative*. See Donnan 1930: 419–20.
    1732. *A Description of the Coasts of North and South-Guinea; and of Ethiopia Interior, Vulgarly Angola: Being a New and Accurate Account of the Western Maritime Countries of Africa, in Six Books*. London: Churchill.

Barbour, Bernard and Michell Jacobs 1985. "The Mi'raj: A Legal Treatise on Slavery by Ahmad Baba." In *Slaves and Slavery in Muslim Africa, Volume 1, Islam and Ideology of Enslavemen*, edited by J.R. Willis. London: Frank Cass.

Barnes, Sandra T. 1997. "Gender and the Political Support and Protection in Precolonial Africa." In *Queens, Queen Mothers*. See Kaplan 1997.

Bascom, William R. and Melville Herskovits (editors) 1959. *Continuity and Change in African Cultures*. Chicago, IL: University of Chicago Press.

Basden, George T. 1912. "Notes on the Ibo Country and the Ibo People, Southern Nigeria." *The Geographical Journal*, Vol. 39, No. 3: 241–47.

— 1925. "Notes on the Ibo Country, Southern Nigeria." *Geographical Journal*, Vol. 65, No. 1: 32–41.

— 1966. *Niger Ibos*. London: Frank Cass.

Baum, Robert 1999. *Shrines of the Slave Trade: Diola Religion and Society in Precolonial Senegambia*. Oxford: Oxford University Press.

Bay, Edna 1977. "The Royal Women of Abomey" Ph. D. diss., Boston University.

— 1997a. "Dahomian Political Exile and the Atlantic Slave Trade." In *Identifying Enslaved Africans*. See Lovejoy 1997.

— 1997b. "The Kpojito or 'Queen Mother' of Precolonial Dahomey." In *Queens, Queen Mothers*. See Kaplan 1997.

— 1998. *Wives of Leopard: Gender, Politics, and Culture in the Kingdom of Dahomey*. Charlottesville, VA: University of Virginia Press.

Bay, Edna and Nancy J. Hafkin (editors) 1975. *African Studies Review*. Vol. 18, No. 3: Special Issue on Women in Africa.

Becker, Charles 1988. "Les effects démographiques de la traite des esclavages en Sénégambie: esquisse d'une histoire des peuplements du VVII e à la fin du xixe siècle." In *De la Traite*. See Daget 1988.

Beckles, Hilary McD. 1989. *Natural Rebels: A Social History of Enslaved Black Women in Barbados*. London: Zed Press.

Becroft [Beecroft], John 1836. "Substance of a Letter Received from J. Becroft, Esq., Relative to His Recent Assent of the Quorra." *The Journal of the Royal Geographical Society*, Vol. 6, Pt. 2: 424–26.

Becroft [Beecroft], Captain et al. 1844. "Details of Explorations of the Old Calabar River, in 1841 and 1842." *The Journal of the Royal Geographical Society*, Vol. 14: 260–83.

Behrendt, S.D. 1997. "The Annual Volume and Regional Distribution of the British Slave Trade, 1780–1807." *Journal of African History*, Vol. 38, No. 2: 187–211.

— 1998. "Long-Run Patterns in the Shipping of Slaves." Presented at Transatlantic Slavery and the African Diaspora: Using the W.E.B. DuBois Institute Dataset of Slaving Voyages, Omohundro Institute of Early American History and Culture, Williamsburg, Virginia, September 11–13.

Berlin, Ira 1998. *Many Thousands Gone: The First Two Centuries of Slavery in North America, Cambridge*, MA: Harvard University Press.

Blackburn, Robin 2005. "The True Story of Equiano," *The Nation*, Vol. 281, No. 17, November 21:33–37.

Blake, William O. 1861. *The History of Slavery and the Slave Trade, Ancient and Modern. The Forms of Slavery that Prevailed in Ancient Nations,*

Particularly Greece and Rome. The African Slave Trade and the Political History of Slavery in the United States Compiled from Autthentic Materials. Columbus, OH: H. Milner.
Blindloss, Harold 1898. *In the Niger Country.* Edinburgh and London: William Blackwood and Sons.
Bloch, Marc 1975. *Slavery and Serfdom in the Middle Ages* trans. William R. Beer. Berkeley, CA: University of California Press.
Belasco, Bernard I. 1980. *The Entrepreneur as Culture Hero: Preadaptations in Nigerian Economic Development.* New York: Praeger Publishers.
Bennett, Lt. Gov. B. 1704. "Lieutenant Governor Benjamin Bennett to the Board of Trade," August 4, 1708. See Donnan 1931:48.
Bentor, Eli 1994. "Aro Ikeji Festival: Toward a Historical Interpretation of a Masquirade Festival," Ph.D. diss., School of Fine Arts, Indiana University.
Biobaku, Saburi O. 1965. *The Egba and Their Neighbors 1847–1872.* Oxford: Clarendon Press.
Board of Trade 1709. "Report on the Trade to Africa." *See Donnan* 1931: 49–81.
Bohannan, Paul and Laura Bohannan 1968. *Tiv Economy.* Evanston, IL: Northwestern University Press.
Bold, Edward 1822. *The Merchant's and Mariner's African Guide.* Salem, MA: Cushing and Appleton.
Bosman, William 1705. *A New and Accurate Description of the Coast of Guinea.* London: James Knapton.
Boston, J.S. 1968. *The Igala Kingdom.* Oxford: Oxford University Press.
Bottomore, Thomas B. 1964. *Elites and Society.* Middlesex, UK: Penguin.
  1971. *Sociology: A Guide to problems and Literature.* New York: Pantheon Books.
Bowser, Frederick P. 1974. *The African Slave in Colonial Peru 1524–1650.* Palo Alto, CA: Stanford University Press.
Bridges, A.F.B. n.d. *So We Used to Do.* Rhodes House MSS. Afr. s. 1881(1): "Bridges Papers."
Brown, Carolyn A. 1996. "Testing the Boundaries of Marginality: Twentieth-Century Slavery and Emancipation Struggles in Nkanu, Northern Igboland, 1920–29." *Journal of African History*, Vol. 37, No.1: 51–80.
Bugg, John 2006. Review of *Equiano, The African: Biography of a Self-Made Man.* In *Eighteenth Century Studies*, Vol. 39, No. 4: 571–73.
Burdo, Adolphe 1880. *Niger et Bénué: Voyage dan l'Afrique Central.* Paris: E. Plon.
Burns, Alan C. 1922 (compiler). *The Nigeria Handbook 1922–23.* Lagos: Government Printer.
Byrd, Alexander X. 2006. "Eboe, Country, Nation, and Gustavus Vassa's Interesting Narrative." *William and Mary Quarterly*, Vol. 63, No. 1:123–48.
  2008. *Captives and Voyages: Black Migrants Across the Eighteenth-Century British Atlantic.* Baton Rouge: Louisiana State University Press.
Canot, Captain Theodore 1928. *Adventure of an African Slaver: Being a True Account of the life Captain Theodore Canot, Trader in Gold, Ivory & Slaves on the Coast of Guinea: His Own Story as Told in the Year 1854 to Brantz Mayer & Now Edited with an Introduction by Malcom Cowley.* Garden City, NY: Garden City Publishing Co., Inc.

Carlston, K.S. 1968. *Social Theory and African Tribal Organization: The Development of Socio-Legal Theory.* Chicago, IL: University of Illinois Press.

Carretta, Vincent. 1999. "Olaudah Equiano or Gustavus Vassa? New Light on an Eighteenth Century Question of Identity." *Slavery and Abolition*, Vol. 20, No. 3: 96–105.

2005. *Equiano the African: Biography of a Self-Made Man.* Athens, Georgia: The University of Georgia Press.

2009. Colloquy with the Author: Vincent Carretta and "Equiano, the African." *Studies in Eighteenth-Century Culture*, Vol. 38:2–7.

Carrey, Bryccan, "Where Was Olaudah Equiano Born (And Why Does It Matter?)": www.brycchancarey.com/equiano/nativity.htm (accessed July 30, 2009).

Chambers, Douglas B. 1997. "'My Own Nation': Igbo Exiles in the Diaspora." *Slavery and Abolition*, Vol. 18, No. 1: 72–97.

2002. "The Significance of the Igbo in the Bight of Biafra Slave Trade: A Rejoinder to Northrup's 'Myth Igbo'," *Slavery and Abolition*, Vol. 23, No.1: 101–20.

2005. *Murder at Montpelier: Igbo Africans in Virginia.* Jackson: University of Mississippi Press.

Chikezie, D.O. 1977. Transcripts of oral interview. See G.C. Mmeregini 1978.

Chinyele, N. 1972. Transcripts of oral interview. See Nwankwo, J.C. 1973.

Chuku, Gloria I. 1989. "The Rise and Fall of Aro Business Oligarchy from 15th Century to 20th Century." MA thesis, Department of History, University of Port Harcourt.

2005. *Igbo Women and Economic Transformation in Southeastern Nigeria, 1900–1960.* New York: Routledge.

Chukwura, N. 1977. Transcripts of oral interview. See Modebe, I.P. 1978.

Clarke Letter – Book, no. 76. In *Douments Illustrative ...*, Vol. 3. See Donnan 1932:326–27.

CMS A 3/O 1923.

CO 520/6/33280.

CO 520/8/30543: Morrisey, "Cross River Division, Slave Markets," August 1, 1901.

CO 520/14: "Memorandum Concerning the Aro Expedition Detailing Circumstances that Led to It and the Results Which It is Anticipated Will Ensure Therefrom."

Cohen, Abner 1969. *Custom and Politics in Urban Africa: A Study of Hausa Migrants in Yoruba Towns*, London: Routledge and Kegan Paul.

1971. "Cultural Strategies in the Organization of Trading Diasporas." In *Development of Indigenous Trade.* See Meillassoux 1971b.

Cohen, Ronald 1981. "Evolution, Fission, and the Early State." In *The Study of the State* edited by H.J.M. Claessen and P. Skalník. The Hague: Mouton Publishers.

Cole, William 1862. *Life in the Niger, or, the Journal of an African Trader.* London: Saunders, Otley, and Co.

Constanzo, Angelo 2003. "'Neither a Saint, a Hero, Nor a Tyrant," paper presented at the conference "Olaudah Equiano: Representation and Reality," Kingston University-upon-Thames, March 22.

Cookey, Sylvanus 1974. *King Jaja of the Niger Delta: His Life and Times, 1821–1891*, New York: NOK Publishers Ltd.
Cooper, Frederick 1996. "Race, Ideology, and the Perils of Comparative History." *American Historical Review*, Vol. 101, No. 4: 1124–38.
Coquery-Vidrovitch, Catherine 1997. *African Women: A Modern History*, trans. Beth Gillian Raps. Boulder, CO: Westview Press.
Coquery-Vidrovitch, Catherine and Paul E. Lovejoy 1985a. *The Workers of African Trade*. Beverly Hills, CA: Sage.
Coquery-Vidrovitch, C. and Paul E. Lovejoy 1985b. "The Workers of Trade in Precolonial Africa." In *The Workers of African Trade*. See Coquery-Vidrovitch and Lovejoy 1985a.
Cotterell, Harry n.d. "Reminiscences of One Connected with the West African Trade from 1863–1910." In *Trading in West Africa 1840–1920* edited by P.N. Davies. London: Croom Helm, 1976.
Cowan, A.A. 1935. "Early Trading Conditions in the Bight of Biafra, Part I." *Journal of the Royal African Society*, Vol. 34, No. 137: 391–402.
  1936. "Early Trading Conditions in the Bight of Biafra, Part II." *Journal of the Royal African Society*, Vol. 35, No. 138: 53–64.
Craton, Michael 1978. *Searching for the Invisible Man: Slaves and Plantation Life in Jamaica*. Cambridge, MA: Harvard University Press.
Crosbies and Trafford et al. 1762. "Capn. Ambrose Lace." See G. Williams 1897: 486–88.
Crow, Hugh 1830. *Memoirs of the Late Captain Hugh Crow*. London: Longman, Rees, Orme, Brown, and Green.
Crowder, Michael 1978. *The Story of Nigeria*. London: Faber and Faber.
Crowther, Samuel and J. C. Taylor 1859. *The Gospel on the Banks of the Niger. Journals and Notes of the Native Missionaries Accompanying the Niger Expedition of 1857–1859*. London: Dawson of Pall Mall.
Curtin, Philip D. 1969. *The Atlantic Slave Trade: A Census*. Madison, WI: University of Wisconsin Press.
  1971a. "The Slave Trade and the Atlantic Basin: Intercontinental Perspectives." In *Key Issues*. See Huggins et al. 1971.
  1971b. "Pre-Colonial Trading Networks and Traders: The Dianhanké." In *Development of Indigenous Trade*. See Meillassoux 1971b.
  1975. *Economic Change in Precolonial Africa: Senegambia in the Era of the Slave Trade*. Madison, WI: University of Wisconsin Press.
  1976. "Measuring the Atlantic Slave Trade Once Again: A Comment." *Journal of African History*, Vol. 17, No. 4: 595–605.
  1984. *Cross-Cultural Trade in World History*. Cambridge: Cambridge University Press.
  1990. *The Rise and Fall of the Plantation Complex: Essays in Atlantic History*. Cambridge: Cambridge University Press.
  1993. "The Tropical Atlantic in the Age of the Slave Trade." In *Islamic and European Expansion* edited by M. Adas. Philadelphia, PA: Temple University Press.
Curtin, Philip D. and Jan Vansina 1964. "Sources of the Nineteenth Century Atlantic Slave Trade." *Journal of African History*, Vol. 2: 185–208.

Daget, Serge 1988a. *De la traite à l'esclavage du XVIIIème au XIXème Siècle*, Tome 1, Acts du Colloque International sur la Traite des Noirs, Nantes 1985, Centre de recherche sur l'Histoire du Monde Atlantique, Société Française d'Histoire d'Outre-Mer.

1988b. *De la traite à l'esclavage du XVIII eme au XIXeme Siècle*, Tome 2, Acts du Colloque International sur la Traite des Noirs Nantes 1985, Centre de recherche sur l'Histoire du Monde Atlantique Société Française d'Histoire d'Outre-Mer.

Davidson, Basil 1961. *Black Mother: The Years of the African Slave Trade*. Boston and Toronto: Little, Brown and Company.

1971. "Slaves or Captives? Some Notes on Fantasy and Fact." In *Key Issues*. See Huggins et al. 1971.

1978. *Africa in Modern History*. Middlesex, UK: Penguin.

Dayrell, E. 1911. "Further Notes on Nsibidi Signs with their Meanings from Ikom District, Southern Nigeria." *Journal of the Royal Anthropological Institute*, Vol. 41: 521–40.

De Carli, Denis 1704. "A Voyage to Congo." In *A Collection of Voyages and Travels, Volume One*, compiled by Awnsham Churchill and John Churchill. London: Thomas Astley.

De Gregori, Thoma R. 1969. *Technology and the Economic Development of the Tropical African Frontier*. Cleveland, OH: The Press of Case Western Reserve University.

De Sandoval, P. Alonso [1627] 1956. *De Instauranda Aethiopum Salute: El Mundo de la Esclavitud Negra en America*. Bogota: Empresa Nacional de Publicaciones.

Department of State and Official Bodies (England) 1890. *Report by Major Macdonald of His Visit as Her Majesty's Commissioner to the Niger and Oil Rivers*. London: Foreign Office.

Dickson, Kwamina B. 1969. *A Historical Geography of Ghana*. London: Cambridge University Press.

Dike, John O. 1996. Interview, Ndiawa, Arondizuogu, February 15.

Dike, K. Onwuka 1956. *Trade and Politics in the Niger Delta 1830–1885*. Oxford: Clarendon Press.

1959. "John Beecroft, 1790–1854: Her Britanic Majesty's Consul to the Bights of Benin and Biafra 1849–1854." *Journal of the Historical Society of Nigeria*, Vol. 1, No. 1: 5–14.

Dike, K. Onwuka and Felicia I. Ekejiuba 1978. "The Aro State: A Case Study of State Formation in Southeastern Nigeria." *Journal of African Studies*, Vol. 5, No. 1: 268–300.

1990. *The Aro of South-Eastern Nigeria, 1650–1980: A Study of Socio-Economic Formation and Transformation in Nigeria*. Ibadan, Nigeria: Ibadan University Press Ltd.

Dike, P.C. 1986. "Igbo Traditional Social Control and Sanctions." In *Igbo Jurisprudence*. See AhIajoku Lecture (Onugaotu) Colloquium 1986.

Domar, Evesy 1970. "The Causes of Slavery and Serfdom: A Hypothesis." *Journal of Economic History*, Vol. 30, No. 1: 13–32.

Donnan, Elizabeth 1930. *Documents Illustrative of the History of the Slave Trade to America*, Vol. 1 1441–1700. Washington, DC: Carnegie Institution of Washington.
  1931. *Documents Illustrative of the History of the Slave Trade to America*, Vol. 2, *The Eighteenth Century*. Washington, DC: Carnegie Institution of Washington.
  1932. *Documents Illustrative of the History of the Slave Trade to America*, Vol. 3, New England and the Middle Colonies. Washington, DC: Carnegie Institution of Washington.
  1935. *Documents Illustrative of the History of the Slave Trade to America*, Vol. 4, *The Border Colonies and the Southern Colonies*. Washington, DC: Carnegie Institution of Washington.
Drake, D.K. 1976. "The Liverpool-African Voyage c. 1790–1807: Commercial Problems." In *Liverpool*. See Anstey and Hair 1976.
Duignan, Gerard 1995. Interview, Mission House at Kimmage, Dublin, Republic of Ireland.
Duke, Antera 1956. "The Diary (1785-8) of Antera Duke." In *Efik Traders of Old Calabar*. See Forde 1956.
  1956. *Efik Traders of Old Calabar, Containing the Diary of Antera Duke, an Efik Slave-Trading Chief of the Eighteenth Century* edited by G.I. Jones. London: Oxford University Press.
Eades, J.S. 1993. *Strangers and Traders: Yoruba Migrants, Markets and the State in Northern Ghana*. Edinburgh: Edinburgh University Press.
Easterfield, M. 1993. "Introduction." See Uku 1993.
Ebosi, C.C. n.d. Transcripts of oral interview. See Ohaegbu, U.E. 1991.
Ebu, A.A. 1972. Transcripts of oral interview. See Northrup 1972–1973.
Echemazi, Nwamuo 1996. Interview, Atani, Arochukwu, February 24.
Echeruo, Michael 1979. "Ahamefula – A Matter of Identity." *Ahiajoku Lecture 1979*, Owerri, Ministry of Information and Social Development.
Economic History Services. http://eh.net/hmit/ukcompare/ (accessed March 30, 2010)
Edwards, Bryan 1793. *The History, Civil and Commercial, of the British Colonies in the West Indies; in Two Volumes* Vol. 2. London: John Stockdale.
Egboh, Fidelia N. 1987. "A Pre-Colonial History of Akokwa." BA thesis, History Department, University of Nigeria, Nsukka.
Eke, S.O. 1978. "An Economic History of Isuochi in the Nineteenth Century (Agriculture, Craft and Trade)." BA thesis, History Department, University of Nigeria, Nsukka.
Ekechi, Felix K. 1981. "Aspects of the Palm Oil Trade at Oguta (Eastern Nigeria), 1900–1950." *African Economic History*, No. 10: 35–65.
  1994. "Pawnship in Igbo Society." *Pawnship in Africa: Debt Bondage in Historical Perspective* edited by T. Falola and P.E. Lovejoy. Boulder, CO: Westview Press.
Ekeh, Peter E. 1990. "Social Anthropology and Two Contrasting Uses of Tribalism in Africa." *Comparative Studies in Society and History*, Vol. 32, No. 4: 660–700.

Ekejiuba, Felicia I. 1967. "Omu Okwei, the Merchant Queen of Ossomari: A Biographical Sketch." *Journal of the Historical Society of Nigeria*, Vol. 3, No. 4: 633–46.

1972a. "The Aro Trade System in the Nineteenth Century." *Ikenga*, Vol. 1, No. 1: 11–26.

1972b. "The Aro System of Trade in the Nineteenth Century." *Ikenga*, Vol. 1, No. 2: 10–21.

1972c. "Igba Ndu, Igbo Mechanism of Social Control and Adjustment." *African Notes*, Vol. 8, No. 1.

1986. "Aro Trade before the Twentieth Century." In *Arochukwu History*. See J.O. Ijoma 1986a.

1991. "High Point of Igbo Civilization: The Arochukwu Period." In *Groundwork of Igbo History*. See Afigbo 1991b.

Ekejiuba, Maxwell 1996. Interview, Ndianiche-Obinetiti, Arondizuogu, March 4.

Ekeke, J.I. et al. 1973. Transcripts of oral interview. See Northrup 1972–1973.

Ekkehart, Schlicht 1998. *On Custom in the Economy*. Oxford: Clarendon Press.

Eku, J.U. 1972. Transcripts of oral interview. See Northrup 1972–1973.

Ekwobi, John Nwawho 1996. Interview, Ndiukwu, Arondizuogu, April 11.

Eltis, David 1978. "The Atlantic Slave Trade, 1821–1843." Ph.D. diss., University of Rochester.

1979. "The Direction and Fluctuation of the Transatlantic Slave Trade, 1821–1843: A Revision of the 1845 Parliamentary Paper." In *The Uncommon Market*. See Gemery and Hogendorn 1979.

1983. "Forced and Coerced Transatlantic Migrations: Some Comparisons." *American Historical Review*, Vol. 88, No. 2: 251–80.

1986. "Fluctuations in the Age and Sex Ratios of Slaves in the Nineteenth-Century Transatlantic Slave Traffic." *Slavery and Abolition*, Vol. 7, No. 3:257–72.

1987. *Economic Growth and the Ending of the Transatlantic Slave Trade*. New York: Oxford University Press.

1998. "Gender and the Slave Trade in the Early Modern Atlantic World." Presented at Transatlantic Slavery and the African Diaspora: Using the W.E.B. DuBois Institute Dataset of Slaving Voyages, Omohundro Institute of Early American History and Culture, Williamsburg, Virginia, September 11–13.

1989a. "Fluctuations in Mortality in the Last Half Century of the Transatlantic Slave Trade." *Social Science History*, Vol. 13, No. 3: 315–40.

1989b. "Trade between Western Africa and the Atlantic World before 1870: Estimates of Trends in Value, Composition and Direction." *Research in Economic History*, Vol. 12: 197–239.

1993. "Europeans and the Rise and Fall of Slavery in the Americas: An Interpretation." *American Historical Review*, Vol. 98, No. 5: 1399–1423.

1995. "The Volume and African Origins of the British Slave Trade before 1714." *Cahiers d'Etudes Africaines*, Vol. 35, Nos. 2–3 :617–27.

2000. *The Rise of African Slavery in the Americas*. New York: Cambridge University Press.

Eltis, David, Stephen D. Behrendt, David Richardson and Herbert S. Klein. Voyages: The Trans-Atlantic Slave Trade Database. www.slavevoyages.org (Accessed June 7, 2010).

Eltis, David and David Richardson (editors) 2008. *Extending the Frontiers: Essays on the New Transatlantic Slave Trade Database*, New Haven, CT: Yale University Press.

Eltis, David and Stanley Engerman 1992. "Was the Slave Trade Dominated by Men?" *Journal of Interdisciplinary History*, Vol. xxiii, No. 2: 237–57.

   1993. "Fluctuations in Sex and Age Ratios in the Transatlantic Slave Trade, 1663–1864." *Economic History Review*, Vol. 46, No. 2:308–23.

Eltis, David and Lawrence C. Jennings 1988. "Trade between Western Africa and the Atlantic World in the Pre-Colonial Era." *American Historical Review*, Vol. 93, No. 4: 936–59.

Eltis, David, Paul Lovejoy and David Richardson 1999. "Slave-Trading Ports: Towards an Atlantic-Wide Perspective." In Law and Strickrodt (editors), *Ports of the Slave Trade*.

Eltis, David and David Richardson 1995a. "The Structure of the Transatlantic Slave Trade, 1595–1867." Presented at the Social Science History Meeting.

   1995b. "Total Factor Productivity in the Transatlantic Slave Trade." *Explorations of Economic History*, Vol. 32, No. 4: 465–84.

Eltis, David and David Richardson 1997. "West Africa and the Transatlantic Slave Trade: New Evidence of Long-Run Trends," *Slavery and Abolition*, Vol. 18, No. 1: 16–35.

Emecheta, Buchi 1977. *The Slave Girl*. London: Allison and Busby.

Emeruwa, S.O. 1992. "The History of Aro-Ajatakiri, Oboro in Ikwuano Local Government Area from 1901 to the Present." NCE project (History), Alvan Ikoku College of Education, Owerre.

Enekwa, Eugene 1996. Interview, Ndianiche-nde-Ezeana, Arondizuogu, April 8.

Eni, Humphrey O. 1973. *The Ujari People of Awka District*, Onitsha, University Publishing Company.

Equiano, Olaudah 1995. *The Interesting Narrative of the Life of Olaudah Equiano Written by Himself* (edited with an Introduction by Robert Allison). Boston, MA: Bedford Books/St. Martin's Press.

Erim, Erim O. 1981. *Idoma Nationality, 1600–1900: Problems in Studying the Origins and Development of Ethnicity*. Enugu, Nigeria: Fourth Dimension.

Eshiet, D.K. 1973. Transcripts of oral interview. See Northrup 1972–1973.

Essien, O.E. 1991. "The Ibibio Language: Classification and Dialects." In *The Ibibio: An Introduction to the Land, the People and their Culture* edited by Monday Abasiattai. Calabar, Niger: Alphonsus Akpan.

Esu, U. 1973. Transcripts of oral interview. See Northrup 1972–1973.

Eze, C. 1987. "The Aro of Nneato." NCE *thesis*, Alvan Ikoku College of Education, Owerri.

Ezeana, Adaoha 1996. Interview, Ndiamazu-Uno, Arondizuogu, March 10.

Ezeana, Obioma 1996. Interview, Ndiamazu-Uno, Arondizuogu, March 10.

Ezeijezie, U. 1976. Transcripts of oral interview. See Ezenibe, R.A.O. 1977.

Ezeike, B.I. 1981. "Ekwulobia from the Earliest Times to 1910." BA thesis, History Department, University of Nigeria, Nsukka.

Ezeilo, J. 1980. Transcripts of oral interview. See Ezeike, B.I. 1981.
Ezekwerempi, J. 1976. Transcripts of oral interview. See Anaedobe, M.M. 1977.
Ezeliora, Bernadette 1994. *Traditional Medicine in Amesi*. Enugu, Nigeria: Cecta (Nig) Limited.
Ezenibe, R.A. O. 1977. "Igboukwu from the Earliest Times to 1920: Origins, Migrations, Settlement and Inter-Group Relations." BA thesis, History Deparment, University of Nigeria, Nsukka.
Ezenkwele, E. 1976. Transcripts of oral interview. See Anaedobe, M.M. 1977.
Ezenwadiugwu, E. 1976. Transcripts of oral interview. See Anaedobe, M.M. 1977.
Ezenyem, C.E. 1981. "Social Stratification in Idemili L.G.A. up to the End of the Colonial Era." BA thesis, History Department, University of Nigeria, Nsukka.
Ezenyenenwe, E. 1976. Transcripts of oral interview. See Ezenibe, R.A.O. 1977.
Ezeone, H. 1976. Transcripts of oral interview. See Ezenibe, R.A.O. 1977.
Eziokwu, B. 1991. Transcripts of oral interview. See U.E. Ohaegbu 1991.
Fage, John D. 1969. "Slavery and the Slave Trade in the Context of West African History." *Journal of African History*, Vol. 10, No. 3: 393–404.
  1975. "The Effect of the Export Slave Trade on African Populations." In *The Population Factor*. See Moss and Rathbone 1975.
  1980. "Slaves and Society in Western Africa, c. 1445–c. 1700." *Journal of African History*, Vol. 21, No. 3: 289–310.
  1991. "Hawkins' Hoax? A Sequel to 'Drake's Fake'," *History in Africa*, Vol. 18:83–91.
Falconbridge, Alexander 1788. *An Account of the Slave Trade on the Coast of Africa*. London : J. Phillips.
Falola, Toyin 1984: *The Political Economy of a Pre-Colonial African State: Ibadan, 1830–1900*. Ile-Ife, Nigeria: University of Ife Press.
Falola, Toyin and Paul E. Lovejoy (editors) 1994. *Pawnship in Africa: Debt Bondage in Historical Perspective*. Boulder, CO: Westview Press.
Finley, Moses I. 1968. "Slavery." *The International Encyclopedia of the Social Sciences*. New York: The Macmillan Company and The Free Press.
Floyd, B. 1969. *Eastern Nigeria: A Geographical Review*. New York: Frederick A. Praeger.
Fogel, Robert W. and Stanley L. Engerman 1974. *Time on the Cross: The Economic of American Negro Slavery*. Boston, MA and Toronto: Little, Brown and Company.
Forde, D. 1950. "Ethnographic Survey of Africa: Foreword." *Ibo and Ibibio-Speaking Peoples*. See Forde and Jones 1950.
  1953. "The Cultural Map of West Africa: Successive Adaptations to tropical Forests and Grasslands," *Transactions of the New York Academy of Sciences*, Vol. 15, No. 6: 206–19.
  (editor) 1956. *Efik Traders of Old Calabar*. London: Oxford University Press.
Forde, Daryl and G.I. Jones 1950. *The Ibo and Ibibio-Speaking Peoples of South-Eastern Nigeria*. London: Oxford University Press.
Fox, A.J. 1964. *A Short History of Uzuakoli by Students of the Methodist College, Uzuakoli, under the Direction of A.J. Fox*. London: Oxford University Press.

Fraser, J. 1790. Testimony, 29 January. See Lambert 1975b.
Galenson, David W. 1986. *Traders, Planters, and Slaves: Market Behaviour in Early English America*. Cambridge: Cambridge University Press.
Gallwey, Lt. Col. 1902. "Political Report in Connection with the Aro Field Force Operations by Lt. Col. Gallwey." CO 520/14/18725, April 1, 1902.
Geggus, David 1989. "Sex Ratio, Age and Ethnicity in the Atlantic Slave Trade: Data from French Shipping and Plantation Records." *Journal of African History*, Vol. 30, No. 1:23–44.
Gemery, Henry A. and Jan Hogendorn 1974. "The Atlantic Slave Trade: A Tentative Economic Model." *Journal of African History*, Vol. 15, No. 2: 223–46.
Gemery, Henry A. and Jan Hogendorn (editors) 1979. *The Uncommon Market: Essays in the Economic History of the Slave Trade*. New York: Academic Press.
Genuine "Dicky Sam" 1884. *Liverpool and Slavery: An Historical Account of the Liverpool-African Slave Trade*. Liverpool: A. Bowker and Sons.
Gile, Zac O. n.d. "Indigenous and Adapted African Vegetables," *International Society for Horticultural Science*. http://www.actahort.org/members/showpdf?session=7671
Glover, J.H. with A.C.G. Hastings 1926. *The Voyage of the Dayspring*. London: John Lane.
Gomez, Michael A. 1998. *Exchanging Our Country Marks: The Transformation of African Identities in the Colonial and Antebellum South*. Chapel Hill, NC: University of North Carolina Press.
   2003. "A Quality of Anguish: The Igbo Response to Enslavement in the Americas," in *Trans-Atlantic Dimensions of Ethnicity*. See Lovejoy and Trotman 2003.
Goodlife, F.A. 1933. "Intelligence Report on the Otanzu, Okigwe Division, Owerri Province, 1933." NAE – 28935 CSE 1/1/5.
   1952. *Rhodes House Mss. Afr. s.* 1753(2): Goodlife Papers.
Goody, J. 1980. *Technology, Tradition and the State in Africa*. Cambridge: Cambridge University Press.
Gose, Peter 1994. *Deathly Waters and Hungry Mountains: Agrarian Ritual and Class Formation in an Andean Town*. Toronto: University of Toronto Press.
Grainger, James 1764. *The Sugar-Cane: A Poem. In Four Books. With Notes*. London: R. and J. Dodsley.
Green, Magaret M. 1964. *Ibo Village Affairs*. London: Frank Cass.
Greene, Sandra 1996. *Gender, Ethnicity and, Social Change on the Upper Slave Coast*. Portsmouth, NH: Heinemann.
Grier, S.M. 1922. "Grier Papers." *Rhodes House MSS. Afr. s.* 1379, Box 3/6: 661–42.
Guyer, Jane I. 1980. "Food, Cocoa, and the Division of Labor by Sex in Two West African Societies," *Comparative Studies in Society and History*, Vol. 22, No. 3:355–73.
Hair, Paul E.H. 1963. "Koelle at Freetown: An Historical Introduction." In *Polyglotta*, see Koelle 1963.
   1965. "The Enslavement of Koelle's Informants." *Journal of African History*, Vol. 6, No. 2: 193–203.

1967. "Ethnolinguistic Continuity on the Guinea Coast." *Journal of African History*, Vol. 8, No. 2: 247–68.

Hair, Paul E.H., Adam Jones and Robin Law 1992a. *Barbot on Guinea: The Writings of Jean Barbot on West Africa 1678–1712*, Vols. 1 and 2. London: the Hakluyt Society.

1992b. "Introduction." In *Barbot on Guinea*. See Hair, P.E.H., A. Jones and R. Law 1992a.

Hall, Gwendolyn Midlo 1998. "Ethnic Selectivity in the African Slave Trade to Louisiana: Comparing the Du Bois Database with the Louisiana Slave Database." Presented at Transatlantic Slavery and the African Diaspora: Using the W.E.B. DuBois Institute Dataset of Slaving Voyages, Omohundro Institute of Early American History and Culture, Williamsburg, Virginia, September 11–13.

2005. *Slavery and African Ethnicities in the Americas: Restoring the Links*. Chapel Hill, NC: University of North Carolina Press.

Hargreaves, Susan M. 1987. "The Political Economy of Nineteenth Century Bonny: A Study of Power, Authority, Legitimacy and Ideology in a Delta Trading Community from 1700–1914." Ph.D. diss., Centre of West African Studies, University of Birmingham.

Harms, Robert 1978. "Slave Systems in Africa," *History in Africa*, Vol. 5: 327–35.

Hartley, C.W.S. 1977. *The Oil Palm (Elaeis Guineensis Jacq.)* (2nd edition). London: Longman.

Hastings, A.C.G. 1925. *Nigerian Days*. London: John Lane, The Bodley Head Limited.

[1857] 1926. *The Voyage of the Dayspring being the Journal of the Late Sir John Hawley Glover, R.N., G.C.M.G., together with Some Account of the Expedition up the Niger River in 1857*. London: John Lane – The Bodley Head Limited.

Hausner, J. et al. (editors) 1993. *Institutional Frameworks of Market Economies*. Aldershot, Avebury.

Hawkins, John 1970. *A History of a Voyage to the Coast of Africa, and the Travels into the Interior of that Country; Containing Particular Descriptions of the Climate and Inhabitants, and Interesting Particulars Concerning the Slave Trade*. London: Frank Cass.

Hawthorne, Walter 2003. *Planting Rice and Harvesting Slaves: Transformations along the Guinea-Bissau Coast, 1400–1900*. Portsmouth, NH: Heinemann.

Henderson, Helen K. 1997. "Onitsha Woman: The Traditional Context for Political Power." In *Queens, Queen Mothers*. See Kaplan 1997.

Henderson, Richard N. 1972. *The King in Every Man: Evolutionary Trends in Onitsha Ibo Society and Culture*. New Haven, CT: Yale University Press.

Herskovits, Melville J. 1936. "The Significance of West Africa for Negro Research." *Journal of Negro History*, Vol. 21, No. 1:15–30.

Heslop, I.R.P. 1936. "Intelligence Report on the Nkalu Clan, Orlu District, Okigwi Division, Owerri Province." *NAE* CSE 1/85/6197A.

Henige, David 1982. *Oral Historiography*. Madison, WI: University of Wisconsin Press.

1986. "Measuring the Immesurable: The Atlantic Slave Trade, West African Population and the Pyrrhonian Critic." *Journal of African History*, Vol. 27, No. 2: 295–313.

Higman, Barry W. 1976. *Slave Population and Economy in Jamaica*. Cambridge: Cambridge University Press.

Hilton, Anne 1983. "Family and Kinship among the Kongo South of the Zaïre River from the Sixteenth to the Nineteenth Centuries." *Journal of African History*, Vol. 24, No. 2: 189–206.

Hippisley, John 1764. *On the Populousness of Africa*. London: T. Lownds.

Hobhouse, Isaac et al. 1725. "Instructions to Captain William Barry," 7 October. In *Documents Illustrative*. See Donnan 1931.

Hobsbawm, Eric 1971. "From Social History to the History of Society." *Daedalus*, Vol. 100, Winter:20–45.

Hogendorn, Jan 1996. "Economic Modelling of Price Differences in the Slave Trade between the Central Sudan and the Coast." *Slavery and Abolition*, Vol. 17, No. 3: 209–22.

Hollden, Capt. E. 1723. "Captain Edward Hollden to the Owners of the Grayhound," 30 April. In *Documents Illustrative*. See Donnan 1931: 299–300.

Hopkins, A. G. 1968. "Economic Imperialism in West Africa: Lagos, 1880–92." *Economic History Review*, Vol. 21, No. 3:580–606.

1973. *An Economic History of West Africa*. London: Longman.

Horton, James Africanus B. 1863. *West African Countries and Peoples, British and Native. With the Requirements Necessary for Establishing that Self Government Recommended by the Committee of the House of Commons, 1865; and a Vindication of the African Race*. London: W.J. Johnson.

Horton, W. Robin G. 1954. "The Ohu System of Slavery in a Northern Ibo Village-Group." *Africa* 24: 311–36.

1976. "Stateless Societies in the History of Africa." In *History of West Africa, Volume One* (2nd edition). Essex: Longman.

Huggins, Nathan I. et al. (editors) 1971. *Key Issues in the Afro-American Experience*. New York: Harcourt Brace Jovanovich, Inc.

Hutchinson, John and John McEwan Dalziel 1928. *Flora of West Africa*, Vol. 1, Part 2. London: Crown Agents for the Colonies.

Hutchinson, Thomas J. 1855. *Narrative of an Expedition of the Niger, Tshadda, and Binue Exploration Including a Report on the Position and Prospects of Trade up those Rivers with Remarks on the Malaria and Fevers of Western Africa*. London: Longman, Brown, Green, and Longmans.

1858. *Impressions of Western Africa with Remarks on the Diseases of the Climate and a Report on the Peculiarities of Trade up the Rivers in the Bight of Biafra*. London: Longman, Brown, Green, Longmans, and Roberts.

1861. *Ten Years Wanderings among the Ethiopians*. London: Hurst and Blackett.

Ibemere, T. n.d. Transcripts of oral interview. See Ohaegbu, U.E. 1991.

Ibok, N. 1973. Transcripts of oral interview. See Northrup 1972–1973.

Idiong, B.U. et al. 1973. Transcripts of oral interview. See Northrup 1972–1973.

Ifediora, O. 1987. "Aspects of the Pre-Colonial history of Awka." BA thesis, History Department, University of Nigeria, Nsukka.

Ifemesia, Chieka C. 1959. "British Enterprise on the Niger 1830–1869." Ph.D. diss., University of London.

1978. *Southeastern Nigeria in the Nineteenth Century: An Introductory Analysis*. New York: NOK Publishers.

1979. *Traditional Humane Living among the Igbo: An Historical Perspective*. Enugu, Nigeria: Fourth Dimension.

Igbokwe, Edwin M. 2001. "Between Conservation and Production: Traditional Ware Yam Cultivation in Igbo-Etiti." *Nigeria Indigenous Knowledge and Development Monitor*, July. http://www.iss.nl/ikdm/IKDM/IKDM/9-2/igbokwe.html

Igwe, C.E. 1992. "The History of Ndiuche (in Ideato Local Governement Area) 1900–1960." BA thesis, History Department, University of Nigeria, Nsukka.

Igwe, D. 1992. Transcripts of oral interview. See C.E. Igwe 1992.

Igwe, Michael Sunday 1996. Interview, Ndiamazu-Uno, Arondizuogu, February 18.

Igwegbe, Richard O. 1962. *The Original History of Arondizuogu from 1635 to 1960*. Aba: International Press.

Igwilo, Kanu Okoli 1996a. Interview, Ndiamazu-Ipka-Akaputa, Arondizuogu, March 2.

1996b. Interview, Ndiamazu-Ipka-Akaputa, Arondizuogu, March 3.

Ihimnaegbu, U. 1986. Transcripts of oral interview. See Uwazuruike 1987.

Ijoma, J.Okoro (editor) 1986a. *Arochukwu: History and Culture*. Enugu: Fourth Dimension Publishers.

1986b. "Introduction." In *Arochukwu*. See Ijoma 1986a.

1986c. "Early History." In *Arochukwu*. See Ijoma 1986a.

1986d. "Eze Kanu Oji: A Symbol of Stability." In *Arochukwu*. See Ijoma 1986a.

1994. "The Aro and their Neighbours: A Reconsideration of the Historiography." *Nigerian Heritage*, Vol. 4:36–49.

1996. Personal communication, February 24.

Ijoma, J.Okoro and Owuka N. Njoku 1991. "High Point of Igbo Civilization: The Arochukwu Period." In *Groundwork of Igbo History*. See Afigbo 1991b.

Ike, E. 1985. Transcripts of oral interview. See I.O. Nwankwo 1986.

Ike, Ifeanyi 1996. Interview, Enugu, March 4.

Ike, J. 1972. Transcripts of oral interview. See Nwankwo, J.C. 1973.

Ike, K. 1972. Transcripts of oral interview. See Nwankwo, J.C. 1973.

Ike, Marthina 1995. Interview, Enugu, September 20.

1996a. Interview, Enugu, February 29.

1996b. Interview, Enugu, March 4.

Ike, Michael 1995. Interview, Enugu, September 21.

Ikime, O. 1980 (editor). *Groundwork of Nigerian History*. Ibadan, Nigeria: Heineman Educational Books (Nigeria) Limited.

Iloha, M. 1972. Transcripts of oral interview. See Nwankwo, J.C. 1973.

Imo, Malinda C. 1980. "Headship of Aro-Ndizuogu Community 1900–1960." BA thesis, History Department, University of Nigeria, Nsukka.

Imo, Princewill 2003. Interview, Telephone, February 5.

Inikori, J.E. 1976a. "Measuring the Atlantic Slave Trade: An Assessment of Curtin and and Anstey." *Journal of African History*, Vol. 17, No. 2: 197–223.

1976b. "Measuring the Atlantic Slave Trade: A Rejoinder." *Journal of African History*, Vol. 17, No. 4:607–27.

1978. "The Origins of the Diaspora: The Slave Trade from Africa." *Tarikh*, Vol. 5, No. 4: 1–19.

1979. "The Slave Trade and the Atlantic Economies, 1451–1870." In *The African Slave Trade from the Fifteenth to the Nineteenth Century: Reports and Papers of the Meeting of Experts Organized by UNESCO at Port-au-Prince, Haiti, 31 January to 4 February 1978*. Paris: UNESCO.

1981. "Under-Population in 19th Century West Africa: The Role of the Export Slave Trade." In *African Historical Demography, Volume 11*. See *African Historical Demography*.

Inikori, J.E. (editor) 1982a. *Forced Migration: The Impact of the Export Slave Trade on African Societies*. London: Hutchinson University Library.

1982b. "Introduction." In *Forced Migration*. See Inikori 1982a.

1986. "West Africa's Seaborne Trade, 1750–1850: Volume, Structure and Implications." In *Figuring African Trade*. See Liesegang 1986.

1988. "The Sources of Supply for the Atlantic Slave Exports from the Bight of Benin and the Bight of Bonny (Biafra)." In *De la Traite*. See Daget 1988b.

1992a. "Export versus Domestic Demand: The Determinants of Sex Ratios in the Transatlantic Slave Trade." *Research in Economic History*, Vol. 14: 117–66.

1992b. "The Volume of the British Slave Trade, 1655–1807." *Cahiers d'Etudes Africaines*, Vol. 32, No. 4: 643–88.

Inikori, Joseph E. 1994a. "History in Breath and History in Depth: Grand Theories and Empirical Evidence in the Expanding Historiography of the Atlantic Slave Trade." Paper presented at the Conference on the State of African Diaspora Studies: Present Realities and Future Prospects, University of North Carolina at Chapel Hill, February 18–19.

1994b. "Ideology versus Tyranny of Paradigm: Historians and the Impact of the Atlantic Slave Trade on African Societies." *African Economic History*, No. 22: 37–58.

1998. "The Known, the Unknown, the Knowable, and the Unknowable: Evidence and the Evaluation of Evidence in the Measurement of the Trans-Atlantic Slave Trade." Presented at Transatlantic Slavery and the African Diaspora: Using the W.E.B. DuBois Institute Dataset of Slaving Voyages, Omohundro Institute of Early American History and Culture, Williamsburg, Virginia, September 11–13.

Inikori, Joseph E. and Stanley Engerman (editors) 1992. *The Atlantic Slave Trade: Effects on the Economies, Societies, and Peoples in Africa, the Americas and Europe*. Durham and London: Duke University Press.

Innis, Harold A. 1962. *The Fur Trade in Canada: An Introduction to Canadian Economic History*, based on the Revised Edition and prepared by S.D. Clark and W.T. Easterbrook. New Haven, CT: Yale University Press.

Inokun, J. 1972. Transcripts of oral interview. See Northrup 1972–1973.

International Population Census Publications, Africa, Nigeria: 1950, 1952, 1953, 1957. New Haven, CT: Research and Publication, Inc.

Inyang, J.E. 1973. Transcripts of oral interview. See Northrup 1972–1973.

Ipere, Chief 1983. Transcripts of oral interview. See Alaka 1984.

Ire, O. 1981. Transcripts of oral interview. See Udueze, A.E. 1982.
Iroh, C. 1991. Transcripts of oral interview. See Nwankwo, T. 1991.
Irokobe, M.O. 1977. Transcripts of oral interview. See G.C. Mmeregini 1978.
Irono, M. 1988. *The Life and Times of Thomas Nwafor Irono*, Enugu, Author.
Isangedighi, S. et al. 1973. Transcripts of oral interview. See Northrup 1972–1973.
Isangetighi, J. et al. 1973. Transcripts of oral interview. See Northrup 1972–1973.
Isichei, Elizabeth 1973. *The Ibo People and the Europeans*. London: Faber and Faber.
1976. *A History of the Igbo People*. London: Macmillan.
Isichei, Elizabeth (editor) 1978. *Igbo Worlds: An Anthology of Oral Histories and Historical Descriptions*. Philadelphia, PA: Institute for the Study of Human Issues.
1983. *A History of Nigeria*. Lagos: Longman.
Ita, P.E. 1972. Transcripts of oral interview. See Northrup 1972–1973.
Jackson, R.M. [1826] 1934. *Journal of a Voyage to Bonny River on the West Coast of Africa in the Ship Kingston from Liverpool* edited by Roland Jackson. Letchworth, UK: The Garden City Press Ltd.
James, W. 1988. "Perceptions from an African Slaving Frontier." In *Slavery and Other Forms of Unfree Labour* edited by L.J. Archer. London: Routledge.
Jell-Bahlsen, Sabine 1997. "Eze Mmiri Di Egwu, The Water Monarch is Awesome: Reconsidering the Mammy Water Myths." In *Queens, Queen Mothers*. See Kaplan 1997.
Johnson, Marion 1984. "Commodities, Customs, and the Computer." *History in Africa*, Vol. 11, 359–66.
Johnston, Harry H. 1888a. "A Journey up the Cross River, West Africa." *Proceedings of the Royal Geographical Society*, Vol. 10, No. 7 (July): 435–38.
1888b. "The Niger Delta." *Proceedings of the Royal Geographical Society*, Vol. 10, No. 12 (December): 749–63.
1923. *The Story of My Life*. Indianapolis, IN: The Bobbs-Merrill Company.
Jones, Adam 1995. "Female Slave-Owners on the Gold Coast: Just a Matter of Money?" In *Slave Cultures*. See Palmié 1995a.
Jones, G.I. 1939. "Who Are the Aros?" *Nigerian Field*, Vol. 8, No. 3: 100–03.
1961. "Ecology and Social Structure among the North Eastern Ibo." *Africa*, Vol. 31: 117–34.
1963. *The Trading States of the Oil Rivers*. London: Oxford University Press.
1989. *From Slaves to Palm Oil: Slave Trade and Palm Oil Trade in the Bight of Biafra*. Cambridge: African Studies Centre.
Jones, James 1788. "James Jones to Lord Hawkesbury," 26 July. In *Documents Illustrative*. See Donnan 1931: 589–92.
"Journal of the Arthur, Dec. 5, 1677–May 25, 1678." In *Documents Illustrative*. See Donnan 1930: 226–34.
Kalu, Ogbu 1979. "The Battle of the Gods: Christianization of Cross River Igboland, 1903–1950." *Journal of the Historical Society of Nigeria*, Vol. 10, No. 1: 1–20.

Ihenacho, David Asonye 2004. *African Christian Rises, Volume Two: Eucharistic Inculturation in Igbo Catholicism*. Bloomington, IN: Universe, Inc. http://www.books.google.com

Kalunta, E. 1977. Transcripts of oral interview. See G.C. Mmeregini 1978.

Kanu, C. 1972. Transcripts of oral interview. See Nwankwo, J.C. 1973.

Kanu, J. 1972. Transcripts of oral interview. See Nwankwo, J.C. 1973.

Kanu, Okoro P. 2000. *Pre-British Aro of Arochukwu: Notes and Reflections on an African Civilization*. Houston, TX: USAfrica Books, 2001.

Kanu-Igbo, Ukobasi Francis 1996a. Interview, Enugu, March 6.

  1996b. Interview, Enugu, March 7.

Kanu-Onuoha, Okoro 1996. Interview, Amankwu, Arochukwu, February 24.

Kaplan, Flora Edouwaye S. 1997 (editor). *Queens, Queen Mothers, Priestesses, and Power Case Studies in African Gender*. Annals of the New York Academy of Sciences, Vol. 810. New York: The New York Academy of Social Sciences.

Kea, Ray 1982. *Settlements, Trade and Politics in the Seventh-Century Gold Goast*. Baltimore, MD: Johns Hopkins University Press.

Kilkenny, Roberta W. 1981. "The Slave Mode of Production: Precolonial Dahomey." In *Modes of Production in Africa* edited by D. Crummey and C.C. Stewart. Beverly Hills, CA: Sage Publications.

Klein, Herbert S. 1976. *African Slavery in Latin America and the Caribbean*, New York: Oxford University Press.

  1978. *The Middle Passage: Comparative Studies in the Atlantic Slave Trade*. Princeton, NJ: Princeton University Press.

  1983. "African Women in the Atlantic Slave Trade." In *Women and Slavery*. See Robertson and Klein 1983a.

Klein, Herbert, Stanley Engerman, Robin Baines and Ralph Shlomowitz 2001. "Transoceanic Mortality: The Slave Trade in Comparative Perspective." *William and Mary Quarterly*, Third Series, Vol. 58, No. 1: 93–117.

Klein, Martin A. 1968. *Islam and Imperialism in Senegal: Sine-Saloum, 1847–1914*. Palo Alto, CA: Stanford University Press.

  1971. "Slavery, the Slave Trade, and Legitimate Commerce in Late Nineteenth-Century Africa." *Etudes d'histoire Africaine*, Vol. 2: 5–28.

  1972. "Social and Economic Factors in the Muslim Revolution in Senegambia." *Journal of African History*, Vol. 13, No. 2:419–41.

  1978. "Review Article: The Study of Slavery in Africa." *Journal of African History*, Vol. 19, No. 4: 599–609.

  1983. "Women in Slavery in the Western Sudan." In *Women and Slavery*. See Robertson and Klein 1983a.

  1987. "The Demography of Slavery in Western Soudan: The Late Nineteenth Century." In *African Population and Capitalism*. See Cordell and Gregory 1987.

  1988. "Slave Resistance and Emancipation in Coastal Guinea." In *The End of Slavery*. See Miers and Roberts 1988.

  1992. "The Impact of the Atlantic Slave Trade on the Societies of the Western Sudan." In *The Atlantic Slave Trade*. See Inikori and Engerman 1992.

1998. *Slavery and Colonial Rule in French West Africa*. Cambridge: Cambridge University Press.

2001. "The Slave Trade and Decentralized Societies." *Journal of African History*, Vol. 42, No. 1: 49–65.

Klein, M.A. and P. E. Lovejoy. 1979. "Slavery in West Africa." In *The Uncommon Market*, edited by H. Gemery and J.S. Hogendorn. New York: Academic Press.

Koelle, Sigmund W. [1854] 1963. *Polyglotta Africana*. Graz, Austria: Akademische Druck – U. Verlagsanstalt.

Kopytoff, I. (editor) 1987a. *The African Frontier: The Reproduction of Traditional African Societies*. Bloomington, IN and Indianapolis: Indiana University Press.

1987b. "The Internal African Frontier: The Making of African Political Culture." In *The African Frontier*. See Kopytof 1987a.

Kopytoff, I. and S. Miers 1977. "African 'Slavery' as an Institution of Marginality." In *Slavery in Africa*. See Miers and Kopytoff 1977.

Korieh, Chima (editor) 2008. *Olaudah Equiano and the Igbo: History, Society, and Atlantic Diaspora Connections*. Trenton, NJ: Africa World Press.

Kroll, Catherine 2007. "'Styled *Embrenche*': Marking African Authority in Olaudah Equiano's Interesting Narrative." Unpublished.

Kulikoff, A. 1986. *Tobacco and Slaves: The Development of Southern Cultures in the Chesapeake, 1680–1800*. Chapel Hill, NC and London: University of North Carolina Press.

Kwentoh, N. 1977. Transcripts of oral interview. See Modebe, I.P. 1978.

Laird, Macgregor and R.A.K. Oldfield 1837. *Narrative of an Expedition into the Interior of Africa, by the River Niger, in 1832, 1833, and 1834*, Vol. 1. London: Richard Bentley.

Lamar, H. and L. Thompson (editors) 1981. *The Frontier in History: North America and South Africa Compared*. New Haven, CT: Yale University Press.

Lambert, Sheila 1975a. *House of Commons Sessional Papers of the Eighteenth Century, Volume 68, George III Minutes of Evidence on the Slave Trade 1788 and 1789*. Willington, DE: Scholarly Resources, Inc.

1975b. *House of Commons Sessional Papers of the Eighteenth Century, Volume 71, George III Minutes of Evidence on the Slave Trade 1790*. Willington, DE: Scholarly Resources, Inc.

1975c. *House of Commons Sessional Papers of the Eighteenth Century, Volume 73, George III Minutes of Evidence on the Slave Trade 1790*. Willington, DE: Scholarly Resources, Inc.

Landa, Janet T. 1994. *Trust, Ethnicity, and Identity*. Ann Arbor, MI: University of Michigan Press.

Lander, Richard and John 1832. *Journal of an Expedition to Explore the Course and Termination of the Niger with a Narrative of a Voyage Down that River to its Termination*, Vol. 2. New York: J. and J. Harper.

Latham, A.J.H. 1973. *Old Calabar 1600–1891: The Impact of the International Economy upon a Traditional Society*. Oxford: Clarendon Press.

1978. "Price Fluctuations in the Early Palm Oil Trade." *Jounal of African History*, Vol. 19, No. 2: 213–18.

1986. "Palm Produce from Calabar, 1812–1887, with a Note on the Formation of Palm Oil Prices to 1914." In *Figuring African Trade*. See G. Liesegand 1986.
Law, Robin 1977. "Royal Monopoly and Private Enterprise in the Atlantic Trade: The Case of Dahomey." *Journal of African History*, Vol. 18, No. 4: 555–77.
   1978. "Slaves, Trade, and Taxes: The Material Basis of Political Power in Precolonial West Africa." *Research in Economic Anthropology*, Vol. 1: 37–52.
   1980. *The Horse in West African History*. Oxford: Oxford University Press.
   1991a. "Computing Slave Domestic Prices in Precolonial West Africa: A Methodological Exercise from the Slave Coast." *History in Africa*, Vol. 18: 239–57.
   1991b. *The Slave Coast of West Africa 1550–1750: The Impact of the Atlantic Slave Trade on an African Society*. Oxford: Clarendon Press.
   1992. "Warfare on the West African Slave Coast, 1650–1850." In *War in the Tribal Zone: Expanding States and Indigenous Warfare*, edited by R. Brian Ferguson and Neil L. Whitehead. Sante Fe, NM: School of American Research Press.
   1993. "The Historiography of the Commercial Transition in Nineteenth Century West Africa." In *African Historiography: Essays in Honour of Jacob Ade Ajayi* edited by Toyin Falola. Ikeja, Nigeria: Longman.
Law, Robin (editor) 1995a. *From Slave Trade to "Legitimate" Commerce: The Commercial Transition in Nineteenth-Century West Africa*. Cambridge: Cambridge University Press.
   1995b. "Introduction." In *From Slave Trade*. See Law 1995a.
   1996. "The State and Private Enterprise in Dahomey's Atlantic Trade (Revisited)." Paper delivered at the Harriet Tubman Seminar on Slavery, York University, Toronto, October 28.
   1997. "The 'Nigerian' Hinterland and the African Diaspora." In *Identifying Enslaved Africans*. See Lovejoy 1997.
Law, Robin and Paul E. Lovejoy 1996. "The Changing Dimensions of African History: Reappropriating the Diaspora." Paper delivered at the Harriet Tubman Seminar on African Slavery, York University, Toronto, November 18.
Law, Robin and Silke Strickdot (editors) 1999. *Ports of the Slave Trade (Bights of Benin and Biafra)* University of Sterling, Center of Commonwealth Studies, Occasional Paper Number 6.
Lejeune, Fr. 1901. "The Missions in British Nigeria." *Illustrated Catholic Misions*, Vol. 15, No. 178, February.
   1901. "British Nigeria: Progress of Christian Civilization." *Illustrated Catholic Missions*, Vol. 17, No. 194, June.
Leith-Ross, Sylvia 1939. *African Women*, London: Faber and Faber.
Leonard, Arthur G. 1898. "Notes on a Journey to Bende." *Journal of the Manchester Geographical Society*, 14: 190–207.
   1906. *The Lower Niger and its Tribes*. London: Macmillan.
Leonard, P. 1833. *Records of a Voyage to the Coast of Africa in His Majesty's Ship Dryad*. Edinburgh: William Tait.

Levin, Michael D. 1992. "Speculations on the Pre-Colonial History of the Cross River Basin." *Ikoro*, Vol. 7, Nos. 1 and 2: 97–104.

1997. Personal communication. May.

Lewis, W.A. 1954. "Economic Development with Unlimited Supplies of Labour." *The Manchester School of Economic and Social Studies*, Vol. 22:139–91.

Leyland, Thomas 1803. "Thomas Leyland and Company to Captain Caesar Lawson," 18 July. In *Documents Illustrated*. See Donnan 1931:650–52.

Liesegand, G. (editor) 1986. *Figuring African Trade*. Sankt Augustin, Germany: Kölner Beiträge zur Afrikanistik. 11. Bd.

Littlefield, Daniel C. 1981. *Rice and Slaves: Ethnicity and the Slave Trade in Colonial South Carolina*. Baton Rouge, LA and London: Louisiana State University.

Lovejoy, Paul E. 1979. "Indigenous African Slavery." *Historical Reflections*, Vol. 6, No. 1: 18–61.

1980. *Caravans of Kola*. Zaria: Ahmadu Bello University Press.

Lovejoy Paul E. (editor) 1981a. *The Ideology of Slavery in Africa*. Beverly Hills, CA: Sage.

1981b. "Slavery in the Context of Ideology." See Lvejoy 1981a.

1982a. "Polanyi's 'Ports of Trade': Salaga and Kano in the Nineteenth Century." *Canadian Journal of African Studies*, Vol. 16, No. 2: 245–77.

1982b. "The Volume of the Atlantic Slave Trade: A Synthesis." *Journal of African History*, Vol. 23, No. 4:.473–501.

1983. *Transformations in Slavery: A History of Slavery in Africa*. Cambridge: Cambridge University Press.

Lovejoy Paul E. (editor) 1986. *Africans in Bondage: Studies in Slavery and the SLave Trade*. Madison, WI: African Studies Program, University of Wisconsin.

1989. "The Impact of the Atlantic Slave Trade on Africa: A Review of the Literature." *Journal of African History*, Vol. 30.

1994a. "Background to Rebellion: The Origins of Muslim Slaves in Bahia." *Slavery and Abolition*, Vol. 15, No. 2.

1994b. Personal Communication. April.

Lovejoy Paul E. (editor) 1997. *Identifying Enslaved Africans*. Toronto: Harriet Tubman Center, York University.

2006. "Autobiography and Memory: Gustavus Vassa, alias Olaudah Equiano, the African." *Slavery and Abolition*,Vol. 27, No. 3: 317–47.

Lovejoy, Paul E. and Jan S. Hogendorn 1979. "Slave Marketing in West Africa." In *Uncommon Markets*. See Gemery and Hogendorn 1979.

Lovejoy, Paul E. and D. Richardson 1995a. "Competing Markets for Male and Female Slaves: Prices in the Interior of West Africa, 1750–1850." *International Journal of African Historical Studies*, Vol. 28, No. 2: 261–93.

1995b. "The Initial 'Crisis of Adaptation': The Impact of British Abolition on the Atlantic Slave Trade in West Africa, 1808–1820." In *From Slave*. See Law 1995a.

1996. "'Pawns Will Live When Slaves Are Apt to Dye': Credit, Risk and Trust at Old Calabar in the Era of the Slave Trade." Paper delivered at the Harriet Tubman Seminar on African Slavery, York University, Toronto, October 7.

1997. "Pawns Will Live when Slaves is Apt to Dye": Credit, Slaving and Pawnship at Old Calabar in the Era of the Slave Trade, London School of Economics and Political Science Working Papers in Economic History, No. 37/97, November.

1999. "Trust, Pawnship and Atlantic History: The Institutional Foundations of the old Calabar Slave Trade." *American Historical Review*, Vol. 102: 333–55.

2004. "'This Horid Hole': Royal Authority, Commerce and Credit at Bonny, 1690–1840." *Journal of African History*, Vol. 45, No. 3: 363–92.

Lovejoy, Paul E. and David V. Trotman (editors) 2003. *Trans-Atlantic Dimensions of Ethnicity in the African Diaspora*. London: Continuum.

Lynn, Martin 1981. "Change and Continuity in the British Palm Oil Trade with West Africa." *Journal of African History*, Vol. 22, No. 3: 331–48.

1997. *Commerce and Economic Change in West Africa: The Palm Oil Trade in the Nineteenth Century*. Cambridge: Cambridge University Press.

MacAlister, Donald 1902. "The Aro Country, Southern Nigeria." *Scottish Geographical Magazine*, Vol. 18, No. 12: 631–36.

MacCormack, C.P. 1983. "Slaves, Slave Owners, and Slave Dealers: Sherbro Coast and Hinterland." In *Women and Slavery*. See Robertson and Klein 1983a.

Macdonald, Major 1890. "Notes on Slavery in the Niger and Oil River District." In *Report by Major Macdonald*. See Department of State and Official Bodies (England) 1890.

Macgregor, J.K. 1909. "Some Notes on Nsibidi." *Journal of the Royal Anthropological Institute*, Vol. 39: 209–19.

Maduadichie, Kevin 1996. Interview, Ndiakunwanta-Uno, Arondizuogu, February 11.

Maduagwu, B.O.J. n.d. *Brief History of Umunze*. Onitsha: Appolos Brothers Press.

1996. Interview, Umunze, February 11.

Madubuike, Ihechukwu 1976. *A Handbook of African Names*. Washington, DC: The Continents Press.

Mann, Kristin 2007. *Slaving and the Birth of an African City: Lagos, 1760–1900*. Bloomington, IN: Indiana University Press.

Manning, Patrick 1981. "The Enslavement of Africans: A Demographic Model." *Canadian Journal of African Studies*, Vol. 15, No. 3: 499–526.

1982. *Slavery, Colonialism and Economic Growth in Dahomey, 1640–1960*. Cambridge: Cambridge University Press.

1986. "Slave Trade, 'Legitimate Trade, and Imperialism Revisited: The Control of Wealth in the Bights of Benin and Biafra." In *Africans in Bondage*. See Lovejoy 1986.

1987. "Local versus Regional Impact of Slave Exports on Africa." In *African Population and Capitalism*. See Cordell and Gregory 1987.

1988. "The Impact of Slave Trade Exports on the Populations of the Western Coast of Africa, 1700–1850." In *De la Traite*. See Daget 1988.

1990. *Slavery and African Life*. Cambridge: Cambridge University Press.

1998a. "Louisiana Slavery in Atlantic Context: Demography, Economy, and Culture, 1720–1850." Presented at the American Historical Association Annual Meeting, Seattle, WA, January 10.

1998b. "Volume and National Participation in the Trade." Presented at Transatlantic Slavery and the African Diaspora: Using the W.E.B. DuBois Institute Dataset of Slaving Voyages, Omohundro Institute of Early American History and Culture, Williamsburg, Virginia, September 11–13.

Marks, Shula and Richard Rathbone (editors) 1983. *Journal of African History*, Vol. 24, No. 2: Special Issue on The History of the Family in Africa.

Martin, Anne 1956. *The Oil Palm Economy of the Ibibio Farmer*. Ibadan, Nigeria: Ibadan University Press.

Martin, Susan 1988. *Palm Oil and Protest: An Economic History of the Ngwa Region, South-Eastern Nigeria, 1800–1980*. Cambridge: Cambridge University Press.

1995. "Slave, Igbo Women and Palm Oil Trade in the Nineteenth Century." In *From Slave*. See R. Law 1995a.

Mason, Michael 1969. "Population Density and 'Slave Raiding' – the Case of the Middle Belt of Nigeria." *Journal of African History*, Vol. 10, No. 4:551–64.

Matory, J. Lorand 1984. *Sex and the Empire That Is No More: Gender and the Politics of Metaphor in Oyo Yoruba Religion*. Minneapolis, MN: University of Minnesota Press.

Matthews, H. F. 1922. "Ethnological Report on Okpoto, Egedde, Etc." Rhodes House: MSS Afr. s. 783 Box 2/7 ff 1A – 265.

Mauny, Raymond 1961. "Nigeria as Seen by Leo Africanus, 1526." *Nigeria Magazine*, No. 69, August:189–90.

Mayne, C.J. 1935. "Intelligence Report on the Village of Ndizuogu in the Orlu District of the Okigwe Division, Owerri Province." NAE 12481A-MINLOC 16/1/1326.

Mba, Nina E. 1982. *Nigerian Women Mobilized*. Berkeley, CA: University of California Press.

Mbadiwe, Kingsley O. 1991. *Rebirth of a Nation* (edited by L.I. Agusiegbe). Enugu: Fourth Dimension.

Mbaekwe, J. 1977. Transcripts of oral interview. See Okoroafo, E.S. 1978.

McCall, John C. 2000. *Dancing Histories: Hueristic Ethnography with the Ohafia Igbo*, Ann Arbor, MI: University of Michigan Press.

McPhee, Allan 1971. *The Economic Revolution in British West Africa* (second edition). London: Frank Cass.

Meek, Charles K. 1937. *Law and Authority in a Nigerian Tribe*. London: Oxford University Press.

Mefo, A. and M. Ibe 1972. Transcripts of oral interview. See Northrup 1972–1973.

Meillassoux, Claude 1971a. *The Development of Indigenous Trade and Markets in West Africa*. Glasgow: Oxford University Press.

1971b. "Introduction." In *Development of Indigenous Trade*. See Meillassoux 1971b.

1981. *Maidens, Meal and Money: Capitalism and the Domestic Community*. London: Cambridge University Press.

1982. "The Role of Slavery in the Economic and Social History of Sahelo-Sudanic Africa." In *Forced Migration*. See Inikori 1982.

1983. "Female Slavery." In *Women and Slavery*. See Robertson and Klein 1983a.

Menard, Russel R. and S. Bernard Schwartz 1993. "Why African Slavery? Labour Transition in Brazil, Mexico, and the Carolina Lowcountry." In *Slavery in the Americas* edited byBinder, Wolfgang, Würzburg, Germany: Königshausen and Neumann.

Merem, K. and K. Nwankwo 1973. Transcripts of oral interview. See Northrup 1972–1973.

Merewether, J. and E. Manning 1736. "John Merewether and Edward Manning to Peter Burrell," January 6, 1736. See Donnan 1931: 455.

Metuh, Emefie E. 1973. "The Supreme God in Igbo Life and Worship." *Journal of Religion in Africa*, Vol. 5, No. 1:1–11.

Mgbeahurukwe, M. 1977. Transcripts of oral interview. See Okoroafo, E.S. 1978.

Mgbemena, O. 1991. Transcripts of oral interview. See Theresa Nwankwo 1991.

Mgbemene, A.E.D. 1996. Interview, Amagu, Ajali, April 12.

Miers, Suzanne and Igor Kopytoff (editors) 1977. *Slavery in Africa: Historical and Anthropological Perspectives*. Madison, WI: University of Wisconsin Press.

Miller, Ivor L. 2009. *Voice of the Leonard: African Secret Societies and Cuba*. Jackson: University of Mississippi Press.

Miller, Joseph 1988. *Way of Death: Merchant Capitalism and the Angolan Slave Trade 1730–1830*. Madison, WI: The University of Wisconsin Press.

Minchinton, Walter E. 1976. "The Slave Trade of Bristol with the British Mailand Colonies in North America 1699–1770." In *Liverpool*. See Anstey and Hair 1976.

Mmeregini, E.O. n.d. *The Making of the Legend-Ndiokoroji*, Author.

Mmeregini, G.C. 1978. "Ndiokoroji: The History of an Aro Settlement." BA thesis, History, University of Nigeria, Nsukka.

Mmeregini, R.O. 1977. Transcripts of oral interview. See G.C. Mmeregini 1978.

Mockler-Ferryman, Augustus F. 1902. *British Nigeria: A Geographical and Historical Description of the British Possession Adjacent to the Niger River, West Africa*. London: Cassell and Company, Ltd.

Modebe, I.P. 1978. "Onicha Trade in the 19th Century." BA thesis, History Department, University of Nigeria, Nsukka.

Moitt, Bernard 1989. "Behind the Sugar Fortunes: Women, Labor and the Development of Caribbean Plantations during Slavery." In *African Continuities* (edited by Chiliungu, Simeon Waliaula and Sada Niang). Toronto: Terebi.

Monteith, Archibald. [1853] 1966. "Archibald John Monteith: Native Helper and Assistant in the Jamaica Mission at New Carmel," edited by V. H. Nelson. *Transactions of the Moravian Historical Society*, Vol. 2, No. 1, 1966:29–51.

Moor, Ralph 1902. "Memorandum Concerning the Aro Expedition Detailing Circumstances that Led to It and the Results which It is Anticipated Will Ensue therefrom." CO 520/14, April 24, 1902.

1908. Comment on Lieutenant Steele's "Exploration in Southern Nigeria." *The Geographical Journal*, Vol. 32, March: 22–24.

Morgan, Philip D. 1997. "The Cultural Implications of the Atlantic Slave Trade: African Regional Origins, American Destinations and New World Developments." *Slavery and Abolition*, Vol. 18, No. 1: 122–45.

1998. *Slave Counterpoint: Black Culture in the Eighteenth-Century Chesapeake and Lowcountry*. Chapel Hill, NC: University of North Carloina Press for the Omohundro Institute of Early American History and Culture.

Morley, J. 1790. See Lambert 1975c.

Morris, T. 1730/1 [?]. "Theodore Morris to Isaac Hobhouse." In *Documents Illustrative*. See Donnan 1931: 431–33.

Monye, O.A. 1991. "A Biography of Late Dr. Kingsley Gabriel Ozuomba Mbadiwe." BA thesis, History Department, Imo State University, Okigwe.

Müller, Birgit 1985. "Commodities as Currencies: The Integration of Overseas Trade into the Internal Trading Structure of the Igbo of South-East Nigeria." *Cahiers d'études africaines*, Vol. 25, No. 97: 57–77.

Mullin, Michael 1992. *Africa in America: Slave Acculturation and Resistance in the American South and the British Caribbean, 1736–1831*. Urbana, IL and Chicago, IL: University of Illinois Press.

Muojekwu, U. 1976. Transcripts of oral interview. See Anaedobe, M.M. 1977.

Muotoh, Aaron 1996. Interview, Ndianiche-nde-Uwakoronye, Arondizuogu, March 10.

Muotoh, Ezekiah O.G. 2000. *Arondizuogu Past and Present*. Okigwe, Nigeria, Muotoh.

Murphy, R. 1989. *Cultural and Social Anthropology: An Overture* (3rd edition). Englewood Cliffs, NJ: Prentice Hall.

Musisi, N.B. 1991. "Women. 'Elite Polygyny,' and Buganda State Formation." *Signs*, Vol. 16, No. 4: 757–86.

NAE 1/1920 – OKIDIST 4/2/1: "Cases of Slave Dealing," D.O. Okigwi, to Resident, Owerri, Oct. 19, 1920.

NAE 1/1920 – ORLDIST 4/2/1. "Cases of Slave Dealing."

NAE 3/20 – ORLDIST 4/2/2: "Urualla N.C. –."

NAE 4/1920 – OKIDIST 4/2/3: "Native Staff."

NAE 6/1927A – CSE 1/12/1. "Matters in Okigwi Division."

NAE 17/1922 – OKIDIST 4/4/11. "Various Petitions and Complaints."

NAE 31 OKIDIST 4/4/23. "Annual Reports – Okiwgwe Division."

NAE 32/21 – OKIDIST 4/3/38. "Quaterly Reports," 1921.

NAE 35/1920 – OKIDIST 4/2/32: "Land Cases."

NAE 38/22 OKIDIST 4/4/29. "Uruala Native Court."

NAE 45/19 – OKIDIST 4/1/32: "Marriages."

NAE 46/1920 – OKIDIST 4/2/41. "Land Cases & Instructions &c. – Re."

NAE 52/19 – ORLDIST 4/1/38. "Statistic of Population."

NAE 65/1924 – OKIDIST 4/6/58. "Okigwi Division – Annual Report 1924."

NAE 81/27 – OKIDIST 4/9/70. "Anthropological Report on the Aros of Ndizuogu and Others," March 31, 1927.

NAE 101/1928 – OKIDIST 4/10/74. "Annual Report 1928."

NAE 12481A – MINLOC 16/1/1326. "Intelligence Report on the Village of Ndizuogu in the Orlu District of the Okigwi Division, Owerri Province."

NAE 28935 – CSE 1/1/5: "Intelligence Report on the Otanzu, Okigwi Division, Owerri Province, 1933."

Sources Cited

NAE ARODIV – 20/1/15: "Anthropologists' Papers on Aro Origin. Discussion and the Basis of the Widespread of Aro Influence, 1927."
NAE Conf. E 17/11 – CALPROF 13/4/7. "Report on Special Action, Messages & Escorts for Okigwe."
NAE CSE – 1/1/5 28935.
NAE CSE – 1/85/6197A. "Intelligence Report on the Nkalu Clan, Orlu District, Okigwi Division, Owerri Province."
NAE EP 1248 – MINLOC 6:1.306. "Intelligence Report on the Ndizuogu Village Area, orlu District, Okigwe Division, Owerri Province."
NAE EP 1281 – MINLOC 6/1/306.
NAE MILGOV – 13/1/17: "Mbanasataw-Awka Division, 1936."
NAE OKIDIST – 4/4/11 17/1922. "Various Petitions and Complaints."
NAE OKIDIST – 14/1/32 45/19. "Marriages."
NAE OKIDIST – 14/1/38 52/19. "Statistic of Population."
NAE OKIDIST – 19/1/1: "Intelligence Book Okigwi Division, 1908–25."
NAE ONPROF – 7/16/150: "Awka Division Intelligence Notes on the Towns of Ajlli Native Court Area 1929."
NAE OR/C/823 – ORLDIST 3/1/359. "Ndizuogu Intelligence & Reorganization Record."
NAE ORLDIST – 14/1/1: "Intelligence Book 1911."
NAE ORLDIST – 14/1/2.
NAE ORLDIST – 14/1/3.
Nair, K.K. 1972. *Politics and Society in Southeastern Nigeria 1841–1906: A study of Power, Diplomacy and Commerce in Old Calabar*. London: Frank Cass.
Ndubuisi, Okoro 1996. Interview, Ugbo, Arochukwu, February 25.
Newbury, C.W. 1969. "Trade and Authority in West Africa from 1850 to 1880." In *Colonialism in Africa 1870–1960*, Vol. 1, edited by L.H. Gann and P. Duignan. London: Cambridge University Press.
Newmark, S. Daniel 1957. *Economic Influences on the South African Frontier*. Palo Alto, CA: Stanford University Press.
Nieboer, H.J. 1900. *Slavery as an Industrial System: Ethnological Researches*. The Hague: Martinus Nijhoff.
Niger Expedition 1842. *Church Missionary Record*, Vol. 13, No. 3: 53–62.
Njoku, J.E. 1978. *A Dictionary of Igbo Names, Culture and Proverbs*, Washington, DC: University Press of America.
Njoku, Onwuka N. 1991. "Igbo Economy and Society." In *Groundwork of Igbo History*. See Afigbo 1991.
    2000. *Ohafia: A Heroic Igbo Society*. Okigwe, Nigeria: Kalu Oyeoku.
Nkagbu, M. 1981. Transcripts of oral interview. See A.E. Udueze 1982.
Ngene, O. 1972. Transcripts of oral interview. See Nwankwo, J.C. 1973.
Nlebedum, S. 1977. Transcripts of oral interview. See G.C. Mmeregini 1978.
Nnolim, Simon Alagbogu 2007. *The History of Umuchu*. Raleigh, NC: Lulu.
Noah, M.E. 1980. *Old Calabar: The City State and the Europeans, 1800–1885*. Uyo, Nigeria: Scholars Press.
Northrup, David 1972. "The Growth of Trade among the Igbo before 1800." *Journal of African History*, Vol. 13, No. 2: 217–36.
    1972–1973. "A Collection of Interviews Conducted in Southeastern Nigeria in 1972–1973."

1978a. "African Mortality in the Suppression of the Slave Trade: The Case of the Bight of Biafra." *Journal of Interdisciplinary History*, Vol. 9, No. 1: 47–64.
1978b. *Trade Without Rulers: Pre-Colonial Economic Development in South-Eastern Nigeria.* Oxford: Clarendon Press.
1976. "The Compatibility of the Slave and Palm Oil Trades in the Bight of Biafra." *Journal of African History*, Vol. 17, No. 3: 353–64.
1979. "Nineteenth-Century Patterns of Slavery and Economic Growth in Southeastern Nigeria." *International Historical Studies*, Vol. 12, No. 1: 1–16.
1981. "The Ideological Context of Slavery in Southeastern Nigeria in the 19th Century." In *The Ideology of Slavery.* See Lovejoy 1981a.
2000. "Igbo and Myth Igbo: Culture and Ethnicity in the Atlantic World, 1600–1850," *Slavery and Abolition*, Vol. 21, No. 3:1–20.
Nwabueze, E. 1984. "Igbo Masquerade Performance and the Problem of Alien Intervention: Transition from Cult to Theatre." *Ufahamu*, Vol. 14, No. 1: 75–92.
Nwabughuogu, A. 1982. "From Wealthy Enterpreneurs to Petty Traders: African Middlemen in Eastern Nigeria, 1900_1950." *Journal of African History*, Vol. 23, No. 3: 365–79.
Nwala, T. Uzodinma 1985. *Igbo Philosophy.* Lagos: Lantern Books.
Nwamba, P. 1973. Transcripts of oral interview. See Isichei 1978.
Nwana, Harry A.P. n.d. *Arondizuogu Traditional Values.* Lagos: Lumex Industrial Press.
Nwana, Pita [1933] 1950. *Omenuko.* London: Longman.
Nwangwu, G.I. 1991. Transcripts of oral interview. See Ohaegbu, U.E. 1991.
Nwankwo, Aloy 1996. Interview, Boston, MA, USA, December 18.
Nwankwo, C. 1972. Transcripts of oral interview. See Nwankwo, J.C. 1973.
Nwankwo, Cyril 1996. Interview, Ndiamazu-Ijoma-Igbo, Arondizuogu, March 2.
Nwankwo, Emmanuel 1996. Interview, Ndiakaeme-Uno, Arondizuogu, March 10.
Nwankwo, I.O. 1986. "A History of Aro Settlements in Ihiala." BA thesis, Department of History, University of Nigeria, Nsukka.
Nwankwo, J.C. 1973. "The Early Settlement of Ndikelionwu and its Neighbourhood." BA thesis, History Department, University of Nigeria, Nsukka.
Nwankwo, Theresa 1991. "Economic Activities of Arondizuogu from Pre-Colonial Era to 1960." NCE, project, Alvan Ikoku College of Education, Owerri, September.
Nwankwo, Uduekwesi Eunice 1996. Interview, Ndiakaeme-uno, Arondizuogu, March 3.
Nwapa, Flora 1997. "Priestesses and Power among the Riverine Igbo." In *Queens, Queen Mothers.* See Kaplan 1997.
Nwaubani, Ebere 1994. "Chieftaincy among the Igbo: A Guest on the Center-Stage." *International Journal of African Historical Studies*, Vol. 27, No. 2: 347–71.
Nwauwa, Apollos O. 1990. "The Dating of the Aro Chiefdom: A Synthesis of Correlated Genealogies." *History in Africa*, Vol. 17: 227–45.

1991. "Integrating Arochukwu into the Regional Chronological Structure." *History in Africa*, Vol. 18: 297–310.

1992. "On the Aro Colonial Primary Source Material: A Critique of the Historiography." *History in Africa*, Vol. 19: 377–85.

1995. "Aro Secondary Source Material: A Biblio-Historiographical Review." *Ife Journal of History*, Vol. 2, No. 1: 106–17.

Nwene, J. 1972. Transcripts of oral interview. See Nwankwo, J.C. 1973.

Nwoga, D.I. 1984. "Nka Na Nzere: The Focus of Igbo World View." *1984 Ahiajoku Lecture*, Owerri, Imo State Ministry of Information, Culture, Youth and Sports.

Nwokeji, G. Ugo 1997a. "Biafra Markets and Slaves: The Aro and the Atlantic Slave Trade, c. 1750 to 1890." Presented at the conference, "West Africa and the Americas: Repercussions of the Slave Trade," held at the University of West Indies, Mona-Kingston, Jamaica, February 20–22.

1997b. "Household and Market Persons: Servitude and Banishment in the Making of the Biafra Diasporas, c. 1750 and 1890." Presented at "The Black Atlantic: Race, Nation, and Gender," seminar series, Rutgers Centre for Historical Analysis, October 7. (Also presented at the Canadian Council of Area Studies Learned Societies Conference, Memorial University of Newfoundland, June 4–7.)

1997c. "'Did We Bring Land with Us from Aro?': The Contradictions of Mmuba among the Aro of Nigeria, c. 1750–1890." In *Identifying Enslaved Africans*. See Lovejoy 1997.

1997d. "A Note on the Aro Diaspora." *Kwenu: For the Advancement of Igbo Historical Heritage and Linguistic Legacy*, Vol. 1, No. 2 (December), East Orange, New Jersey.

1998a. "African Conceptions of Gender and the Slave Traffic." Presented at Transatlantic Slavery and the African Diaspora: Using the W.E.B. DuBois Institute Dataset of Slaving Voyages, Omohundro Institute of Early American History and Culture, Williamsburg, Virginia, September 11–13.

1998b. "The Slave Emancipation Problematic: Igbo Society and the Colonial Equation." *Comparative Studies in Society and History*, Vol. 40, No. 2: 318–55.

2000a. "The Atlantic Slave Trade and Population Density: A Historical Demography of the Biafra Hinterland." *Canadian Journal of African Studies*, Vol. 34, No. 3, 616–55.

2000b. "Caste, Slavery, and Postslavery in Igboland." In *Afrika 2000* (CD-ROM), edited by U. Engel, Adam Jones and Robert Kappel, University of Leipzig, Germany.

2001. "Revisiting Olaudah Equiano's Identity," *African Studies Association Annual Meeting*, Houston, TX, November 15–18.

2006. Review of *Equiano the African: Biography of a Self-Made Man* by Vincent Carretta. Athens, Georgia: The University of Georgia Press, 2005. *Journal of American History*, Vol. 93, No. 3:840–41.

2009. Colloquy with the Author: Vincent Carretta and "Equiano, the African." *Studies in Eighteenth-Century Culture*, Vol. 38: 7–8.

Forthcoming. "Slavery in Non-Islamic West Africa." In Eltis, David and Stanley L. Engerman (editors), *Cambridge World History of Slavery*, Vol. 3. New York: Cambridge University Press.

Nwokeji, G. Ugo 1999. "The Biafran Frontier: Trade, Slaves, and Aro Society, C. 1750–1905." Ph.D. Diss., University of Toronto.

Nwokeji, G. Ugo and David Eltis 2002a. "The Roots of the African Diaspora: Methodological Considerations in the Analysis of Names in the Liberated African Regsters of Sierra Leone and Havana." *History in Africa*, Vol. 29: 365–79.

2002b. "Characteristics of Captives Leaving the Cameroons for the Americas, 1822–37." *Journal of African History*, Vol. 43, No. 2: 191–210.

Nwokeji, Orizu M. 1996. Interview, Ndiamazu-Uno, Arondizuogu, April 12.

Nwokoye-Emesuo, Azubuike Nkemakonam. (a.k.a. Periccomo). Interview, Nde-Ogbuonyeoma-nde-Uche, Arondizuogu, April 11.

Nworji, N. 1986. Transcripts of oral interview. See Ifediora 1987.

Nwosu, D.C. 1986. "The History of Arondizuogu from the Earliest Times to 1920." NCE project, History Department, Alvan Ikoku College of Education, Owerri.

Nzekwu, Onuora 1961. "Kola Nuts." *Nigeria Magazine*, No. 71, 1961: 298–306.

Nzom, O. 1977. Transcripts of oral interview. See G.C. Mmeregini 1978.

Obi-Buenyi, Okonkwo Eze 1986. Transcript of Interview. In Nwokebi, Emeka Obiora 1987. "Ichi: The Pre-Colonial History." BA Thesis, Department of History, University of Nigeria, Nsukka.

Obi, F. 1972. Transcripts of oral interview. See Nwankwo, J.C. 1973.

Obichere, Boniface 1988. "Slavery and the Slave Trade in the Niger Delta Cross River Basin." In *De la Traite*. See Daget 1988.

Obiechina, Emmanuel 1994. "Nchetaka: The Story, Memory and Continuity of Igbo Culture." *Ahiajoku Lecture 1994*, Owerri, Ministry of Information and Social Development.

Obinani, Fabian (a.k.a. Fiber) 1996. Interview, Ndinjoku, Arondizuogu, March 17.

Obong, U.U. 1972. Transcripts of oral interview. See Northrup 1972–1973.

Odung, I.A. 1972. Transcripts of oral interview. See Northrup 1972–1973.

Ofonagoro, Walter I. 1972. "The Opening of Southern Nigeria to British Trade, and Its Consequences: Economic and Social History, 1881–1916." Ph.D. diss., Columbia University.

1978. "Notes on the Ancestry of Mbanaso Okwaraozurumba Otherwise Known as Jaja of Opobo, 1821–1891." *Journal of the Historical Society of Nigeria*, Vol. 9, No. 3: 145–56.

Ogbomo, Onaiwu W. 1997. *When Men and Women Mattered: A History of Gender Relations among the Owan of Nigeria*. Rochester, NY: University of Rochester Press.

Ogbukagu, Ik. N. 1997. *Traditional Igbo Beliefs and Practices*. Owerri, Nigeria: Novelty Industrial Enterprises Ltd.

Ogbuozobe, J. 1985. Transcripts of oral interview. See Ogbuozobe, P.N. 1986.

Ogbuozobe, N. 1985. Transcripts of oral interview. See Ogbuozobe, P.N. 1986.

Ogbuozobe, P.N. 1986. "Achina: A Consideration of Pre-Colonial Intergroup Relationships." BA thesis, History Department, University of Nigeria, Nsukka.
Ogedengbe, K. Nwachukwu 1971. "The Aboh Kingdom of the Lower Niger c. 1650–1900." Ph.D. diss., History, University of Wisconsin.
— 1977. "Slavery in Nineteenth Century Aboh." In *African Slavery*. See Miers and Kopytoff 1977.
Oguagha, P.A. 1991. "The Igbo in the Igala and Idoma Studies." In *Groundwork of Igbo*. See Afigbo 1991b.
Ogude, S.E. 1982. "Facts into Fiction: Equiano's Narrative Reconsidered." *Research in African Literatures*, Vol. 13, No. 1: 31–43.
— 2003. Personal communication.
Oguocha, Ike 1996. Igbonet. Electronic listserv. Specific date temporarily misplaced.
Ohadike, Donatus C. 1988. "The Decline of Slavery among the Igbo People." In *The End of Slavery in Africa*. See Miers and Roberts 1988.
— 1991. *The Ekumeku Movement: Western Igbo Resistance to the British Conquest of Nigeria, 1883–1914*. Athens, OH: Ohio University Press.
— 1994. *Anioma: A Social History of the Western Igbo People*. Athens, OH: Ohio University Press.
Ohaegbu, D. 1991. Transcripts of oral interview. Ohaegbu, U.E. 1991.
Ohaegbu, U.E. 1991. "The History of Umuduru Egbeaguru from the Earliest Times to the Present." NCE project, Alvan Ikoku College of Education, Owerri.
Ohia, Uche 2007. *Patriotism and Community Development: A History of Arondizuogu Patriotic Union*. Aba, Nigeria: Silverduck Services Limited.
Oji, D. 1978. Transcripts of oral interview. See Okpara, R.E. 1979.
Oji, K. 1972. Transcripts of oral interview. See Northrup 1972–1973.
Oji, Nwankwo and Fidelis Okereke 1996. Interview, Ndianyake, Arondizuogu, March 16.
Ojiako, Udechukwu 2010. "Genealogy of Ojiako Family of Adazi-Nnuwku, Generated from Oral and Written History." March 25 (via email).
— 2010. Personal communication, March 21.
Ojiaku, Mazi Okoro 2008. *Yesteryear in Umu-Akha: History and Evolution of an Igbo Community (1665–1999)*. Charleston, NC: Booksurge Publishing.
Ojike, M. 1946. *My Africa*. New York: The John Day Company.
Ojo, G.J. Afolabi 1966. *Yoruba Culture: A Geographical Analysis*. Ile-Ife, Nigeria: University of Ife Press.
Okafor, Chinyere 1986. "Aro Diaspora: A Cultural and Historical Overview." In *Arochukwu*. See Ijoma 1986a.
Okafor, E.O. 1978. "Alor Wars in the Nineteenth Century." NCE project, Alvan Ikoku College of Education, Owerri.
Okafor, J. 1999. "The Use of Farmer Knowledge in Non-Wood Forest Product Research," *Non-Wood Forest Products of Central Africa: Current Research Issues and Prospects for Conservation and Development*, FAO Corporate Document Depository. http://www.fao.org/docrep/x2161e/x2161e13.htm.
Okeke, E.C. et al. 2009. "The Igbo Traditional Food System Documented in Four States in Southeastern Nigeria." In Indigenous Peoples' Food Systems, edited

by Harriet V. Khunlein et al., *Food and Agriculture Organization of the United Nations Center for Indigenous Peoples' Nutrition and Environment.* ftp://ftp.fao.org/docrep/fao/012/i0370e/i0370e13.pdf

Okeke, I. Romeo 1986. *The "Osu" Caste Concept in Igboland.* Enugu: Access Publishing.

Okely, Judith 1996. *Own or Other Culture.* London: Routledge.

Okere, L.C. 1983. *The Anthropology of Food in Rural Igboland, Nigeria: Socioeconomic and Cultural Aspects of Food and Food Habit in Rural Igboland.* New York: University of America Press.

Okereke, M. 1991. Transcripts of oral interview. See Nwankwo, T. 1991.

Okereke, Thomas Okoro 1996. Interview, Ndimoko, Arondizuogu, March 16.

Okigbo, B.N. 1980. "Plants and Food in Igbo Culture." *1980 Ahiajoku Lecture*, Owerri, Imo State Ministry of Information, Culture, Youth and Sports.

Okigbo, P.N.C. 1986. "Towards a Reconstruction of the Political Economy of Igbo Civilization." *Ahiajoku Lecture 1986*, Owerri, Imo State Ministry of Information, Culture, Youth and Sport.

Okoli, Clifford 1996. Interview, Ndiamazu-Ikpa-Ocha, Arondizuogu, February 11.

Okoli, E.N. 1977. "A History of Mazi Okoli Udozuka (Agadagbachiriuzo)." *S.U.A. Education Week.* See Students' Union Arondizuogu 1977.

Okoli, J.C. 1977. "Pre-Colonial History of Achina in Aguata Local Government Area, Anambra State." NCE project, Alvan Ikoku College of Education, Owerri.

Okoli, Nwambego Magareth 1996. Interview, Ndinduvwuisi, Arondizuogu, March 8.

Okoli, N. 1972. Transcripts of oral interview. See Nwankwo, J.C. 1973.

Okori, A. 1972. Transcripts of oral interview. See Northrup 1972–1973.

Okorie, N. 1991. Transcripts of oral interview. See Nwankwo, T. 1991.

Okoro, Elizabeth 1996. Interview, Amankwu, Arochukwu, February 25.

Okoro, F.E.S. 1973. Transcripts of oral interview. See Northrup 1972–73.

Okoro, G. Ohiaeri 1996. Interview, Amankwu, Arochukwu, February 23.

Okoro, Jacob Ogbonna 1996. Interview, Amankwu, Arochukwu, February 24.

Okoro, Jonathan G. 1985. *A Brief History of Arondizuogu* Aba. Nigeria: Precision Graphics.

1996. Interview, Ndiejezie, Arondizuogu, February 4.

Okoroafo, E.S. 1978. "An Economic History of Isuochi in the Nineteenth Century (Agriculture, Crafts and Trade). BA thesis, History Department, University of Nigeria, Nsukka.

Okoroafor, O. 1972. Transcripts of oral interview. See Isichei 1978.

Okoroji, Emmanuel Ezimoha 1996. Interview, Ujari, Arochukwu, February 25.

Okpala, D. 1976. Transcripts of oral interview. See Anaedobe, M.M. 1977.

Okpara, R.O. 1979. "Economic and Social History of Oro c. 1800–1916." NCE project (History), Alvan Ikoku College of Education, Owerri.

Oldendorp, Christian Georg Andreas [1777] 1995a. *Geschichte der Mission der Evangelischen Brüder auf den Caraibischen Inseln S. Thomas, S. Croix und S. Jan, Teil I*, edited by N.L. von Zinzendorf, Hildesheim, George Olms Verlag.

[1777] 1995b. *Geschichte der Mission der Evangelischen Brüder auf den Caraibischen Inseln S. Thomas, S. Croix und S. Jan, Teil II*, edited by N.L. von Zinzendorf, Hildesheim, George Olms Verlag.

[1777] 2000. *Historie der caribischen Inseln Sanct Thomas, Sanct Crux und Sanct Jan, inbesondere der dasigen Neger und der Mission der evangelischen Brüder under denselben* (modern edition edited by Gudrun Meier, Stephan Palmié, Peter Stein and Horst Ulbricht). Abhandlungen und Berichte des Staatlichen Museums für Völkerkunde Dresden: Verlag für Wissenschaft und Bildung.

1987. *History of the Mission of the Evangelical Brethren on the Caribbean Islands of St. Thomas, St. Croix, and St. John*, edited by Johann Jacob Bossard; translated by Arnold R. Highfield and Vladimir Barac. Ann Arbor, MI: Karoma Publishers, Inc.

Oldfield, R.K. 1837. "A Brief Account of an Ascent of the Old Calabar River in 1836." *Journal of the Royal Geographical Society*, Vol. 7: 195–98.

Olisa, C. G. 1990. *Ossomari: A Kingdom of the Lower Niger Valley (1640–1986)*. Obosi, Nigeria: Chukwuemeka G. Olisa.

Onokala, P.C. 1994. "The Development of Road Transport Network and Trade in Igbo-Ukwu Region." *Nigerian Heritage*, Vol. 3: 115–30.

Onukwube, G.O. 1978. Transcripts of oral interview. See G.C. Mmeregini 1978.

Onwuejeogwu, M. Angulu. 1975. *The Social Anthropology of Africa: An Introductio*. London: Heinemann.

1981. *An Igbo Civilization: Nri Kingdom and Hegemony*. London: Ethnographica.

1987. "Evolutionary Trends in the History of the Development of the Igbo Civilization in the Culture Theatre of Igboland in Southern Nigeria." *Ahiajoku Lecture 1987*, Owerri, Imo State Ministry of Information.

Onyeahankeya, N. 1977. Transcripts of oral interview. See G.C. Mmeregini 1978.

Onyeama, Dilibe 1982. *Chief Onyeama: The Story of an African God*. Enugu: Delta.

Onyekwelu, Menankiti 2001. *The History and Culture of Amaokpala*. Nigeria: MacMena and Rose International Ltd.

Onyemara, S. 1977. Transcripts of oral interview. See G.C. Mmeregini 1978.

Onyenkpa, C.O. 1981. "A Historical Survey of Isuikwuato before 1900: Origins, Patterns of Migration and Settlement, and Political Organization." BA thesis, History Department, University of Nigeria, Nsukka.

Onyensoh, U.C. 1985. "Aro Settlements in Ngwaland." BA thesis, History Department, University of Nigeria, Nsukka.

Onyenuche, J.C. n.d. Transcripts of oral interview. See Ohaegbu, U.E. 1991.

Onyilagha, J. 1985. Transcripts of oral interview. See P.N. Ogbuozobe 1986.

Onyiukah, E.M. 1983. "Trade and Trade Routes in Nineteeth Century Isuikwuato." BA thesis, History Department, University of Nigeria, Nsukka.

Oppong, Christine (editor) 1983. *Female and Male in West Africa*. London: George Allen & Unwin.

Oriji, John N. 1977. "A History of Ngwa People: Social and Economic Development in an Igbo Clan." Ph.D. diss., Rutgers University.

1981. "Oracular Trade, Okonko Secret Society and the Evolution of Decentralized Authority among the Ngwa-Igbo of Southeastern Nigeria." *Ikenga*, Vol. 5, No. 1: 35–52.

1982. "A Re-Assessment of the Organization and Benefits of the Slave and Palm Produce Trade amongst the Ngwa-Igbo." *Canadian Journal of African Studies*, Vol. 16, No. 3: 523–48.

1983. "A Study of the Slave and Palm Produce Trade amongst the Ngwa Igbo." *Cahiers d'Etudes Africaines*, Vol. 23, No. 3: 311–28.

1987. "The Slave Trade, Warfare and Aro Expansion in the Igbo Hinterland." *Transafrican Journal of History*, Vol. 16: 151–66.

1990. *Traditions of Igbo Origin: A Study of Pre-Colonial Population Movements in Africa*. New York: Peter Lang.

1994. *Traditions of Igbo Origin: A Study of Pre-Colonial Population Movements in Africa* (revised ed.). New York: Peter Lang.

Orji, B.N.N. 1978. "Politics and Trade in Pre-Colonial Arondizuogu." BA thesis, History Department, University of Nigeria, Nsukka.

Ottenberg, Phoebe 1959. "The Changing Economic Position of Women among the Afikpo Ibo." In *Continuity and Change in African Cultures*. See Bascom and Herskovits.

Ottenberg, Simon 1958. "Ibo Oracles and Intergroup Relations." *Southwestern Journal of Anthropology*, Vol. 14, No. 3:295–317.

1959. "Ibo Receptivity to Change." In *Continuity and Change in African Cultures*. See Bascom and Herskovits.

1971. *Leadership and Authority in an African Society: The Afikpo Village-Group*. Seattle, WA and London: University of Washington Press.

Oyewumi, Oyeronke 1997. *The Invention of Women: Making an African Sense of Western Gender Discourses*. Minneapolis, MN: University of Minnesota Press.

Ozurumba, M. 1980. Transcripts of oral interview. See Udeagha, N.N. 1980.

Palmer, C. 1981. *Human Cargoes: The British Slave Trade to Spanish America, 1700–1739*. Urbana, IL: University of Illinois Press.

Palmié, Stephan (editor) 1995a. *Slave Cultures and Cultures of Slavery*. Knoxville: The University of Tennessee Press.

1995b. "Introduction." In *Slave Cultures*. See Palmié 1995a.

Parker, Isaac 1790. See Lambert 1975c.

Partridge, C. 1905. *Cross River Natives: Being Some Notes on the Primitive Pagans of Obubra Hill District, Southern Nigeria*. London: Hutchinson and Co.

Pascalis, F. "Recommendations." See Hawkins 1970.

Patterson, O. 1982. *Slavery and Social Death*. Cambridge, MA: Harvard University Press.

1984. "Slavery: The Underside of Freedom," *Slavery and Abolition*, Vol. 5, No. 2: 87–104.

Phillips, Captain Thomas 1693. "Abstract of a Voyage along the Coast of Guinea to Whidaw, the Island of St. Thomas, and thence to Barbadoes, in 1693." *Collection of Voyages and Travels*, Vol. 2. London: Thomas Astley, pp. 387–416.

Piot, Charles 1996. "Of Slaves and the Gift: Kabre Sale of Kin during the Era of the Slave Trade." *Journal of African History*, Vol. 37, No. 1: 31–49.

Polanyi, Karl 1957. "The Economy as Instituted Process." In *Trade and Market*. See Polanyi et al. 1957a.
  1963. "Ports of Trade in Early Societies." *Journal of Economic History*, Vol. 23, No. 1:33–45.
Polanyi, Karl et al. 1957a. *Trade and Market in the Early Empires: Economies in History and Theory*. New York: The Free Press.
Polanyi, Karl. 1957b. "The Place of Economies in Society." In *Trade and Market*. See Polanyi et al. 1957a.
Reynolds, Edward 1974. *Trade and Economic Change on the Gold Coast, 1807–1874*. Harrow, UK: Longman.
Richardson, David 1976. "Profits in the Liverpool Slave Trade: The Accounts of William Davenport, 1757–1784." In *Liverpool*. See Anstey and Hair 1976.
  1989a. "The Eighteenth Century British Trade: Estimates of its Volume and Coastal Distribution in Africa." *Research in Economic History*, Vol. 12: 151–95.
  1989b. "Slave Exports from West and West-Central Africa, 1700–1800: New Estimates of Volume and Distribution." *Journal of African History*, Vol. 30, No. 1: 1–22.
  1997. Personal communication, Kingston, Jamaica, February 20.
  2001. "Shipboard Revolts, African Authority, and the Atlantic Slave Trade." *William and Mary Quarterly*, Third Series, Vol. 58, No. 1: 69–92.
Richardson, David and S.D. Behrendt 1995. "Inikori's Odyssey: Measuring the British Slave Trade, 1655–1807." *Cahiers d'Etudes Africaines*, Vol. 34, Nos. 2–3: 599–615.
Richardson, David and David Eltis 1997. "Patterns of Slave Shipments from West Africa: Comparing the Gold Coast, Bight of Benin, and Bight of Biafra, 1660–1867." Presented at the conference "West Africa and the Americas: Repercussions of the Slave Trade," The University of the West Indies, Mona, Kingston, Jamaica, February 20.
Roberts, Richard 1980. Production and Reproduction of Warrior States: Segu Bambara and Segu Tokolor, c. 1712–1890." *International Journal of African Historical Studies*, Vol. 13, No. 3:389–419.
  1984. "Women's Work and Women's Property: Household Social Relations in the Maraka Textile Industry of the Nineteenth Century." *Comparative Studies in Society and History*, Vol. 26: 229–50.
  1987. *Warriors, Merchants, and Slaves: The State and the Economy in the Middle Niger Valley, 1700–1914*. Palo Alto, CA: Stanford University Press.
Robertson, Claire 1983. "Post-Proclamation Slavery in Accra: A Female Affair?" In *Women and Slavery*. See Robertson and Klein 1983a.
Robertson, Claire C. 1984. *Sharing the Same Bowl: A Socioeconomic History of Women and Class in Accra, Ghana*, Bloomington, IN: Indiana University Press.
Robertson, Claire and Martin Klein (editors) 1983a. *Women and Slavery in Africa*. Madison, WI: University of Wisconsin Press.
  1983b. "Introduction." In *Women and Slavery*. See Robertson and Klein 1983a.

Rodney, Walter 1966. "African Slavery and Other Forms of Social Oppression on the Upper Guinea Coast in the Context of the Atlantic Slave Trade." *Journal of African History*, Vol. 7, No. 3: 431–43.
  1967. *West Africa and the Slave Trade*, Historical Society of Tanzania Paper No. 2, East African Publishing House.
  1970. *A History of the Upper Guinea Coast 1545–1800*. London: Oxford University Press.
Röschenthaler, Ute M. 2006. "Translocal cultures: The slave trade and cultural transfer in the Cross River region." *Social Anthropology*, Vol. 14, No. 1: 71–91.
Ross, Robert 1983. *Cape of Torments: Slavery and Resistance in South Africa*. London: Routledge & Kegan Paul.
Royal African Company 1721. "The Royal African Company: Committee Report on the State of Trade." See Donnan 1931: 250–56.
  "The Royal African Company, 1672." In *Documents Illustrative*. See Donnan 1930: 192–93.
Russell, J. 1972. Transcripts of oral interview. See Northrup 1972–1973.
Ryder, A.F.C. 1980. "The Trans-Atalantic Slave Trade." In *Groundwork of Nigerian History*. See Ikime 1980.
Sargent, Robert A. 1999. *Economics, Politics and Social Change in the Benue Basin c. 1300–1700*. Enugu: Fourth Dimension.
Schön and Crowther 1960. "Iboland and the Slave Trade." In *Nigerian Perspectives*. See Hodgkin 1960.
Shankland, T.M. 1933. "Intelligence Report on the Aro Clan." NAE ARODIV – 3/1/55.
Shaw, Thurstan. 1970a. *Igbo-Ukwu: An Account of Archaeological Discoveries in Eastern Nigeria*, Vol. 1. London: Faber and Faber.
  1970b. *Igbo-Ukwu: An Account of Archaeological Discoveries in Eastern Nigeria*, Vol. 2. London: Faber and Faber.
  1978. *Nigeria: Its Archeology and Its Early History*. London: Thames and Hudson.
Shelton, Austin J. 1968. "Onojo Ogboni: Problems of Identification and Historicity in the Oral Traditions of the Igala and Northern Nsukka Igbo of Nigeria." *Journal of American Folklore*, Vol. 81: 243–57.
  1971. *The Igbo-Igala Boderlad: Religion and Social Control in Indigenous African Colonialism*. Albany: State University of New York Press.
Shepherd, V. 1993. "Alternative Husbandry: Slaves and Free Labourers on Livestock Farms in Jamaica in the Eighteenth and Nineteenth Centuries." *Slavery and Abolition*, Vol. 14, No. 1.
Sheridan, Richard B. 1994. *Sugar and Slavery: An Economic History of the British West Indies, 1623–1775*. Barbados: Canoe Press.
  Short History of Umunem Otolo Nnewi. Onitsha: Tabansi Press (no author, n.d.).
Snelgrave, Captain William 1730. "A New Account of Some Parts of Guinea and the Slaves-Trade in 1730." *Collection of Voyages and Travels*, Vol. 2. London: Thomas Astley, pp. 485–519.
  [1734] 1971. *A New Account of Some Parts of the Coast of Guinea, and the Slave Trade*. London: Frank Cass.

Sobel, Michal 1987. *The World they Made Together: Black and White Values in Eighteenth-Century Virginia*. Princeton, NJ: Princeton University Press.

Sowell, Thomas 1996. *Migrations and Cultures: A Worldview*. New York: Basic Books.

Sparks, Randy J. 2002. "Two Princes of Calabar: An Atlantic Odyssey from Slavery to Freedom." *William and Mary Quarterly*, 3rd Series, Vol. 59, No. 3: 555–84.

Starke, T. 1702. "Answer of Thomas Starke to James Westmore." See Donnan 1935:

Stede, E. and S. Gascoigne 1679. "Edwyn Stede and Stephen Gascoigne to the Royal African Company." See Donnan 1930: 249.

1682/3. "Edwyn Stede and Stephen Gascoigne to the Royal African Company." See Donnan 1930: 304–05.

Steel, Edward A. 1908. "Explorations in Southern Nigeria." *Geographical Journal*, Vol. 32, March: 6–21.

Stevenson, R.F. 1968. *Population Growth and Political Systems in Tropical Africa*, New York and London: Columbia University Press.

Students' Union Arondizuogu (compiler) 1977. *S.U.A. Education Week*. Nsuka: University of Nigeria.

Sundiata, Ibrahim 1996. *From Slaving to Neoslavery: The Bight of Biafra and Fernando Po in the Era of Abolition*, Madison, WI: University of Wisconsin Press.

Tamari, T. 1991. "The Development of Caste Systems in West Africa." *Journal of African History*, Vol. 32, No. 2: 221–50.

Talbot, P. Amaury. 1912. *In the Shadow of the Bush of the Nigerian Political Service*. New York: George H. Doran.

[1923] 1967. *Life in Southern Nigeria: The Magic, Beliefs and Customs of the Ibibio Tribe*. London: Frank Cass & Co. Ltd.

1926a. *The Peoples of Southern Nigeria: A Sketch of their History, Ethnology and Languages, with an Abstract of the 1921 Census*, Vol. 1. London: Oxford University Press.

1926b. *The People of Southern Nigeria: A Sketch of their History, Ethnology and Languages, with an Abstract of the 1921 Census*, Vol. 2. London: Humphrey Milford.

1926c. *The Peoples of Southern Nigeria: A Sketch of their History, Ethnology and Languages, with an Abstract of the 1921 Census*, Vol. 3. London: Humphrey Milford.

1926d. *The Peoples of Southern Nigeria: A Sketch of their History, Ethnology and Languages, with an Abstract of the 1921 Census*, Vol. 4. London: Humphrey Milford.

Thésée, Françoise 1986. *Les Ibo l'Amélie: Destinée d'une Cargaison de Traite Clandestine à la Martinique, 1822–1838*. Paris: Editions Caribéennes.

Thompson, Vincent B. 1987. *The Making of the African Diaspora in the Americas*. London: Longman.

1995. "The Phenomenon of Shifting Frontiers: The Kenya-Somalia Case in the Horn of Africa, 1880s-1970s." *Journal of Asian and African Studies*, Vol. 30, Nos. 1–2:1–40.

Thornton, John K. 1977. "Demography and History in the Congo Kingdom." *Journal of African History*, Vol. 18, No. –: 507–30.
1980. "The Slave Trade in Eighteenth Century Angola – Effects on Demographic Structures." *Canadian Journal of African Studies*, Vol. 14, No. 3: 417–28.
1981. "The Demographic Effect of the Slave Trade on Western Africa 1500–1850." In *Afrrican Historical Demography*, Vol. 11. See *African Historical Demography*.
1983. "Sexual Demography: The Impact of the Slave Trade on Family Structure." See Robertson and Klein 1983.
1991. "African Dimensions of the Stono Rebellion." *American Historical Review*, Vol. 96, No. 4: 1101–13.
1992b. "The Kongo Civil Wars and the Slave Trade: Demography and History Revisited, 1718–1844." Millersville, PA: University of Pennsylvania.
1996. "African Background of the Slave Cargo of the Henrietta Maria." MS.
1998. *Africa and Africans in the Making of the Atlantic World, 1400–1800*, Cambridge: Cambridge University Press.
1998. "From the General to the Particular: Ethnicity and History in the Slave Trade." Presented at Transatlantic Slavery and the African Diaspora: Using the W.E.B. DuBois Institute Dataset of Slaving Voyages, Omohundro Institute of Early American History and Culture, Williamsburg, Virginia, September 11–13.
Thorp, Daniel B. 1988. "Chattel with a Soul: The Autobiography of a Moravian Slave Author(s)." *The Pennsylvania Magazine of History and Biography*, Vol. 112, No. 3: 433–51.
Torrington, Arthur 2005. "Equiano Was Not Born in Africa"? *Every Generation*: www.everygeneration.co.uk.
Trade Wind Fruits: http://www.tradewindsfruit.com/ (accessed on July 29, 2009).
Trouillot, Michel-Rolph 2001. "The Anthropology of the state in the Age of Globalization: Close Encounters of the Deceptive Kind." Current Anthropology, Vol 42, 1: 125–38.
Ubah, C.N. 1987. "Changing Patterns of Leadership among the Igbo, 1900–1960." *Transafrican Journal of History*, Vol. 16: 167–84.
Uche, Jonas Ekemezie 1996. Interview, Ndiuche, Arondizuogu, March 17.
Uche, S.I. 1988. "Akokwa and Her Neighbours in the Pre-Colonial Period." BA thesis, History Department, Imo State University, Okigwe.
Uchendu, Victor C. 1965. *The Igbo of Southeastern Nigeria*. Toronto: Holt, Rinehart and Winston.
1977. "Slaves and Slavery in Igboland, Nigeria." In *Slavery in Africa* edited by S. Miers and I. Kopytoff. Madison, WI: University of Wisconsin Press.
Udeagha, C.O. 1987. "Trade and Trade Routes within the Okigwe Area in the 19th Century." *Transafrican Journal of History*, Vol. 16: 78–91.
Udeagha, N.N. 1980. "A History of Ihube from the Earliest Times to 1928." BA thesis, History Department, University of Nigeria, Nsukka.
Udensi, O. 1991. Transcripts of oral interview. See Nwankwo, T. 1991.
Udo, Edet A. 1983. *Who Are the Ibibio?*, Onitsha, Nigeria, Africana – FEP Publishers Limited.
Udo, J. 1972. Transcripts of oral interview. See Northrup 1972–1973.

Udo, R.K. 1970. *Geographical Regions of Nigeria*, Berkeley, CA: University of California Press.
Udonyah, E. 1972. Transcripts of oral interview. See Northrup 1972–1973.
Udueze, A.E. 1982. "The Economy of Uturu in the Nineteenth Century." BA thesis, History Department, University of Nigeria, Nsukka.
Ufere, Kemdi George 1996. Interview, Ndiumazu-Uno, Arondizuogu, March 3.
Ugboaja, I. 1985. Transcripts of oral interview. See I.O. Nwankwo 1986.
Ukonu, M.C. 1979. "A History of Owerre-Ezukala from 1800–1960." NCE project, Alvan Ikoku College of Education, Owerri.
Uku, Edward K. 1993. *Seeds in the Palm of Your Hand*. Madison, WI: University of Wisconsin, African Studies Program.
Ukwu, Ukwu I. 1967. "The Development of Trade and Marketing in Iboland." *Journal of the Historical Society of Nigeria*, Vol. 2.
  1969. "Markets in Iboland." In *Markets in West Africa*, by B.W. Hodder and U.I. Ukwu. Ibadan, Nigeria: Ibadan University Press.
Umeafonta, E. 1976. Transcripts of oral interview. See Ezenibe, R.A.O. 1977.
Umeh, C.S. 1984. "Uga and Her Neighbours up to 1905." BA thesis, History Department, University of Nigeria, Nsukka.
Umeukeje, U. 1976. Transcripts of oral interview. See Anaedobe, M.M. 1977.
Umo, R. Kanu n.d. [1947?]. *History of Aro Settlements*. Lagos: Mbonu Ojike.
Umunnakwe, Georgina U. 1995. *Interview, Bayswater*. London: July 8–9.
Uriem, C.T. 1980. Transcripts of oral interview. See Onyenkpa, C.O. 1981.
Uwazuruike, P.N. 1987. "A Historical Survey of Okwe-Okigwe during the Pre-Colonial Period." BA thesis, History Department, University of Nigeria, Nsukka.
Uya, Okon E. 1984. *A History of Oron People of the Lower Cross River Basin*. Oron, Nigeria: Manson Publishing Company.
Van Nyendael, David 1702. "A Description of *Rio Formosa*, or the River of Benin." See Bosman 1705.
Vansina, Jan 1961. *Oral Tradition: A Study in Historical Methodology* (trans. H.M. Wright). London: Routledge and Kegan Paul.
  1985. *Oral Tradition as History*. Madison, WI: University of Wisconsin Press.
Venour, Capt. W.J. 1902. "The Aro Country in Southern Nigeria." *Geographical Journal*, Vol. 20.
Vickery, Lt. C.E. 1906. "A West African Expedition." *The United Service Magazine*, Vol. 33 (New Series), April–September: 552–62.
Waddell, Hope M. [1863] 1970. *Twenty-Nine Years in the West Indies and Central Africa: A Review of Missionary Work and Adventure* (2nd edition), London: Frank Cass.
Walker, Capt. J.B. 1871. "Notes on the Old Calabar and Cross Rivers." *Proceedings of the Royal Geographical Society*, Vol. 16, No. 2 (Session 1871–72): 135–37.
  1875. "Notes on a Visit, in May 1875, to the Old and Qua Rapids." *Proceedings of the Royal Geographical Society*, Vol. 20, No. 3: 224–30.
Walsh, Lorena 1997. *From Calabar to Carter's Grove: The History of a Virginia Slave Community*. Charlottesville, VA: University of Virginia Press.

Walvin, James 1992. *Black Ivory: A History of British Slavery*. London: HarperCollins Publishers.
  1997. *Questioning Slavery*. London: Routledge.
Wamuo, J.W. 1973. Transcripts of oral interview. See Northrup 1972–1973.
Wariboko, W.E. 1991. "New Calabar and the Forces of Change ca 1850–1945." Ph.D. diss., Centre of West African Studies, University of Birmingham.
Wariboko, Waibinte 1999. "New Calabar: The Transition from Slave-to Produce-Trading and the Political Problems in the Eastern Niger Delta, 1848–1891." In Law and Strickrodt (eds.), *Ports of the Slave Trade*.
Warner-Lewis, Maureen 2007. *Archibald Monteath: Igbo, Jamaican, Moravian*. Kingston, Jamaica: The University of West Indies Press.
Wax, Daniel D. 1973. "Preferences for Slaves in Colonial America." *Journal of Negro History*, Vol. 58, No. 4: 371–401.
  1978. "Black Immigrants: The Slave Trade in Colonial Maryland." *Maryland Historical Magazine*, Vol. 73, No. 1: 30–45.
Williams, Eric 1944. *Capitalism and Slavery*. Chapel Hill, NC: University of North Carolina Press.
Williams, Gomer 1897. *History of the Liverpool Privateers and Letters of Marque with an Account of the Liverpool Slave Trade*. London: William Heinemann.
White, D.G. 1985 *Ar'n't I a Woman?: Female Slaves in the Plantation South*, New York, Norton.
White, H.C. 1995. *Where Do Languages Come From? – Switching Talk*, Columbia University, Centre for the Social Sciences, No. 202.
Whitford, John [1877] 1967. *Trading Life in Western and Central Africa* (2nd edition). London: Frank Cass.
Wipper, Audrey (editor) 1972. *Canadian Journal of African Studies*, Vol. 6, No. 2: Special Issue on the Roles of African Women: Past, Present and Future.
Wolf, Eric R. 1982. *Europe and the People without History*. Berkeley, CA: University of California Press.
Zeleza, Paul T. 1993. *A Modern Economic History of Africa, Volume 1: The Nineteenth Century*. Dakar, Senegal: Council for the Development of Social Science Research in Africa (CODESRIA).

Index

Italic page numbers indicate maps or tables.

Abo state/society, XVIn2, 14, 24, 32
abolitionist movement, 219, 220
    See also British abolition of slave trade
Achebe, Chinua, 160, 217–218n8
    Things Fall Apart, 86n8, 163
Acholonu, Catherine, 217–218, 217–218n8
Adams, John, 138, 138n29, 166, 197
adultery, 135
Afigbo, Adiele, 8–9, 18, 50, 212, 218
Afikpo slave market, 13n22, *61*, 64
African diaspora in the Americas, XVII
Africanus, Leo, 166n28
agawhu. *See* merchant-warlords
age structure of slave trade, 11, 144–148, 150, 156, 161, 176, 209
    See also boys as slaves; children as slaves; girls as slaves
agency, XVII, 6n8, 56, 76, 79, 204
agriculture
    See also kolanuts; palm oil trade; yams
    of the Aro, 7, 102–103, 105–107, 178, 188
    and civil war, 191
    and food shortages, 188
    gender division of labor in, XVIII, 149, 152–153, 156, 159–161, 169–170, 176
    in the Igbo heartland, 88
    and immigration, 80
    slave labor in, 183
    vs. the trading society, 102
    and warfare, 189–190
Agwu, Eze (Aro king), 15n27

Ajana (deity), 106
Akamnonu, Oliver
    Taste of the West, 158n18
Akpa ethnic group, XIV, 26–31, 30n17, 79
Akuma, (Aro king), 15, 15n27
Ala (deity), XV–XVII, XVIn2, XVIn3
Alagoa, Ebiegberi Joe, 211
Allied War (Ogu Omakoba), 190–191, 190–191n29
amadi (class), 64, 66, 100–102, 104, 112, 128, 197, 214, 215n5
Amadiume, Ifi, 158
Amaigbo (town), XVIn2
Amankwu (dialect), 108
Amankwu (lineage-group), 28, *61*, 62, 62–63, 97
Amaokpala people, 90n15, 163–164n23, 194–195
Amazu (Isuogu's dependent), 57, 93, 93n17, 97, 200n45
the Americas
    captives deported to, XXIII, 4–5, 32, 117, 119, 124–125, 128, 141–142, 197
    demand for captives in, XVII, 20, 22–23, 33–37, 42–47, 117–118, 197, 204, 207
    Igbo slaves in, 44, 125
    plantations in, 33, 37, 42–43, 45, 118–120, 147
    slave standards in, 125–126
    slave traders from, 117
amuda (class), 101

265

Ana (deity), XV, XVIn3, 105–109, 106n34
Andrew the Moor, 141–142
Angelo, Michael, 154
Anglo-Aro relations (post-Atlantic slavery), 7–8
Angola, 117, 151
Ani (deity). See Ala; Ana
antislavery task force, 210
Anya. A.O., 164n25, 165n27
architecture of the Aro, 191–192, 192n33, 197, 217
archival sources. See *under* sources overview
Aro, rise of
  first phase (1600-1720s), 26–37, 64
  second phase (1740s-1807), 37–45, 64
Aro agriculture, 7, 102–103, 105–106, 178, 188
Aro central council (Ọkpankpọ), 27, 54, 65, 75–76, 78, 96, 206
  See also Aro diaspora/expansion; Aro organization
Aro commercial organization. See Aro organization; Aro trade networks/diasporas
Aro culture, XIV–XVII, XVIn2, XVIn3, 1–3, 16, 18–19, 22–26, 82–83, 95–97
Aro diaspora settlements
  and agriculture, 188
  Aro influence continued by, 184
  and Arochukwu, 115–116
  vs. centralization, 15–16
  cultural interpretations of, 19
  as free cities, 188n27
  immigrant populations of, 2–3, 16
  institutions of, 76–80, 98
  lineage-groups of, 6, 60, 61, 62, 76, 90–93, 102, 108
  and the Nri-Awka region, 124
  overviews, XVIn2, 54–64
Aro diaspora/expansion
  See also Aro central council; Aro organization; Aro regional dominance; Aro trade networks/diasporas; Arochukwu region; Atlantic slave trade; Biafra hinterland; culture formation; Igbo ethnic group; Igboland
  and agriculture, 188
  alliances in, 64–71
  Aro influence continued by, 184

and the Aro slave trade, 178
and Aro state structures, 11–19
Arondizuogu lineage-groups in, 102
and the Biafra geocultural landscape, XVIII
cohesion of, 17
and cultural deviation, 100–107
culture formation in, 83–84, 100–101
economic vs. political, 13, 206
and human proliferation, 71–75
hybridity in, XV
and the Ikeji festival, 102
incest in, 103–104
and indigenous slavery, 25
lineage-groups in, 60–62, 61, 62, 76, 184
linkages with Arochukwu, 96–100, 115
on the Niger River, 54
and Nigerian cultural studies, 18
oppression and spiritual life in, 198
origins of, 26–27
the osu in, 198
political economy of, 71
and private enterprise, 15, 56, 64–71
and regional slave preferences, 125
and the slave trade, XVII–XVIII, 15, 20–21, 45, 54, 115–116, 178
slave trade routes during, 50–51, 66n16
state-sponsored, 15–16
strategies of, 56
systems in, 115
timing and location of, 57–64
and warfare, 15, 68–71, 106–107, 188–189, 193
and women slave ratios, 177
Aro economic imperialism, 13n22, 206
  See also Aro diaspora/expansion; Aro trade networks/diasporas
Aro identity, XV, 18–19, 42–45, 55, 77, 83–84, 178–179, 206
Aro imperialists, 77, 206
Aro languages and dialects, XVII, 60–62, 61, 62, 73, 76, 78n34, 107–111
Aro lineage-groups, 6, 12, 15, 60, 61, 62–63, 68, 76
Aro merchant-warlords, 58, 65–66, 66n16, 68, 189, 194
  See also warfare
Aro militarization. See Aro warfare
The Aro of Southeastern Nigeria (Dike and Ekejiuba), 11
Aro organization

Index

See also Aro diaspora/expansion; Aro regional dominance; Aro trade networks/diasporas
  and the Aro's ascendancy, 80
  in Atlantic scholarship, 6, 8
  and the Atlantic slave trade, 34–35, 45, 54, 115–116, 204
  characteristics of, 204
  as economic/political, 13, 206
  and the Ekpe, 77–78
  overview, 11–19
  state characteristics of, XIV, 204
  as trade network/diaspora, XVIII, 115–116
Aro political economy, 2, 11, 117
Aro politics/political organization, XVII, XXIII–XXIV, XVIn3, 11–14, 16–17, 23–24, 26, 30, 53–56, 75–76, 195, 206
Aro regional dominance, 181, 186–187
  See also Aro diaspora/expansion; Aro organization; Aro slave trade
Aro script (nsibiri), 6, 78n34, 211
Aro slave trade
  See also Aro diaspora/expansion; Atlantic slave trade; Biafra hinterland; domestic slave trade; slave traders
  and the Aro economy, 71, 207
  and the Aro political economy, 2, 26
  vs. Aro warfare, 6, 179
  British abolition of, 2–3, 181–184
  and British imperialism, 181–185
  and culture formation, 83
  dominance of, XIV, 1–3, 11, 22–23, 31, 75
  and the Ekpe, 79
  emerging, 34–35
  and firearms, 196
  human commodity in, 104
  and human proliferation, 72
  indigenous, 6–7
  institutions of, 75–80, 132–143
  labor pools of, 188
  and the Nri-Awka, 80, 94
  overviews, 118–128, 134–143
  and the palm oil trade, 183–184
  as punishment/reprisal, 76, 81, 99, 118, 131n14, 132, 140n35, 195
  routes of, 50–51
  slave demographics in, 2
  slaves' cultures absorbed in, 94–95, 197
  and social mobility, 197
  women in, 154, 157, 173
Aro statehood, 11–19
Aro trade diasporas. *See* Aro trade networks/diasporas
Aro trade networks/diasporas
  See also Aro organization; Aro regional dominance
  and agriculture, 188
  and Aro rule, 173, 206
  and the Atlantic slave trade, 23–26
  Bende market as central to, 31
  British encroachment on, 185–186, 186n19, 203
  combined, XIV
  as defining Aro characteristic, 17, 206
  elements of, 54–56
  free cities in, 188n27
  in the hinterland, 10
  regional context overview, 53–81
  in southern Igboland, 10
  as study focus, XIV, 11, 18
Aro warfare, 12, 65, 68–71, 106–107, 178–181, 187–196, 188n26, 203
  See also Cross River Igbo warriors; merchant-warlords; warfare
Aro-Anglo relations (post-Atlantic slavery), 7–8
  See also British headings
Arochukwu region
  See also Aro diaspora settlements; Aro diaspora/expansion; Aro trade networks/diasporas
  architecture of, 191
  and the Atlantic slave trade, 23
  class structure in, 100–101
  cultural developments in, 83
  and cultural deviation, 100–107, 113
  early ethnic groups in, 87n10
  formation/consolidation of, 6, 20, 31–32, 53
  Ibiniukpabi oracle in, 77
  Igbo ascendancy in, 100
  Igbo-Akpa confederacy in, 26, 31
  and Igboland, XVII, XVn1
  Ikeji festival in, 102–103
  immigration into, 26–27, 32, 53
  indigenous slavery in, 25
  languages and dialects of, 107–112, *109–110*

Arochukwu region (*Cont.*)
  lineage-groups of, 27, 55, 63, 101, 191
  linkage groups of, 96–100
  marriage possibilities in, 104
  as place vs. ethnic group, 18–19
  politics/political culture of, 66, 100
  shrines originating in, 200
  slavery in, 24, 50–51, 65–67, 71, 75, 123
  structure in, 28
  as trade diaspora center, 54
  twin taboo in, 104, 104n32
  zoning in, 63
Arondizuogu diaspora settlement
  agriculture in, 103, 105–106
  ancestors of, 72, 102
  and the Atlantic slave trade, 87n9
  colonial domination resisted by, 106
  cultural development in, 83
  and cultural deviation, 100–107
  establishment of, 20, 29–30n15, 57–60, 66, 66n16, 70
  founding of, 1, 57, 60
  Ikeji festival in, 102–103, 102n31
  immigrants in, 115
  landscape surrounding, 85
  languages and dialects of, 107–112, 109–110, 111n39
  as largest Aro settlement, 1, 13n22, 83
  leadership, 59–60
  lineage-groups of, 60, 62, 89, 90–93, 92, 102, 102n31, 184, 200n45, 214–215
  merchant-warlords revered in, 193
  multiple lineage-group shrines in, 200, 200n45
  Nri-Awka cultural impact in, 107, 200
  osu caste system in, 198–200, 199n40, 200n44
  and the Owa community, 74–75, 75n29
  Patriotic Union (APU), 102n31
  population of, 3n2, 58, 66n16, 90, 94
  power shift in, 114
  skilled slaves in, 122–123
  slavery and population expansion in, 94
  slavery ending in, 199
  trade diaspora in, 56–58, 60, 62
  and twin taboo, 105
  and warfare, 107, 191
Asante state, 12, 23, 123, 163n21, 165
asylum. *See* slave defections
Atani people, 63, 185
Atlantic economic context, 179–181

Atlantic slave trade
  See also Aro slave trade; Biafra slave trade; indigenous slavery
  and Aro diaspora/expansion, 19, 22–26, 32, 35–36, 51, 53–54, 58–60, 66, 70–71, 82, 115–116, 118, 125, 204–206
  and Aro organization, 34–35, 45, 54, 115–116, 204
  and the Aro political economy, 117
  and Arochukwu, 23
  and the Arondizuogu settlement, 87n9
  captives destined for, 117
  and domestic slavery, 25, 130
  end of, 6, 126, 131, 181, 196–197, 202–203, 205, 207–208
  expansions and shifts, 22–26
  and gender inequality, 177
  gender structure of, 10
  in hinterland vs. coastal areas, 7, 23, 38, 45–52
  and human sacrifice, 201
  and the Ibibio, 32
  and the Ibiniukpabi oracle, 76
  and the Igbo, XV, 4n4, 5, 20, 32, 42, 51, 58, 70–71
  vs. indigenous slavery, 5, 24–25, 117–118, 181–182, 197
  and kolanuts, 170
  overview, 4–7
  vs. palm oil trade, 3
  slavery prior to, 87n9
  suppression of, 119
  Trans-Atlantic Slave Trade Database of, 150
  volume of, 33
Atta dynasty, 50
autochthonous communities, XVIn2, 85
Awa (Izuogu's son), 60, 112–114, 215–216n5
Awka trading group, 57, 70, 77–78, 108
  See also Nri-Awka region
Ayanma displays, 115

Baikie, William, 133, 135
Barbados, 35, 42
Barbot family, records kept by, 31, 34–36, 34n20, 78, 88, 142
Basden, G.T., 153, 159–160
Bello, Mohammed, 139–140
Bende slave market, 4, 6, 8, 31, 34, 50, 56, 79, 191

Index

Benin kingdom, 12, 25, 31, 43, 64–65n14, 149, 151–152, 168, 168n31
Bentor, Eli, 19, 83, 212
Bermuda, 35
Biafra hinterland
　Aro control in, 15, 22, 53, 75
　Aro expansion into, XVIII, 2–3, 6, 9–10, 18–19, 45, 50–51, 58, 205, 207
　British encroachment into, 185
　captives drawn from, 50
　map of, XI
　population of, XIX, 22, 188
　and the slave trade, 7, 23–24, 43, 45–52, 75, 119, 134
　zoning of, 60–64
Biafra slave trade
　See also Aro slave trade; Atlantic slave trade; gender structure of slave trade; Igbo ethnic group; Igboland; indigenous slavery; slave traders
　in the Biafra hinterland, 7, 23–24, 43, 45–52, 75, 119, 134
　historiography of, 7–19
　mental models in, 118
　overview, XIII–XIV, XVIII, 4–7
　quantitative date on, 150–151, *151*
Bight of Benin, XIII, 38, 39, *151*, 159, 168, 170, 176–177, 180
Bight of Biafra
　See also Aro diaspora/expansion; Aro's rise; Atlantic slave trade; Biafra hinterland; historiography; slave ships
　British incursions into, 181–188, 187n21
　captives exported from, XIII–XIV, *XIV*, 4n4, 5, 22, 33, 33–42, *38*, *41*, 46, 123–125, 140, 143, 151
　economy of, 180
　evidence of slavery from, 119
　indigenous slavery in, 24
　kidnapping in, 127–130
　map, XI
　political economy of, XVII, 9, 11, 21
　regional relationships, 20–21
　slave prices in, 36, 36
　slave trade ended in, 202
　turnaround rates in, 37–38, *39*
　warfare/violence overview, 178–203
　women slaves exported from, *151*
blunderbusses, 29–32
　See also firearms
Bonny (state and slave port)
　Aro trade oriented toward, 60
　captives departing from, 46
　captives loaded per vessel in, *41*
　civil war's effect on, 14–15
　documentation on, 154, 156
　female slaves exported from, 158–159
　as historical focus, 23
　Igbo slaves exported from, 51, 159
　lineage-groups of, *61*
　loading times in, 40
　percentage of slave exports, *155*
　preeminence of, 5–6, 20, 44–48, 51, 60, 159
　resistance among slaves brought to, 132
　routes to and from, 50–52
　vs. trans-Saharan slave trade, 166
　trust system in, 78
　voyage times to England, 37
Bosman, William, 127
boys as slaves, 36, 137, 151, *155*, 156, 171
　See also children as slaves; gender structure of slave trade; girls as slaves
Brass (slave port), 23, 47, 49–51
Bristol (England), 42–46, 48, 145, 208
British abolition of slave trade, XVIII, 2–3, 4n4, 6, 181–184
British Anti-Slavery Squadron, 118
British Aro Expedition (1901-02), 3, 29, 179, 199n40
British Board of Trade, 36
British Caribbean, 5
British colonial antislavery efforts, 158n18
British colonial rule, 98, 106, 111, 158n18
British imperialism, 178–179, 181–188, 187n21, 206–207
British incursions in Biafra, 181–188, 187n21
British Niger Expeditions, 105, 133
British slave trade, 4, 4n4, 43–46, 48
British theories on the Aro, 8
Burdo, Adolphe, 199n40

Cameroon (Bight of Biafra subregion), 44, 46, 47, 78, 79, 156, 156n15, 163
Cape Lopez, Gabon, XIII
capitalism, 115
Carew, W.E., 88, 88n12
Carli, Denis de, 151–152
Carretta, Vincent, 218–221
Casement, Roger, 186n19, 191
caste systems, 198–199, 200n43, 200n44

Chambers, Douglas, 58
Chesapeake Bay, 1, 5, 43, 58
Chi (deity), XV–XVII, XVIn2, XVIn3
children as slaves, 57
  See also boys as slaves; gender structure of slave trade; girls as slaves
  in Atlantic vs. domestic slave trade, 144–148, 154, 157
  captured in warfare, 127, 129, 161–162, 205
  kidnapped, 131
  parents' sale of, 95
  as punishment/reprisal, 134, 195
  ratios, 171–172
  and slave wives, 158, 158n18
  in the West-Central African slave trade, 147
Chima, Eze, 214
Christianity, 115, 217–218n8
Chukwu (deity), 55, 61, 76, 185, 199n40
  See also Ibiniukpabi oracle
Church Missionary Society (CMS), 88, 118, 210
civil war. See warfare, civil
class structures, 100–101
coastal states slave trade, 7, 23, 32, 45–52, 118–119
  See also slave traders
Cohen, Abner, 17
Cohen, Ronald, 16–17
colonialism, 115, 217–218n8
  See also British colonial rule
conspicuous consumption, 201, 201n46
Constazo, Angelo, 220
Cookey, Sylvanus, 25
Cooper, Fred, 21n34
Corisco (slave port), 46
Cotterell, Harry, 180–181
Cowan, A, A., 185
Cross River Igboland, XVIn2, 5–6, 13n22, 18, 26–27, 30n15, 31, 50, 68, 70, 89n14
  See also Igboland
Cross River Igbo warriors, 127, 132, 162, 190, 192–193, 195–196, 206, 211
  See also Aro warfare; warfare
Cross River region, XIV–XV, 1, 6, 20, 26–27, 30n17, 51, 54, 78–79, 156, 186–187, 187n21
Crow, Hugh, 43, 138–139, 153
Cuba, 78
cultural aftershocks overview, 178–203
cultural deviations in the frontier, 100–107
culture formation overview, 82–116
currency systems, 36, 53
Curtin, Philip, 174n35

Dahomey state, 16, 64n14, 123, 138, 152, 169
Davenport, William, 44
decadence, 196–202
demand for captives/slaves. See the Americas; European demand for captives; plantations
demographic impacts, XVIII–XIX
deportees overview, 117–143
dialect formation, 107–115
Dickson, Kwamina, 170
Dike, Eze John, II, 59–60, 60n9
Dike, K. Onwuka, XXIV, 9, 14–16, 25n10, 26, 53, 65, 66n16, 206
  The Aro of Southeastern Nigeria (co-author), 11
division of labor. See gender division of labor
documentary historical sources, XXIII–XXIV
domestic slavery, i, 6–7, 25, 43, 87, 119–122, 130, 182–183, 185, 197, 201
  See also indigenous slavery; market persons; slave wives; woman as slaves
Duignan, Reverend Father, 210–211
the Dutch, 35

economic aftershocks overview, 178–203
economic necessity of slavery, 141–143
Edwards, Bryan, 42
Efik societies, 24n7, 78, 149n7
Egbocha (Awa's mother), 112–114, 215n5
Ejiofo of Oba, 194
Ekeh, Peter, 12n20
Ekejiuba, Felicia, XXIV, 14–16, 25n10, 26, 65, 66n16, 158n18
  The Aro of Southeastern Nigeria (co-author), 11
Ekpe society, 2, 6, 6n8, 10, 20, 20n33, 45, 75, 77–79, 78n35, 96, 115, 140, 140n34, 211
Eltis, David, 47, 209
Emecheta, Buchi, 122
  Slave Girl, 158n18
Emesinwa, Oti, 57, 66, 66n16, 199
English America colonies, 4
  See also the Americas

Enugu (Igbo city/state), XVIn2, 125, 200n45
Equiano, Olaudah, 25, 43, 67, 86, 128n12, 133, 191, 217-221, 217-218n8, 220n10
Interesting Narrative, 217
ethnic heterogeneity, 15
ethnically homogenous middlemen groups (EHMGs), 17
ethnolinguistic diversity, XIV, XVII
European demand for captives, XVII, XXIII, 20, 22, 34-37, 42, 46-47, 117, 197, 207
European presence in Atlantic Africa, 35, 178-179, 181-188
Ewe ethnic group, 148
Expanded Online Trans-Atlantic Slave Trade Database (slavevoyages.org), 4n4, 40, 209
Eyamba, King, 182
Eyo (King), 182
Eze Aro (King), 54, 99, 206
Eze as title, 15n27
Ezeagwu confederacy group, 27, 27n13, 28
Ezeanakwe, Ezenne, 195
Ezeliora, Bernadette, 72
Ezenwali (King of Nri), 193
Eze-Ogo (King), 97, 123

Falconbridge, Alexander, 37, 127, 132-133, 159
female husbands, 158, 158n18
firearms, 26, 32n18, 187, 190-191, 195-196, 196n37, 206
See also blunderbusses
Forde, Daryll, 18-19, 194
Fraser, James, 132
frontiers, 3, 20, 32, 58, 84, 84n3, 92-96, 103-104, 106, 111
See also trading frontier overview
funeral rites, 98, 98n25, 193, 195, 201

Gabon (slave port), XIII, 46
Gallwey, Major, 186n19
Gambia (slave port), 41
gender division of labor, XVIII, 11, 149-154, 156n15, 161, 161n20, 176, 182-183
gender structure of slave trade
See also boys as slaves; children as slaves; girls as slaves; slave wives; women; women as slaves
and the Atlantic slave trade, 205

documentation on, limited, 130
overview, 144-177
as study focus, XVIII, 10-11, 209
genealogies as source studies, 214-217
girls as slaves, 36, 150, 155, 158n18, 171-173
See also boys as slaves; gender structure of slave trade
Gold Coast, 23, 38, 39, 127, 148-149, 150n8, 151, 160-161, 165-170, 174, 176, 202
Gomez, Michael, 42
Goody, Jack, 120
Gose, Peter, 207
Grainger, James, 43
Grazilhier, John, 31, 34
Greene, Sandra, 148
Guerin, Mary, 219
Guyer, Jane I, 161n20

Hair, Paul, 34n20, 118, 128, 175
Hall, Gwendolyn, 43-44
Hamitic hypothesis, 8
Hausa ethnic group, 17, 55, 115, 162-163, 163n21, 165-170, 165n27, 166n28, 176
head hunting, 196, 201
hinterland. See Biafra hinterland
Hippisley, John, 4, 174n35
historiography of the Biafra slave trade, 7-19, 23
See also sources overview
Hogendorn, Jan, 10
Holy Ghost Fathers (Dublin), 210
household slaves. See domestic slavery
human proliferation (mmuba), 2, 71-75, 105n33
human sacrifice, 134, 198, 200-202
Hutchinson, Thomas, 182
hybridity, XIV-XV

Ibibio ethnic group
and the Aro, XIV-XV, 27, 79, 187-188
and the Atlantic slave trade, 32
in civil war, 26, 32
dominance of, 5
and the Ekpe, 79
gender division of labor among, 152-153
identity of, XXIII
immigration of, 26
kolanuts' importance to, 163n22

Ibibio ethnic group (*Cont.*)
  in Nigeria, 5
  population of, 5n6
  slavery in, 119, 136
  subgroups of, 149n7
  yam cultivation among, 159–160
Ibibioland, 1–2, 6, 18, 20, 34, 67, 97, 134, 190
Ibiniukpabi oracle, 6, 9, 30, 54, 75–77, 81, 96, 135, 184–185, 187, 199n40
  See also Chukwu
Ibom dialect, 108
Ibom Isii confederacy group, 27–29, 27n13, 28
Ibom lineage-group, 61, 62
Ibom people, 63
Idozuka, Okoro, 189, 193
Igala kingdom, XV, 14–15, 50, 53, 54, 167
Igba ndu (covenant), 67–68, 80
Igbo, Obasi Bassey, 212
Igbo ethnic group
  See also Atlantic slave trade; Cross River Igbo warriors; preexisting societies
  and Aro identity, 42–45
  ascendancy of, 100
  in the Atlantic slave trade, XV, 4n4, 20, 32, 42, 51, 70–71
  in civil war, 26, 32
  culture of, XIII–XVI, XVn1, XVIn2, 82–84
  egalitarian norms of, 140
  gender division of labor among, 152–153, 159
  historiography of, 7–11
  identity of, XXIII
  kolanuts cultivated by, 148–149, 163–165, 165n27, 170, 205
  languages of, XV, 26, 78, 107–111, 107–108nn37-38
  lineage-group, 27
  and the Middle Belt region, 9
  in Nigeria, 5
  and the osu, 198–200
  politics in, 14, 140
  slavery in, 87, 119
  slavery terminology in, 120
  slaves from, 36, 42–45, 47, 52, 69–70, 122, 166, 176
  subcultures of, 18
  terminologies for White people/Europeans, 217–218n8
  twin taboo in, 104–105

  war specialists among, 192
  in West Niger, XVIn2
  yams cultivated by, 148–149, 159, 205
Igbo-Abamaba subculture, 18
Igbo-Ibibio-Efik borderland, XVII
Igbo-Ibibio-Ejagham borderland, XIV–XV
Igboland
  See also Arondizuogu diaspora settlement; Atlantic slave trade; Cross River warrior groups
  agriculture in, 88
  the Aro in, 3, 6, 10–11, 13n22, 19, 20, 51–52, 57–58, 60, 62, 69–71, 80, 82–83, 124, 184
  Arochukwu homeland in, XVII, XVn1
  and the Atlantic slave trade, 5, 20, 51, 58, 70–71, 199
  autochthonous communities of, XVIn2
  Cross River region of, 5–6, 13n22, 18, 20, 26–27, 29–30n15, 50–51, 58, 68, 89n14
  dialects in, 3
  as Equiano birthplace, 218, 220, 220n10
  force used in, 68–71
  and immigration, 10, 26, 80
  indigenous slavery in, 25
  marriage possibilities in, 104
  merchant-warlords in, 194
  missionary societies in, 210
  nucleus of, XVI
  the osu in, 199–200
  slavery in, 123
  slaves from, 51–52, 58, 69–70
  societies of, XV, 3
  southern, XVI, 10, 57, 158
  subcultures of, 18
  trade routes through, 50–52
  warriors from, 5–6, 68, 70, 131
  women slaves in, 158
Igbonet (electronic interactive medium), 107n37
Igbo-Ukwu (people/town), XVIn2, 57, 69, 80, 111, 166
Igga (state/society), XVIn2
Igwe, Michael Sunday, 59
Iheme (Izuogu's dependent), 57, 92, 93n17, 113–114, 124
Iheme lineage-group, 57, 200n45
Ihenacho, Asonye, 163–164n23
Ihiala settlement, 62, 63n13, 195
Ihu homage rite, XVIn3, 2, 98–100, 98n26, 103, 215

Index

Ijeoma, Okoli (of Arondizuogu), 194–195n35
Ijeoma, Okoli (of Ndeikelionwu/Ndieni), 189, 190–193, 190n29, 194–195n35
Ijo state, 11
Ijoma, J. Okoro, 195n36, 200, 200n44
Ikeji festival, XVIn3, 2, 19, 96, 98, 102–103, 102n31, 115
Ikpa-Ora community, 70
Ikperikpe (war drum), 122, 193
immigration
  See also Aro diaspora/expansion
  and agriculture, 80
  and the Akpa, 26, 30
  among the amuda, 101
  into Aro settlements, 2–3, 16
  into Arochukwu, 26–27, 32, 53
  and the Bight of Biafra, XIX, XXIII
  and cultural assimilation, 79, 94–95
  and cultural transposition, 105–106
  hinterland slaveholders developing from, 24
  of the Ibibio, 26
  and Igboland, 10, 26, 80
  and the Jukun, 30n17
  languages and dialects, 107
  and the Nri-Awka region, 83, 89n14, 114, 171–172, 184
  population densities causing, 80
  skilled slaves among, 122–123
  and slave trade expansion, XXIV
  of women, forced, 160
incest, 2, 103–104
indigenous slavery, 5, 14, 24–25, 117–119, 141, 181–182, 197
  See also Atlantic slave trade; domestic slavery; market persons; slave traders
Inikori, Joseph, 7, 25, 147
Inokun settlement, 13n22, 18, 20, 56
institutions of the slave trade, 75–80, 132–143
Interesting Narrative (Equiano), 217
Isichei, Elizabeth, 10, 108, 194, 211
Isieke (town), 217, 217n8
Islam, 55, 166, 202
Isu group, 85, 85n4, 90
Iwerre region, 26
  See also Arochukwu region; Unene region
Izuogu. *See* Mgbokpo, Izuogu
Izuogu, Eze, 212

Izuogu, Mazi. *See* Mgbokpo, Izuogu

Jaja (King), 185
Jamaica, 4n4, 35, 42, 108n38
James, F.S., 186n19
Jewish trade diaspora, 55
Jones, G.I., 9, 18–19, 30, 34n20
judicial processes, 76–78, 135, 138, 143, 162, 199n40, 206–207, 210
Jukun state, 30, 30n17, 79, 167, 168n31

Kanu, Okoro, 15n27
Kanu-Igbo, Ukobasi, 199n42
Kanu-Onuoha, 98n25
kidnapping, 2, 118, 124, 126–132, 128n12, 137, 143, 162, 189, 194, 205, 207
King William. *See* Pepple (King)
kinship, 68, 80, 94, 107n37, 114, 120–121, 124, 171, 215
Klein, Herbert, 119
Klein, Martin, 12n20
Koelle, Sigmund, 118, 128–130, 134–135, 135n25, 137, 175
kolanuts
  in the Atlantic slave trade, 170
  and British incursion, 187
  cultural significance of, XV–XVII, XVIn3, 149, 163–164, 163–164n23, 163n21, 164n24, 168–169n32, 205
  and the Hausa, 162–163, 165, 176
  and the Igbo, 148–149, 163–165, 164n25, 165n27, 170, 205
  reverence for, 149
  in rites and festivals, 98n26, 163, 163n23, 164n24
  and the slave trade, XVI, XVIII
  species of, 165, 165n26
  and trans-Saharan commerce, 162–163, 168–170
  and the trans-Saharan slave trade, 149, 176
  and warfare, 163–164n23
Kongo Kingdom, 13, 152, 154, 166–167, 175
Kopytoff, Igor, 25n9, 84, 92, 95, 120
Kwararafa state, 30–32, 167

languages and dialects. *See* Aro languages; Arochukwu; Arondizuogu diaspora settlement; culture formation; Igbo ethnic group; Nri-Awka region
Latham, John, 24n7, 31

Law, Robin, 34n20, 64n14
law and order, 132–140
Leonard, Arthur, 8, 186n19, 191
leveling mechanisms, 14
lexicostatistics, 107–108, *109–110*
lineage-groups
  Amankwu, 28, *61*, 62, 62–63, 97
  Aro, 6, 12, 15, 60, 62–63, 68, 76, 99
  of Aro diaspora settlements, 6, 60–62, *61*, *62*, *76*, 90–93, 102, 108
  Aro diaspora/expansion, 6
  Aro influence continued by, 184
  Arochukwu, 27, 55, 63, 101, 108, 191
  Arondizuogu, 60, 62, 89, 90–93, 92, 102, 102n31, 184, 200, 200n45, 214–215
  Bonny, *61*
  founded by the amadi, 100–102
  Ibom, 62
  Igbo, 27
  Iheme, 27, 200n45
   interviews in, 214
   and kidnapping, 128
  Ndiakaeme, 105
  Ndiakunwanta, 93, 95
  Ndiamazu, 92–93, 93n17, 97, 99, 200n45
  Ndiawa, 92, 101, 113–114, 215
  Ndi-Iheme, 92–93, 114
  Ndiejezie, 93
  Nri-Awka, 103, 124
  Otusi, 27–29, 27n13, 76
  shrines of, 200, 200n44
  synchronic relations among members, 217
  Ujari, *61*, 62, 87n10, 123
  unified by the Ihu rite, 99
  warfare among, 191
linkage institutions, 2, 75, 96–100
Liverpool (England), 43–44, 46, 48, 136–139, 145, 208
Lovejoy, Paul, XXIII–XXIV, 10, 20, 47, 170, 219–220

Madeira, Victor, 217
Maduagwu, B.O.J., 89–90n14
male slaves, 5, 11, 22, 36, 43, 144, 150–155, 161–162, 170, 173
  See also boys as slaves; gender structure of slave trade; women as slaves
Mann, Kristin, 168n32

Manning, Patrick, 175n36, 210
market persons, 117, 119, 121–123, 131n17, 132, 141
  See also domestic slavery; household slavery; indigenous slavery
marriage, 59, 68, 103–104, 107, 142, 158, 158n18, 173, 175, 201, 210
  See also partial exogamy
Martin, Susan, 158
Mathews, H.F., 29, 29–30n15, 31–32
Mauny, Raymond, 166n28
Mayne, C.J., 85
Mazi (Consul), 15, 64–65, 64n14
Mazi Izuogu. *See* Mgbokpo, Izuogu
mbia (Aro spheres of influence), 6
McCall, John, 107n37
means of enslavement, XVIII, 119, 122, 130–131, 132n19, 143–144, 161–162, 205
Meek, Charles, 159, 190
Meillassoux, Claude, 73, 75
merchant-warlords, 68, 178, 188n27, 189, 190, 192–194, 206
  See also Aro merchant-warlords
Mgbemene, Amos Egwuekwe D., 192n33
Mgbokpo, Izuogu
  amadi status of, 66
  ancestors of, 66, 66n16
  in Arochukwu, 97, 99
  as Arondizuogu founder, 1, 57, 60, 99–101
  descendents/dependents, 92–93, 93n17, 101–102, 104, 112–114, 215–216, 215n5, 216n7
  in Isu-Ora conflict, 90
  lineage-groups, 101, 104, 112
  as merchant-warlord, 193
  as slave trader, 97
  as warrior, 70
Mgbori, Owuu, 20n32
Middle Belt region, XV, 9, 14, 31–32, 50, 79, 159, 165–168, 184, 184n13
Middle Passage, 219
Miers, Suzanne, 25n9, 95, 120
migration. *See* immigration
Miller, Joseph, 117, 174
missionary societies, 210
Mmeruonye, Udoji, 212
mmuba (human proliferation), 2, 71–75, 105n33
Monteith, Archibald, 108n38, 131n17

Index

Moor, Ralph, 185–186
mortality rates of slaves, 22, 47

Ndeikelionwu (Ndieni settlement), 20n32, 63, 172, 184, 189–192, 190n29
Ndeikelionwu people, 20n32, 163–164n23, 164
ndị (group/people), 1
Ndiakaeme lineage-group, 105
Ndiakunwanta lineage-group, 93, 95
Ndiamazu lineage-group, 92–93, 93n17, 97, 99, 200n45
Ndiawa lineage-group, 92, 101, 113–114, 215
Ndi-Iheme lineage-groups, 92–93, 114
Ndiejezie lineage-group, 93
Ndieni diaspora cluster, XVIn3, 13n22, 20, 20n32, 56–58, 62, 63, 66, 95, 106, 184, 190–191
Ndiuche dialect, 112
Ndiuche lineage-group, 92, 101, 112–115, 215, 215n5
Ndizuogu. *See* Arondizuogu diaspora settlement
Ndoki society, XVIn2
New Calabar (state and slave port), 23, 31, 34–37, 46, 46–52, 60, 61, 78, 130, 132, 154, 155, 156
New Men, 194
Ngwa, Fritz-Canute, 156n15
Ngwa society, XVIn2, 67, 154
Ngwaland, 78, 135n25, 183n7
Niger Delta/River, XIII, 6–7, 30, 50–51, 54, 156, 159, 181, 186, 187n21
Niger Expeditions (British), 105, 133
Niger riverine states, 11, 14–15, 20, 32, 53, 54, 185, 210
Niger slave markets, 50, 184
Niger slave route, 50
Nigeria, XIII, 1, 4–5, 9, 18, 50, 56, 63, 75, 79, 96, 104n32, 123, 163, 169
  See also Hausa ethnic group
Nkwere trading group, 57, 79, 125, 195
Nna Atọ (Three Fathers) council, 27, 206
Nnachi (Aro pioneer), 60, 66n16
Northrup, David, XXIV, 12n21, 13–17, 13n22, 63n13, 79–80, 97, 211
  Trade without Rulers, 11–12
Nri, Eze (King), 15n27, 193
Nri cultural hegemony, 82

Nri-Awka people
  as Aro dependents, 57
  culture of, 103, 189–190, 200
  ichi markings on, XVIn2
  languages and dialects of, 108, 109–110, 111, 111n39
  lineage-groups of, 103, 124
  personality cult among, 190
  politics of, 190
  slave market of, 62
  and warfare, 190
Nri-Awka region
  Aro exchange structures in, 57
  Aro expansion into, 124
  and the Aro frontier, 20, 58, 94–96, 104
  Aro slave trade in, 80, 94
  Arondizuogu and immigrants from, 184
  Arondizuogu culture influenced by, 107, 200
  Arondizuogu market control in, 62
  and cultural deviations, 104
  cultural politics in, 112–114, 123–125
  Igbo norms in, 104
  Ihiala settlement in, 62, 63n13
  and the Ihu homage rite, 103–105
  and immigration, 83, 89n14, 114, 171–172, 184
  merchant-warlords from, 193
  and the Ndieni cluster, 20n32, 57, 184
  and the Oda deity, 72
  slavery impetus in, 80
  slaves from, 114, 123–125
  slaves of status in, 138, 138n29
  warfare/violence in, 69, 74, 189–190, 193, 195–198, 205–206
  women of, 173
nsibiri (Aro script). *See* Aro script
nucleation, 92, 92–93
Nwabughuogu, Anthony, 187n21
Nwankwo, Theresa, 3n2
Nwaoma, Ofọdọbendu, 141–142
Nwauwa, Apollos, 29–30n15
Nwokoye-Emesuo, Nkemakonam (Perricomo), 98
Nzekwu, Onuora, 163, 168–169n32

Obegu (town), 187
Obiechina, Emmanuel, 212
Oda (diety), 72–73
Ogbuofelu (slave), 198
Ogirisi, Mbgawho, 199

Ogude, S.E., 218, 220n10
Oguta society/state, XVIn2, 24, 32, 56, 61, 185
Ohafia people, 26, 70, 89–90n14, 107n37, 135, 135n25
ohu (slave/slave class), 101, 120
Oil Rivers Protectorate, 186
Ojike, Mbonu, 188n26
Okafor, Chinyere, 103
Okennachi confederacy group, 27–29, 27n13, 28
Okereke, Ozigbo, 189
Okereke, Thomas, 115n40
Okigwe District, 3n2, 63, 188n26, 210
Okoli, Nwambego, 91
Ọkọnkọ society. See Ekpe society
Okoro, J. G., 192n33, 200, 216
Okoro, Jacob Ogbonna, 63, 97, 97n24
Okoro, Jonathan G., 58–59, 192n33, 214–216, 216n7
Okoroji (Aro merchant-warrior), 123, 197
Okoroji (Ndikoroji founder), 98, 184
Okoroji, Emmanuel, 123
Okoroji, Ezumoha, 192n33
Ọkpankpọ (Aro central council). See Aro central council
Okwaraeze (Ndiokwareze founder), 20n32
Okwei, Omu, 158n18
Old Calabar (state and slave port), *41*
  as Biafra's principal port, 34, 40
  vs. Bonny's preeminence, 5–6, 20, 45–48, 51, 60, 159
  British slave trade in, 44
  captives departing from, *41*, 46, *155*, 156–157, 156n15
  documentation on, 154, 156
  Ekpe society in, 20n33, 78
  enslaved princes returning to, 139
  female slaves departing from, 157
  as study focus, 23
Oldendorp, Christian Georg Andreas, 5, 58, 86–87, 113, 118–119, 128–130, 198, 217, 221
Onitsha state, XVIn2, 14–15, 18, 32, 69, 111
Onwuejeogwu, M. Angulu, 10n18, 15n27, 190, 193
Onyeama of Eke, 194
Opobo (state and slave port), 23, 49, 185
Opobo state, 23, 49, 185

Ora community, 69–70, 90
oral historical sources, XXIII–XXIV, 2, 209, 211–217
Oriji, John, XVIn2, 6n8
Oron people, 140–141n35, 149, 149n7, 159
Osai (King), 133
Osomari state, 14, 24, 32
osu caste system, 198–200, 200n43, 200n44
Ottenberg, Simon, 94, 206
Ọtụsị lineage-groups, 27–29, 27n13
overseas slave trade. See Atlantic slave trade
Owa community, 74–75, 75n29, 190, 194–195, 217
Oyewumi, Oyeronke, 161n20
Oyo state, 12, 23

palm oil trade, 3, 6, 49, 149n7, 174, 176, 178, 180–185, 188, 202–203
palm wine, 67, 85–88, 87n10, 98n26
Palmer, Colin, 42
panyaring (kidnapping), 127
Parker, Isaac, 126
partial exogamy, 72–73, 104
  See also marriage
Paschal, Michael Henry, 219
Patterson, Orlando, 95
pax (trading), 23, 53
Pepple (King), 137, 139, 182–183, 201n46
personality cults, 190
plantations, 33, 37, 42–43, 45, 118, 119, 120, 147, 183, 208
Polanyi, Karl, 17–18, 64–65, 64n14
polygyny, 11, 173–175, 174n35, 210
Portugal, 42n25
preexisting societies, 84–90, 85n4, 87n9, 103, 106, 108, *109–110*, 114, 194, 199
preferences for slaves, 20, 43–44, 47, 118, 122–126, 147–148, 171, 173–174
prices for slaves. See slave prices
private enterprise, 15, 56, 64–71
profits from slave trade, 2, 46, 118, 122, 134, 136, 148, 160, 182, 186, 194, 201, 207

Raphael-Hernandez, Heike, 217
rebellion. See resistance to slavery
resistance to slavery, 38–39, 48, 69–70, 197–198
revolt. See resistance to slavery
Richardson, David, 20, 38, 47

Rodney, Walter, 137–138
Rolf-Trouillot, Michel, 16
Royal African Company (RAC), 35–36, 36n23

Sandoval, Alonso de, XVn1, 4n4, 32, 217, 221
Sargent, Robert, 10, 21n34, 30n17
Senegambia region, 38–40, 39, 55, 64n14, 127, 131, 138, 153, 161–162, 198
Seven Years War, 207
Shaw, Thurstan, XVIn2, 15n27, 69
Sierra Leone, 7, 38–39, 39, 118, 125, 134–135, 168, 175
Slave Coast, 127, 148, 174
slave defections, 189
Slave Girl (Emecheta), 158n18
slave owners, 74, 118, 121, 123, 197
slave prices, 22, 36, 36, 44–45, 48, 207
slave ships
  British, 4, 44–46, 48
  loading rates, XVIII, 45–46, 52, 209
  sizes/loads of, 39–42, 41
  turnaround rates, 5, 34, 37–40, 39, 42, 44, 46–47
slave suicide, 42, 132–133
slave trade routes, 50–51, 66–67, 66n16, 167
slave traders, 37, 117–118, 123, 139, 179, 201, 201n46
  See also Aro slave trade; coastal states slave trade; indigenous slavery
slave wives, 157–158, 158n18, 161, 174, 199, 205
  See also women as slaves
slavery, means of, 132–143
Slavery and Social Death (Patterson), 95
slavery as economic necessity, 141–143
slavery as punishment/reprisal, 76, 81, 99, 118, 131n14, 132–140, 140n35, 171, 195
slavery terminology, 120, 127
slaves, skilled, 122–123
slavevoyages.org (Trans-Atlantic Slave Trade Database), 4n4, 40, 209
Snelgrave, William, 34, 132, 142
social death, 95
sources overview, 209–221
  See also historiography of the Biafra slave trade
Southeast African slave trade, 38, 39

Sowell, Thomas, 68
state and diaspora, 11–19
steamships, 180
Stevenson, Robert, 16
sugar, XIII–XIV, 22, 182
suicide among slaves, 42, 132–133

taboos, 3, 104, 125, 133, 140n35, 163n23, 165, 193
Talbot, Amaury, 8, 163n22
Taste of the West (Akamnonu), 158n18
taxonomies, 18, 56, 83
Things Fall Apart (Achebe), 86n8, 163
Thornton, John, 4n4, 25n9, 130, 153–154, 217
Three Fathers (Nna Atọ) council, 27, 206
titled societies, XXIII–XXIV, 18
Tiv ethnic group, 159, 167
trade callers, 80, 188n27
trade diasporas. *See* Aro trade networks/diasporas
trade routes, 1, 50–51, 163
Trade without Rulers (Northrup), 11–12
trading frontier overview, 82–116
transatlantic slave trade. *See* Atlantic slave trade
Trans-Atlantic Slave Trade Database (www.slavevoyages.org), 4n4, 40, 150, 209
trans-Saharan commerce, 162–163, 166–168, 176
trans-Saharan slave trade, 21, 149, 162, 165–170, 176
trust system, 5, 45, 78
turnaround rates. *See* slave ships, turnaround rates
Turner, A., 186n19
twin taboo, 104–105, 104n32, 105n33

Uburu slave market, 50, 61, 79
Uche (Izuogu's son), 112–114, 215, 215–216n5
Uche, S.U., 88n12
Uchendu, Victor, 160, 172
Udozuka, Okoro, 91, 93–94, 98n25, 192, 199
Ufere, Ikelionwu, 58
Ugwuoba people, 70n23, 194, 194n35
Ujari dialect, 108
Ujari lineage-group, 61, 62, 87n10, 123

Ujari people, 20n32, 62–63, 106, 106n36, 190, 199
Ujari region, 57, 58n8, 62, 66, 87n10, 98, 190–191, 199
Ukwu, Ukwu I., 9, 80
Umo, Kanu, 61, 115, 199n40
Umu Chukwu (children of God), 76, 81
Unene region, 26, 30
  See also Arochukwu region; Iwerri region
Upper Guinea Coast, 127, 160–162
upper Imo River region, 1, 51, 57, 70, 84–85, 85n4, 107, 122, 184, 216

Vansina, Jan, 211
Vassa (Equiano slave name). See Equiano, Olaudah
Vavilov, Nikolai, 164n25
violence. See Aro warfare; British imperialism; Nri-Awka region, warfare/violence in; warfare
vocabulary comparisons, 107–108

war captives, 70, 127–130, 143, 161–162, 205, 207
War of Jenkin's Ear, 207
warfare
  See also Aro merchant-warlords; Aro warfare; Cross River Igbo warriors; Nri-Awka region; women
  and the age structure of slavery, 11
  and agriculture, 189–190
  among lineage-groups, 191
  and Aro diaspora/expansion, 15, 68–71, 106–107, 188–189, 193
  and Aro identity, 178–179
  and Aro slave trade, 6, 179
  Aro state created by, 15
  and Aro trade, 68
  and Arondizuogu, 107, 191, 193
  civil, 2, 13, 15, 26, 32, 91, 179, 190–191
  and decadence, 196–202
  and the end of the slave trade, 202
  and firearms, 196
  and the gender structure of slavery, XVIII, 11, 205
  and the Igbo-Akpa alliance, 26
  in Igboland, 68–71
  and the indigenous economy, 11
  and kolanuts, 163n23
  Nri-Awka model of, 190
  Otusi̇' roles in, 27, 29
  and the slave economy, 148
  and slavery, 118, 126–132, 157, 161–162, 188–189, 205
Warner Lewis, Maureen, 108
West African states, XIII, 23
West Niger, XVIn2, 80, 184
West-Central African slave trade
  as capital resource, 73
  children in, 147
  dependents in, 117, 127
  end of, 202
  prominence of, XIII, 4n4, 38, 39, 209
  and slave wives, 174
  women in, 160–161, 174–175
Western Sudan, 131
Whitford, John, 182
Whydah (slave port), 40
Windward Coast, 37–39
women
  See also gender division of labor; gender structure of slave trade
  as business assets, 173
  cursed with barrenness, 187
  as domestic slaves, 148
  economic roles of, 151–152
  forced immigration of, 160
  in human proliferation, 73
  in the Ihu rite, 99
  in the indigenous economy, 11
  political power of, 114
  and restrictive marriage practices, 104
  as sacrificial victims, 112–113
  and the twin taboo, 104–105
  as war captives, 127, 161–162
  and yam cultivation, 160
women as slaves
  See also slave wives
  in Atlantic vs. domestic slave trade, 144–148
  Biafra exports of, 5, 22
  as marginal, 148
  preferences for, 43, 147
  in quantitive data, 150–151
  ratios, 149, 151, 156–158, 160–161, 169, 176–177, 183, 205
  values of, 161
  and warfare, 205
  women owners of, 158, 199

yam festivals, 88, 88n13, 97n23, 98n26, 102–103
yams

cultivation of, 88, 96, 153n12, 159–160
cultural significance of, 205
and the gender division of labor, 149, 160
and the Ibibio, 159–160
and the Igbo, 148–149, 159–160, 164n25, 205

reverence for, XV–XVII, 19, 149, 159–160
as ritual gifts, XVIn3
species of, 166
Yoruba culture, 161, 161n20, 168–169, 168–169n32, 176, 217–218n8

UNIVERSITY OF ST. THOMAS LIBRARIES